Towards Understanding the Qur`an

Vol. IV

SURAHS 10-16

English version of

Tafhim al-Qur`an

SAYYID ABUL A`LA MAWDUDI

Translated and Edited by
Zafar Ishaq Ansari

assisted by

A.R. Kidwai

MARKAZI MAKTABA ISLAMI PUBLISHERS, NEW DELHI-25

ISBN 0 86037 230 8 (PB)
ISBN 0 86037 231 6 (HB)

Translated and edited by Zafar Ishaq Ansari
Cover illustration: Rashid Rahman

British Library Cataloguing in Publication Data

Maududi, Sayyid Abul A`la
Towards Understanding the Qur`an
Peges: 424
Vol. 4, Surahs 10-16
1. Islam, Koran: Critical Studies
I. Title. II. Ansari, Zafar Ishaq
III. Islamic Foundation. IV. Tafhim al-Qur`an. English
297` 1226

ISBN 0 -86037-231-6
ISBN 0-86037-230-8 Pbk

Human Welfare Trust Publication No. 107

First Reprint in India- 1990
Reprint - January 1994
Reprint - September 1997
Reprint - January 1999

Published by

Markazi Maktaba Islami Publishers.
D 307, Abul Fazl Enclave, Jamia Nagar, Okhla
New Delhi-110025 Ph: 6911652

Rs. 175.00

Printed at Dawat Offset, Delhi-6, Ph.: (011) 3267573

NOT TO BE SOLD OUTSIDE INDIA

Contents

TRANSLITERATION TABLE

Consonants. Arabic

initial: unexpressed
medial and final: ء '

ء	'	د	d	ض	ḍ	ك	k
ب	b	ذ	dh	ط	ṭ	ل	l
ت	t	ر	r	ظ	ẓ	م	m
ث	th	ز	z	ع	'	ن	n
ج	j	س	s	غ	gh	ه	h
ح	ḥ	ش	sh	ف	f	و	w
خ	kh	ص	ṣ	ق	q	ي	y

Urdu and Persian the same except the following:

پ	p	ڈ	ḏ	ژ	z̲
ٹ	ṯ				
چ	ch	ڑ	ṟ	گ	g

Vowels, diphthongs, etc.

short: ـَ a; ـِ i; ـُ u.

long: ـَا ā ـُو ū ـِي ī ـِيّ īy

diphthongs: ـَوْ aw

ـَيْ ay

Editor's Preface

This is the fourth volume of *Towards Understanding the Qur'ān* and comprises *Sūrahs* 10–16 (*Yūnus, Hūd, Yūsuf, al-Ra'd, Ibrāhīm, al-Ḥijr* and *al-Naḥl*). It is unfortunate that the time-lapse between the publication of the third and fourth volumes is even greater than that between the publication of the second and third volumes.

The present volume has been prepared with the able assistance of Dr. A.R. Kidwai, who originally translated the notes of *Tafhīm* into English. That draft served as the base out of which the present manuscript developed after a long and thoroughgoing process of editing and re-editing. While credit for this assistance goes to Dr. Kidwai, the responsibility for the present draft, with whatever inadequacies it might contain, rests with the present writer alone. As for the English rendering of the meaning of the text of the *sūrahs,* the work is exclusively this writer's.

In this volume, as in the previous ones, an attempt has been made to consistently provide adequate documentation. In documenting *Ḥadīth* we have followed the system of A.J. Wensinck in his *Concordance*. However, instead of referring to the number of the *'Bāb'* of a tradition – a practice followed by Wensinck – we have preferred to mention the title of the *'Bāb'*. It may also be noted that while referring to other explanatory notes from different works of *Tafsīr,* we have referred to the verse and *sūrah* in connection with which the notes in question were written rather than to the volume and page numbers of the *Tafsīr* works cited. As for the Bible, all quotations have been taken from its *Revised Standard Edition*. Furthermore, we have retained in this volume the features we introduced in the previous volumes of this work, namely Maps, Glossary of Terms, Biographical Notes, and Bibliography.

In finalizing the manuscript, I have greatly benefited from the editorial suggestions of Miss Susanne Thackray. Dr. A.R. Kidwai also kindly looked at the draft and favoured me with useful critical comments. Whenever I was in need of academic assistance, my friend, Dr. Mahmood Ahmad Ghazi, Director General, Dawah Academy, International Islamic University, Islamabad, ungrudgingly allowed me to draw upon his vast resource of learning. In providing documentation and in preparing Biographical Notes and Glossary of Terms, I received valuable assistance from my colleague, Mr. A.R. Ashraf Baloch of the Islamic Research Institute. Mr. Amjad Mahmood of the Islamic Research Institute and Mr. Tahir Farkhan Ahmad of the Computer Centre of the International Islamic University, Islamabad assiduously typed the manuscript many times. Mr. E.R. Fox rendered valuable assistance in technical editing and proofreading and Mr. Naiem Qaddoura in setting the Arabic material.

Last, but not least, I am grateful to my wife and to my children – Asma, Yasir, Sarah, and Anas – in encouraging me by their expression of pride and appreciation, and by putting up, with stoic dignity, with what seems to them to be my 'workaholic' habits and which inevitably prevent me from giving them in fullness what I owe them – attention and company. The gratitude I owe my wife, of course, is far too deep to be adequately expressed in words for she has been a constant source of strength, happiness and peace of mind during the last thirty-three years of our shared life. To all these and many others who assisted and encouraged me, I record my profound sense of gratitude. May Allah bless them all.

It goes without saying that the upbringing and prayers of my parents have had a hand in anything good that I ever did, including this humble effort to serve the Qur'ān. It is sad that when this volume sees the light of day it will no longer be possible for me to gratefully present to my father – as I always did in the past – the first copy of every published work of mine immediately after receiving it from the press. This is because in December 1991 he went far beyond my access; leaving the confines of this world, he headed to the wide expanses of another world, and hopefully God's grace and mercy. For his departed soul and for my mother, who survives him and remains a major guiding light and inspiration, I raise my hands in fervent prayer: 'My Lord! Bestow on them Your Mercy even as they cherished me when I was small' (*Banū Isrā'īl* 17: 24).

Islamabad **Zafar Ishaq Ansari**
Jūmadá al-Ūlá, 1413
November 1992

N.B. ► *refers to the continuation of the paragraph adopted by Mawdūdī in the Urdu translation.*

Sūrah 10

Yūnus

(Jonah)

(Makkan Period)

Title

The title of this *sūrah* is derived from verse 98 which refers to the Prophet Yūnus (Jonah). As usual, the title has nothing more than a symbolic significance; it by no means signifies that the *sūrah* is focused on the story of Prophet Yūnus (peace be on him).

Place of Revelation

Traditions inform us that the whole *sūrah* was revealed in Makka and this is also corroborated by the contents of the *sūrah* itself. It is, however, contended by a number of scholars that some of the verses were revealed in Madina. Such a view seems to be based on very superficial information and unsubstantiated conjecture. For a careful study of the *sūrah* demonstrates that it does not comprise several discourses revealed on different occasions. On the contrary, the contents convey the distinct impression of being parts of a single, coherent discourse, all of which was presumably revealed in one piece. The subjects contained within the *sūrah* also clearly indicate that it was revealed during the Makkan period of the Prophet's life.

Period of Revelation

Although we have not been able to find any tradition which significantly identifies the period in which the *sūrah* was revealed, the subjects discussed within it do seem to suggest that it was revealed during the last phase of the Prophet's stay in Makka. The tenor of the discourse indicates that at the time of its revelation, hostility to the Prophet's Message by his opponents had become quite intense. It seems as if the Prophet's opponents had lost their patience and were no longer in a mood to allow him and his followers to remain alive in their midst. They had become so hostile to the Prophet (peace be on him) and his teachings that it could hardly be imagined that teaching and admonition would ever direct them to the right path. Thus, the time had come for them to be severely warned that if they continued to reject the Prophet (peace be on him) they would inevitably face a dire end. It is features such as these that indicate that this particular *sūrah* belongs to the last phase of the Makkan period of the Prophet's life. However, it is also clear that this *sūrah* pre-dates those *sūrahs* which were revealed just prior to *Hijrah*. The *sūrahs* of the latter kind are known for their explicit or implicit references to *Hijrah*.

Once we know the period of revelation of the *sūrah*, there is hardly any need to discuss its circumstantial context since that has already been mentioned in our introductory remarks to *Sūrahs al-An'ām* and *al-A'rāf*. (See *Towards Understanding the Qur'ān*, vol. II, pp. 210–13; and vol. III, pp. 1–2 – Ed.)

Subject Matter

The main subjects of the discourse are motivated by the three-fold purpose of communicating the Basic Message, urging people to respond to it positively and warning them against rejecting or opposing it.

The discourse opens by referring to the unbelievers' sense of wonderment that someone who was no more than a human being, one like themselves, was the vehicle for communicating God's Message. This had prompted them to brand the Prophet (peace be on him) a sorcerer even though there was nothing weird or exotic about the Message itself, nor did it seem to have any connection with sorcery or soothsaying.

The Message merely consisted of two vital truths. First, that the One God Who had brought the universe into being and Who holds its reins is the Lord and Master of all mankind, and He alone has the right to be served and worshipped by His creatures. Second, that the present life will be followed by another life when all human beings will be resurrected, will be called to account regarding their actions, and will be judged according to their conduct. As a result those who take God as their Lord and act righteously in compliance with His revealed guidance will be rewarded, and those who act contrary to that command will be punished. The contents of the Prophet's Message are true irrespective of whether people accept it or not. The Prophet (peace be on him) had no axe to grind: he was simply calling people to accept the Message and to change their lives accordingly. Acceptance of the Message would be to their own benefit and its rejection would inevitably hurt them.

Main Themes

These introductory remarks are succeeded by the following themes which appear in a definite sequence:

1. First, arguments aimed at supporting the doctrines of *tawḥīd* (unity of God) and the Hereafter are proffered. These are intended to satisfy the minds of people who are mainly interested in guarding themselves against false ideas and their evil consequences rather than scoring points off their adversaries in a debate.
2. Misconceptions about the teachings on *tawḥīd* and the Hereafter are removed. People are warned about their heedlessness and apathy which stood in the way of their recognizing the truth.
3. Doubts created about the Prophet (peace be on him) are shown to be baseless and the objections raised against his Message are refuted.
4. People are forewarned about the dire consequences they will face in the Next Life if they fail to take heed and mend their ways in the present life.
5. People are warned that the present life is akin to a term of examination, a term that will end with their breathing their last breath of life. If they reject the Prophet's Message and thus fail in the examination to which they have been subjected, the opportunity for success will be irretrievably lost. The advent of the Prophet (peace be on him) and the communication of truth through the Qur'ān has provided people with an opportunity that is at once highly valuable and of crucial importance since it is the only one they have. Hence, if they fail to avail themselves of that opportunity they are bound to suffer in the eternal life of the Hereafter.
6. Attention is drawn to the many manifestations of rank ignorance of the truth, and to the several errors of belief and practice which arise because of the failure to live in accord with Divine Guidance.

In this connection the stories of the Prophets Noah and Moses (peace be on them) are narrated – the one of Noah in brief and that of Moses in some detail – in order to demonstrate the following points:

1. The unbelievers' attitude towards the Prophet Muḥammad (peace be on him) resembles the attitude displayed by the unbelievers in the past towards the Prophets Noah and Moses (peace be on them). This being so, the contemporaneous unbelievers are also bound to meet the fate of their predecessors.

2. The Prophet Muḥammad (peace be on him) and his followers were at that time utterly helpless and weak. This should not, however, lead the unbelievers to the mistaken belief that their present state will endure. It would be a mistake on their part not to realize that the Prophet (peace be on him) enjoyed the support of the same God Who had once supported Moses and Aaron. And there also can be no mistaking the fact that He has the power to turn the tables against the unbelievers in a way which is even beyond the grasp of their imagination.

3. The unbelievers should remember that each person has been granted a term within which he may repent and mend his ways. It is of no avail, however, if someone were to repent when in the throes of death – a lesson which is quite evident from what happened to Pharaoh. (See verses 90–2 below – Ed.)

4. The Prophet's followers are told not to lose hope because they are weak and facing very severe hostility. They are also instructed how to operate in the circumstances which confront them. Moreover, they are warned in forceful terms that if Allah, out of His mercy, were to deliver them from their present state of abject suffering, they should guard against following in the footsteps of the Israelites.

The *sūrah* concludes with a declaration that the beliefs and way of life which God has directed His Messenger to follow, constitute the right way for all, a way which may not be altered by anyone. Those who accept this way will do so to their own advantage. Conversely, those who choose to stumble in error will end up hurting only themselves.

In the name of Allah, the Merciful, the Compassionate.

(1) *Alif. Lām. Rā.* These are the verses of the Book overflowing with wisdom.[1]

(2) Does it seem strange to people that We should have revealed to a man from among themselves, directing him to warn the people (who lie engrossed in heedlessness); and to give good news to the believers that they shall enjoy true honour and an exalted status with their Lord?[2] (Is this so strange that) the deniers of the truth should say: 'This man is indeed an evident sorcerer'?[3]

الٓرۚ تِلۡكَ ءَايَٰتُ ٱلۡكِتَٰبِ ٱلۡحَكِيمِ ١
أَكَانَ لِلنَّاسِ عَجَبًا أَنۡ أَوۡحَيۡنَآ إِلَىٰ
رَجُلٖ مِّنۡهُمۡ أَنۡ أَنذِرِ ٱلنَّاسَ وَبَشِّرِ ٱلَّذِينَ
ءَامَنُوٓاْ أَنَّ لَهُمۡ قَدَمَ صِدۡقٍ عِندَ رَبِّهِمۡۗ
قَالَ ٱلۡكَٰفِرُونَ إِنَّ هَٰذَا لَسَٰحِرٞ
مُّبِينٌ ٢

---

1. This introductory statement carries a subtle note of warning. For the unbelievers, out of their sheer stupidity looked upon the Qur'ān which was presented to them by the Prophet (peace be on him) as merely a literary masterpiece, an embodiment of spellbinding poetic imagination, a fascinating discourse on a very sublime, illusive plane in the manner of soothsayers. The unbelievers are told that such notions are pure misconceptions. On the contrary, the Qur'ānic verses are part of a Book which abounds in wisdom. Hence, if they disregard the Qur'ān, they are merely depriving themselves of a treasure-house of wisdom.

2. The unbelievers are asked why they are astonished that a human being has been designated to warn other human beings. Would it have been reasonable to designate some angel, *jinn* or animal rather than a human being to warn other human beings? Similarly, is there anything weird or exotic about the appointment of a Prophet? For if people are found engrossed in error and are oblivious to the truth, what then is truly strange: that their Creator and Lord should make arrangements to guide them or let them continue stumbling in their error? And if Divine Guidance is made available to human beings, does it not stand to reason that it is those who follow, rather than those who reject it,

(3) Surely your Lord is Allah, Who created the heavens and the earth in six days, then established Himself on the Throne (of His Dominion), governing all affairs of the universe.[4] None may intercede with Him except after obtaining His leave.[5] Such is Allah, your Lord; do therefore serve Him.[6] Will you not take heed?[7]

إِنَّ رَبَّكُمُ ٱللَّهُ ٱلَّذِى خَلَقَ ٱلسَّمَٰوَٰتِ وَٱلْأَرْضَ فِى سِتَّةِ أَيَّامٍ ثُمَّ ٱسْتَوَىٰ عَلَى ٱلْعَرْشِ يُدَبِّرُ ٱلْأَمْرَ مَا مِن شَفِيعٍ إِلَّا مِنۢ بَعْدِ إِذْنِهِۦ ذَٰلِكُمُ ٱللَّهُ رَبُّكُمْ فَٱعْبُدُوهُ أَفَلَا تَذَكَّرُونَ ۝٣

that deserve to be held in honour and esteem? Those who express their astonishment at this should reconsider what it is that truly merits astonishment.

3. The unbelievers' allegation that the Prophet (peace be on him) is a sorcerer is devoid of even an iota of truth. The mere fact that a person, by dint of his capacity to express himself effectively, influences people and captivates their hearts and minds does not warrant being called a sorcerer. What is worth considering is the purpose for which he employs his oratorical skill, and the kind of influence that his oration has on the audience. Any orator who uses his skill for an evil purpose will naturally be considered a demagogue, an unbridled and irresponsible speaker. For his only interest lies in casting a spell over his audience, even if he might have to resort to making false and exaggerated statements or saying things that are altogether unjust.

The discourse of such speakers is bereft of all wisdom. For all it aims to do is to hoodwink and bamboozle the gullible masses. Such speakers have no coherent set of ideas to offer. What they say is full of contradiction and incoherence. Such speakers lack moderation and lean towards extremism. For their purpose is to prove their capacity to spellbind their audiences by verbal flamboyance or to intoxicate them with inflammatory eloquence in order to pit one group against another. Such oratory is not conducive to moral improvement, and the lives of the audience are by no means reformed. Neither does the eloquence of such speakers bring about any healthy change in the outlook of the audience nor in the quality of their lives. In fact, such eloquence may even have an evil and corrupting influence.

In sharp contrast to all this, the Prophet's oration is characterized by wisdom and coherence, balance and moderation of the highest order, and strict adherence to the truth. Each word of the Prophet (peace be on him) is pregnant with purposiveness and manifests a keen sense of proportion. In addition, all his oration is directed to just one purpose – to guide and reform mankind. In all that he says there is no trace of any concern for worldly interests – personal, familial or national. He only warns people against the evil consequences of their heedlessness and invites them to something that would lead to their own well-being. Furthermore, the effect of the Prophet's oration on his audience is radically different from that of sorcerers. For, all those who accept the Prophet's message undergo a change for the better; their moral conduct improves, and all in all they become oriented to righteousness and benevolence. It was, therefore, for the Prophet's detractors to consider whether sorcerers achieve such results and whether their professional skills are directed towards such noble purposes.

4. There is no reason to believe that after having created everything God chose to consign Himself to the limbo of unconcern. On the contrary, after His great act of creation He established Himself on the Throne and holds the reins of the entire universe so that He not only reigns but in fact also effectively rules over the universe. The Qur'ān considers it a colossal error – an error to which the ignorant have succumbed – to believe that after creating the universe God either left it to run on its own, or entrusted its affairs to others to govern it as they please. On the contrary, the Qur'ān emphasizes that it is God Who is directing all the affairs of His creation; that all power effectively rests with Him alone. The Qur'ān constantly drives home the point that God alone has all authority so that all that takes place in the universe or in any part of it takes place by His command or His leave. God's relationship with the universe is not simply that He created it; rather the reins of the universe are with Him and He is in effective and continual control of its affairs. It is He alone Who keeps the universe in existence and it is He alone Who directs it as He pleases. (See *Towards Understanding the Qur'ān*, vol. III, *al-A'rāf*, nn. 41–2, pp. 33–4.)

5. No one is in a position to interfere with God in His governance of the universe, or has the power to effectively intercede with God on anyone else's behalf and to prevail upon Him to change any of His decisions. Nor is anyone in such a position of power with God that his intercession would make or unmake anyone else's destiny. The utmost that a person can do is to pray to God. However, the acceptance or non-acceptance of such prayers rests solely with Him. No one is so powerful that his desire will, of necessity, always prevail with God, nor does anyone's intercession bind God to act according to the former's desire.

6. After emphasizing the given fact of God's lordship in the first part of the verse, man is now informed of its logical consequences. Since all authority rests solely with God, it is incumbent upon man to serve Him exclusively. God's lordship embraces the three-fold attributes of His being (i) the Sustainer, (ii) the Master, and (iii) the Sovereign. In like manner, the term *'ibādah* embraces the three-fold corresponding implications that man should (i) worship, (ii) serve, and (iii) obey God.

(4) To Him is your return.[8] This is Allah's promise that will certainly come true. Surely it is He Who brings about the creation of all and He will repeat it[9] so that He may justly reward those who believe and do righteous deeds; and that those who disbelieve may have a draught of boiling water and suffer a painful chastisement for their denying the truth.[10]

إِلَيْهِ مَرْجِعُكُمْ جَمِيعًا وَعْدَ ٱللَّهِ حَقًّا
إِنَّهُۥ يَبْدَؤُا۟ ٱلْخَلْقَ ثُمَّ يُعِيدُهُۥ لِيَجْزِىَ ٱلَّذِينَ
ءَامَنُوا۟ وَعَمِلُوا۟ ٱلصَّٰلِحَٰتِ بِٱلْقِسْطِ وَٱلَّذِينَ
كَفَرُوا۟ لَهُمْ شَرَابٌ مِّنْ حَمِيمٍ
وَعَذَابٌ أَلِيمٌۢ بِمَا كَانُوا۟
يَكْفُرُونَ ﴿٤﴾

'Ibādah, in the first sense, implies that since God alone is the Sustainer, it is to Him that man should offer his thanks, it is to Him that he should address all his prayers, it is to Him that he should bow in love and devotion and reverence. In the second sense, *'ibādah* denotes that since God alone is the Master, it behoves man that he should live as His slave, that he should not act independently of, let alone in defiance of Him, that he should refuse to be the slave of anyone other than God, both in thought and in deed. In its third sense, *'ibādah* means that since God alone is the Sovereign, man should obey His command, follow His Law, and abstain from arrogating sovereignty to himself or anyone other than Him.

7. Since man has been informed of the fundamental truths and has been shown the right way, there is no justification for him to remain engrossed in those false conceptions which have caused him to act in a manner altogether inconsistent with the reality.

8. The Prophet's teachings comprise two fundamental doctrines: (i) that God alone is man's Lord and hence man should worship Him, and (ii) that man is bound to return to his Lord in the Next Life wherein he will be made to render an account to his Lord. This particular verse focuses on the second of these two doctrines.

9. This Qur'ānic statement combines the enunciation of a basic doctrine with its supporting argument. The doctrine that is being enunciated here is that God will resurrect man. This is supported by the argument that it is God Who brought about the creation in the first place. All those who believe that the original creation was an act of God can neither consider it impossible nor

(5) He it is Who gave the sun radiance and the moon light, and determined the stages (for the waxing and waning of the moon) that you may learn the calculation of years and the reckoning of time. Allah has created all this with a rightful purpose (rather than out of play). He expounds His signs for the people who know. (6) Surely in the alternation of the night and the day and in all that Allah has created in the heavens and the earth there are signs for the people who seek to avoid (error of outlook and conduct).[11]

هُوَ ٱلَّذِى جَعَلَ ٱلشَّمْسَ ضِيَآءً
وَٱلْقَمَرَ نُورًا وَقَدَّرَهُۥ مَنَازِلَ لِتَعْلَمُوا۟
عَدَدَ ٱلسِّنِينَ وَٱلْحِسَابَ ۚ مَا خَلَقَ
ٱللَّهُ ذَٰلِكَ إِلَّا بِٱلْحَقِّ ۚ يُفَصِّلُ ٱلْءَايَٰتِ
لِقَوْمٍ يَعْلَمُونَ ﴿٥﴾ إِنَّ فِى ٱخْتِلَٰفِ ٱلَّيْلِ
وَٱلنَّهَارِ وَمَا خَلَقَ ٱللَّهُ فِى ٱلسَّمَٰوَٰتِ
وَٱلْأَرْضِ لَءَايَٰتٍ لِّقَوْمٍ
يَتَّقُونَ ﴿٦﴾

---

irrational to believe that God can and will create afresh. The only ones who might be inclined to deny such a possibility are those atheists who presumably out of aversion to the irrational religious practices of the priests, have succumbed to the absurd doctrine of creation without a Creator.

10. The present verse sets forth the rationale of resurrection. The preceding verses had conclusively established that resurrection is possible, that there is no reasonable ground to dub it as a far-fetched idea. Drawing upon the above, the verse under consideration points out that the requirements of justice and reason can only be fulfilled by resurrection, and that this calls for a repetition of the original act of creation by God.

The point that is being made here is that those who accept God as their One and the Only Lord and truly live in service and devotion to Him deserve to be fully rewarded for their righteous conduct. Likewise, those who reject the truth and act according to their own whim deserve to be duly punished for their unrighteous conduct. The present life is so constituted that reward and punishment are not being meted out and cannot be meted out in the manner described above. This is a plain fact, and one which is evident to all except those who are obstinate. This being the case, reason and justice demand fresh creation in order that such reward and punishment be meted out. (For further

(7) Surely those who do not expect to meet Us, who are gratified with the life of the world and content with it, and are heedless of Our signs, (8) their abode shall be the Fire in return for their misdeeds.[12]

إِنَّ ٱلَّذِينَ لَا يَرْجُونَ لِقَآءَنَا وَرَضُوا۟ بِٱلْحَيَوٰةِ ٱلدُّنْيَا وَٱطْمَأَنُّوا۟ بِهَا وَٱلَّذِينَ هُمْ عَنْ ءَايَٰتِنَا غَٰفِلُونَ ۝٧ أُو۟لَٰٓئِكَ مَأْوَىٰهُمُ ٱلنَّارُ بِمَا كَانُوا۟ يَكْسِبُونَ ۝٨

elaboration see *Towards Understanding the Qur'ān,* vol. III, *al-A'rāf,* n. 30, pp. 23–6; see also *Hūd,* n. 105 below – Ed.)

11. This provides yet another argument in support of the doctrine of the Hereafter. The argument is derived from the orderly nature of the universe. This vast universe – the handiwork of God – is spread out before our eyes. It is full of signs of God's power and wisdom such as those which underlie the sun and the moon and the alternation of night and day. Even a superficial glance at the universe is enough to convince one that the Creator of this enormous universe is not at all like a child who creates something to play with and after enjoying it for a while whimsically destroys it. For it is quite evident that every act of the Creator is characterized by order and wisdom, and that a strong purposiveness underlies everything, even a speck of dust. Now, since the Creator is All-Wise – as is evident from His creation – it is absurd to assume that He Who has also invested man with reason, moral consciousness and free-will, will not call man to account for his conduct; that He will altogether disregard the need for retribution arising from man's responsibility which in turn stems from his inherent rational and moral endowments.

Apart from expounding the doctrine of the Hereafter, the above verses also adduce the following three arguments in support of that doctrine:

First, a persuasive case is made out in support of the possibility of a second life. The basis of the argument is that the creation of man in the first instance is indicative of God's creative power. (There is no reason to believe that God has become bereft of that power of creation, and hence would be unable to create man afresh – Ed.)

Second, the Next Life is needed in order that man might be rewarded or punished in consideration of his performance, whether good or bad. Both justice and reason seem to call for a new life wherein everyone would be able to see, in a fair manner, the consequence of his deeds.

Third, that the Next Life, which is a requirement of justice and reason, will certainly come to pass. This is because the Creator, Who created man and the universe, is All-Wise, and it is inconceivable that such a Being will not respond to an unmistakable requirement of justice and reason.

After careful consideration it appears that the above are the only possible arguments that might be adduced and they suffice to establish that there is life after death. The only possible question that remains, after having established that the Next Life is demanded by both reason and justice, and also that it is a requisite of God's wisdom, is whether it is possible to visually observe the Next Life in the manner in which people observe other objects. Now it should be clearly understood that this inability will remain during the present phase of existence. The reason for it is that God asks man to believe in certain truths and such a demand in respect of objects which can be observed with human eyes would be utterly meaningless. The test to which man has been put consists precisely of this: whether man can affirm certain truths which belong to the suprasensory realm by the use of his rational faculties.

Another point which has been stated in this context also deserves serious consideration. This is embodied in the following Qur'ānic statement: 'He expounds His signs for the people who know' (*Yūnus* 10: 5); '. . . and in all that Allah has created in the heavens and the earth there are signs for the people who seek to avoid (error of outlook and conduct)' (*Yūnus* 10: 6). This means that God in His infinite wisdom has seen to it that in the multifarious phenomena of existence there should be plenty of signs which betoken the hidden realities underlying that phenomena. However, not all men will be able to benefit from those signs. Those who will be able to benefit are those (i) who liberate themselves from prejudices and seek knowledge with the help of the natural endowments bestowed upon them by God, and (ii) those who are keen not to fall into error and who earnestly seek to adhere to the right way.

12. Here again a doctrine has been put forth along with its supporting argument. (For another such instance see n. 9 above – Ed.) The statement that is being made here is that rejection of the doctrine of the Hereafter necessarily entails the punishment of Hell, and the argument that is being proffered in support of it is that those who are oblivious to the Hereafter commit, because of their disbelief in it, evil deeds which can only lead to them suffering the torments of Hell. This argument is corroborated by the entire record of man's past. It is quite clear that the lives of those who do not believe that they will not be held to account by God for their deeds; who work on the assumption that life is merely confined to the span of worldly existence; who measure human success or failure only in terms of the extent of material comfort, fame and power that a person is able to enjoy; who under the influence of such materialistic notions do not even care to pay attention to those signs of God which point to reality, assume an altogether wrong direction with the result that their life is vitiated. Hence they live a totally unbridled life, develop the worst possible character traits, and fill God's earth with injustice and corruption, with sin and transgression, and ultimately end up meriting the punishment of Hell.

It will be seen that whereas the three arguments mentioned earlier were of a theoretical nature the above argument about the Hereafter is drawn from human experience itself. Although in the present verse the argument is found only in an implicit form, it is spelt out at several other places in the Qur'ān. The argument essentially is that unless man's character rests on the consciousness and conviction that he will have to render an account for all his deeds to God, both man's individual and collective behaviour will fail to have sound basis and direction. It would seem, therefore, to be worth asking: why is this so? Why is it that once this consciousness and conviction are altogether ended or greatly enfeebled, the human character turns to iniquity and corruption? Had affirmation of the Hereafter not been in conformity with reality, and conversely, had its denial not been opposed to it, then the evil consequences flowing from the denial of the Hereafter would not have been found with such unfailing regularity. If adherence to a proposition invariably leads to good results, and failure to adhere to it invariably leads to evil consequences, then this definitely proves the proposition to be true.

In an attempt to refute the above argument it is sometimes contended that even atheists who reject the Hereafter and follow a materialistic approach to life often lead lives that are on the whole good and decent, that they hold themselves free from corruption and injustice. Not only that but also that their actual conduct is characterized by righteousness and benevolence. However, only a little reflection will make apparent the fallacy underlying this argument. For if one were to examine any atheistic or materialistic philosophy or ideology one will not find in them any basis for righteous behaviour which draws such lavish praise from so-called 'righteous' atheists. Nor can it be established by logical reasoning that an atheistic philosophy of life provides any incentive to embrace such virtues as truthfulness, trustworthiness, honesty, faithfulness to one's commitment, benevolence, generosity, preferring the interests of others to one's own, self-restraint, chastity, recognition of the rights of others, and fulfilment of one's obligations. The fact is that once God and the Hereafter are relegated to oblivion, the only practicable course left for man is to anchor his morality on utilitarianism. All other philosophical ideas which are expounded are merely theoretical embellishments and have no relevance for man's practical life.

As for utilitarian morality – no matter how hard we might try to broaden its scope – it does not go beyond teaching man that he ought to do that which will yield to him or to his society some worldly benefit. Now since utility is the criterion of all acts, such a philosophy tends to make man cynical, with the result that in order to derive benefits, he will not differentiate between truth and lie; between trustworthiness and treachery; between honesty and dishonesty; between loyalty and perfidy; between observing justice and committing wrong. In short, a person under the spell of utilitarian ideas will be ready to do a thing or its opposite, depending on what serves his interests best. The conduct of the British is illustrative of this stance. It is sometimes contended that though the British have a materialistic outlook on life and generally do not believe in the Hereafter, they are more truthful, fairer, and more straightforward and faithful to their commitment.

The fact, however, is that the tenuous character of moral values under a utilitarian moral philosophy is amply illustrated by the character of the British.

(9) Surely those who believe (in the truths revealed in the Book) and do righteous deeds their Lord will guide them aright because of their faith. Rivers shall flow beneath them in the Gardens of Bliss.[13] (10) Their cry in it will be: 'Glory be to You, Our Lord!', and their greeting: 'Peace!'; and their cry will always end with: 'All praise be to Allah, the Lord of the universe.'[14]

إِنَّ الَّذِينَ ءَامَنُوا وَعَمِلُوا
الصَّٰلِحَٰتِ يَهْدِيهِمْ رَبُّهُم
بِإِيمَٰنِهِمْ تَجْرِى مِن تَحْتِهِمُ
الْأَنْهَٰرُ فِى جَنَّٰتِ النَّعِيمِ ﴿٩﴾
دَعْوَىٰهُمْ فِيهَا سُبْحَٰنَكَ اللَّهُمَّ
وَتَحِيَّتُهُمْ فِيهَا سَلَٰمٌ وَءَاخِرُ
دَعْوَىٰهُمْ أَنِ الْحَمْدُ لِلَّهِ
رَبِّ الْعَٰلَمِينَ ﴿١٠﴾

For their actual conduct clearly shows that they do not consider moral values to have any intrinsic worth. This is evident from the fact that even those values which are held by the British to be good in their individual lives are brazenly flouted when they act as a nation. Had the qualities of truthfulness, justice, honesty and faithfulness to one's committed word been regarded as intrinsic virtues, it would have been altogether out of the question for the elected rulers of Britain to cynically violate all moral principles in governmental and international affairs and yet continue to retain the confidence of the British people. Does such a behaviour of a people who do not take the Hereafter seriously prove that they do not believe in absolute moral values? Does it also not prove that, guided by concern for material interests, such people are capable of following mutually opposed views simultaneously?

Nevertheless, if we do find some people who, in spite of their not believing in God and the Hereafter, consistently adhere to some moral virtues and abstain from evil, there should be no mistaking that their righteous conduct and piety represents the continuing influence which religious ideas and practices have over them – even if unconsciously – rather than their subscription to a materialistic philosophy of life. If they possess any portion of the wealth of morality, there can be no doubt that it was stolen from the treasure-house of religion. It is ironical that such persons are now using the same wealth derived from religious sources, to promote an irreligious way of life. We consider this an act of theft because irreligiousness and materialism are altogether bereft of morality.

13. This Qur'ānic statement calls for serious reflection. The sequence of ideas presented here is also quite significant because answers have been

systematically provided to a number of highly relevant basic questions. Let us look at these answers in their sequence. Why will the righteous enter Paradise? The answer is: because they have followed the straight way in their worldly life. That is, in all matters and in every walk of life, in all affairs relating to the personal or collective life they have been righteous and have abstained from false ways.

This gives rise to another question: how were the righteous able to obtain a criterion that would enable them to distinguish, at every turn and crossroad of life, between right and wrong, between good and evil, between fair and unfair? And how did they come to have the strength to adhere to what is right and avoid what is wrong? All this, of course, came from their Lord Who bestowed upon them both the guidance which they needed to know the right way and the succour required to follow it. In answer to why their Lord bestowed upon them this guidance and succour, we are reminded that all this was in consideration for their faith.

It is also made clear that this reward is not in lieu of merely a verbal profession to faith, a profession that is no more than a formal acceptance of certain propositions. Rather, the reward is in consideration for a faith that became the moving spirit of a believer's character and personality, the force that led him to righteous deeds and conduct. We can observe in our own physical lives that a person's survival, state of health, level of energy, and joy of living all depend upon sustenance from the right kind of food. This food, once digested, provides blood to the veins and arteries, provides energy to the whole body and enables the different limbs to function properly.

The same holds true of man's success in the moral domain. It is sound beliefs which ensure that he will have the correct outlook, sound orientation and right behaviour that will ultimately lead to his success. Such results, however, do not ensue from that kind of believing which either consists of a mere profession to faith, or is confined to some obscure corner of man's head or heart. The wholesome results mentioned above can only be produced by a faith which deeply permeates man's entire being, shaping his mental outlook, even becoming his instinct; a faith which is fully reflected in his character, conduct and outlook on life. We have just noted the importance of food. We know that the person who, in spite of eating remains like one who has not partaken of any food, would not be able to enjoy the healthy results that are the lot of the person who has fully assimilated what he ate. How can it be conceived that it would be different in the moral domain of human life? How can it be that he who remains, even after believing, like the one who does not believe, will derive the benefit and receive the reward meant for those whose believing leads to righteous living?

14. This should remove any misconceptions about Paradise which seem to have been formed by some people of frail understanding. Subtly, the verse suggests that when people are admitted to Paradise, they will not instantly pounce upon the objects of their desire as the starved and hungry are wont to do when they observe food. Nor will they frantically go about giving vent to their

(11) Were Allah[15] to hasten to bring upon men (the consequence of) evil in the way men hasten in seeking the wealth of this world, their term would have long since expired. (But that is not Our way.) So We leave alone those who do not expect to meet Us that they may blindly stumble in their transgression. ▶

۞ وَلَوْ يُعَجِّلُ ٱللَّهُ لِلنَّاسِ ٱلشَّرَّ ٱسْتِعْجَالَهُم بِٱلْخَيْرِ لَقُضِىَ إِلَيْهِمْ أَجَلُهُمْ ۖ فَنَذَرُ ٱلَّذِينَ لَا يَرْجُونَ لِقَآءَنَا فِى طُغْيَٰنِهِمْ يَعْمَهُونَ ﴿١١﴾

lusts, impatiently demanding their cherished objects of enjoyment – beautiful women, wine, dissolute singing and music. The fact is that the men of faith and righteousness who are admitted to Paradise will be those who, during their life in the world, have embellished their lives with sublime ideas and noble deeds, who have refined their emotions, who have oriented their desires in the right direction, and who have purified their conduct and character. Thus, the nobility which they have developed in their personalities will shine in even greater splendour when they set their feet in the pure and clean environment of Paradise. Those same traits which characterized their behaviour in the world will appear with even greater lustre.

The favourite occupation of such people in Paradise will be the same as during their life on the earth – to celebrate the praise of God. Likewise, their relationships in Paradise will be imbued with feelings of mutual harmony and concern for each other's well-being as had been the case in this world.

15. These introductory remarks are followed by a discourse which comprises the admonition and explanation of certain important points. For a fuller appreciation of the discourse, it is better to take note first of the following points about its background.

First, that the prolonged and acute famine which had virtually destroyed the people of Makka had ended just a little before the revelation of these verses. The famine was so severe that even the most arrogant leaders of the Quraysh had been humbled. As a result, idol-worship had declined and people turned increasingly, with prayer and sincere supplication, to the One True God. The famine was so acute that at one stage Abū Sufyān had approached the Prophet (peace be on him) with a request to implore God to deliver them from the calamity. However, no sooner had the famine ended and heavy rains brought about a rich harvest and prosperity than the Makkans reverted to their old evil habits, to their rebellion against God, to their hostile machinations against

(12) And (such is man that) when an affliction befalls him, he cries out to Us, reclining and sitting and standing. But no sooner than We have removed his affliction, he passes on as though he had never cried out to Us to remove his affliction. Thus it is that the misdeeds of the transgressors are made fair-seeming to them. ▶

وَإِذَا مَسَّ ٱلْإِنسَٰنَ ٱلضُّرُّ دَعَانَا لِجَنۢبِهِۦٓ أَوْ قَاعِدًا أَوْ قَآئِمًا فَلَمَّا كَشَفْنَا عَنْهُ ضُرَّهُۥ مَرَّ كَأَن لَّمْ يَدْعُنَآ إِلَىٰ ضُرٍّ مَّسَّهُۥ كَذَٰلِكَ زُيِّنَ لِلْمُسْرِفِينَ مَا كَانُوا۟ يَعْمَلُونَ ﴿١٢﴾

Islam. Those who had turned to God for a short while once again became engrossed in their former apathy and wickedness. (See also *al-Naḥl* 16: 113; *al-Mu'minūn* 23: 75–7; and *al-Dukhān* 44: 10–16. See also al-Bukhārī, *Abwāb al-Istisqā', Bāb idhā istashfa'a al-Mushrikūn bi al-Muslimīn 'ind al-Qaḥṭ* – Ed.)

Second, whenever the Prophet (peace be on him) warned the Makkans of God's punishment as a consequence of their rejecting the truth, they retorted by asking: why had God's punishment not befallen them there and then? Why was it being delayed?

In response, the Qur'ān states that when it comes to punishing human beings God does not resort to the same haste which He resorts to when He wants to show mercy. The Makkans had seen that God had quickly halted the famine when they had prayed for its removal. They thought that if they were considered by God to be an evil people, He would have afflicted them with a calamitous punishment as soon as they had asked for it, or as soon as they engaged in rebellion against God. But that is not God's way. No matter how rebellious a people become, God grants them ample time to make amends. He also warns them over and over again and grants them a long respite. It is only when leniency has run its full course that His law of retribution comes into action. In sharp contrast to this is the attitude of men of low mettle. This is amply reflected in the ways of the rebellious ones among the Quraysh. When they encountered a disaster, they remembered God and bewailed and bemoaned of the same to Him. As soon as hard times were over, however, they forgot everything about God. It is precisely this kind of behaviour by different nations which invites God's punishment.

(13) Surely We destroyed the nations (which had risen to heights of glory in their times) before you[16] when they indulged in wrong-doing[17] and refused to believe even when their Messengers brought clear signs to them. Thus do We recompense the people who are guilty. (14) Now We have appointed you as their successors in the earth to see how you act.[18]

وَلَقَدْ أَهْلَكْنَا ٱلْقُرُونَ مِن قَبْلِكُمْ
لَمَّا ظَلَمُوا۟ ۙ وَجَآءَتْهُمْ رُسُلُهُم
بِٱلْبَيِّنَٰتِ وَمَا كَانُوا۟ لِيُؤْمِنُوا۟ ۚ كَذَٰلِكَ
نَجْزِى ٱلْقَوْمَ ٱلْمُجْرِمِينَ ﴿١٣﴾ ثُمَّ
جَعَلْنَٰكُمْ خَلَٰٓئِفَ فِى ٱلْأَرْضِ
مِنۢ بَعْدِهِمْ لِنَنظُرَ كَيْفَ
تَعْمَلُونَ ﴿١٤﴾

16. In Arabic, the word *qarn,* which occurs in the above verse, usually denotes 'the people of a given age'. However, the word in its several usages in the Qur'ān, connotes a 'nation' which, wielded in its heyday, whether fully or partially, the reins of world leadership. When it is said that a certain nation was 'destroyed' this does not necessarily mean its total annihilation. When any such nation suffers the loss of its ascendancy and leadership, when its culture and civilization become extinct, when its identity is effaced, in fact, when such a nation disintegrates and its component parts become assimilated into other nations, then it is fair to say that it has suffered destruction.

17. The expression *ẓulm* (wrong-doing, injustice) in the above verse has not been used in the limited sense in which it is generally used. Instead, here the word embraces the whole range of sins which consists of man exceeding the limits of service and obedience to God. (For further explanation see *Towards Understanding the Qur'ān,* vol. I, *al-Baqarah,* 2, n. 49, p. 64 – Ed.)

18. One should not lose sight of the fact that the immediate addressees of the present discourse were the people of Arabia. Here they are told that all previous nations were granted the opportunity to show their potential to do good. Instead, they took to wrong-doing and rebellion and rejected the message of the Prophets who had been raised solely to guide them. Thus they failed in the test to which they were put by God and were accordingly removed from the scene of history. Now the turn of the Arabs has come and they have also been granted the opportunity to prove their worth. They have also been put to the same test to which the previous nations had been put and in which they

(15) And whenever Our clear revelations are recited to them, those who do not expect to meet Us say: 'Bring us a Qur'ān other than this one, or at least make changes in it.'[19] Tell them (O Muḥammad): 'It is not for me to change it of my accord. I only follow what is revealed to me. Were I to disobey my Lord, I fear the chastisement of an Awesome Day.'[20] ▶

وَإِذَا تُتْلَىٰ عَلَيْهِمْ ءَايَاتُنَا بَيِّنَٰتٍ قَالَ
ٱلَّذِينَ لَا يَرْجُونَ لِقَآءَنَا ٱئْتِ
بِقُرْءَانٍ غَيْرِ هَٰذَآ أَوْ بَدِّلْهُ قُلْ
مَا يَكُونُ لِىٓ أَنْ أُبَدِّلَهُۥ مِن تِلْقَآئِ
نَفْسِىٓ إِنْ أَتَّبِعُ إِلَّا مَا يُوحَىٰٓ إِلَىَّ إِنِّىٓ
أَخَافُ إِنْ عَصَيْتُ رَبِّى عَذَابَ يَوْمٍ
عَظِيمٍ ﴿١٥﴾

had failed. If the people of Arabia want to avoid meeting a similarly tragic fate, they would be well advised to avail themselves of the opportunity granted them, to learn the lessons from the history of the previous nations, and to avoid the mistakes which led to the undoing of many in the past.

19. This statement of the unbelievers was based, first of all, on the misconception that the Qur'ān, which the Prophet (peace be on him) presented to them as the 'Word of God', was in fact a product of his own mind which he had ascribed to God merely to invest it with authority. Moreover, they wanted to impress upon the Prophet (peace be on him) that the contents of his message were of little practical, worldly use. The emphasis on the unity of God, on the Life to Come and on the moral principles which people were asked to follow – all these were of no practical consequence to them. They virtually told the Prophet (peace be on him), that if he wanted to lead them he should come forth with something that would be of benefit to them and ameliorate their worldly life. And if this was not possible, then he should at least show some flexibility in his attitude which would enable them to strike a compromise with him by effecting mutual accommodation between the Makkan unbelievers and the Prophet (peace be on him) himself.

In other words, the Makkans felt that the Prophet's doctrine of God's unity should not totally exclude their polytheism; that his conception of devotion to God should be such as to allow them some scope for their worldliness and self-indulgence; that the call to believe in the Hereafter should be such that it might still be possible for them to behave in the world as they pleased and yet entertain the hope of somehow attaining salvation in the Next World. Likewise, the absolute and categorical nature of moral principles enunciated

(16) Tell them: 'Had Allah so willed, I would not have recited the Qur'ān to you, nor would Allah have informed you of it. I have spent a lifetime among you before this. Do you, then, not use your reason?[21] ▶

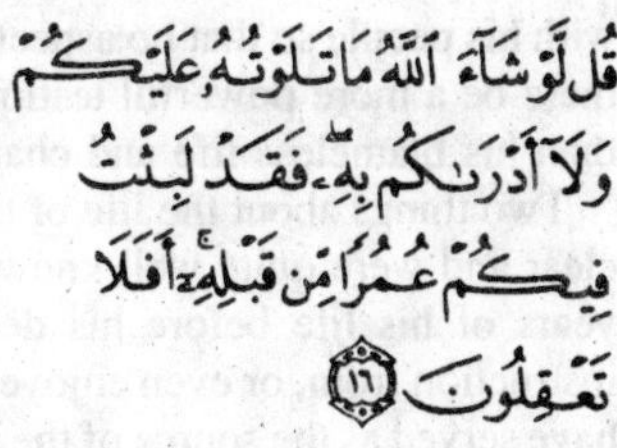

by the Prophet (peace be on him) was also unpalatable to them. They wanted moral principles to be propounded in a manner that would provide concessions to their predilections and biases, to their customs and usages, to their personal and national interests, and to the lusts and desires that they wished to satisfy.

In effect, they suggested a compromise according to which one sphere of life should be earmarked as 'religious', and in this sphere men should render to God what rightfully belongs to Him. Beyond this sphere, however, it should be left to people's discretion to run their worldly affairs as they pleased. It seemed altogether outrageous to them that the doctrines of the unity of God and accountability in the Hereafter should embrace the whole gamut of human life, and that man should be asked to subject himself entirely to the Law of God.

20. This is the Prophet's response to what has been said above (see n. 19 above). It is made clear that the Prophet (peace be on him) was not the author of the Qur'ān; and that since it had only been revealed to him, he had no authority therefore to make any alteration in it whatsoever. It is also made clear that the question was not one that could be the subject of any bargain. The unbelievers should either accept the faith propounded by the Prophet (peace be on him) *in toto* or reject it *in toto*.

21. This is indeed a very weighty argument in refutation of the unbelievers' allegation that the Prophet (peace be on him) had himself authored the Qur'ān and subsequently ascribed it to God. So far as other arguments are concerned, they might be considered as somewhat remote. But the argument based on the life and character of the Prophet (peace be on him) was particularly weighty since the Makkans were thoroughly familiar with the whole of his life. Before his designation as a Prophet, he had spent a full forty years in their midst. He was born in their city. They had observed his childhood, and then his youth, and it was in their city that he had reached his middle age. He had also had a variety of dealings with them. He had had social interaction, business transactions, matrimonial ties, and relationships of every conceivable nature

with his people so that no aspect of his life was hidden from their view. Could there be a more powerful testimony to the truth of his claim to prophethood than his blameless life and character?

Two things about the life of the Prophet (peace be on him) were especially clear and were quite well known to all Makkans. First, that during the forty years of his life before his designation as a Prophet, he had received no instruction from, or even enjoyed the company of learned people which could have served as the source of the ideas which began to flow, as would a stream, from his lips as soon as he claimed, at the age of forty, that he had been designated as a Prophet. Before that he was never seen to have been concerned with the problems, or to have discussed the subjects, or to have expressed the ideas which frequently recur in the Qur'ān. In fact none of his closest friends and relatives had foreseen in his pre-Prophetic life any signs indicative of the great message which he suddenly started to preach at the age of forty. These pieces of evidence, taken together, provide incontrovertible evidence that the Qur'ān is not a product of the Prophet's mind; that it had come to the Prophet (peace be on him) from without. For no human being can produce something for which traces of growth and evolution are not found in the earlier period of his life.

This explains the fact that when some of the more crafty Makkan unbelievers realized the sheer absurdity of their allegation that the Prophet (peace be on him) was the author of the Qur'ān, they chose to propagate that there must be some other person who had taught the Prophet (peace be on him) the Qur'ān. Such a statement, however, was even more preposterous since they failed to convincingly point out who that other person was who was the true source of the Qur'ān. Even leaving aside Makka, the fact is that there was not a single person throughout the length and breadth of Arabia who possessed the competence needed for the authorship of the Qur'ān. Had such an extraordinary person existed, how could he have remained hidden from the sight of others?

Second, the pre-Prophetic life of Muḥammad (peace be on him) clearly shows him to be a man of exceptionally high moral character for there was not the least trace of any evil – whether lies, deceit, vile cunning or trickery. On the contrary, all those who came into contact with the Prophet (peace be on him) were impressed by him as a person of flawless character, as one utterly truthful and trustworthy.

An illustration in point is the incident related in connection with the re-building of the Ka'bah five years before his designation as a Prophet. There was a serious dispute between the various families of the Quraysh on the question as to who should have the privilege of placing the Black Stone in its place in the edifice of the Ka'bah. In order to reach an amicable accord, they resolved that they would abide by the ruling given by the first person who entered the Ka'bah the following day. The next day people saw it was the Prophet (peace be on him) who was the first to enter. They exclaimed: 'Here is a trustworthy man (*amīn*). We agree [to follow his ruling]. He is Muḥammad.' (Ibn Sa'd, *al-Ṭabaqāt,* vol. 1, p. 146 – Ed.) Thus, before designating

(17) Who, then, is a greater wrong-doer than he who forges a lie against Allah or rejects His signs as false?[22] Surely the guilty shall not prosper.'[23]

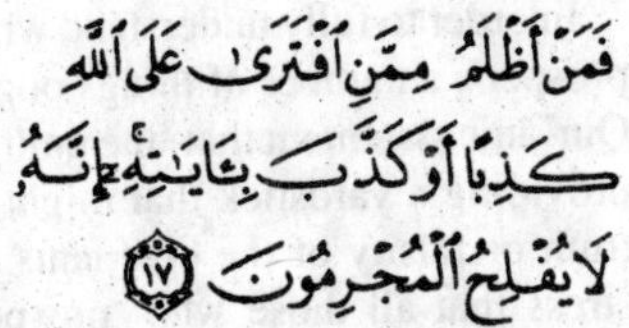

Muḥammad (peace be on him) as a Prophet, God had the whole body of the Quraysh testify to his trustworthiness. No room was left, therefore, for suspecting that he who had never resorted to lying or deceit throughout his life would suddenly resort to fabricating a gigantic lie; that he would first compose something, then deny that it was his work, and would then ascribe it to God.

In view of the above, God directs the Prophet (peace be on him) to ask the unbelievers to use their brains before levelling such a stupid allegation against him. For the Prophet (peace be on him) was after all no stranger to them; he had spent virtually a whole lifetime in their midst. In view of the well-known and uniformly high level of his conduct and character, how could it even be conceived that he would falsely ascribe the Qur'ān to God if God had not actually revealed it to him. (For further elaboration see *al-Qaṣaṣ* 28, n. 109.)

22. If the verses of the Qur'ān were in fact not from God but had been composed by the Prophet (peace be on him) who then claimed them to be from God, the Prophet would be guilty of the worst kind of wrong. But if, on the contrary, the Qur'ān was the word of God, those who rejected it as false must be regarded as the worst kind of wrong-doers.

23. The Qur'ānic term *falāḥ* (prosperity, success) used in the above verse has been understood by some to signify such things as longevity, worldly prosperity and other worldly attainments. Under this false impression, they tend to believe that if a claimant to prophethood attains material prosperity and longevity or if his message is spread around, then he ought to be considered a genuine Prophet because he has indeed attained 'prosperity'. Had he been an impostor, it is argued, he would soon have been assassinated, or would have starved to death, and, in any case, his message would not have spread around. Such an absurd line of argument can only be pursued by those who are altogether ignorant of the concept of *fālāḥ* (prosperity) as envisaged in the Qur'ān, who are unaware of God's law of respite regarding evil-doers, and who are altogether unappreciative of the special meaning in which the term has been employed in the present context.

In order to fully understand what is meant by saying that 'the guilty shall not prosper', a number of things ought to be borne in mind. In the first place, the Qur'ānic statement that 'the guilty shall not prosper' is not made with a view to providing a yardstick that might be applied by people so as to determine the truth or falsity of the claimants of prophethood. The verse does not seek to stress that all those who 'prosper' after claiming to be a Prophet are truly Prophets, and that those who do not prosper after making such a claim are not so. The point of emphasis here is altogether different. Here the Prophet (peace be on him) is being made to say that since he knows fully that those guilty of inventing lies against Allah could not prosper, he would not dare make any claim to prophethood if such a claim was false.

On the other hand, the Prophet (peace be on him) also knew that the unbelievers were guilty of rejecting the true signs of God and of declaring a true Prophet of God to be an impostor. In view of that monstrous guilt, it was quite apparent to the Prophet (peace be on him) that they would not prosper.

Moreover, the Qur'ānic term *falāḥ* (prosperity, success) has not been used in the limited sense of worldly success. Rather, it denotes that enduring success which admits of no failure regardless of whether one is able to achieve success in the present phase of one's existence or not. It is quite possible that someone who calls people to falsehood might enjoy life and flourish in a worldly sense, and he might even be able to attain a substantial following for his message. But this is not true prosperity or success; rather it constitutes total loss and failure. Contrarily, it is also possible that someone who calls people to the truth might be exposed to much persecution and be overwhelmed by pain and suffering. It is possible that even before he is able to create any significant following, he is continually subjected to persecution and torture. In the Qur'ānic view, such an apparently tragic end constitutes the very zenith of such a person's success rather than his failure.

Moreover, it should be remembered that it has been amply elucidated in the Qur'ān that God does not punish evil-doers instantly; that He rather grants them a fair opportunity to mend their ways. Not only that, if the evil-doers misuse the respite granted by God to perpetrate further wrongs, they are sometimes granted an even further respite.

In fact, at times a variety of worldly favours are bestowed upon such evil-doers in order that the potential for wickedness inherent in them might be fully exposed by their actions, proving that they do indeed deserve a very severe punishment. Hence, if an impostor continues to enjoy periods of respite and if worldly favours are lavished upon him this should not in any way give rise to the notion that he is on the right path.

In the same way as God grants respite to other evil-doers, He also grants respite to impostors. There are no grounds whatsoever for believing that the respite granted to other evil-doers would not be granted to those impostors who lay false claim to prophethood. We may well call to mind that Satan himself has been granted a respite until Doomsday. It has never been indicated that although Satan is granted a free hand to misguide human beings, as soon as he

(18) They worship, beside Allah, those who can neither harm nor profit them, saying: 'These are our intercessors with Allah.' Tell them (O Muḥammad): 'Do you inform Allah of something regarding whose existence in the heavens or on the earth He has no knowledge?[24] Holy is He and He is exalted far above what they associate with Him in His divinity'.

وَيَعْبُدُونَ مِن دُونِ ٱللَّهِ مَا لَا يَضُرُّهُمْ وَلَا يَنفَعُهُمْ وَيَقُولُونَ هَٰٓؤُلَآءِ شُفَعَٰٓؤُنَا عِندَ ٱللَّهِ قُلْ أَتُنَبِّـُٔونَ ٱللَّهَ بِمَا لَا يَعْلَمُ فِى ٱلسَّمَٰوَٰتِ وَلَا فِى ٱلْأَرْضِ سُبْحَٰنَهُۥ وَتَعَٰلَىٰ عَمَّا يُشْرِكُونَ ١٨

---

throws up an impostor claiming prophethood such a venture is instantly nipped in the bud.

In order to refute the view expressed above it is possible that someone may refer to the following verse of the Qur'ān:

> Now if he [i.e. Muḥammad] would have made up, ascribed some sayings to Us, We would indeed have seized him by the right hand, and then indeed would have cut his life-vein (*al-Ḥāqqah* 69: 44–6).

Even a little reflection makes it obvious that the verse in question does not contradict the view we have expressed above. For, what the present verse says relates to a principle which God follows in dealing with true Prophets. Were any such Prophet to falsely claim something to be a revelation from God, he would instantly be seized by God's wrath. To argue to the contrary that all those who are not seized by God's wrath are necessarily genuine Prophets is simply a logical fallacy devoid of any justification. For the threat of instant Divine wrath embodied in this verse is applicable only to true Prophets, and not to impostors who, like other evil-doers, are granted a respite.

This can be well understood if we bear in mind the disciplinary rules laid down by different governments for their officials. It is obvious that those rules are not enforced in respect of ordinary citizens. Were the latter to lay any false claim to being a government official, he would be subjected to the normal rules of the criminal code relating to the conviction of those who are guilty of fraud rather than to the disciplinary rules meant for government officials. Under this analogy, an impostor who claims to be a Prophet, would be dealt with by God along with other evil-doers who commit evil, and who, as we know, are not necessarily punished immediately.

(19) Once all men were but a single community; then they disagreed (and formulated different beliefs and rites).[25] Had it not been that your Lord had already so ordained, a decisive judgement would have been made regarding their disagreements.[26]

وَمَا كَانَ ٱلنَّاسُ إِلَّآ أُمَّةً وَٰحِدَةً فَٱخْتَلَفُوا۟ ۚ وَلَوْلَا كَلِمَةٌ سَبَقَتْ مِن رَّبِّكَ لَقُضِىَ بَيْنَهُمْ فِيمَا فِيهِ يَخْتَلِفُونَ ١٩

In any case, as we have pointed out earlier, the verses quoted above were not revealed so as to provide the criterion to judge the truth of anyone who lays claim to prophethood. This verse should not be considered to mean that if a celestial hand stretches forth to cut off the life-vein of a claimant to prophethood, such a person is an impostor; and if that does not happen, he is a genuine Prophet. Such a weird criterion would have been needed only if no other means were available to judge the genuineness of a claimant to prophethood. But as things stand, a Prophet is known by his character, by his work, and by the contents of his message.

24. To say that something is not known to God amounts to saying that it does not exist. For, quite obviously, all that exists is known to God. The above verse thus subtly points out the non-existence of any intercessors on behalf of unbelievers insofar as God does not know that there exist any in the heavens, or on the earth who would intercede on behalf of the unbelievers. That being so, who are those intercessors about whose existence and whose power of intercession with God the unbelievers wanted to inform the Prophet (peace be on him)?

25. For further elaboration see *Towards Understanding the Qur'ān,* vol. I, *al-Baqarah* 2, n. 230, pp. 165–6, and *ibid.*, vol. II, *al-An'ām* 6, n. 24, pp. 228–9 – Ed.

26. The fact is that God has wilfully kept reality beyond the ken of man's sense-perception. This was done so as to test whether man, by making proper use of his reason, conscience and intuition, is able to find the right way. As a logical corollary of this, God allows those who decide to follow any other way rather than the right one to do so. Had this not been the case, the reality could have been instantly unmasked and that would have put an end to all disagreements relating to the issue.

(20) They say: 'Why was a sign not sent down upon the Prophet from His Lord?'[27] Tell (such people): 'The realm of the Unseen belongs to Allah. Wait, then; I shall wait along with you.'[28]

وَيَقُولُونَ لَوْلَآ أُنزِلَ عَلَيْهِ ءَايَةٌ مِّن رَّبِّهِۦ فَقُلْ إِنَّمَا ٱلْغَيْبُ لِلَّهِ فَٱنتَظِرُوٓاْ إِنِّى مَعَكُم مِّنَ ٱلْمُنتَظِرِينَ ﴿٢٠﴾

This statement has been made in order to remove a major misconception. Many people feel disconcerted today, as they felt disconcerted at the time when the Qur'ān was revealed, by the fact that there are found different religions in the world and that the followers of each of these are convinced that their religion alone is the true one. People have been puzzled as to how to determine which religion is the right one and which is not.

In this regard, the Qur'ānic view which is being articulated here is that multiplicity of religions does not constitute the original state of things, that it is a relatively later development in human history. Initially, all mankind professed a single religion, and that religion was the true one. Later on, people began to disagree regarding the truth and this gave rise to different religions and creeds. Now it is not likely that God would dramatically appear before them and reveal the reality to them directly during the present phase of their worldly existence. For, the very purpose of the present life is to test people. And this test consists of finding out who discovers the reality – even though it is beyond the reach of the senses – with the help of his reason and common sense.

27. The word 'sign' in the verse refers to the proof which supports a person's claim that he is a true Prophet and that his teaching is truly from God. In this connection it ought to be remembered that the demand of the unbelievers that the Prophet (peace be on him) should bring forth some sign to support his claim to be a Prophet was not made with sincerity. Their position was not that of a group of sincere people who were otherwise keen to accept the truth as soon as it became apparent to them, and who were ready to mould their own conduct, habits and social life according to its requirements, and all that they were waiting for was some sign, some proof, that would create in them a genuine conviction. The fact, on the contrary, was that the unbelievers' demand for miraculous signs was merely a pretext which they proffered in order to rationalize their disbelief. For they were sure to reject every sign, regardless of what that sign was, as unconvincing. Since they were hardened unbelievers, they were not prepared at all to accept such unseen truths as the unity of God and the Hereafter which would have led them to give up their

(21) No sooner than We bestow mercy on a people after hardship has hit them than they begin to scheme against Our signs.[29] Tell them: 'Allah is swifter in scheming. Our angels are recording all your intriguing.'[30] ▶

وَإِذَآ أَذَقۡنَا ٱلنَّاسَ رَحۡمَةً مِّنۢ بَعۡدِ ضَرَّآءَ
مَسَّتۡهُمۡ إِذَا لَهُم مَّكۡرٌ فِيٓ ءَايَاتِنَا قُلِ
ٱللَّهُ أَسۡرَعُ مَكۡرًاۚ إِنَّ رُسُلَنَا يَكۡتُبُونَ
مَا تَمۡكُرُونَ ٢١

unrestrained freedom to live as they pleased, and would have subjected their lives to a set of moral restrictions.

28. The Prophet's statement conveys the idea that he had faithfully presented to them whatever God had revealed to him. As for the things which had not been revealed to the Prophet (peace be on him) they constitute *ghayb* (the realm of the unseen). Now, it is only God and none else who can decide whether to reveal any part of the *ghayb* ('the unseen') or not. Hence, if some people's believing was contingent upon their observing the signs which God had not revealed, then they might as well keep waiting indefinitely for those signs. The Prophet (peace be on him) would also wait and see whether God would yield to their adamant demands for miraculous signs or not.

29. This again alludes to the famine which was referred to earlier in verses 11–12 of the present *sūrah*. The unbelievers are virtually being told that it did not behove them to ask for any miraculous sign. For, not long ago they had suffered from a famine during which they had abjured faith in those very deities whom they had earlier considered their intercessors with God. They had seen with their own eyes how their cherished deities had failed them. They had clearly seen the extent of the supernatural powers of those very deities at whose altars they made offerings and sacrifices in the firm belief that their prayers would be answered and their wishes realized. They had seen – and that too in the recent past – that none of those deities had any power; that all power in fact lay with God alone.

It was because of this experience that they had begun to address all their prayers to God alone. Was all this not enough of a sign to convince the unbelievers about the truth of the teachings of the Prophet Muḥammad (peace be on him)? And yet, despite clear signs, the unbelievers waxed arrogant. No sooner was the famine over and they were blessed with outpourings of rain which put an end to their misery than they reverted to their unbelief. They also sought to offer a wide variety of fanciful explanations about why the famine had hit them and why they were subsequently delivered from it. They resorted to all this in order that they might rationalize their adherence to polytheistic

(22) He it is Who enables you to journey through the land and the sea. And so it happens that when you have boarded the ships and they set sail with a favourable wind, and the passengers rejoice at the pleasant voyage, then suddenly a fierce gale appears, and wave upon wave surges upon them from every side, and people believe that they are surrounded from all directions, and all of them cry out to Allah in full sincerity of faith: 'If You deliver us from this we shall surely be thankful.'[31] (23) But no sooner than He delivers them than they go about committing excesses on the earth, acting unjustly. Men! The excesses you commit will be of harm only to yourselves. (Enjoy, if you will) the fleeting pleasure of this world; in the end you shall all return to Us, and then We shall tell you what you did. ▶

هُوَ ٱلَّذِى يُسَيِّرُكُمْ فِى ٱلْبَرِّ وَٱلْبَحْرِ حَتَّىٰٓ إِذَا
كُنتُمْ فِى ٱلْفُلْكِ وَجَرَيْنَ بِهِم بِرِيحٍ
طَيِّبَةٍ وَفَرِحُوا۟ بِهَا جَآءَتْهَا رِيحٌ
عَاصِفٌ وَجَآءَهُمُ ٱلْمَوْجُ مِن كُلِّ
مَكَانٍ وَظَنُّوٓا۟ أَنَّهُمْ أُحِيطَ بِهِمْ دَعَوُا۟
ٱللَّهَ مُخْلِصِينَ لَهُ ٱلدِّينَ لَئِنْ أَنجَيْتَنَا مِنْ
هَٰذِهِۦ لَنَكُونَنَّ مِنَ ٱلشَّٰكِرِينَ ﴿٢٢﴾
فَلَمَّآ أَنجَىٰهُمْ إِذَا هُمْ يَبْغُونَ فِى ٱلْأَرْضِ
بِغَيْرِ ٱلْحَقِّ يَٰٓأَيُّهَا ٱلنَّاسُ إِنَّمَا بَغْيُكُمْ
عَلَىٰٓ أَنفُسِكُم مَّتَٰعَ ٱلْحَيَوٰةِ ٱلدُّنْيَا
ثُمَّ إِلَيْنَا مَرْجِعُكُمْ فَنُنَبِّئُكُم بِمَا كُنتُمْ
تَعْمَلُونَ ﴿٢٣﴾

beliefs and practices and evade believing in the One True God. Quite obviously what good can any miraculous sign be to those who had corrupted their conscience so thoroughly?

30. It needs to be clearly understood as to what is meant by attributing 'scheming' to God in the present verse. It simply means that if the unbelievers refuse to accept the truth and to alter their conduct accordingly, God will still grant them the respite to go about their rebellious ways. God will also lavish upon them the means of subsistence and other bounties as long as they live. All this will keep them in a state of intoxication. However, whatever they do

(24) The example of the life of this world (which has enamoured you into becoming heedless to Our signs) is that of water that We sent down from the heaven which causes the vegetation of the earth, which sustains men and cattle, to grow luxuriantly. But when the earth took on its golden raiment and became well adorned and the owners believed that they had full control over their lands Our command came upon them by night or by day, and We converted it into a stubble, as though it had not blossomed yesterday. Thus do We expound the signs for a people who reflect. ▶

إِنَّمَا مَثَلُ ٱلْحَيَوٰةِ ٱلدُّنْيَا كَمَآءٍ أَنزَلْنَٰهُ مِنَ
ٱلسَّمَآءِ فَٱخْتَلَطَ بِهِۦ نَبَاتُ ٱلْأَرْضِ مِمَّا
يَأْكُلُ ٱلنَّاسُ وَٱلْأَنْعَٰمُ حَتَّىٰٓ إِذَآ أَخَذَتِ
ٱلْأَرْضُ زُخْرُفَهَا وَٱزَّيَّنَتْ وَظَنَّ
أَهْلُهَآ أَنَّهُمْ قَٰدِرُونَ عَلَيْهَآ
أَتَىٰهَآ أَمْرُنَا لَيْلًا أَوْ نَهَارًا فَجَعَلْنَٰهَا
حَصِيدًا كَأَن لَّمْ تَغْنَ بِٱلْأَمْسِ ۚ
كَذَٰلِكَ نُفَصِّلُ ٱلْءَايَٰتِ لِقَوْمٍ
يَتَفَكَّرُونَ ٢٤

during their state of intoxication will be imperceptibly recorded by the angels of God. All this will go on till the very last moments of their lives and then they will be seized by death and will be asked to render an account of their deeds.

31. This particular 'sign' which testifies to the truth of belief in the One True God is innate in human nature and hence can be witnessed by all. However, as long as the means of self-indulgence are plentiful, man tends to forget God and exults in his worldly enjoyment. But as soon as the means which have led him to his worldly efflorescence are gone, even the most die-hard polytheists and atheists begin to appreciate this innate sign testifying that there indeed is a God Who has His firm grip over the universe, and that it is the One True God alone Who is all-powerful and Who holds sway over all that exists. (For details see *Towards Understanding the Qur'ān*, vol. II, *al-An'ām* 6, n. 29, pp. 231–3 – Ed.)

(25) (You are being lured by this ephemeral world) although Allah calls you to the abode of peace[32] and guides whomsoever He wills to a straight way. (26) For those who do good there is good reward and more besides;[33] neither gloom nor humiliation shall cover their faces. They are the people of the Garden and in it they shall abide. (27) Those who do evil deeds, the recompense of an evil deed is its like,[34] and humiliation shall spread over them and there will be none to protect them from Allah. Darkness will cover their faces as though they were veiled with the dark blackness of night.[35] These are the people of the Fire and in it they shall abide. ▶

وَٱللَّهُ يَدْعُوٓا۟ إِلَىٰ دَارِ ٱلسَّلَٰمِ وَيَهْدِى مَن
يَشَآءُ إِلَىٰ صِرَٰطٍ مُّسْتَقِيمٍ ﴿٢٥﴾ ۞ لِّلَّذِينَ
أَحْسَنُوا۟ ٱلْحُسْنَىٰ وَزِيَادَةٌ ۖ وَلَا يَرْهَقُ
وُجُوهَهُمْ قَتَرٌ وَلَا ذِلَّةٌ ۚ أُو۟لَٰٓئِكَ أَصْحَٰبُ
ٱلْجَنَّةِ ۖ هُمْ فِيهَا خَٰلِدُونَ ﴿٢٦﴾ وَٱلَّذِينَ
كَسَبُوا۟ ٱلسَّيِّـَٔاتِ جَزَآءُ سَيِّئَةٍۭ بِمِثْلِهَا
وَتَرْهَقُهُمْ ذِلَّةٌ ۖ مَّا لَهُم مِّنَ ٱللَّهِ مِنْ
عَاصِمٍ ۖ كَأَنَّمَآ أُغْشِيَتْ وُجُوهُهُمْ قِطَعًا
مِّنَ ٱلَّيْلِ مُظْلِمًا ۚ أُو۟لَٰٓئِكَ أَصْحَٰبُ ٱلنَّارِ ۖ
هُمْ فِيهَا خَٰلِدُونَ ﴿٢٧﴾

---

32. God calls man to the path which would ensure for him his entry into the 'Abode of Peace' in the Hereafter. The expression *Dār al-salām* which literally means the 'Abode of Peace', stands for Paradise, whose inhabitants shall be secure against every calamity, loss, sorrow or suffering.

33. Apart from rewarding human beings in proportion to the good deeds that they have done, God also confers upon them, out of His sheer grace and bounty, a reward which is far in excess of their good deeds.

34. The manner in which the evil ones will be treated is quite different from the way in which the righteous will be treated. As we have seen, the reward of the righteous will be far in excess of their good deeds. However, so far as the evil-doers are concerned, their punishment will be strictly in proportion to the evil they have committed, not even an iota more than that. (For further elaboration see *al-Naḥl* 16, n. 109a.)

(28) And the Day when We shall muster them all together, We shall say to those who associated others with Allah in His divinity: 'Keep to your places – you and those whom you associated with Allah.' Then We shall remove the veil of foreignness separating them.[36] Those whom they had associated with Allah will say: 'It was not us that you worshipped. (29) Allah's witness suffices between you and us that (even if you worshipped us) we were totally unaware of your worshipping us.'[37] ▶

وَيَوْمَ نَحْشُرُهُمْ جَمِيعًا ثُمَّ نَقُولُ
لِلَّذِينَ أَشْرَكُوا مَكَانَكُمْ أَنتُمْ
وَشُرَكَاؤُكُمْ فَزَيَّلْنَا بَيْنَهُمْ وَقَالَ
شُرَكَاؤُهُم مَّا كُنتُمْ إِيَّانَا تَعْبُدُونَ
﴿٢٨﴾ فَكَفَىٰ بِاللَّهِ شَهِيدًا بَيْنَنَا
وَبَيْنَكُمْ إِن كُنَّا عَنْ عِبَادَتِكُمْ
لَغَافِلِينَ ﴿٢٩﴾

35. This refers to the darkness and gloom that covers the faces of the criminals after they have been seized and after they have lost all hope of escaping God's punishment.

36. The words of the Qur'ānic text are فَزَيَّلْنَا بَيْنَهُمْ. Some Qur'ān-commentators have interpreted these words to signify that God will sunder the relationship that has come to exist in the worldly life between false deities and their polytheistic devotees with the result that one will not show any solicitude to the other. But such an interpretation is not consistent with the Arabic literary usage. According to Arabic usage, the words suggest that God will cause the one to become distinct from the other. It is this sense which is reflected in our translation: '. . . We shall remove the veil of strangeness from among them'. What is meant by this is that false deities and their devotees will confront each other, and it will become quite clear as to what distinguishes one group from the other. The polytheists will come to know those they considered to be their gods, and the false deities will also come to know those who had worshipped them.

37. This shows how the false gods will react to their worshippers. Angels who had been declared gods and goddesses and therefore, worshipped, the *jinn,* the spirits, the forefathers of yore, the Prophets, and the saints and martyrs who were considered to share with God some of His attributes, will all disavow

(30) Thereupon everyone shall taste the recompense of his past deeds. All shall be sent back to Allah, their true Lord, and then all the falsehoods they had fabricated will have forsaken them.

(31) Ask them: 'Who provides you with sustenance out of the heavens and the earth? Who holds mastery over your hearing and sight? Who brings forth the living from the dead and the dead from the living? Who governs all affairs of the universe?' They will surely say: 'Allah.' Tell them: 'Will you, then, not shun (going against reality)?' (32) Such, then, is Allah, your true Lord.[38] And what is there after truth but error? How, then, are you being turned away?[39]

هُنَالِكَ تَبْلُوا۟ كُلُّ نَفْسٍ مَّآ أَسْلَفَتْ ۚ
وَرُدُّوٓا۟ إِلَى ٱللَّهِ مَوْلَىٰهُمُ ٱلْحَقِّ ۖ وَضَلَّ
عَنْهُم مَّا كَانُوا۟ يَفْتَرُونَ ﴿٣٠﴾ قُلْ مَن
يَرْزُقُكُم مِّنَ ٱلسَّمَآءِ وَٱلْأَرْضِ أَمَّن
يَمْلِكُ ٱلسَّمْعَ وَٱلْأَبْصَـٰرَ وَمَن يُخْرِجُ
ٱلْحَىَّ مِنَ ٱلْمَيِّتِ وَيُخْرِجُ ٱلْمَيِّتَ مِنَ
ٱلْحَىِّ وَمَن يُدَبِّرُ ٱلْأَمْرَ ۚ فَسَيَقُولُونَ ٱللَّهُ ۚ
فَقُلْ أَفَلَا تَتَّقُونَ ﴿٣١﴾ فَذَٰلِكُمُ ٱللَّهُ
رَبُّكُمُ ٱلْحَقُّ ۖ فَمَاذَا بَعْدَ ٱلْحَقِّ إِلَّا
ٱلضَّلَـٰلُ ۖ فَأَنَّىٰ تُصْرَفُونَ ﴿٣٢﴾

their devotees. They will tell the latter in quite plain terms that they were not even aware that they were being worshipped; that even if they had been prayed to, called upon or cried out to, or had had offerings or sacrifices made in their name, or who had had reverence, adoration, prostration, rituals or ceremonies performed out of devotion for them, none of these had ever reached them.

38. Since it is God alone Who has the power to do all that has been mentioned here – the provision of livelihood, the bestowing of vision and hearing, the granting of life and causing death, and since even the unbelievers affirmed that it is Allah alone Who causes all that, then it is obvious that He alone deserves to be held as the true Lord, Provider and Master of man, and hence the Only One Who deserves to be worshipped. How, then, can any others than Allah – those who have no share in any of the things mentioned above – be considered to have any share in His Lordship?

(33) Thus the word of your Lord is fulfilled concerning the transgressors that they shall not believe.[40]

(34) Ask them: 'Is there any among those whom you associate with Allah in His divinity who brings about the creation of all beings in the first instance and will then repeat it?' Tell them: 'It is Allah Who brings about the creation of all beings and will then repeat it.[41] How are you, then, being misled?'[42]

كَذَٰلِكَ حَقَّتْ كَلِمَتُ رَبِّكَ عَلَى
ٱلَّذِينَ فَسَقُوٓا۟ أَنَّهُمْ لَا يُؤْمِنُونَ
٣٣ قُلْ هَلْ مِن شُرَكَآئِكُم مَّن يَبْدَؤُا۟
ٱلْخَلْقَ ثُمَّ يُعِيدُهُۥ ۚ قُلِ ٱللَّهُ يَبْدَؤُا۟
ٱلْخَلْقَ ثُمَّ يُعِيدُهُۥ ۖ فَأَنَّىٰ تُؤْفَكُونَ ٣٤

39. Addressing the generality of the unbelievers, the Qur'ān inquires: 'How, then, are you, being turned away?' The question that is posed here makes it clear that it is not the unbelievers themselves who are guilty of turning away, rather they are being made to turn away from the right way and that this is happening under the influence of some person or group who is engaged in misleading people. It is for this reason that in effect people are being asked: 'Why should they go about blindly following those who are out to mislead people? Why should they not use their brains and think for themselves why they are being turned in a direction which is contrary to reality?'

This mode of questioning, with some modifications, appears on a number of occasions in the Qur'ān. On all such occasions the question has been asked in the passive voice. This was presumably to avoid a pointed reference to those who were actually engaged in misleading people. This should make it possible for people who had held these leaders of misguidance in considerable esteem to consider the matter dispassionately. Such a mode should also spare them any provocation that might impair their capacity to think about the issue coolly. For it is quite obvious that pointed references to specific persons might have been exploited so as to provoke people by pointing out that their venerated forefathers and religious mentors were being maliciously criticized and attacked.

This manner of address – the use of the passive rather than the active voice and the avoidance of pointed references to specific persons as the ringleaders of misguidance and mischief – embodies a valuable piece of wisdom for those who seek to invite others to accept the Message of Islam.

(35) Ask them: 'Are there among ones whom you associate with Allah in His divinity those who can guide to the truth?'[43] Say: 'It is Allah alone Who guides to the truth.' Then, who is more worthy to be followed – He Who guides to the truth, or he who cannot find the right way unless others guide him to it? What is wrong with you? How ill do you judge!

قُلْ هَلْ مِن شُرَكَآئِكُم مَّن يَهْدِىٓ إِلَى ٱلْحَقِّ قُلِ ٱللَّهُ يَهْدِى لِلْحَقِّ أَفَمَن يَهْدِىٓ إِلَى ٱلْحَقِّ أَحَقُّ أَن يُتَّبَعَ أَمَّن لَّا يَهِدِّىٓ إِلَّآ أَن يُهْدَىٰ فَمَا لَكُمْ كَيْفَ تَحْكُمُونَ ﴿٣٥﴾

40. Even though God's Message has been elaborated with the help of clear and easy-to-understand arguments, those who have already made up their minds against it will continue in their stubbornness and will simply refuse to accept it.

41. The unbelievers did acknowledge that God alone had brought everything into existence in the first instance, that none of those who had been associated with God in His divinity had any part in it. As for resurrection, which simply amounts to repeating the initial act of creation, it is quite evident that He Who has the power to create, also has the power to repeat; anything else would be inconceivable. All this is so reasonable and clear that in their heart of hearts even rank polytheists were convinced of its truth. Yet they were hesitant to affirm it for if they did so, it would make it difficult for them to deny the existence of the Hereafter.

It is for this reason that in response to the earlier question (see verse 31 above) it has been mentioned that the unbelievers acknowledge that God alone brought about the creation. But with regard to the question of repeating that creation, it is the Prophet (peace be on him) who has been asked here to proclaim that it is God alone Who brought about the original creation and it is He Who will create again.

42. The unbelievers are being asked to see reason. For on the one hand they themselves recognize that it is Allah alone Who causes their birth and death, and on the other, they are being misdirected by their so-called religious leaders into believing that they ought to worship and adore others than Allah.

43. This verse raises an important issue which should be grasped well. Man's necessities in his worldly life are not confined to subsistence, to the provision of shelter and clothing, to protection from calamities, hardships and losses. Man also needs something else, and this is his direst need. This is the need to know how to live in the world; how he should relate with himself and the powers and potentialities with which he has been endowed; how he should relate with the resources of the world which have been placed under his control, with the innumerable human beings with whom he comes into contact, and with the order of the universe as a whole within which, willy-nilly, he has to operate.

Man needs to know all this so as to ensure the achievement of overall success in his life and to see to it that his energies and efforts do not count for naught. To ensure that his energies and efforts are not misdirected or employed in a manner that would lead to his destruction. This right way – the way that provides guidance concerning all the above questions – constitutes 'the truth', and the guidance which directs man to this truth is 'the true guidance'. Now, the Qur'ān asks the unbelievers, who had rejected the Prophet's Message, whether any of their deities whom they worshipped besides God, could direct them to 'the truth'? The answer to this question is obviously in the negative.

In order to understand this it must be remembered that the deities they worshipped besides God can be divided into two broad categories:

1. The first category consists of the gods and goddesses, and those living or dead persons, whom people worship. People turn to them believing that they are capable of satisfying their needs in a supernatural way and of protecting them from calamities. But as far as guiding people to the right way is concerned, it is quite obvious that false gods had never provided any such guidance. Even the worshippers of those gods had never sought such guidance from them, nor did the polytheists ever claim that those gods taught them anything relating to morality, social conduct, culture, economy, polity, law and justice.
2. The second category consists of those outstanding people who lay down the principles and laws which others follow. Such persons are doubtlessly leaders of others. But are they really those who lead people to the truth? Does the knowledge of any of those leaders encompass all that needs to be known in order to lay down sound principles for the guidance of mankind? Do any of them possess the breadth of vision that takes into account the whole gamut of issues relating to human life? Can any one of them claim to be free of those biases, those personal or national pre-occupations, those interests and desires, inclinations and predilections which prevent people from laying down perfectly just laws for human society? As it is, since the answer to these questions is in the negative – and since the answer of any sensible person to these questions could never be in the positive – how can any of those human beings be considered to be dependable sources of guidance to the truth?

(36) Most of them only follow conjectures;[44] and surely conjecture can be no substitute for truth. Allah is well aware of whatever they do.

(37) And this Qur'ān is such that it could not be composed by any unless it be revealed from Allah. It is a confirmation of the revelation made before it and a detailed exposition of the Book.[45] Beyond doubt it is from the Lord of the universe.

وَمَا يَتَّبِعُ أَكْثَرُهُمْ إِلَّا ظَنًّا إِنَّ الظَّنَّ لَا يُغْنِي مِنَ الْحَقِّ شَيْئًا إِنَّ اللَّهَ عَلِيمٌ بِمَا يَفْعَلُونَ ﴿٣٦﴾ وَمَا كَانَ هَٰذَا الْقُرْآنُ أَن يُفْتَرَىٰ مِن دُونِ اللَّهِ وَلَٰكِن تَصْدِيقَ الَّذِي بَيْنَ يَدَيْهِ وَتَفْصِيلَ الْكِتَابِ لَا رَيْبَ فِيهِ مِن رَّبِّ الْعَالَمِينَ ﴿٣٧﴾

It is for this reason that the Qur'ān asks people whether any of their gods could lead them to the truth? This question, combined with the previous ones, helps man to arrive at a definitive conclusion concerning the whole question of religion. If one were to face the question with a clear mind, it is evident that man stands in dire need of One to Whom he could look up to as his Lord; One in Whom he could seek refuge and Whose protection he could solicit; One Who might answer his prayer and grant his supplication; One to Whom, notwithstanding the undependable nature of the worldly means of support, he could turn to for effective help and support. The questions posed above inevitably lead to the conclusion that this need can be met by none other than God.

In addition, man also stands in need of a guide who might teach him the principles of righteous conduct, who might teach him the laws that he might follow with full confidence. Even here it is quite clear that God alone can meet this need of man. Once these matters become clear, there remains no justification to adhere either to polytheistic religions or to secular principles of morality, culture and polity.

44. Those who, in disregard of God's guidance, invented religions, developed philosophies and prescribed laws to govern human life did not do this with the help of any definite knowledge that they possessed; rather, it would be the result of their conjecture and fancy. Likewise, those who followed their religious and worldly leaders did so not because they fully knew and fully understood all that the latter espoused. Rather, they followed those

(38) Do they say that the Messenger has himself composed the Qur'ān? Say: 'In that case bring forth just one *sūrah* like it and call on all whom you can, except Allah, to help you if you are truthful.'[46]

أَمْ يَقُولُونَ ٱفْتَرَىٰهُ قُلْ فَأْتُوا۟ بِسُورَةٍ مِّثْلِهِۦ وَٱدْعُوا۟ مَنِ ٱسْتَطَعْتُم مِّن دُونِ ٱللَّهِ إِن كُنتُمْ صَـٰدِقِينَ ﴿٣٨﴾

leaders merely on the gratuitous assumption that whatever was being taught by those great people, and whatever had been recognized as 'right' by their own forefathers, must indeed be true.

45. The statement that it is 'a confirmation of the revelation made before it' underscores that the Qur'ān lays no claim of introducing anything novel, of coming forth with any innovation at variance with the fundamental teachings already communicated to man through the Prophets (peace be on them). The Qur'ānic claim merely consists of confirming and authenticating those teachings. Had the Qur'ān been the product of the imagination of the founder of an altogether new religion, the outcome of a creative brain, it would have borne traces of novelty in order to emphasize its distinctiveness.

The second part of the statement, namely that the Qur'ān is a 'detailed exposition of the Book' is equally significant. What this means is that the Qur'ān elaborates those fundamental teachings which constitute the core and essence of all the scriptures (*al-kitāb*); that is, those teachings which have been sufficiently elucidated in the Qur'ān so that they might be grasped by people and penetrate their hearts; and additionally, it has been shown how those teachings could be applied to practical life.

46. It is generally believed that the challenge embodied in this verse has a reference merely to the eloquence, rhetoric and other literary qualities of the Qur'ān. Were one to read the writings of Muslim scholars in connection with the explanation of this verse, it is not surprising that people should entertain such a misunderstanding.

However, the Qur'ān is far above claiming its uniqueness and inimitability merely on the grounds of its literary merits. Although there can be no doubt about the literary excellence of the Qur'ān, the main ground on which it is claimed that no human being could produce a book like it has to do with its contents and teaching. The Qur'ān alludes, in many places, to those characteristics of its inimitability which could not have been conferred upon it by man, thus hinting that those characteristics could have no other source but God Himself. We have explained, in the course of this work, all such allusions

(39) In fact they arbitrarily rejected as false whatever they failed to comprehend and whose final sequel was not apparent to them.[47] Likewise had their predecessors rejected the truth, declaring it falsehood. Do observe, then, what was the end of the wrong-doers. (40) Of those some will believe and others will not. Your Lord knows best the mischief-makers.[48] (41) And if they reject you as false, tell them: 'My deeds are for myself and your deeds for yourselves. You will not be held responsible for my deeds, nor I for your deeds.'[49]

بَلْ كَذَّبُوا۟ بِمَا لَمْ يُحِيطُوا۟ بِعِلْمِهِۦ وَلَمَّا
يَأْتِهِمْ تَأْوِيلُهُۥ ۚ كَذَٰلِكَ كَذَّبَ ٱلَّذِينَ
مِن قَبْلِهِمْ ۖ فَٱنظُرْ كَيْفَ كَانَ
عَٰقِبَةُ ٱلظَّٰلِمِينَ ﴿٣٩﴾ وَمِنْهُم
مَّن يُؤْمِنُ بِهِۦ وَمِنْهُم مَّن لَّا يُؤْمِنُ
بِهِۦ ۚ وَرَبُّكَ أَعْلَمُ بِٱلْمُفْسِدِينَ ﴿٤٠﴾
وَإِن كَذَّبُوكَ فَقُل لِّى عَمَلِى وَلَكُمْ
عَمَلُكُمْ ۖ أَنتُم بَرِيٓـُٔونَ مِمَّآ أَعْمَلُ
وَأَنَا۠ بَرِىٓءٌ مِّمَّا تَعْمَلُونَ ﴿٤١﴾

in the Qur'ān. In order to avoid repetition, we would like at this stage to avoid engaging in any discussion on that subject. (For further explanation see *al-Ṭūr* 52, nn. 26–7.)

47. There can only be two justifiable grounds for those who wish to reject the Qur'ān as a false scripture: either they should have definite knowledge to the effect that it is a fabrication or they should be able to demonstrate that the statements made by, or the information contained in it, are false. But as things stand, neither of these two reasons is available. For none can contend, on the basis of definite knowledge, that the Book had been authored by someone who, in his turn, falsely attributed it to God. Nor has anyone been able to penetrate the realms of the suprasensory world and claim, on that basis, that they know for sure that this Book contains false information; that whereas in fact there are several gods, this Book claims that there is none other than the One God; that all its statements about matters such as the existence of God and angels are counter to reality. Nor has anyone returned to life after having suffered death to contend that the Qur'ānic statement about the reckoning and reward and punishment in the Next Life is false. Those who continue to decry the Qur'ān as false are in fact doing so merely on grounds of conjecture, even though they

(42) Of them some seem to give heed to you; will you, then, make the deaf hear even though they understand nothing?[50] (43) And of them some look towards you; will you, then, guide the blind, even though they can see nothing?[51] ▶

وَمِنْهُم مَّن يَسْتَمِعُونَ إِلَيْكَ أَفَأَنتَ تُسْمِعُ
ٱلصُّمَّ وَلَوْ كَانُوا۟ لَا يَعْقِلُونَ ﴿٤٢﴾
وَمِنْهُم مَّن يَنظُرُ إِلَيْكَ أَفَأَنتَ
تَهْدِى ٱلْعُمْىَ وَلَوْ كَانُوا۟
لَا يُبْصِرُونَ ﴿٤٣﴾

---

do this with an air of confidence which at times creates the impression that statements about the fakeness and falsity of the Qur'ānic teachings are scientifically established facts.

48. The statement that 'Your Lord knows best the mischief-makers' underscores an important fact about unbelievers. Those unbelievers could certainly silence others into not carrying the discussion any further by openly admitting that they had failed to grasp the teaching of the Qur'ān and hence it was not possible for them to sincerely believe in it. God, however, is well aware even of the things that are hidden, even those that are in the deepest recesses of their hearts and minds. He knows how each person has sealed his mind and heart against accepting any truth; how he has sought to immerse himself in heedlessness; how he has managed to suppress his conscience; how he has prevented the testimony of the truth from affecting his heart; how he has destroyed the innate capacity of his mind to accept the truth; how he has heard the call of the truth and has turned a deaf ear to it; and how, despite his ability to understand the Message of God, he has made no effort to do so. Such people cherish their biases and prejudices, their lusts and desires, their worldly advantages and the interests which can be procured only by supporting falsehood, much more than by accepting the truth. Such people can hardly be considered to have innocently succumbed to a 'mistake'. On the contrary, they are rank 'mischief-makers'.

49. Since every individual is himself accountable for his deeds, there is no point in engaging in unnecessary discussions which are often actuated by obduracy. For if the Prophet (peace be on him) was indeed inventing lies, he would bear the evil consequence of such an action. On the other hand, if his opponents were denying the truth, their action will not hurt the Prophet (peace be on him), but rather hurt themselves.

50. In its most elementary sense even animals are possessed of the faculty of hearing. But 'hearing' in its true sense is applicable only when the act of

hearing is accompanied with the attention required to grasp the meaning of what one hears, and with the readiness to accept it if it is found reasonable. Those who have fallen prey to prejudices, who have made up their minds that they will not hear, let alone accept anything, howsoever reasonable it might be, if it goes against their inherited beliefs and behaviour-patterns, or is opposed to living a life of heedlessness, as the animals do, or who focus all their attention on the gratification of their palate, or who recklessly pursue their lusts in total disregard of all consideration of right and wrong may also be rightly characterized as incapable of hearing. Such people are not deaf of hearing, but their minds and hearts are certainly deaf to the truth.

51. The import of the statement is substantially the same as that made above. The limb called the 'eye' is of little service if it serves no other purpose than that of observation. For the eye, as an instrument of observation, is also available to animals and they use it solely for that purpose. What is of true worth is the mental eye which ought to enable man to see not only that which is apparent and evident, but also that which is beyond that. If a man is not possessed of this mental eye – which is the true eye – then even though he might be able to observe in the literal sense of the word, he cannot be considered to be one who truly sees.

Both these verses are addressed to the Prophet (peace be on him). But it is to those whom he wanted to reform rather than directly to himself that the reproach was directed. Moreover, the purpose of the statement is not just to reproach. The pinching sarcasm which has been employed in the statement aims at awakening the slumbering humanity of people so that they may be able to take heed.

The manner of the discourse brings to mind the image of a righteous man who lives in the midst of a corrupt people. He is a man who maintains for himself extremely high standards of character and conduct. At the same time, he attempts, out of sincerity and goodwill, to awaken his fellow-beings to realize the low depths to which they have sunk. He also seeks to explain to them, out of sincere concern for them, how evil their ways of life are. And above all, he highlights for them the contours of the right way of life. But the people around him are such that they are neither inspired to righteousness by his practical and righteous example, nor do they pay any heed to his earnest counsel and admonition. The purpose of what has been said here, viz. '. . . will you, then, make the deaf hear even though they understand nothing?' should be understood in the above context.

This statement resembles the remark of someone who, feeling disgusted when he finds his friend fails to make people hear his earnest exhortations, throws up his hands in exasperation and says: 'Are you not wasting your time, my friend, trying to make the deaf hear, or trying to direct the blind to the right path? The ears that would make them listen to the voice of the truth are sealed; the eyes that could have made them perceive the truth have been blinded.' The purpose of so saying is not to reproach that righteous person for his sincere exhortation nor to prevent him from making his efforts to reform people. What

(44) Surely Allah does not wrong men; they rather wrong themselves.[52] (45) (But today they are oblivious of everything except enjoyment of worldly life.) And on the Day when He will muster all men together, they will feel as though they had been in the world no more than an hour of the day to get acquainted with one another.[53] (It will then become evident that) those who called the lie to meeting with Allah[54] were utter losers and were not rightly-directed. ▶

إِنَّ ٱللَّهَ لَا يَظۡلِمُ ٱلنَّاسَ شَيۡـٔٗا وَلَٰكِنَّ
ٱلنَّاسَ أَنفُسَهُمۡ يَظۡلِمُونَ ﴿٤٤﴾ وَيَوۡمَ
يَحۡشُرُهُمۡ كَأَن لَّمۡ يَلۡبَثُوٓاْ إِلَّا سَاعَةٗ مِّنَ
ٱلنَّهَارِ يَتَعَارَفُونَ بَيۡنَهُمۡۚ قَدۡ خَسِرَ ٱلَّذِينَ
كَذَّبُواْ بِلِقَآءِ ٱللَّهِ وَمَا كَانُواْ
مُهۡتَدِينَ ﴿٤٥﴾

underlies this sharp remark is the faint hope that perhaps such people would be shaken out of their slumber.

52. God has generously endowed people with all that is needed to help them distinguish between truth and falsehood – ears, eyes, and hearts. But some people have become virtual slaves to their lusts and are utterly spellbound by the allurements of a worldly life. By so doing, they have caused their eyes to go blind, their ears to become deaf, and have perverted their hearts to such a degree that they have become bereft of the capacity to distinguish between what is good and what is evil, what is right and what is wrong, and have debilitated their conscience to such a degree that it has ceased to have any effect on their lives.

53. A time will come when such people will, on the one hand, come face to face with the infinite life of the Hereafter, and on the other, they will look back at their past worldly life and realize how puny it was as compared to the life ahead. It is then that they will comprehend what folly they have committed by ruining their eternal future for the sake of ephemeral pleasures and benefits in this worldly life.

54. This refers to the unbelievers' rejection that a time will come when everyone will have to stand before God for His judgement.

(46) Whether We let you see (during your lifetime) some of the chastisement with which We threaten them, or We call you unto Us (before the chastisement strikes them), in any case they are bound to return to Us. Allah is witness to all what they do.

(47) A Messenger is sent to every people;[55] and when their Messenger comes, the fate of that people is decided with full justice; they are subjected to no wrong.[56]

وَإِمَّا نُرِيَنَّكَ بَعْضَ الَّذِي نَعِدُهُمْ أَوْ نَتَوَفَّيَنَّكَ
فَإِلَيْنَا مَرْجِعُهُمْ ثُمَّ اللَّهُ شَهِيدٌ عَلَىٰ
مَا يَفْعَلُونَ ﴿٤٦﴾ وَلِكُلِّ أُمَّةٍ
رَسُولٌ فَإِذَا جَاءَ رَسُولُهُمْ قُضِيَ
بَيْنَهُمْ بِالْقِسْطِ وَهُمْ
لَا يُظْلَمُونَ ﴿٤٧﴾

55. The Qur'ānic expression *ummah* is not to be taken in the narrow sense in which the word 'nation' is used. The word *ummah* embraces all those who receive the message of a Messenger of God after his advent. Furthermore, this word embraces even those among whom no Messenger is physically alive, provided that they have received his message. All those who, after the advent of a Messenger, happen to live in an age when the teachings of that Messenger are extant or at least it is possible for people to know about what he had taught, constitute the *ummah* of that Messenger. Besides, all such people will be subject to the law mentioned here (see verse 47 and n. 56). In this respect all human beings who happen to live in the age which commences with the advent of Muḥammad (peace be on him) onwards are his *ummah* and will continue to be so as long as the Qur'ān is available in its pristine purity. Hence the verse does not say: 'Among every people there is a Messenger.' It rather says: 'There is a Messenger for every people.'

56. When the message of a Messenger of God reaches a people the stage is set and they are left with no valid excuse for not believing. Everything has already been done to communicate the truth to these people and so all that remains is to wait for God's decision to inflict His punishment upon them. And so far as God's judgement is concerned, it is marked with absolute justice. All those who obey that Messenger and mend their behaviour are deemed worthy of God's mercy. On the contrary, those who reject his teaching are considered deserving of His punishment, depending on God's will, both in this world and the Hereafter.

(48) They say: 'If what you promise is true, when will this threat be fulfilled?' (49) Tell them: 'I have no power to harm or benefit even myself, except what Allah may will.[57] There is an appointed term for every people; and when the end of their term comes, neither can they put it off for an hour, nor can they bring it an hour before.'[58] (50) Tell them: 'Did you consider (what you would do) were His chastisement to fall upon you suddenly by night or by day? So why are the culprits seeking to hasten its coming? (51) Is it only when this chastisement has actually overtaken you that you will believe in it? (And when the chastisement will surprise you), you will try to get away from it, although it is you who had sought to hasten its coming.' ▶

وَيَقُولُونَ مَتَىٰ هَٰذَا ٱلْوَعْدُ إِن كُنتُمْ
صَٰدِقِينَ ﴿٤٨﴾ قُل لَّآ أَمْلِكُ لِنَفْسِى
ضَرًّا وَلَا نَفْعًا إِلَّا مَا شَآءَ ٱللَّهُ لِكُلِّ أُمَّةٍ
أَجَلٌ إِذَا جَآءَ أَجَلُهُمْ فَلَا يَسْتَـْٔخِرُونَ
سَاعَةً وَلَا يَسْتَقْدِمُونَ ﴿٤٩﴾ قُلْ أَرَءَيْتُمْ
إِنْ أَتَىٰكُمْ عَذَابُهُۥ بَيَٰتًا أَوْ نَهَارًا مَّاذَا
يَسْتَعْجِلُ مِنْهُ ٱلْمُجْرِمُونَ ﴿٥٠﴾ أَثُمَّ
إِذَا مَا وَقَعَ ءَامَنتُم بِهِۦٓ ءَآلْـَٰٔنَ وَقَدْ كُنتُم
بِهِۦ تَسْتَعْجِلُونَ ﴿٥١﴾

57. In response to the unbelievers' query, the Prophet (peace be on him) makes it clear that he had never claimed that he himself would come forth with the judgement mentioned above, or that it lay in his power to afflict people with punishment. There was no point, therefore, in asking him when the final judgement against them would come to pass. The warning of punishment had been given by God rather than by the Messenger. Hence it lay only in God's power to decide when His judgement should come to pass, and in which form God would execute His warning to punish unbelievers.

58. God does not act in haste in judging a people. He does not summarily punish or reward people the very moment they reject or accept a Messenger's call. Instead, God grants a long respite both to individuals and to nations. He

(52) The wrong-doers will then be told: 'Suffer now the abiding chastisement. How else can you be rewarded except according to your deeds?'

(53) They ask you if what you say is true? Tell them: 'Yes, by my Lord, this is altogether true, and you have no power to prevent the chastisement from befalling.' (54) If a wrong-doer had all that is in the earth he would surely offer it to ransom himself. When the wrong-doers perceive the chastisement, they will feel intense remorse in their hearts.[59] But a judgement shall be made with full justice about them. They shall not be wronged. ▶

ثُمَّ قِيلَ لِلَّذِينَ ظَلَمُوا ذُوقُوا عَذَابَ
الْخُلْدِ هَلْ تُجْزَوْنَ إِلَّا بِمَا كُنتُمْ
تَكْسِبُونَ ﴿٥٢﴾ ۞ وَيَسْتَنبِئُونَكَ
أَحَقٌّ هُوَ قُلْ إِي وَرَبِّي إِنَّهُ لَحَقٌّ وَمَا
أَنتُم بِمُعْجِزِينَ ﴿٥٣﴾ وَلَوْ أَنَّ لِكُلِّ
نَفْسٍ ظَلَمَتْ مَا فِي الْأَرْضِ لَافْتَدَتْ
بِهِ وَأَسَرُّوا النَّدَامَةَ لَمَّا رَأَوُا الْعَذَابَ
وَقُضِيَ بَيْنَهُم بِالْقِسْطِ وَهُمْ
لَا يُظْلَمُونَ ﴿٥٤﴾

grants them plenty of time to reflect upon and understand the Message, and to mend their ways. Often the term fixed for this purpose spans several centuries. For it is God alone Who knows best what is the right term for a people. However, once that term – which has been determined by God with full justice – is over, and the individual or nation concerned does not give up its rebellious attitude, God's judgement is enforced. The time for the enforcement of such judgement can never come a moment before or after the time fixed for it by God.

59. Throughout their lives the unbelievers denied that they would be resurrected and called to account by God. Considering the Next Life a mere illusion, they wasted their lives on vain pursuits and levelled all kinds of allegations against the Prophets who had forewarned them that the Next Life would inevitably come to pass. All this notwithstanding, a moment will come when they will find themselves face to face with the Next Life. When such a moment comes they will be totally unnerved. In view of their evil deeds, their conscience will intimate to them the end they are going to meet. Speechless and

(55) Indeed all that is in the heavens and the earth belongs to Allah. And most certainly Allah's promise will be fulfilled, though most men are not aware. (56) He it is Who gives life and causes death, and to Him shall you all be returned.

(57) Men! Now there has come to you an exhortation from your Lord, a healing for the ailments of the hearts, and a guidance and mercy for those who believe. (58) Tell them (O Prophet!): 'Let them rejoice in Allah's grace and mercy through which this (Book) has come to you. It is better than all the riches that they accumulate. (59) Did you consider that the sustenance which Allah had sent down for you[60] of your own accord you have declared some of it as unlawful and some as lawful?'[61] Ask them: 'Did Allah bestow upon you any authority for this or do you forge lies against Allah?[62]

أَلَآ إِنَّ لِلَّهِ مَا فِي ٱلسَّمَٰوَٰتِ وَٱلۡأَرۡضِۗ
أَلَآ إِنَّ وَعۡدَ ٱللَّهِ حَقّٞ وَلَٰكِنَّ أَكۡثَرَهُمۡ
لَا يَعۡلَمُونَ ٥٥ هُوَ يُحۡيِۦ وَيُمِيتُ وَإِلَيۡهِ
تُرۡجَعُونَ ٥٦ يَٰٓأَيُّهَا ٱلنَّاسُ قَدۡ
جَآءَتۡكُم مَّوۡعِظَةٞ مِّن رَّبِّكُمۡ وَشِفَآءٞ
لِّمَا فِي ٱلصُّدُورِ وَهُدٗى وَرَحۡمَةٞ
لِّلۡمُؤۡمِنِينَ ٥٧ قُلۡ بِفَضۡلِ ٱللَّهِ
وَبِرَحۡمَتِهِۦ فَبِذَٰلِكَ فَلۡيَفۡرَحُواْ هُوَ
خَيۡرٞ مِّمَّا يَجۡمَعُونَ ٥٨ قُلۡ
أَرَءَيۡتُم مَّآ أَنزَلَ ٱللَّهُ لَكُم
مِّن رِّزۡقٖ فَجَعَلۡتُم مِّنۡهُ
حَرَامٗا وَحَلَٰلٗا قُلۡ ءَآللَّهُ أَذِنَ
لَكُمۡۖ أَمۡ عَلَى ٱللَّهِ تَفۡتَرُونَ ٥٩

haggard, their hearts will begin to sink out of remorse and regret. Those who had staked their all on vain fancies, and had refused to take any heed of the admonition of their well-wishers, whom else can they blame except themselves for the catastrophe that will confront them?

60. The word *rizq* is often used in daily parlance to denote 'eatables'. Hence, many people think that the reproach embodied in the present verse is

directed merely against the wrong customs that have come into vogue in that narrow realm of behaviour which is confined to the dining room. It is not only those who are ignorant but also those who are learned about Islam that are victims of this misconception.

However, use of the word *rizq* in Arabic is not confined to eatables. It is used in a broad sense, and covers all the things that are granted to man by God for his use. Whatever God has conferred on man thus constitutes his *rizq,* including his offspring. In the works of the branch of knowledge called *Asmā' al-Rijāl* (which is part of the *Ḥadith* Sciences), we find, among the transmitters of traditions, several names such as *Rizq, Ruzayq,* and *Rizq Allāh* which signify the recipients of God's bounty. In the famous invocative prayer اللّٰهُمَّ أَرِنَا الحَقَّ حَقًّا وَارْزُقْنَا اتِّبَاعَهُ 'O God: Show us the truth and grant us the strength (*urzuqnā*) to follow it', the *rizq* that a person seeks from God is the strength to follow the truth after God has enabled him to perceive it. Here *rizq* has been used to mean the conferment of the bounty of knowledge on someone. In a tradition we have been told that Allah sends an angel to the womb of every expectant mother and that he writes down what the *rizq,* the life-span, and deeds of the to-be-born child are to be (see al-Bukhārī, *Kitāb Bad' al-Khalq, Bāb Dhikr al-Malā' ikah* – Ed.). It is quite obvious that the word *rizq* here does not signify merely the eatables that child will receive during its life-time; it rather signifies the totality of the things that it will receive. We also find the expression وَمِمَّا رَزَقْنَاهُمْ يُنْفِقُونَ in the Qur'ān. (See *al-Baqarah* 2: 3; *al-Anfāl* 8: 3 – Ed.)

It is, therefore, a serious mistake to consider *rizq* as being confined to the realm of the kitchen and the dining table. Likewise, it is a mistake, and quite a serious one to think that God disapproves only if those rules in the domain of food are broken and does not mind if people do so in other domains of life.

The error that people so commit has very grave consequences. As a result of this misconception, an important principle of Islam has been lost sight of. For it is owing to this misconception that while lawfulness or otherwise in regard to eating and drinking is considered a seriously religious issue, even highly religious people, let alone ordinary Muslims, feel no serious repugnance about the notion that in the collective sphere of life man has the right to lay down the rules of his behaviour. Even the most learned and pious religious scholars feel no revulsion against legislating without reference to God and His Book. Nor do they feel that such legislation is as sharply in conflict with Islam as one's laying down what is lawful and what is unlawful in matters of food and drink.

61. The purpose of the verse is to make people realize what an enormous act of rebellion people are committing by laying down, of their own accord, the limits that are lawful and those that are unlawful. Are they not conscious of the fact that human beings and all that they possess belong to Allah? If they are conscious of it, how can it be considered justifiable for men to lay down as to how they should use the possessions bestowed upon them by Allah? What would their own opinion be about the servant who claims that he has the full right to lay down the rules for the disposal of his master's property, and who

(60) Think how those who invent lies against Him will be treated on the Day of Judgement? Allah is bountiful to men yet most of them do not give thanks.[63]

وَمَا ظَنُّ ٱلَّذِينَ يَفْتَرُونَ عَلَى ٱللَّهِ
ٱلْكَذِبَ يَوْمَ ٱلْقِيَٰمَةِ إِنَّ
ٱللَّهَ لَذُو فَضْلٍ عَلَى ٱلنَّاسِ وَلَٰكِنَّ
أَكْثَرَهُمْ لَا يَشْكُرُونَ ٦٠

---

believes that his master has no right to determine anything? Were a person's own servant to make such a claim about his master, how would the latter react to it? As for the servant who goes so far as even to deny that he is a servant or denies that he is answerable to a master, or who denies that the property under his care belongs to his master, he is guilty of an even greater monstrosity, and is beyond the scope of our discussion here. What is being discussed is the case of one who, on the one hand, acknowledges that he is the servant of a master and that the property in his possession has been entrusted to him by the master, and rightfully belongs to the master. Notwithstanding this acknowledgement, the servant claims that he has the right to lay down, independently of the master, the rules for using that property.

62. If the master had authorized the servant to use his property as the latter wished and to lay down the rules for so doing as he pleased, the servant would have been justified in doing so. But do these people really have any evidence to prove that they had been granted any such authorization by their master? Or is it that such a claim was backed by no such authorization? If they do not have any evidence to produce such an authorization, they are guilty not only of rebellious behaviour, but also of lies and fabrications.

63. It is indeed an act of utmost favour on the part of the master that he informs his servant of the attitude he should adopt to the master's house and to other belongings and even with regard to his own self as he is able to obtain God's good pleasure and how he would be able to escape his wrath and punishment. But many servants are not sufficiently grateful to their master for this favour. It seems that the right thing would have been for the master to have left his properties at the servant's disposal without informing him of what would lead to reward and what would lead to punishment. He should then have kept a secret watch over his servants and punished those who work contrary to his desire – a desire which had not even been made known to them. The fact is that if the master had put his servants to such a severe test none would have escaped his punishment.

(61) (O Prophet!) What-
ever you may be engaged in,
whether you recite any portion
of the Qur'ān, or whatever
else all of you are doing, We
are witnesses to whatever you
may be occupied with. Not
even an atom's weight escapes
your Lord on the earth or in the
heaven, nor is there anything
smaller or bigger than that,
except that it is on record in a
Clear Book.[64] (62) Oh, surely the friends of Allah have
nothing to fear, nor shall they
grieve – (63) the ones who
believe and are God-fearing.
(64) For them are glad tidings
in this world and in the Hereafter. The words of Allah shall
not change. That is the
supreme triumph. (65) (O
Prophet!) Let not the utterances of the opponents distress you. Indeed all honour is
Allah's. He is All-Hearing,
All-Knowing.

وَمَا تَكُونُ فِي شَأْنٍ وَمَا تَتْلُوا مِنْهُ مِن قُرْءَانٍ
وَلَا تَعْمَلُونَ مِنْ عَمَلٍ إِلَّا كُنَّا عَلَيْكُمْ
شُهُودًا إِذْ تُفِيضُونَ فِيهِ وَمَا يَعْزُبُ عَن
رَّبِّكَ مِن مِّثْقَالِ ذَرَّةٍ فِي ٱلْأَرْضِ وَلَا فِي
ٱلسَّمَآءِ وَلَآ أَصْغَرَ مِن ذَٰلِكَ وَلَآ أَكْبَرَ إِلَّا
فِي كِتَٰبٍ مُّبِينٍ ﴿٦١﴾ أَلَآ إِنَّ أَوْلِيَآءَ ٱللَّهِ
لَا خَوْفٌ عَلَيْهِمْ وَلَا هُمْ يَحْزَنُونَ
﴿٦٢﴾ ٱلَّذِينَ ءَامَنُوا۟ وَكَانُوا۟
يَتَّقُونَ ﴿٦٣﴾ لَهُمُ ٱلْبُشْرَىٰ فِي ٱلْحَيَوٰةِ
ٱلدُّنْيَا وَفِي ٱلْءَاخِرَةِ لَا تَبْدِيلَ
لِكَلِمَٰتِ ٱللَّهِ ذَٰلِكَ هُوَ ٱلْفَوْزُ
ٱلْعَظِيمُ ﴿٦٤﴾ وَلَا يَحْزُنكَ قَوْلُهُمْ
إِنَّ ٱلْعِزَّةَ لِلَّهِ جَمِيعًا هُوَ ٱلسَّمِيعُ
ٱلْعَلِيمُ ﴿٦٥﴾

64. The purpose of the statement is to console the Prophet (peace be on him) and to warn his enemies. On the one hand, the Prophet (peace be on him) is being reassured that the resoluteness, diligence and perseverance which characterize his efforts in preaching the truth and attempting to reform people is well known to God. It can hardly be conceived that after entrusting to the Prophet (peace be on him) a perilous task that God would leave him alone, unassisted. God knows full well all what the Prophet (peace be on him) does, and is also well aware of how others behave towards him. At the same time what is being said also constitutes a warning to the Prophet's opponents. If they obstruct the efforts of the Messenger of the truth, of one engaged in reforming mankind out of sincerity and goodwill, there is no reason for them to assume that no one is observing

(66) Verily whoever dwells in the heavens or the earth belongs to Allah. Those who invoke others beside Allah, associating them with Him in His divinity, only follow conjectures and are merely guessing. (67) It is Allah alone Who has made the night that you may rest in it, and has made the day light-giving. Surely in that there are signs for those who give heed (to the call of the Messenger).[65]

أَلَآ إِنَّ لِلَّهِ مَن فِى ٱلسَّمَٰوَٰتِ وَمَن
فِى ٱلْأَرْضِ ۗ وَمَا يَتَّبِعُ ٱلَّذِينَ
يَدْعُونَ مِن دُونِ ٱللَّهِ شُرَكَآءَ ۚ
إِن يَتَّبِعُونَ إِلَّا ٱلظَّنَّ وَإِنْ هُمْ إِلَّا
يَخْرُصُونَ ﴿٦٦﴾ هُوَ ٱلَّذِى جَعَلَ لَكُمُ
ٱلَّيْلَ لِتَسْكُنُوا۟ فِيهِ وَٱلنَّهَارَ
مُبْصِرًا ۚ إِنَّ فِى ذَٰلِكَ لَءَايَٰتٍ لِّقَوْمٍ
يَسْمَعُونَ ﴿٦٧﴾

their deeds, or that they will never be called to account. They ought to take heed for all their deeds are being duly recorded on the Divine Scroll.

65. What is being said here in a summary fashion requires some elaboration. The statement refers to philosophical inquiry which aims at discovering the reality underlying the physical phenomena of the universe. All those who do not look up to revelation in order to know what such reality is, have to fall back, willy-nilly, on philosophical inquiry. Whether a person ends up with atheism, polytheism or monotheism, he perforce has recourse to philosophical inquiry of some sort in order to arrive at some conclusion about reality. Likewise, the worth of the religious doctrines propounded by the Prophets can also be determined by resort to philosophical reflection after which a person is likely to arrive at some conclusion as to whether the reality to which the physical phenomena allude makes any sense or not. The soundness of the conclusion at which a person arrives totally depends, however, on the soundness of the method of philosophical inquiry that is adopted. If the method is sound, so would the conclusion be; and *vice versa.*

Let us now examine the methods that were adopted by different groups in this pursuit. Of these, the method used by the polytheists is based on superstition. As for the gnostic and ascetic hermits, even though they flaunt meditation as their characteristic method and claim their ability to penetrate the reality that lies beyond the phenomenal veil, their quest is based merely on conjecture. Likewise, what they claim to have observed is actually a product of their fancy. Swayed by it, they mistake their fancies for the truth.

Now, philosophers are guided in their quest for reality by speculation which, it would seem, is nothing less than conjecture. But realizing that their conjecture has no respectable ground upon which to stand, philosophers provide the crutches of logical reasoning and phoney rationalism to support their quest, and give it the imposing title of philosophical inquiry.

Then we come across scientists. In their own field, they resort to scientific methods of inquiry, but as soon as they enter the realm of the metaphysical, they abandon this method and proceed with guesswork and conjecture.

The outlook of all these groups is impaired, afflicted with bias and prejudice of one sort or another. This makes them impervious to everything which is alien to them with the net result that they cling adamantly to their cherished ways.

The Qur'ān brands this kind of intellectual quest as essentially fallacious. It tells such people that the real cause of their malady is guesswork and conjecture in their pursuit of reality, and that they do not heed the reasonable counsel of others because of their deep-seated prejudices. The result is not only are they incapable of independently grasping reality, but their prejudice renders them incapable of arriving at any sound judgement regarding it even when it is expounded by the Prophets.

In sharp contrast to these fallacious methods, the Qur'ān lays down an altogether different method to guide men in their quest of reality. This requires, first of all, that one should heed with open ears and consider with open minds the statements of those who claim to be expounding their doctrine about reality not on the basis of speculation or conjecture, nor on the basis of meditation or intuitive conviction, but on the basis of 'knowledge'. They should then proceed to consider the phenomena which form a part of man's observation or experience of the universe (called *āyāt* – signs – in the Qur'ānic parlance); to systematize all that they come to know in this manner and to seriously reflect whether the phenomena seem to testify to the reality underlying the phenomena to which these people [i.e. the Prophets] have drawn their attention. If one finds sufficient grounds to affirm the truths propounded by the Prophets, why on earth should anyone contradict such truths? In our view, this very method is the basis of the philosophy of Islam and it is regrettable that even Muslim philosophers abandoned it and set out to follow in the footsteps of Plato and Aristotle.

Not only does the Qur'ān urge people, over and over again, to follow this method, but by frequently drawing attention to the physical phenomena and then showing how right conclusions can be derived from them, it also seems to train them to follow this method. Were one to consider even the present verse by way of example one would encounter reference to a couple of physical phenomena – night and day. The alternation of day and night is the outcome of an absolutely precise and well-regulated movement of the earth around the sun. This is an incontrovertible sign of the existence of an all-encompassing controller, of an all-powerful Lord Whose dominion embraces the whole universe. This alternation of day and night is also indicative of the infinite wisdom and purposiveness of the Creator since a lot of creatures of the earth depend upon it. This alternation is also indicative of the Providence, Mercy and

(68) They say: 'Allah has taken a son.'[66] Glory be to Him.[67] He is self-sufficient! His is all that is in the heavens and all that is in the earth.[68] Have you any authority to support (that Allah has taken a son)? Do you ascribe to Allah something of which you have no knowledge? (69) Tell them (O Muḥammad!): 'Indeed those who invent lies against Allah will never prosper. (70) They may enjoy the life of this world, but in the end they must return to Us, and then We shall cause them to taste severe chastisement for their disbelieving.'

قَالُوا اتَّخَذَ اللَّهُ وَلَدًا ۗ سُبْحَانَهُ
هُوَ الْغَنِيُّ ۖ لَهُ مَا فِي السَّمَاوَاتِ وَمَا فِي
الْأَرْضِ ۚ إِنْ عِندَكُم مِّن سُلْطَانٍ
بِهَٰذَا ۚ أَتَقُولُونَ عَلَى اللَّهِ مَا
لَا تَعْلَمُونَ ﴿٦٨﴾ قُلْ إِنَّ الَّذِينَ
يَفْتَرُونَ عَلَى اللَّهِ الْكَذِبَ
لَا يُفْلِحُونَ ﴿٦٩﴾ مَتَاعٌ فِي الدُّنْيَا
ثُمَّ إِلَيْنَا مَرْجِعُهُمْ ثُمَّ نُذِيقُهُمُ
الْعَذَابَ الشَّدِيدَ بِمَا كَانُوا
يَكْفُرُونَ ﴿٧٠﴾

Lordship of the Creator since it is evident that He Who has created all beings on earth has also made arrangements to cater to all their requirements.

What this unmistakably proves is that the Creator is the One Who fully controls the entire universe and that far from being arbitrary and capricious, He is Wise. His actions also go to show that in view of His benevolence and providence He alone deserves to be served and worshipped. Also, this alternation of day and night clearly reveals that anything which is subject to the system of alternation of night and day is a servant and not the Lord. All this being the testimony of the natural phenomena, how can it ever be entertained that the religious doctrines developed by polytheists on the basis of their guesswork and conjecture have even a shred of legitimacy?

66. In the preceding verses, the polytheists were reproached for basing their religious doctrines on guesswork and conjecture, and then failing to examine, on scientific grounds, whether those doctrines were backed up by any supporting proof or not. In this verse, the Christians and followers of some other religions are being taken to task for another error – for their designating someone, again by resort to sheer conjecture, as God's son.

67. This Arabic expression سُبْحَانَ اللهِ is used both in its literal sense and also by way of exclamation. As an exclamatory expression it emphasizes one's

utter amazement about God. In its literal sense, it signifies that God is free of every defect and flaw. The above verse in question employs both meanings. For, apart from expressing amazement at the notion that God took someone as His son, it also stresses the perfection, the absolute flawlessness of God. Since God is perfect and flawless, how does it make any sense to say that He took someone as His son?

68. In refuting the notion that God took anyone as His son, three arguments are advanced: (i) God is free of all defects; (ii) God is All-Sufficient; and (iii) all that is in the heavens and in the earth belongs to Him.

A brief elucidation of these statements will enable one to appreciate the meaning and significance of what is being said here. To be a son can have only two meanings: either he has sprung from his father's loins, that is, he is his father's son in the true sense of the term, and thus of his father's loins, or that he is not a son in the literal sense of the word but has merely been adopted as such. Now, if someone is considered to be a son of God in its true, literal sense, that would obviously amount to considering God akin to a mortal. Like any other mortal, God is conceived to belong to one gender or the other, and to stand in need of a spouse, and of some sort of conjugal relationship to enable the birth of offspring, and thus to ensure the continuity of his progeny. Alternatively, God is believed to have adopted someone as His son. Such a statement could either mean that God is akin to that issueless human who resorts to adoption in order that the adopted son might inherit Him and thus secure Him against the loss that would ensue from his being issueless, or at least partially offset that loss. The other possibility is that God also has certain emotional predilections and it is for this reason that He has fallen in love with one of His creatures to the extent of adopting him as His son. In each of the above-mentioned cases, the concept of God is marred by investing Him with several flaws, defects and weaknesses, and He is conceived as One lacking self-sufficiency, as One Who perforce must depend on others.

Hence, the opening part of the verse clearly proclaims God to be free of all defects, deficiencies and weaknesses which people ascribe to Him. This is followed by saying that God is All-Sufficient, that is, He is free of all those needs which impel an issueless mortal to adopt someone as his son. This is further followed by the assertion that all that is in the heavens and in the earth belongs to God and hence all human beings, without any exception, are His servants and bondsmen. This makes it clear that there is no personal relationship between God and any of His creatures that would prompt Him to choose any, to the exclusion of others, for elevation to the level of godhead. For sure, He holds certain people, on grounds of their merit, to be dearer than others. But God's love for someone does not mean that he is lifted up from the rank of being God's servant to becoming His associate and partner in godhead. What God's special love for some person means can be gauged from the following verse of the Qur'ān: 'Oh, surely the friends of Allah have nothing to fear, nor shall they grieve – the ones who believe and are God-fearing. For them are glad tidings in this world and in the Hereafter' (see verses 62–4 above).

(71) And narrate to them the story of Noah[69] when he said to his people: 'My people! If my living in your midst and my effort to shake you out of heedlessness by reciting to you the revelations of Allah offend you, then remember that I have put all my trust in Allah. So draw up your plan in concert with those whom you associate with Allah in His divinity, leaving no part of it obscure, and then put it into effect against me, and give me no respite.[70] (72) When you turned your back on my admonition (what harm did you cause me?) I had asked of you no reward, for my reward lies only with Allah, and I am commanded to be of those who totally submit (to Allah)'

۞ وَاتْلُ عَلَيْهِمْ نَبَأَ نُوحٍ إِذْ قَالَ
لِقَوْمِهِ يَا قَوْمِ إِن كَانَ كَبُرَ عَلَيْكُم
مَّقَامِي وَتَذْكِيرِي بِآيَاتِ اللَّهِ
فَعَلَى اللَّهِ تَوَكَّلْتُ فَأَجْمِعُوا
أَمْرَكُمْ وَشُرَكَاءَكُمْ ثُمَّ لَا يَكُنْ
أَمْرُكُمْ عَلَيْكُمْ غُمَّةً ثُمَّ اقْضُوا
إِلَيَّ وَلَا تُنظِرُونِ ﴿٧١﴾ فَإِن
تَوَلَّيْتُمْ فَمَا سَأَلْتُكُم مِّنْ
أَجْرٍ إِنْ أَجْرِيَ إِلَّا عَلَى اللَّهِ
وَأُمِرْتُ أَنْ أَكُونَ مِنَ
الْمُسْلِمِينَ ﴿٧٢﴾

69. In the preceding verses a combination of convincing arguments and persuasive instruction was employed to drive home to the people that their intellectual outlook and way of life were faulty. As opposed to that, the right way for mankind was highlighted and it was shown why that way was right. Thereafter, attention was paid to candidly exposing the attitude which the unbelievers had adopted during the past eleven years: instead of mending their ways in the light of the reasonable criticism to which they had been subjected and in response to the right guidance offered to them, they became inveterate enemies of the very man who was expounding a message that could ensure their salvation and who sought their well-being and had no axe of his own to grind. Regrettably, they responded to his arguments by throwing brickbats and answered his sincere counsels by hurling filthy abuses at him. They found even the existence of this man in their midst, of one whose main fault was that he called a spade a spade, absolutely insufferable. They virtually said that if in a

(73) But they rejected Noah, calling him a liar. So We saved him and those who were with him in the Ark, and made them successors (to the authority in the land), and drowned all those who had rejected Our signs as false. Consider, then, the fate of those who had been warned (and still did not believe).

(74) Then We sent forth after him other Messengers, each one to his people. They brought to them clear signs, but they were not such as to believe in what they had rejected earlier as false. Thus do We seal the hearts of those who transgress.[71]

فَكَذَّبُوهُ فَنَجَّيْنَٰهُ وَمَن مَّعَهُۥ فِى ٱلْفُلْكِ
وَجَعَلْنَٰهُمْ خَلَٰٓئِفَ وَأَغْرَقْنَا ٱلَّذِينَ
كَذَّبُوا۟ بِـَٔايَٰتِنَا فَٱنظُرْ كَيْفَ كَانَ عَٰقِبَةُ
ٱلْمُنذَرِينَ ﴿٧٣﴾ ثُمَّ بَعَثْنَا مِنۢ بَعْدِهِۦ رُسُلًا
إِلَىٰ قَوْمِهِمْ فَجَآءُوهُم بِٱلْبَيِّنَٰتِ فَمَا
كَانُوا۟ لِيُؤْمِنُوا۟ بِمَا كَذَّبُوا۟ بِهِۦ مِن قَبْلُ
كَذَٰلِكَ نَطْبَعُ عَلَىٰ قُلُوبِ
ٱلْمُعْتَدِينَ ﴿٧٤﴾

group of blind persons there is anyone possessed of sight, the only right course for him is to blind himself rather than try to restore the vision of others. And if such a person refused to do so, it was for them to pluck out his eyes and make him blind like themselves.

No direct comment is made here with regard to the attitude of those people. Instead, God asks His Prophet (peace be on him) to narrate to them the story of Noah. Through this story the unbelievers would be able to see clearly their own predicament as well as the predicament of the believers.

70. Faced with determined opposition from the unbelievers, Noah made it quite clear that he would not cease to strive for his cause, regardless of what the unbelievers might do for it is in God that he put his trust. (Cf. *Hūd* 11: 55.)

71. 'Those who transgress' mentioned in the present verse are those who, once they commit a wrong, cling to it out of adamance and obstinacy. These are the ones who, out of sheer arrogance and egotism, would like to stick to the stand they once took even if it was erroneous. Such people remain unmoved

(75) Then, after them,[72] We sent forth Moses and Aaron to Pharaoh and his chiefs with Our signs, but they waxed proud.[73] They were a wicked people. (76) And when truth came to them from Us, they said: 'Indeed this is plain sorcery.'[74] ▶

ثُمَّ بَعَثْنَا مِنۢ بَعْدِهِم مُّوسَىٰ وَهَٰرُونَ إِلَىٰ فِرْعَوْنَ وَمَلَإِي۟هِۦ بِـَٔايَٰتِنَا فَٱسْتَكْبَرُوا۟ وَكَانُوا۟ قَوْمًا مُّجْرِمِينَ ﴿٧٥﴾ فَلَمَّا جَآءَهُمُ ٱلْحَقُّ مِنْ عِندِنَا قَالُوٓا۟ إِنَّ هَٰذَا لَسِحْرٌ مُّبِينٌ ﴿٧٦﴾

even by the most reasonable arguments. As a result, they become victims of a curse and are never able to find the right way.

72. For a full appreciation of the story of Moses and Pharaoh, see the explanatory notes in *Towards Understanding the Qur'ān*, vol. III, *al-A'rāf* 7, n. 83 ff. The points elucidated in these notes will not be repeated here.

73. Intoxicated by their riches, political power and glory they considered themselves to be well above the level of ordinary human beings. Thus, instead of humbly submitting themselves to God, they waxed proud.

74. The response of the Pharaonites to the Prophet Moses (peace be on him) was exactly the same as the response of the Makkan unbelievers to the Prophet (peace be on him). This response has been mentioned earlier (see verse 2 above) in these words: 'This man is indeed an evident sorcerer.'

The context makes it clear that the Prophets Moses and Aaron (peace be on them) were entrusted with the same mission which had formerly been entrusted to Prophet Noah (peace be on him), then to the Prophets who followed him and finally to the Prophet Muḥammad (peace be on him) who was the last in the chain of such Prophets.

From the outset, the thrust of the *sūrah* has been the same – that man should take God, the Lord of the universe, and Him alone, as his Lord and as the sole object of his worship, service and obedience, and that he has to render to Him an account of all his deeds. Now, those who had rejected the message of the Prophet (peace be on him) are being told that their well-being as well as that of all human beings rests on affirming their belief in the One True God and in the Hereafter, a belief which has been invariably expounded by the Prophets down the ages. Man's well-being depends on affirming this belief, and on fashioning his entire behaviour on the basis of that.

This constitutes the pivotal point of the whole *sūrah*. The reference to other Prophets (peace be on them) in this *sūrah* by way of historical illustration indicates that the message of all the Prophets was the same as the one embodied

(77) Moses said: 'Do you say this about the truth after it has come to you? Is this sorcery? You call this sorcery although sorcerers never come to a happy end.'[75] (78) They replied: 'Have you come to turn us away from the way of our forefathers that the two of you might become supreme in the land?[76] We shall never accept what the two of you say.' ▶

قَالَ مُوسَىٰٓ أَتَقُولُونَ لِلْحَقِّ لَمَّا جَآءَكُمْ ۖ أَسِحْرٌ هَـٰذَا وَلَا يُفْلِحُ ٱلسَّـٰحِرُونَ ﴿٧٧﴾ قَالُوٓا۟ أَجِئْتَنَا لِتَلْفِتَنَا عَمَّا وَجَدْنَا عَلَيْهِ ءَابَآءَنَا وَتَكُونَ لَكُمَا ٱلْكِبْرِيَآءُ فِى ٱلْأَرْضِ وَمَا نَحْنُ لَكُمَا بِمُؤْمِنِينَ ﴿٧٨﴾

---

in this *sūrah*. The Prophets Moses and Aaron (peace be on them) had conveyed the same message to Pharaoh and his chiefs. Had the mission of these two Prophets been merely to liberate a specific nation, as some people are inclined to believe, reference to this event for the purpose of historical illustration would have been quite discordant with the context in which it occurs. There can be no doubt that the mission of Moses and Aaron partially aimed at bringing about the liberation of the Israelites (then, a Muslim people) from the domination of an unbelieving nation. This was, however, a secondary rather than the central purpose of raising those Prophets. According to the Qur'ān the main objective of the mission of these two Prophets was the same as that of all other Prophets. An objective which has been clearly set forth in the following verses of: 'Go to Pharaoh for he has certainly transgressed all bounds (of servitude to Allah). And say to him: "Would you rather be purified; and that I guide you to your Lord that you may fear Him" ' (*al-Nāzi'āt* 79: 17–19).

Now, since Pharaoh and his nobles did not respond positively to this call, the Prophet Moses (peace be on him) was ultimately left with no other choice but to secure the liberation of his people, who were Muslims, and to take them away from the area dominated by Pharaoh. This was of course a fairly important event, and the Qur'ānic narration of it also treats it as such. However, all those who are not inclined to view the detailed teachings of the Qur'ān in isolation from its general principles, can never commit the mistake of considering the liberation of a people to be the *basic* purpose of raising a Prophet whereas inviting people to the true faith is of secondary significance. (For further details see *Ṭā Hā* 20: 44–52; *al-Zukhruf* 43: 46–56; and *al-Muzzammil* 73: 15–16.)

(79) And Pharaoh said (to his) men: 'Bring every skilled sorcerer to me.' (80) And when the sorcerers came Moses said to them: 'Cast whatever you wish to cast.' (81) Then when they had cast (their staffs), Moses said: 'What you have produced is sheer sorcery.[77] Allah will certainly reduce it to naught. Surely Allah does not set right the work of the mischief-makers. (82) Allah vindicates the truth by His commands, howsoever much the guilty might detest that.'

وَقَالَ فِرْعَوْنُ ٱئْتُونِي بِكُلِّ سَٰحِرٍ عَلِيمٍ
٧٩ فَلَمَّا جَآءَ ٱلسَّحَرَةُ قَالَ لَهُم مُّوسَىٰٓ
أَلْقُوا۟ مَآ أَنتُم مُّلْقُونَ ٨٠ فَلَمَّآ أَلْقَوْا۟
قَالَ مُوسَىٰ مَا جِئْتُم بِهِ ٱلسِّحْرُ إِنَّ ٱللَّهَ
سَيُبْطِلُهُۥٓ إِنَّ ٱللَّهَ لَا يُصْلِحُ عَمَلَ
ٱلْمُفْسِدِينَ ٨١ وَيُحِقُّ ٱللَّهُ ٱلْحَقَّ
بِكَلِمَٰتِهِۦ وَلَوْ كَرِهَ ٱلْمُجْرِمُونَ ٨٢

75. In view of the apparent similarity between sorcery and miracle the Israelites hastily branded Moses (peace be on him) a sorcerer. In relegating Moses to the role of a sorcerer, however, these simpletons ignored the fact that the character and conduct as well as the motives underlying the activity of sorcerers are entirely different from those of the Prophets. Is it consistent with the known character of a sorcerer that he should fearlessly make his way to the court of a tyrant, reproach him for his error, and summon him to exclusively devote himself to God and to strive for his self-purification? What would rather seem to be consistent with the character of a sorcerer is that if he had gained access to the courtiers he would have gone about flattering them, soliciting their help in securing an opportunity to show his tricks. And if ever he succeeded in finding his way to the royal court, he would probably have resorted to flattery in an even more abject and dishonourable manner, would have made himself hoarse in publicly praying for the long life and abiding glory of the ruler, and would then have humbly pleaded that he might be allowed to perform his show. And once the show was over, he would have disgracefully stretched forth his hands in the style of a beggar, entreating for an appropriate award.

All this has been condensed into the succinct statement that 'sorcerers never come to a happy end'.

76. Had the sole demand of Moses and Aaron (peace be on him) been the liberation of the Israelites, Pharaoh and his courtiers would not have suspected

(83) None but a few youths[78] of Moses' people accepted him,[79] fearing that Pharaoh and their own chiefs would persecute them. Indeed Pharaoh was mighty in the land, he was among those who exceed all limits.[80]	فَمَآ ءَامَنَ لِمُوسَىٰٓ إِلَّا ذُرِّيَّةٌ مِّن قَوْمِهِۦ عَلَىٰ خَوْفٍ مِّن فِرْعَوْنَ وَمَلَإِيْهِمْ أَن يَفْتِنَهُمْ ۚ وَإِنَّ فِرْعَوْنَ لَعَالٍ فِى ٱلْأَرْضِ وَإِنَّهُۥ لَمِنَ ٱلْمُسْرِفِينَ ﴿٨٣﴾

that the spread of these Prophets' message would transform the religion of the land and that the supremacy of Pharaoh and his courtiers would be undermined. What made them uneasy was the fact that Prophet Moses (peace be on him) was inviting the people of Egypt to the true faith and that this posed a threat to the whole polytheistic way of life which was the very cornerstone of the predominance of Pharaoh and his chiefs and clergy. (For further details see *Towards Understanding the Qur'ān, al-A'rāf* 7, n. 44 and *al-Mu'min* 40, n. 43 – Ed.)

77. What Moses (peace be on him) presented before the court was no sorcery; rather it was the sorcerers who had made a show of their tricks of sorcery.

78. The word *dhurrīyah* used in this verse literally means 'offspring'. We have, however, rendered this into English as 'a few youths'. We have preferred this translation because the Qur'ān employed this particular expression so as to convey the idea that it was a few youths – male and female – who had the courage of their convictions to embrace and champion the truth in those perilous times whereas their parents and the more elderly members of the community were unable to do so. The older segment of the population was too deeply concerned with its materialistic interests, too engrossed in worldliness and too eager to enjoy a life of security to stand by the truth when that seemed to invite all kinds of peril. On the contrary, this older generation tried to persuade the young ones to stay away from Moses for the simple reason that it would invite the wrath of Pharaoh upon themselves and upon others.

The Qur'ān underscores this point, for once again those who came forward and courageously supported the Prophet (peace be on him) were not the elderly. They were rather a few courageous Makkan youths. Those who embraced Islam at this very early period in its history – the period of revelation of these verses – and who supported the message of truth despite fierce persecution, were all young people. This group was altogether bereft of the aged doters of a life free of peril and hazard. 'Alī ibn abī Ṭālib, Ja'far ibn al-'Aqīl, Zubayr, Ṭalḥah, Sa'd ibn abī Waqqāṣ, Muṣ'ab ibn 'Umayr, 'Abd

Allāh ibn Mas'ūd were all young people and each one of them, at the time of embracing Islam, was under twenty. Likewise, 'Abd al-Raḥmān ibn 'Awf, Bilāl and Ṣuhayb were all in their twenties while Abū 'Ubaydah ibn al-Jarrāḥ, Zayd ibn Ḥārithah, 'Uthmān ibn 'Affān and 'Umar ibn al-Khaṭṭāb were between thirty and thirty-five years of age. The oldest among these Companions was Abū Bakr, and when he embraced Islam he too was no older than thirty-eight. 'Ammār ibn Yāsir was the same age as the Prophet (peace be on him), and only one Companion, 'Ubaydah ibn Ḥārith al-Muṭṭalibī was older than he.

79. The words فَمَا آمَنَ لِمُوسَىٰ which occur in the present verse have given rise to the misunderstanding that all the Israelites were unbelievers, and that in the early phases of Moses' 'prophethood' only a very few persons were believers. The use of the preposition لِ, when applied to إِيمَان signifies 'to obey and follow someone'. What these words, therefore, mean is that except for a few young people none in the whole nation of Israel was prepared to accept Moses as his leader, to follow him and support him in his Islamic mission. The part of the verse which follows makes it quite clear that this was not because they had any doubts about the veracity of Moses (peace be on him) or about the truth of his mission. The only reason for them not joining hands with him was that they – especially their elders and nobles – were unwilling to risk Pharaoh's fierce persecution.

These people both in terms of pedigree and faith, belonged to the *ummah* of Abraham, Isaac, Jacob and Joseph (peace be on them) and were, therefore, Muslims. Yet the long subjugation of the Israelites had created such moral degeneration and faint-heartedness among them that they had been rendered altogether incapable of championing the cause of faith and truth or of opposing falsehood and unbelief, or even supporting those who had set out to champion that cause. The overall attitude of the Israelites during the whole of this conflict between Moses and Pharaoh may be gauged by the following statement in the Bible:

> They met Moses and Aaron, who were waiting for them, as they came forth from Pharaoh; and they said to them, 'The Lord look upon you and judge, because you have made us offensive in the sight of Pharaoh and his servants, and have put a sword in their hand to kill us' (*Exodus* 5: 20–1).

According to the Talmud, the Israelites used to tell the Prophets Moses and Aaron (peace be on them):

> 'Yea', said the overburdened children of Israel to Moses and Aaron, 'we are like a lamb which the wolf has carried from its flock, the shepherd strives to take it from him, but between the two the lamb is pulled to pieces; between ye and Pharaoh will we all be killed' (H. Polano, *The Talmud Selections*, p. 152).

(84) Moses said: 'My people! If you believe in Allah and are truly Muslims[81] then place your reliance on Him alone.' (85) They replied:[82] 'We place our reliance on Allah. Our Lord! Do not make us a trial for the oppressors,[83] (86) and deliver us, through Your mercy, from the unbelievers.'

وَقَالَ مُوسَىٰ يَٰقَوْمِ إِن كُنتُمْ ءَامَنتُم بِٱللَّهِ فَعَلَيْهِ تَوَكَّلُوٓا۟ إِن كُنتُم مُّسْلِمِينَ ﴿٨٤﴾ فَقَالُوا۟ عَلَى ٱللَّهِ تَوَكَّلْنَا رَبَّنَا لَا تَجْعَلْنَا فِتْنَةً لِّلْقَوْمِ ٱلظَّٰلِمِينَ ﴿٨٥﴾ وَنَجِّنَا بِرَحْمَتِكَ مِنَ ٱلْقَوْمِ ٱلْكَٰفِرِينَ ﴿٨٦﴾

The Qur'ān also refers to much the same when it mentions what the Israelites said to Prophet Moses (peace be on him):

> We were oppressed before your coming to us and after it (*al-A'rāf* 7: 129).

80. The word مُسْرِفِين which has been used here signifies transgressors, those who exceed the limits. But this literal translation hardly conveys the true spirit of the word. For it has been used to refer to those who, in order to achieve their objectives, are not deterred from using any means, howsoever evil they may be. Such people do not mind committing injustice, or indulging in acts of moral turpitude. They are also wont to go to any extent in pursuing their desires. Once they have something in mind, they simply know no bounds.

81. Such an address could, obviously, not be directed to a community of unbelievers. The Prophet Moses' statement makes it absolutely clear that the Israelites of those days were believers. Accordingly, Moses (peace be on him) exhorted them not to be unnerved by Pharaoh's might, that they put their trust in God's power if indeed they were true believers as they claimed.

82. This was the reply of the youths who came forward to support Moses (peace be on him). It is evident from the context that the ones who said: 'We place our reliance on Allah' were not the 'wrong-doing folk' [mentioned in the present verse] but the 'youths' [mentioned in verse 83 above].

83. The supplication of these devout youths: 'Our Lord! Do not make us a trial for the oppressors', covers a very wide range of meanings. Whenever a people rise to establish the truth in the midst of prevalent falsehood, they encounter oppressors of all sorts. On the one hand, there are protagonists of falsehood who would like to crush the standard-bearers of the truth with all the

(87) And We directed Moses and his brother: 'Prepare a few houses for your people in Egypt, and make your houses a direction for men to pray, and establish Prayer,[84] and give glad tidings to the men of faith.'[85]

وَأَوۡحَيۡنَآ إِلَىٰ مُوسَىٰ وَأَخِيهِ أَن تَبَوَّءَا لِقَوۡمِكُمَا بِمِصۡرَ بُيُوتٗا وَٱجۡعَلُواْ بُيُوتَكُمۡ قِبۡلَةٗ وَأَقِيمُواْ ٱلصَّلَوٰةَۗ وَبَشِّرِ ٱلۡمُؤۡمِنِينَ ٨٧

force at their disposal. There is also a sizeable group of people who claim to champion the truth but who, despite their claim to be its devotees, are so cowed by the all-round supremacy of falsehood that they look upon the struggle to make the truth prevail as an unnecessary, futile and absurd pursuit. Such people are inclined, in order to somehow justify their insincerity to the cause of the truth, to prove that those who are engaged in the struggle to make the truth prevail are in fact in error. By so doing they seek to calm the uneasiness felt by their conscience concerning the desirability of struggling for the cause of the truth. Over and above all these are the common people who observe, as silent spectators, the encounter between truth and falsehood, and ultimately support the party which appears to be winning regardless of what aspect that party supports.

In this scenario, every reverse that the votaries of the truth suffer, every affliction or hardship that they endure, any mistake that they commit, and any weakness that they show becomes a cause of trial for all these groups. If the votaries of the truth are crushed or defeated, the protagonists of falsehood jubilantly claim that it was they, rather than those whom they opposed, who were in the right. The lukewarm supporters of the truth would cry: 'Look! Did we not foretell that the conflict with such mighty forces would merely result in a loss of many precious lives, that it would be an act of sheer self-destruction, an act of wanton suicide, which has not been made incumbent on us by the Law of God. So far as the fundamental requirements of faith are concerned, they are being fulfilled by the performance of basic religious duties and rituals. As for the rulers, however oppressive they may be, they did not prevent them from performing those duties.' As for the masses, their attitude is that the truth is known by the fact that it achieves victory. Hence, if a group comes forth as triumphant, the fact of its triumph proves that it was in the right. Similarly, if in the course of a struggle, the protagonists of the truth commit any lapse or betray any weakness in the face of heavy odds, or if even a single person succumbs to any act of immorality, this provides a good many opponents with a pretext to cling to falsehood. If the struggle meets with failure, people are so wont to lose heart that it becomes extremely difficult for any similar movement to rise for a

(88) Moses prayed:[86] 'Our Lord! You bestowed upon Pharaoh and his nobles splendour[87] and riches[88] in the world. Our Lord! Have You done this that they may lead people astray from Your path? Our Lord! Obliterate their riches and harden their hearts that they may not believe until they observe the painful chastisement.'[89] (89) Allah responded: 'The prayer of the two of you is accepted. So keep steadfast, and do not follow the path of the ignorant.'[90]

وَقَالَ مُوسَىٰ رَبَّنَآ إِنَّكَ ءَاتَيْتَ
فِرْعَوْنَ وَمَلَأَهُۥ زِينَةً وَأَمْوَٰلًا فِى
ٱلْحَيَوٰةِ ٱلدُّنْيَا رَبَّنَا لِيُضِلُّوا۟ عَن
سَبِيلِكَ ۖ رَبَّنَا ٱطْمِسْ عَلَىٰٓ أَمْوَٰلِهِمْ
وَٱشْدُدْ عَلَىٰ قُلُوبِهِمْ فَلَا يُؤْمِنُوا۟ حَتَّىٰ
يَرَوُا۟ ٱلْعَذَابَ ٱلْأَلِيمَ ﴿٨٨﴾ قَالَ قَدْ أُجِيبَت
دَّعْوَتُكُمَا فَٱسْتَقِيمَا وَلَا تَتَّبِعَآنِّ
سَبِيلَ ٱلَّذِينَ لَا يَعْلَمُونَ ﴿٨٩﴾

very long time. Viewed against this background, the prayer of the companions of Moses (peace be on him) appears very meaningful: 'Our Lord! Do not make us a trial for the oppressors.' This prayer sought from God His grace that would protect them from their shortcomings and weaknesses, and would render their struggle successful in this world in order that their very existence might become a blessing for fellow human beings rather than a means, in the hands of oppressors, to inflict harm.

84. The Qur'ān-commentators disagree about the meaning of this verse. After carefully considering the actual words of the verse and reflecting over the context in which these words were said, I have come to the conclusion that perhaps because of the oppression prevailing in Egypt, and because the faith of the Israelites had become quite weak, congregational prayer had become defunct among both the Israeli and Egyptian Muslims.* The abandonment of congregational prayer was a major cause of the disintegration of their collective entity and the virtual extinction of their religious life. That is why Moses (peace be on him) was directed to re-establish congregational prayer and to construct or acquire a few houses in Egypt specifically for that purpose.

*The author's expression 'Egyptian Muslims' denotes those Egyptians who had embraced the faith of the Prophets, the faith of Moses (peace be on him) – Ed.

The reason for such a directive is that when a group of Muslims falls prey to degeneration and dissolution, the necessary effort to revive their religious spirit and to restore their shattered integrity, if it is to conform to a truly Islamic pattern, must begin with the revival of congregational prayer.

The directive to 'make your houses a direction for men to pray' suggests, in my opinion, that these prayer-houses should become pivotal points for the entire people. That the directive to 'establish Prayer' immediately follows this statement means that rather than offer Prayer at different places, they should congregate in the houses set aside for Prayer and perform it collectively. For certainly one of the implications of the expression 'to establish Prayer' which frequently occurs in the Qur'ān, is its observance in congregation.

85. Moses (peace be on him) was directed to banish those feelings of despair, awe and dismay which had seized the believers. To 'give glad tidings' encompasses the whole range required by this task.

86. These verses are related to the early period of Moses' (peace be on him) mission whereas the prayer itself probably belongs to his last days in Egypt. The intervening period spans several years, the detailed events of which have not been mentioned here. At other places in the Qur'ān, however, there are references to the events that took place in that intervening period.

87. This alludes to the pomp and splendour and the glamour of cultural refinement because of which people had become enamoured of them and their life-style, and which had created in the former an irrepressible urge to ape the ways of the latter.

88. This refers to the abundance of material resources which are available to the unbelievers to execute their plans, whereas the believers, insofar as they lack those resources, are forced to defer the execution of their plans.

89. This prayer, as we have pointed out earlier (see n. 86 above), was made by the Prophet Moses (peace be on him) during his very last days in Egypt. Moses resorted to this prayer when, although Pharaoh and his nobles had witnessed a series of signs betokening the truth, and even though Moses (peace be on him) had made the truth all too patently clear to them, they still obdurately persisted in their hostility to it. Moses' prayer that God may 'obliterate their riches and harden their hearts' is a prayer that Prophets are wont to make at a time when they are faced with opposition like that mentioned above. The prayer is substantially in accord with God's own judgement against those who obdurately oppose the truth – that they may never be enabled to have faith.

90. Those who are ignorant of reality and who have no grasp of the beneficent considerations underlying God's decisions are liable to misunderstand things. Such people observe the weakness of the forces that stand for

(90) And We led the Children of Israel across the sea. Then Pharaoh and his hosts pursued them in iniquity and transgression until Pharaoh cried out while he was drowning: 'I believe that there is no god but Allah in Whom the Children of Israel believe, and I am also one of those who submit to Allah.'[91] (91) (Thereupon came the response): 'Now you believe, although you disobeyed earlier and were one of the mischief-makers.▶

۞ وَجَـٰوَزْنَا بِبَنِىٓ إِسْرَٰٓءِيلَ ٱلْبَحْرَ
فَأَتْبَعَهُمْ فِرْعَوْنُ وَجُنُودُهُۥ بَغْيًا
وَعَدْوًا ۖ حَتَّىٰٓ إِذَآ أَدْرَكَهُ ٱلْغَرَقُ
قَالَ ءَامَنتُ أَنَّهُۥ لَآ إِلَـٰهَ إِلَّا ٱلَّذِىٓ
ءَامَنَتْ بِهِۦ بَنُوٓا۟ إِسْرَٰٓءِيلَ وَأَنَا۠ مِنَ
ٱلْمُسْلِمِينَ ﴿٩٠﴾ ءَآلْـَٔـٰنَ وَقَدْ
عَصَيْتَ قَبْلُ وَكُنتَ
مِنَ ٱلْمُفْسِدِينَ ﴿٩١﴾

truth as against the forces of falsehood. They observe that those who seek to make the truth prevail suffer a series of reverses. By way of contrast, they observe the dazzling worldly success of those who stand for falsehood. On such occasions they fall prey to several misconceptions. They begin to suspect that perhaps God Himself wants that His rebels should continue to hold sway over the earth, that perhaps even He – Who Himself is the Truth – is not willing to support the truth in its encounter with falsehood. Under the influence of such a fallacious line of reasoning, they conclude that the struggle for establishing the hegemony of the truth is an exercise in futility. They feel, therefore, satisfied with the freedom to practise religious principles in a very narrow domain of human life; this is provided within the framework of a system of life which is based on denial of the true faith and the 'right' to violate the injunctions of God.

In the present verse God has directed Moses (peace be on him) and his followers not to fall prey to such erroneous ideas. God's directive, as embodied in this verse, amounts to saying that people should patiently persist in their efforts in the face of adverse circumstances, lest they also fall prey to the same mistake as committed by those who lack knowledge and wisdom.

91. Though this event is not mentioned in the Bible, it is explicitly recorded in the Talmud in the following words: 'Who is like Thee, O Lord, among the gods?'

(92) We shall now save your corpse that you may serve as a sign of warning for all posterity,[92] although many men are heedless of Our signs.'[93]

فَٱلۡيَوۡمَ نُنَجِّيكَ بِبَدَنِكَ لِتَكُونَ لِمَنۡ
خَلۡفَكَ ءَايَةٗۚ وَإِنَّ كَثِيرٗا مِّنَ ٱلنَّاسِ عَنۡ
ءَايَٰتِنَا لَغَٰفِلُونَ ﴿٩٢﴾ وَلَقَدۡ بَوَّأۡنَا بَنِيٓ
إِسۡرَٰٓءِيلَ مُبَوَّأَ صِدۡقٖ وَرَزَقۡنَٰهُم مِّنَ
ٱلطَّيِّبَٰتِ فَمَا ٱخۡتَلَفُواْ حَتَّىٰ جَآءَهُمُ ٱلۡعِلۡمُۚ
إِنَّ رَبَّكَ يَقۡضِي بَيۡنَهُمۡ يَوۡمَ ٱلۡقِيَٰمَةِ فِيمَا
كَانُواْ فِيهِ يَخۡتَلِفُونَ ﴿٩٣﴾

(93) We settled the Children of Israel in a blessed land,[94] and provided them with all manner of good things. They only disagreed among themselves after knowledge (of the truth had) come to them.[95] Surely your Lord will judge between them on the Day of Resurrection concerning their disagreements.

---

92. Even to this day the exact place where Pharaoh's dead body was found afloat on the surface of the sea is known. Lying on the western coast of the Sinaitic peninsula, it is presently known as the Mount of Pharaoh (Jabal Fir'awn). A warm spring, situated in its vicinity, is also still called the Bath of Pharaoh (Ḥammām Fir'awn) after Pharaoh. Located a few miles away, Abū Zanīmah is identified as the precise spot at which Pharaoh's dead body was found. If the name of the Pharaoh who died by drowning was Minpetah, as has been established by current research, his embalmed body still lies in the museum of Cairo. In 1907 when Sir Grafton Elliot Smith removed bandages from the mummified body of this Pharaoh, it was found to be coated with a layer of salt. This is clear proof of his death by drowning at sea.

93. God continues to confront people with instructive signs, even though most of them, in total disregard of such signs, fail to derive any lesson from them.

94. That is, God provided an abode for them in Palestine for their exodus from Egypt.

95. Here reference is made to the schisms and dissensions which the Israelites caused and the ever new religious cults which they invented. It is

(94) Now, if you are in doubt concerning what We have revealed to you, then ask those who have been reading the Book before you. It is the truth that has come to you from your Lord, so do never become one of those who doubt, (95) or reject the signs of Allah as false, for then you shall be among those who will be in utter loss.[96]

(96) Surely those against whom the word of your Lord has been fulfilled[97] will not believe ▶

فَإِن كُنتَ فِي شَكٍّ مِّمَّآ أَنزَلْنَآ إِلَيْكَ فَسْـَٔلِ
ٱلَّذِينَ يَقْرَءُونَ ٱلْكِتَـٰبَ مِن قَبْلِكَ ۚ
لَقَدْ جَآءَكَ ٱلْحَقُّ مِن رَّبِّكَ فَلَا
تَكُونَنَّ مِنَ ٱلْمُمْتَرِينَ ﴿٩٤﴾ وَلَا تَكُونَنَّ
مِنَ ٱلَّذِينَ كَذَّبُوا۟ بِـَٔايَـٰتِ ٱللَّهِ
فَتَكُونَ مِنَ ٱلْخَـٰسِرِينَ ﴿٩٥﴾ إِنَّ
ٱلَّذِينَ حَقَّتْ عَلَيْهِمْ كَلِمَتُ
رَبِّكَ لَا يُؤْمِنُونَ ﴿٩٦﴾

pointed out here that they had not acted in ignorance of the truth; their actions rather emanated from mischievous designs. For they had been provided by God with the true religion and they knew its fundamental principles, its requirements, and the features which distinguish the true faith from the false ones. They were also well aware of what constitutes disobedience, on what matters man will be held to account by God, and on what principles man should fashion his life. Despite these clear directives the Israelites transformed their true faith into a multitude of religious cults, and developed them all on foundations altogether divergent from those provided by God.

96. Though this admonition is apparently addressed to the Prophet Muḥammad (peace be on him), in point of fact it is directed to those who entertained doubts about the Prophet's message. Reference is made to the People of the Book because the common Arabs were not conversant with the Scriptures. But so far as the People of the Book were concerned, there were doubtlessly some pious religious scholars among them who were in a position to corroborate the fact that the Qur'ānic message was essentially the same as that delivered by the earlier Prophets.

97. The statement 'the word of your Lord has been fulfilled' refers to those who are not interested in seeking truth; who, by dint of their apathy, bigotry, stubbornness, excessive worldliness and total unconcern about the After-life,

(97) even if they witness every single sign that might come to them until they are face to face with the painful chastisement. (98) Did it ever happen that the people of a town believed on seeing God's chastisement and its believing profited them? (There is no such instance) except of the people of Yūnus.[98] When they believed We granted them reprieve from humiliating chastisement in this world,[99] and We let them enjoy themselves for a while.[100]

وَلَوْ جَآءَتْهُمْ كُلُّ ءَايَةٍ حَتَّىٰ يَرَوُا۟
ٱلْعَذَابَ ٱلْأَلِيمَ ﴿٩٧﴾ فَلَوْلَا كَانَتْ قَرْيَةٌ
ءَامَنَتْ فَنَفَعَهَآ إِيمَٰنُهَآ إِلَّا قَوْمَ يُونُسَ
لَمَّآ ءَامَنُوا۟ كَشَفْنَا عَنْهُمْ عَذَابَ
ٱلْخِزْىِ فِى ٱلْحَيَوٰةِ ٱلدُّنْيَا وَمَتَّعْنَٰهُمْ
إِلَىٰ حِينٍ ﴿٩٨﴾

---

make their hearts immune to the truth. God's judgement about such persons is that they will not be blessed with faith.

98. Even though the Prophet Yūnus, called Jonah in the Bible (860–784 BC), was of Israeli descent, he was sent to Iraq in order to guide the Assyrians. The Assyrians are, therefore, called here 'the people of Yūnus'. Ninevah, the famous ancient town, was their capital, a great many ruins of which are still to be found on the left bank of the Tigris, opposite the present city of Mosul. One of the mounds in this area is still named after the Prophet Jonah. The splendour of the Assyrians may be gauged from the fact that their capital, Ninevah, spread over a radius of sixty miles.

99. Although there are allusions to this incident in three places in the Qur'ān, there is no mention of any detail. (See *al-Anbiyā'*, 21: 87–8; *al-Ṣāffāt* 37: 139–48; and *al-Qalam* 68: 48–50.) In view of the above, it cannot be stated with confidence why the Assyrians were singled out for being spared God's punishment even though God's Law is that if a people decide to believe after God has decided to punish them, their believing afterwards does not profit them.

The 'Book of Jonah' in the Bible contains some material relevant to the matter, but unfortunately that information is barely reliable. For, the 'Book of Jonah' is in no sense a heavenly revelation, nor was it even authored by the Prophet Jonah (peace be on him). What actually happened is that some four or

(99) Had your Lord so willed, all those who are on the earth would have believed.[101] Will you, then, force people into believing?[102] (100) No one can believe except by Allah's leave,[103] and Allah lays abomination on those who do not use their understanding.[104]

وَلَوْ شَآءَ رَبُّكَ لَءَامَنَ مَن فِى ٱلْأَرْضِ
كُلُّهُمْ جَمِيعًا ۚ أَفَأَنتَ تُكْرِهُ ٱلنَّاسَ
حَتَّىٰ يَكُونُوا۟ مُؤْمِنِينَ ﴿٩٩﴾ وَمَا
كَانَ لِنَفْسٍ أَن تُؤْمِنَ إِلَّا
بِإِذْنِ ٱللَّهِ ۚ وَيَجْعَلُ ٱلرِّجْسَ
عَلَى ٱلَّذِينَ لَا يَعْقِلُونَ ﴿١٠٠﴾

---

five hundred years after Jonah's death some anonymous person produced the 'Book of Jonah' and had it incorporated into the Bible. Moreover, some of the contents of the 'Book of Jonah' are too absurd to be acceptable. However, were one to reflect on the allusions to the people of Yūnus in the Qur'ān and on the information provided by the 'Book of Jonah', one is inclined to support the view of the Qur'ān-commentators, namely that since the Prophet Jonah (peace be on him) had left his station without obtaining God's permission to do so and since the Assyrians repented and sought pardon from God as soon as they saw the signs of God's impending punishment, God pardoned them.

One of the basic principles mentioned in the Qur'ān concerning God's punishment of the world's nations is that He does not punish any nation until God's Message has been fully conveyed to them so that the people are left with no justification to claim that they were not aware of His Message. (See the Qur'ān, *al-Nisā'* 4: 165 in conjunction with *al-Isrā'* 17: 15 – Ed.) Now in this case, as we can see, the admonition of the Assyrians did not continue till the very end of the period granted to them by God because Prophet Yūnus (peace be on him) migrated from his station. It is presumably for this reason that God in His justice decided not to punish them since all the requisite conditions of punishment had not been fulfilled. (For details see *al-Ṣāffāt* 37, n. 85.)

100. When the Assyrians embraced the true faith, they were granted a fresh lease of life. However, they once again became wayward both in matters of belief and conduct. Though the Prophet Nahum (720–698 BC) warned them, it still had no effect on them. The final warning was delivered to them by the Prophet Zephaniah (709–640 BC) but that too was of no avail. Ultimately, God sent the Medes against them in 612 BC. The king of the Medes, with the assistance of the Babylonians, invaded Assyria. The Assyrian army was routed and besieged within the walls of Nineveh. Although they put up some resistance for a time, the flooded Tigris swept away the city walls, enabling the invaders to break through the defences and capture the city. Subsequently they

(101) Tell them: 'Observe carefully all that is in the heavens and the earth.' But no signs and warnings can avail those who are bent on not believing.[105] (102) What are they waiting for except to witness the repetition of the days of calamity that their predecessors witnessed? Tell them: 'Wait; I too am waiting with you. (103) Then, (when Allah's wrath falls upon the wicked) We save our Messengers and also those who believe. It is incumbent on Us to deliver the believers.'

قُلِ انظُرُوا مَاذَا فِي السَّمَاوَاتِ
وَالْأَرْضِ ۚ وَمَا تُغْنِي الْآيَاتُ
وَالنُّذُرُ عَن قَوْمٍ لَّا يُؤْمِنُونَ
﴿١٠١﴾ فَهَلْ يَنتَظِرُونَ إِلَّا
مِثْلَ أَيَّامِ الَّذِينَ خَلَوْا مِن
قَبْلِهِمْ ۚ قُلْ فَانتَظِرُوا إِنِّي
مَعَكُم مِّنَ الْمُنتَظِرِينَ
﴿١٠٢﴾ ثُمَّ نُنَجِّي رُسُلَنَا وَالَّذِينَ
آمَنُوا ۚ كَذَٰلِكَ حَقًّا عَلَيْنَا
نُنجِ الْمُؤْمِنِينَ ﴿١٠٣﴾

---

set fire to the whole city and its environs. The Assyrian king set his own palace ablaze and was himself burnt to death. This brought to an end the Assyrian empire and civilization. However, recent excavations in the area have brought to light many traces of massive conflagration.

101. Had it been God's will that only those who are true believers and obey God should inhabit the earth and that there should remain no trace of unbelief and disobedience, God would have caused only the faithful and obedient ones to be born. Nor would it have been difficult for Him to providentially direct everyone to faith and obedience in such a manner that it would have been impossible for people to do otherwise. However, there is a profound wisdom underlying man's creation which would have been totally defeated by such a compulsion. For it was God's will to grant man the free-will to make his choice between faith and unbelief, between obedience and disobedience.

102. What has been said here does not mean that the Prophet (peace be on him) sought to compel people into believing whereas God had dissuaded him from doing so. The technique employed in the above verse is the same as employed at many places in the Qur'ān, viz. that although at times certain things are addressed apparently to the Prophet (peace be on him), they are meant, in fact, for the instruction of others. What is being said here is that the Prophet (peace be on him) had been assigned the task of making the right way

abundantly clear to people with the help of convincing arguments. Thus the Prophet (peace be on him) had fulfilled the task assigned to him. Now, if they have no intent to follow the right way, and they feel sure that unless they are overpoweringly compelled to they should know well that it is no part of a Prophet's task. Had God desired that people be made to have faith compulsively, He could have done so without raising any Prophet.

103. All God's bounties are solely at His disposal and one can neither have access to any of these without His leave, nor can one confer them on others. The bounty of having faith and being directed to the right path is also fully contingent upon God's leave. Hence, it is simply inconceivable that without God's leave anyone can attain this bounty or confer it on anyone else. Even if the Prophet (peace be on him) sincerely wants people to believe, it does not lie in his power to accomplish that without God's leave and succour.

104. This fully explains that God's leave and succour are not bestowed on people arbitrarily. God does not capriciously permit or disallow people to embrace faith. There is a definite law – a law that is based on wisdom – according to which God disposes such matters. The law is that those who in their quest for the truth use their reason properly, and in an unbiased manner, are assisted by God. Owing to God's concern, the means of arriving at the truth are made available to them in proportion to the extent of the sincerity of their quest for the truth and their efforts to reach it. They are also granted the succour required for their success in grasping the truth. As for those who are not really in search of the truth, who keep their reason enmeshed in biases, or fail to make use of their reason in their search for the truth, such people are able to find nothing but the abomination of ignorance and misguidance, of false thinking and evil-doing. Their attitude makes it very clear that they merit nothing but ignorance and misguidance and, hence, that is what they are destined for.

105. This is the final and categorical response to the unbelievers. The unbelievers had asked that they be shown some convincing sign that would make them confirm the truth of the Prophet's claim to prophethood. Here they are being told that if the unbelievers had any desire to seek and accept the truth, there are innumerable signs scattered throughout the heavens and the earth, signs that are more than sufficient to convince them about the truth of the Prophet's message. All one needed to do was to look around with open eyes and to reflect on what one observes. Conversely, if there are some people who have no inclination to seek the truth, then no signs – howsoever extraordinary and wonder-provoking they may be – will help them to have faith. For, whenever such people witness any such sign, they cry out, as did Pharaoh and his chiefs, that it is 'plain sorcery' (see verse 76 above). Those who are afflicted with such a sickness, wake up to the truth only when God's punishment befalls them in all its horror. An instance in point is Pharaoh's realization of the truth as he faced death by drowning (see verse 90 above). But to repent only when one is being seized by God's wrath is of no avail.

(104) (O Prophet!) Tell them:[106] 'Men! If you are still in doubt concerning my religion, know that I do not serve those whom you serve beside Allah. I only serve Allah Who will cause (all of) you to die.[107] I have been commanded to be one of those who believe, (105) and to adhere exclusively and sincerely to the true faith,[108] and not to be one of those who associate others with Allah in His divinity.[109] ▶

قُلْ يَٰٓأَيُّهَا ٱلنَّاسُ إِن كُنتُمْ فِى شَكٍّ مِّن دِينِى
فَلَآ أَعْبُدُ ٱلَّذِينَ تَعْبُدُونَ مِن دُونِ ٱللَّهِ
وَلَٰكِنْ أَعْبُدُ ٱللَّهَ ٱلَّذِى يَتَوَفَّىٰكُمْ ۖ وَأُمِرْتُ
أَنْ أَكُونَ مِنَ ٱلْمُؤْمِنِينَ ﴿١٠٤﴾ وَأَنْ أَقِمْ
وَجْهَكَ لِلدِّينِ حَنِيفًا وَلَا تَكُونَنَّ
مِنَ ٱلْمُشْرِكِينَ ﴿١٠٥﴾

106. The theme broached at the beginning of this discourse is now resumed at the point of its conclusion. (Cf. verses 1–10.)

107. The Qur'ānic expression يَتَوَفَّىٰكُمْ literally means 'who causes you to die'. This literal rendering, however, does not convey the spirit of the statement made here. For what is being said amounts to the following:

God is the One Who has the power over your lives and Who enjoys such absolute control over you that as long as He wishes you to remain alive, you live, and no sooner than He signals you to surrender your lives to Him, you do so. It is Him alone that I worship, and it is to His service and obedience that I am bound.

In this context, it should be borne in mind that the Makkan polytheists believed, as do the present-day polytheists, that only God, the Lord of the universe, has the absolute power to cause death, a power that no one else shares with Him. They also believed that even those whom they associated with God in His attributes and authority were all too helpless to avert their own death. It is to be noted that of the numerous divine attributes, this particular attribute of God – viz. that He alone has the power to cause death – is mentioned here alongside the doctrine that men ought to give themselves in total devotion and service to God alone. The reason for it seems to be that in addition to being the statement of an important fact, it also provides a rationale for exclusively serving and worshipping God.

In other words, the statement of the Prophet here amounts to saying that he is exclusively devoted to the service of God since the latter alone has all power

(106) Do not call upon any apart from Allah – on those who have no power to benefit or hurt you. For if you call upon others than Allah you will be reckoned among the wrong-doers. (107) If Allah afflicts you with any hardship, none other than He can remove it; and if He wills any good for you, none can avert His bounty. He bestows good upon whomsoever of His servants He wills. He is All-Forgiving, All-Merciful.'

وَلَا تَدْعُ مِن دُونِ ٱللَّهِ مَا لَا يَنفَعُكَ وَلَا
يَضُرُّكَ فَإِن فَعَلْتَ فَإِنَّكَ إِذًا مِّنَ ٱلظَّٰلِمِينَ
﴿١٠٦﴾ وَإِن يَمْسَسْكَ ٱللَّهُ بِضُرٍّ فَلَا
كَاشِفَ لَهُۥٓ إِلَّا هُوَ وَإِن يُرِدْكَ
بِخَيْرٍ فَلَا رَآدَّ لِفَضْلِهِۦ يُصِيبُ بِهِۦ مَن
يَشَآءُ مِنْ عِبَادِهِۦ وَهُوَ ٱلْغَفُورُ
ٱلرَّحِيمُ ﴿١٠٧﴾

over life and death. Conversely, why should anyone devote himself to worshipping others who, let alone having power over the life and death of others, do not have power even over their own life and death? The rhetorical force of the verse is also significant, for instead of saying that 'He has power over my death', the verse says: 'He has power over your death'. Thus one simple sentence pithily embraces three things – the thesis, its supporting argument, and the exhortation to accept that thesis. Had it been said that: 'I only serve Allah Who has power over my death', its logical implication would have been that in view of the fact that He had control over the Prophet's life and death, the latter should have served only Allah. However, it has been said that: 'I only serve Allah Who has power over your death'. In this form, the implication of the verse is that not only the Prophet but also others should serve only God and this even though they had succumbed to the error of serving others than God.

108. The emphatic form in which people have been urged to adhere to true faith is noteworthy. Here people are not simply being asked to 'embrace the faith', or to 'follow the faith', or to 'become adherents of the faith'. Apparently such expressions were too weak and feeble to convey the idea of a total, firm, and steady adherence to faith as required of man. The actual words of the verse, أَقِمْ وَجْهَكَ لِلدِّينِ حَنِيفاً suggest that one should focus one's attention on the true faith, that one ought not to waver and let one's attention wander, that one ought to refrain from occasionally moving a step forward and another step backward, or turning alternately left and right. What one is rather required to do is to keep

(108) Tell them (O Muḥammad): 'Men! Truth has come to you from your Lord. Whosoever, then, follows the true guidance does so for his own good; and whosoever strays, his straying will be to his own hurt. I am no custodian over you. (109) And follow, (O Prophet!), whatever is revealed to you, and remain patient until Allah brings forth His judgement. He is the best of those who judge.'

قُلْ يَـٰٓأَيُّهَا ٱلنَّاسُ قَدْ جَآءَكُمُ ٱلْحَقُّ
مِن رَّبِّكُمْ فَمَنِ ٱهْتَدَىٰ فَإِنَّمَا يَهْتَدِى
لِنَفْسِهِۦ وَمَن ضَلَّ فَإِنَّمَا يَضِلُّ عَلَيْهَا
وَمَآ أَنَا۠ عَلَيْكُم بِوَكِيلٍ ﴿١٠٨﴾ وَٱتَّبِعْ
مَا يُوحَىٰٓ إِلَيْكَ وَٱصْبِرْ حَتَّىٰ يَحْكُمَ ٱللَّهُ
وَهُوَ خَيْرُ ٱلْحَـٰكِمِينَ ﴿١٠٩﴾

moving straight ahead on the path to which one has been directed. This is clear and forceful enough in itself. However, the Qur'ān does not stop at that. It adds the condition that the attention should be حَنِيفًا, that is, one characterized by exclusive and sincere devotion. What is thus being demanded is that one should adhere to this religion, this way of serving God, this way of life comprising worship, service, servitude, and obedience and in such a way that man's devotion and service to God are total. Once the true faith has been adopted, there should remain no trace of any liking for the false ways which have been forsaken.

109. The Prophet (peace be on him) is asked not to be one of those who associate others with God in His being, His attributes, His claims against His creatures, and His authority over those who set up others than God as partners to God. These others could be either one's own self, or some other person, or a group of persons; a spirit, a *jinn,* an angel, or any tangible or imagined being. Thus, the demand is not just a positive one to follow the path of serving the One True God with total devotion and steadfastness – there is also a negative aspect of the demand – that one ought to detach oneself from those who associate others with God in His divinity in whatever form. Moreover, one is required to be exclusively devoted to God not only in the realm of belief but also in the realm of conduct; not only in the individual but also in the collective sphere of life; not only when one is in a mosque, but also when one is in an educational institution, or in a court of law, or a legislative body, or in stately palaces where political decisions are made, or in market places bristling with trade and

commerce. In short, one should adhere wherever one might be, to the doctrine of exclusive devotion to God. This is a way that should be quite distinct from the way of those who have developed in their lives a hodgepodge of two opposites: devotion to God and devotion to others than God. In short, one who believes in worshipping the One True God alone can never go hand-in-hand with those who believe in polytheism. For how could a Muslim conceivably be satisfied to go step-by-step with, let alone follow the way of those who associate others with God in His divinity? For in the latter eventuality the believer will be unable to fulfil the basic requisite of his faith, viz. the doctrine of monotheism.

Moreover, the Qur'ān asks the believer not only to shun overt but also covert and subtle forms of polytheism. One should be especially cautious about the latter since the consequences of any kind of polytheism are dreadful. Some people, out of their naïvety, however, are inclined to take a light view of covert polytheism, considering it to be of less consequence than the open variety. One should be wary of such complaisance for covert polytheism may, in fact, be even more serious than the open variety. For an enemy out in the open can be more effectively countered than the one who is hidden from sight, or one who masquerades as a friend. One may well ask: which disease is more fatal, the one with the obvious symptoms, or the insidious one which develops within, eating at the vital organs, and yet which shows no external symptoms?

This analogy holds true for the subtle form of polytheism. For the danger of open polytheism, of one that can be easily identified, is obvious to all and sundry. However, it is the subtle form of polytheism whose diagnosis calls for unusual insight and a mature grasp of the requisites of monotheism. For polytheism in its subtle form goes about striking its roots imperceptibly. The result is that in the course of time the roots of the true faith are eaten away even before anyone is alerted to such a dangerous development.

Sūrah 11

Hūd

(Makkan Period)

Period of Revelation

The contents of this *sūrah* give the impression that it was revealed about the same period as *Yūnus*. It is not unlikely that it was revealed immediately in the wake of *Sūrah Yūnus* since the theme of both *sūrahs* is identical. The note of warning given in *Hūd*, however, is even more severe than that in *Yūnus*.

According to a *ḥadīth*, Abū Bakr once told the Prophet (peace be on him): 'I observe you ageing. What is the cause of it?' The Prophet (peace be on him) replied: 'The *sūrahs Hūd* and its sisters have turned my hair grey.'* This shows how hard the time was which then faced the Prophet (peace be on him). For, on the one hand, the unbelieving Quraysh were fully active in their efforts to crush the Prophet's movement. On the other hand, God continually revealed stern warnings of severe punishment if his people did not respond to the truth.

Under such circumstances the Prophet (peace be on him) was consumed by an impending fear. He was overwhelmed with concern that the term granted to his people to mend their ways might suddenly expire and that the moment might suddenly arrive when God would decide to inflict His chastisement upon them. Hence, as one goes

***A tradition in al-Tirmidhī's *Abwāb Tafsīr al-Qur'ān . . . Sūrat al-Wāqi'ah* (tradition no. 6) reads as follows: '*Hūd* and *al-Wāqi'ah* and *al-Mursalāt* and '*Amma yatasā'alūn* and *idhā al-shams kuwwirat* have turned my hair grey' – Ed.**

through the *sūrah,* one feels as if a fierce storm is about to burst through and break down the dykes that had so far contained it. One is also given the impression that the *sūrah* is a last warning to those oblivious of the dire consequences of this impending storm.

Subject Matter and Main Themes

As already stated, the subject on which this *sūrah* is focused is the same as that found in *Yūnus*. The contents can be divided into three headings: firstly, invitation to accept the truth; secondly, admonition; and finally, warning. What distinguishes the present *sūrah* from *Yūnus* is that the emphasis on the invitation to the truth in *Hūd* is less conspicuous; that the element of admonition consists less of arguments than of counsel and advice; and that the element of warning is both more elaborate and more emphatic.

The invitation consists of urging people to follow the Prophet (peace be on him), to give up associating others with God in His divinity, to turn exclusively to God in devotion, worship and service, and to make the fact of accountability to Him in the Hereafter the moving spirit of their lives.

The element of admonition in the *sūrah* is conveyed through a recounting of the tragic end of previous nations. Overly enamoured of the glittering attractions of worldly life, they wilfully rejected the call of God's Messengers. In view of this tragic past record, people are asked to think whether it is necessary for them to follow the same path which invariably led to the utter destruction of previous nations.

The warning element of the *sūrah* is conveyed by virtue of the fact that out of sheer grace God has granted them a reprieve from His punishment. If they continue to fail to mend their ways during the term allocated to them, they will, however, definitely be struck with chastisement. No one will have the power to avert such chastisement. For it will be awesome and will utterly obliterate all except a small group of people – the true men of faith.

The main focus of this *sūrah* was not communicated directly to the people. It was rather communicated by narrating the historical accounts of the people of Noah, the 'Ād, the Thamūd, the people of Lot, the people of Midian, and the Pharaonites. The point that is especially highlighted in these accounts is that when God firmly decides to punish a people, He executes His decision relentlessly. After He has made such a decision, no leniency is shown to the guilty. Mercy is only shown to the righteous. God's wrath spares neither a Prophet's son nor even his own wife if they happen to be unrighteous. At this decisive stage in the encounter between faith and unbelief, the requirements of true faith are extremely exacting. Men of faith are required to disregard affinities of kinship, even those ties which mutually bind a father and his offspring or those which bind spouses. Each person is required to adhere to one bond only – the bond of faith. In the same way that the Divine sword of justice disregards every affinity except that of truth, men of faith must decisively cut asunder all other ties. This was demonstrated fully after a few years by the Makkan Muslim migrants in the Battle of Badr.

In the name of Allah, the Merciful, the Compassionate.

(1) *Alif. Lām. Rā.* This is a Divine Command[1] whose contents have been made firm and set forth in detail[2] – from One Who is All-Wise, All-Aware (2) that you may worship none but Allah. Verily, I have come to you as a warner and a bearer of good news from Him (3) that you may seek forgiveness of your Lord and turn to Him in repentance whereupon He will grant you a fair enjoyment of life until an appointed term,[3] and will bestow favour on everyone who merits favour.[4] But should you turn away (from the truth), I fear for you the chastisement of an Awesome Day. ▶

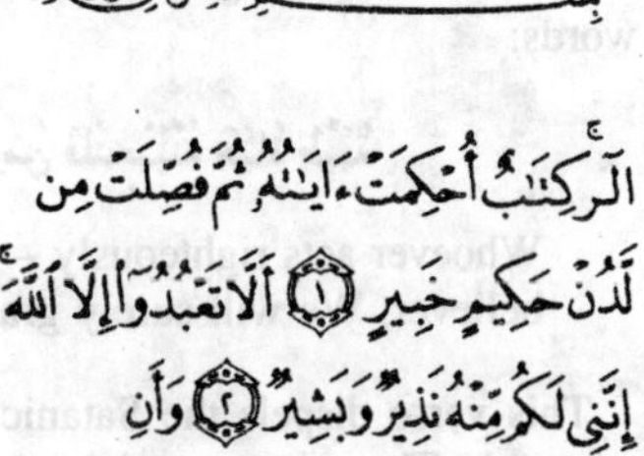

الٓرۚ كِتَٰبٌ أُحۡكِمَتۡ ءَايَٰتُهُۥ ثُمَّ فُصِّلَتۡ مِن
لَّدُنۡ حَكِيمٍ خَبِيرٍ ١ أَلَّا تَعۡبُدُوٓاْ إِلَّا ٱللَّهَۚ
إِنَّنِي لَكُم مِّنۡهُ نَذِيرٞ وَبَشِيرٞ ٢ وَأَنِ
ٱسۡتَغۡفِرُواْ رَبَّكُمۡ ثُمَّ تُوبُوٓاْ إِلَيۡهِ يُمَتِّعۡكُم
مَّتَٰعًا حَسَنًا إِلَىٰٓ أَجَلٖ مُّسَمّٗى وَيُؤۡتِ كُلَّ
ذِي فَضۡلٖ فَضۡلَهُۥۖ وَإِن تَوَلَّوۡاْ فَإِنِّيٓ أَخَافُ
عَلَيۡكُمۡ عَذَابَ يَوۡمٖ كَبِيرٍ ٣

1. In keeping with the context, the word *kitāb* has here been rendered as 'Divine command'. The word *kitāb* in its Arabic usage denotes not only book or inscription, but also writ and command. There are several instances in the Qur'ān of the use of the word in the latter sense. (See, for instance, *al-Baqarah* 2: 235, *al-Ra'd* 13: 38. The significance of 'command' is especially evident from the usage of the *k t b* derivates in the passive tense: see *al-Baqarah* 2: 180, 183, 216, 246, etc. – Ed.)

2. The contents of this 'command' are firm and unalterable. In addition, the Qur'ān is free from the verbosity of orators, the fanciful imagination of poets, the spellbinding rhetoric of litterateurs. Instead, the teachings of the Qur'ān have been set forth with remarkable clarity and precision. Thus, in the Qur'ānic text we do not find even a single word that is superfluous, nor a single word that is lacking. Moreover, the verses expound the teachings of the Qur'ān in such a manner that they are at once elaborate and lucid.

3. If a person turns to God in sincere devotion, He will enable him to spend his life felicitously. God will lavish upon him His bounties, confer a variety of benedictions, provide a life of prosperity, grant peace and tranquillity, and cause him to live honourably rather than in ignominy and disgrace. The same idea has been brought forth elsewhere in the Qur'ān in the following words:

مَنْ عَمِلَ صالحاً مِنْ ذَكَرٍ أو أُنثىٰ وَهُوَ مُؤمِنٌ فَلَنُحيِيَنَّهُ حَياةً طَيِّبَةً

> Whoever acts righteously – whether male or female – the while he is a believer, We will surely grant him a clean life . . . (*al-Naḥl* 16: 97).

This verse dispels the Satanic misconception to which simpletons often succumb. The misconception consists of believing that piety, honesty and responsible behaviour might at the most lead to man's well-being in the Next Life, but they certainly play havoc with his life in the present world. Under this mistaken notion it is believed that good people are inevitably destined to live in abject poverty and utter misery.

In refuting this misconception, God makes it clear that righteous behaviour is conducive to man's success in both worlds. Those who live a righteous and God-fearing life will achieve success and esteemed position in this world as in the Next. For, a position of true honour in this world falls only to those who, out of their devotion to God, act righteously, who are known for their excellent morals, who adhere to propriety in their dealings with others, who are considered by people to be trustworthy, of whom all expect nothing but goodness and benevolence, and of whom none entertains the fear of any evil.

Implicit in the Qur'ānic expression 'a fair enjoyment of life' is another point which should not escape our attention. According to the Qur'ān, 'enjoyment of life' is of two kinds: one, which leads people, who are heedless of God, to temptations with the result that they immerse themselves in worldliness and forget God even more. Thus, 'enjoyment of life', though apparently a divine blessing, proves a curse. It becomes the precursor of God's punishment. This is what the Qur'ān brands as 'illusory enjoyment'. (See *Āl 'Imrān* 3: 185; *al-Ḥadīd* 57: 20 – Ed.)

By contrast, the other kind of enjoyment of life adds to a person's prosperity and physical vitality in such a way that he becomes even more grateful to God. This kind of 'enjoyment of life' prompts man to fulfil the obligations incumbent upon him towards God, towards God's creatures and towards himself. Strengthened by the resources provided by God, man finds himself in a stronger position to effectively promote the cause of good and righteousness and to strive to obliterate evil and mischief. This is the Qur'ānic concept of 'fair enjoyment of life' – an enjoyment which does not end with the life of this world, but extends to the Next Life as well.

4. The more a person excels in moral conduct and good deeds, the higher will be the status that God confers upon him. God does not let anyone's good

(4) Unto Allah is your return, and He has power to do everything.

(5) Lo! They fold up their breasts that they may conceal themselves from Him.[5] Surely when they cover themselves up with their garments Allah knows well what they cover and what they reveal. Indeed He even knows the secrets hidden in the breasts. (6) There is not a single moving creature on the earth but Allah is responsible for providing its sustenance. He knows where it dwells and where it will permanently rest.[6] All this is recorded in a clear Book.

إِلَى ٱللَّهِ مَرْجِعُكُمْ وَهُوَ عَلَىٰ كُلِّ شَىْءٍ
قَدِيرٌ ﴿٤﴾ أَلَآ إِنَّهُمْ يَثْنُونَ صُدُورَهُمْ
لِيَسْتَخْفُوا۟ مِنْهُ أَلَا حِينَ يَسْتَغْشُونَ
ثِيَابَهُمْ يَعْلَمُ مَا يُسِرُّونَ
وَمَا يُعْلِنُونَ إِنَّهُۥ عَلِيمٌۢ بِذَاتِ
ٱلصُّدُورِ ﴿٥﴾ ۞ وَمَا مِن دَآبَّةٍ
فِى ٱلْأَرْضِ إِلَّا عَلَى ٱللَّهِ رِزْقُهَا
وَيَعْلَمُ مُسْتَقَرَّهَا وَمُسْتَوْدَعَهَا
كُلٌّ فِى كِتَٰبٍ مُّبِينٍ ﴿٦﴾

deeds go to waste. In the same way as God does not show any appreciation for evil, He does not show any lack of appreciation for goodness and virtue. In God's kingdom there is no place for the kind of atrocious injustice and stupidity to which a Persian poet has given expression in the following couplet:

> The Arabian steed lies suffering from the wounds of the saddle-pack
> while a golden necklace adorns the neck of a donkey!

God deals with His creatures in such a way that anyone who deserves a reward, is fully granted that reward.

5. When the Prophet's mission became the talk of the day in Makka, some people showed considerable aversion to it, even if they did not actively oppose it. These people were unwilling to listen to the Prophet (peace be on him) and made a point of avoiding him. If they saw him somewhere they would turn their faces away or try to hide themselves. Such people made every effort to avoid any encounter with the Prophet (peace be on him) lest he might invite them to accept his teaching.

(7) And He it is Who created the heavens and the earth in six days – and [before that] His Throne was upon the water[7] – that He may test you, who of you is better in conduct.[8] If you were to say (O Muḥammad): 'All of you will surely be raised after death', then those who disbelieve will certainly say: 'This is nothing but plain sorcery.'[9]

وَهُوَ ٱلَّذِي خَلَقَ ٱلسَّمَٰوَٰتِ وَٱلْأَرْضَ فِي سِتَّةِ أَيَّامٍ وَكَانَ عَرْشُهُۥ عَلَى ٱلْمَآءِ لِيَبْلُوَكُمْ أَيُّكُمْ أَحْسَنُ عَمَلًا وَلَئِن قُلْتَ إِنَّكُم مَّبْعُوثُونَ مِنۢ بَعْدِ ٱلْمَوْتِ لَيَقُولَنَّ ٱلَّذِينَ كَفَرُوٓا۟ إِنْ هَٰذَآ إِلَّا سِحْرٌ مُّبِينٌ ۝٧

The present verse refers precisely to such people; they are portrayed as being frightened at the prospect of facing the truth. Ostrich-like they dug their heads in the sand, fancying that the reality itself had vanished. The fact, however, is that the reality remains, and testifies to the folly of those who hide from it.

6. God is, on the one hand, All-Knowing. He knows exactly where each of His creatures is, be it the nest of a small bird or the hole of a tiny worm. On the other hand, God provides sustenance to all, and provides for them wherever they might be. He is aware at all times of where His creatures spend their lives and where they will breathe their last. It would be sheer stupidity if someone were to think that by resorting to methods such as covering one's face, or closing one's eyes one would be able to escape God's punishment. Even if someone succeeds in eluding the Prophet's observation it is to no avail. For no one can escape God's observation. Nor should anyone entertain the illusion that God is unaware of the fact that the Prophet (peace be on him) was doing his best to communicate the truth to the unbelievers, and that the latter were trying their utmost to clog their ears lest the truth reached them.

7. This is a parenthetical statement which was presumably made in response to some such query: 'If there was a time when the heavens and the earth did not exist, and then they were created – what is it that existed before?' Without explicitly mentioning any such query, an answer is briefly provided. The answer is: before all the heavens and the earth were created there was water everywhere. However, we are not in a position to state with certainty the meaning of the word 'water' used in the verse. Does it mean the 'water' known to us by that name now? Or has it been used metaphorically to refer to matter in

(8) And were We to put off the chastisement from them for a determined period, they will cry out: 'What withholds Him from chastising?' Surely when the day of the chastisement will come, nothing will avert it and the chastisement which they had ridiculed shall encompass them.

(9) If We ever favour man with Our Mercy, and then take it away from him, he becomes utterly desperate, totally ungrateful. ▶

وَلَئِنْ أَخَّرْنَا عَنْهُمُ ٱلْعَذَابَ إِلَىٰٓ أُمَّةٍ مَّعْدُودَةٍ لَّيَقُولُنَّ مَا يَحْبِسُهُۥٓ ۗ أَلَا يَوْمَ يَأْتِيهِمْ لَيْسَ مَصْرُوفًا عَنْهُمْ وَحَاقَ بِهِم مَّا كَانُوا۟ بِهِۦ يَسْتَهْزِءُونَ ﴿٨﴾ وَلَئِنْ أَذَقْنَا ٱلْإِنسَـٰنَ مِنَّا رَحْمَةً ثُمَّ نَزَعْنَـٰهَا مِنْهُ إِنَّهُۥ لَيَـُٔوسٌ كَفُورٌ ﴿٩﴾

its liquid form before it assumed its present form? As for the statement that God's Throne was on water, it means – as far as we have been able to grasp – that God's kingdom was over water.

8. God created the earth and the heavens because He wanted to create man. Furthermore, He created man so as to entrust him with moral responsibility and to invest him with the power of God's vicegerency. Thereafter, it was to be seen how each human being would acquit himself of that responsibility and how he would make use of the power entrusted to him. It is possible to imagine that this was not the purpose of creating man and that God had willed man to have the powers that he now has and yet not put him to any test, nor question him about whether he used the powers granted to him appropriately or not. It is also possible to imagine that man would not be required to render any account to God nor be rewarded or punished for his deeds. It is also possible to imagine that man, who has been encumbered with moral responsibility, would simply end in dust. If all this is true, then we have no alternative but to consider this entire act of creation a senseless ploy, and human life an absolute futility.

9. The unbelievers are so downright foolish that they consider the universe no more than the playhouse of some sportive fellow, and regard themselves merely as pranks to amuse him. They are so elated with this foolish concept that even when they are informed of the true purpose of creation and of their own life in it, they simply laugh it all away. They also go to the extent of flinging the gibe of sorcerer at the Prophet (peace be on him).

(10) And if We let him taste favour after harm has touched him, he says: 'All my ills are gone', and he suddenly becomes exultant and boastful,[10] (11) except those who are patient[11] and act righteously. Such shall have Allah's forgiveness and a great reward.[12]

وَلَئِنْ أَذَقْنَٰهُ نَعْمَآءَ بَعْدَ ضَرَّآءَ مَسَّتْهُ لَيَقُولَنَّ ذَهَبَ ٱلسَّيِّـَٔاتُ عَنِّىٓ ۚ إِنَّهُۥ لَفَرِحٌ فَخُورٌ ﴿١٠﴾ إِلَّا ٱلَّذِينَ صَبَرُوا۟ وَعَمِلُوا۟ ٱلصَّٰلِحَٰتِ أُو۟لَٰٓئِكَ لَهُم مَّغْفِرَةٌ وَأَجْرٌ كَبِيرٌ ﴿١١﴾

10. There are weaknesses in human beings which they themselves can observe if only they engage in self-introspection. It is a measure of man's shallowness and short-sightedness that whenever he has power and wealth he brags and swaggers. In times of prosperity, he becomes incapable of even imagining that his spring can suffer a winter. The result is that whenever he is afflicted with adversity, he is driven to utter despair, becomes an incarnation of grief and despondency so much so that at times he tries to make himself forget his misfortunes by flinging abuses and taunts at God. But when these bad days are over and good days return, he once again becomes boastful. Drunk with success and prosperity, he returns to his old intemperate revelries.

Why has this despicable trait of man been mentioned at this point? The purpose is to subtly remind the Makkan unbelievers of the warning the Prophet (peace be on him) gave them while they enjoyed security and well-being. He warned them that if they continued to disobey God they would be struck by a severe punishment. On hearing this warning, they had burst into laughter and, in effect, said to the Prophet (peace be on him): 'Are you blind to the bounties that are being lavished upon us? Do you not see that the standards of our greatness are fluttering all around? What makes you, then, day-dream that a scourge is about to be let loose upon us?'

This disparaging response to the Prophet's sincere counsel and admonition was an abject expression of man's despicable trait referred to above. God has deferred the infliction of punishment and granted the unbelievers a reprieve in order that they may mend their ways. They, however, failed to seize the opportunity on account of the illusion that their prosperity would endure.

11. This brings out another aspect of 'patience'; a quality in sharp contrast to that undignified trait just mentioned. Those who are patient exhibit poise and equanimity in the midst of vicissitudes of fortune. They do not allow changes of fortune to change their attitude and character. If circumstances are

(12) (O Messenger!) Let it not happen that you omit (to expound) a portion of what was revealed to you. And do not be distressed that they will say: 'Why was a treasure not bestowed upon him?' or 'Why did no angel accompany him?' For you are merely a warner, whereas Allah has control over everything.[13]

فَلَعَلَّكَ تَارِكٌۢ بَعْضَ مَا يُوحَىٰٓ إِلَيْكَ
وَضَآئِقٌۢ بِهِۦ صَدْرُكَ أَن يَقُولُوا۟ لَوْلَآ أُنزِلَ
عَلَيْهِ كَنزٌ أَوْ جَآءَ مَعَهُۥ مَلَكٌ ۚ إِنَّمَآ أَنتَ
نَذِيرٌ ۚ وَٱللَّهُ عَلَىٰ كُلِّ شَىْءٍ وَكِيلٌ ﴿١٢﴾

favourable and they enjoy wealth, power and fame, that does not make them power-drunk. Again, when they are visited with adversity, their dignity is not crushed out of all existence. Whenever God puts them to any test – be it that of prosperity or of adversity – they maintain their dignified posture of moderation. Whatever the circumstance, their mettle never fails them.

12. God forgives the sins of those who are patient and do good and He also rewards them amply for their good deeds.

13. In order to fully understand the verse one should take mental note of the circumstantial background of its revelation. At the time this verse was revealed, Makka was the centre of the Quraysh who had a preponderant influence over the whole of Arabia because of their religious prestige, wealth, trade, and political power. At the very moment when the Quraysh were at the zenith of their power and authority, a Makkan – the Prophet – stood up and vehemently denounced the religion of which they were custodians as a bundle of ignorance and error. He also condemned the social system of which they were standard-bearers, calling it rotten to the core. He also warned them of an impending punishment from God. He emphasized that the only way to avert this punishment was to accept the true faith and righteous order of life which he had expounded to them on God's behalf.

The only thing which this man had to make people believe he had been appointed by God to communicate His message, was the purity of his character and the utter reasonableness of his teaching. In addition, there was apparently nothing in the milieu except the deep-rooted wrongs which had corrupted the religious, moral and social life of the Quraysh that would suggest that God's punishment was close at hand. On the contrary, all portents indicated that the Makkans enjoyed God's plenteous favours and of the deities which they worshipped. Thus, apparently they had every reason to believe that they were on the right path.

(13) Do they say: 'He has invented this Book himself?' Say: 'If that is so, bring ten *sūrahs* the like of it of your composition, and call upon all (the deities) you can other than Allah to your help. Do so if you are truthful.' (14) Then if (your deities) do not respond to your call for help then feel assured that this Book was revealed with the knowledge of Allah, and that there is no true god but Him. Will you, then, surrender (to this truth)?[14]

أَمْ يَقُولُونَ ٱفْتَرَىٰهُ قُلْ فَأْتُوا۟ بِعَشْرِ
سُوَرٍ مِّثْلِهِۦ مُفْتَرَيَٰتٍ وَٱدْعُوا۟ مَنِ
ٱسْتَطَعْتُم مِّن دُونِ ٱللَّهِ إِن كُنتُمْ
صَٰدِقِينَ ﴿١٣﴾ فَإِلَّمْ يَسْتَجِيبُوا۟
لَكُمْ فَٱعْلَمُوٓا۟ أَنَّمَآ أُنزِلَ بِعِلْمِ ٱللَّهِ
وَأَن لَّآ إِلَٰهَ إِلَّا هُوَ فَهَلْ أَنتُم
مُّسْلِمُونَ ﴿١٤﴾

If, under such circumstances, someone in the manner of the Prophet (peace be on him) were to strongly denounce the prevalent way of life, it was hardly surprising that all except a very few right-thinking people who had access to the truth would become his inveterate enemies. This enmity found its expression in a myriad of forms. Some people sought to suppress the Prophet (peace be on him) by resorting to harsh methods of repression. Others tried to undermine his position by false accusations and vicious propaganda. Some discouraged him with their bigoted indifference and frowning, while others resorted to jests, pranks, taunts, and ridicule in order to dismiss his message as absurd.

It is clear that such a hostile attitude would have been heart-breaking for the Prophet (peace be on him). This would have been especially so since the hostility persisted for several years. It is under these trying circumstances that God consoled the Prophet (peace be on him). He comforted him by saying that it is people of low mettle who turn boastful in prosperity and become downcast and despondent in adversity. A worthy person in God's sight pursues righteousness with patience and courage. Hence, the Prophet (peace be on him) should not be shaken by the bigoted opposition, the aversion, the ridicule and mockery, and the foolish objections which he was subjected to by the unbelievers. On the contrary, he should have no hesitation, despite all the opposition he faced, in calling people to the truth revealed by God. In fact, he should not even permit a moment's reluctance in proclaiming the truth for fear that he would be ridiculed for propagating those teachings. Nor should he

(15) Those who seek merely the present world and its adornment.[15] We fully recompense them for their work in this world, and they are made to suffer no diminution in it concerning what is their due. (16) They are the ones who shall have nothing in the Hereafter except Fire.[16] (There they shall come to know) that their deeds in the world have come to naught; and that whatever they have done is absolutely useless.

مَن كَانَ يُرِيدُ ٱلْحَيَوٰةَ ٱلدُّنْيَا
وَزِينَتَهَا نُوَفِّ إِلَيْهِمْ أَعْمَٰلَهُمْ
فِيهَا وَهُمْ فِيهَا لَا يُبْخَسُونَ ﴿١٥﴾
أُوْلَٰٓئِكَ ٱلَّذِينَ لَيْسَ لَهُمْ فِى
ٱلْءَاخِرَةِ إِلَّا ٱلنَّارُ وَحَبِطَ
مَا صَنَعُوا۟ فِيهَا وَبَٰطِلٌ
مَّا كَانُوا۟ يَعْمَلُونَ ﴿١٦﴾

---

shrink from performing his duty to preach because some of those teachings would be too unpalatable for his people even to hear. For the main task of the Prophet (peace be on him) was to continuously state the truth, uncompromisingly and fearlessly, and regardless of those who accepted it and those who did not. Once this duty had been performed, it was pointless worrying whether it would be of any effect. In that regard, the Prophet (peace be on him) ought to place his reliance entirely on God.

14. The argument advanced here serves to establish the divine origin of the Qur'ān as well as the oneness of God. The argument, put succinctly, is as follows:

(i) If the unbelievers thought that the Qur'ān had been authored by some human being, then it ought to be possible for them to compose something which would be the like of it. Now, unbelievers claim that it is the Prophet (peace be on him) – a human being rather than God – who has produced the Qur'ān. In such a case it should be possible for them – for they too are human – to produce such a book. However, despite the repeated challenges for them to produce something like the Qur'ān no one, not even all of them combined, has succeeded in achieving it. The conclusion is quite evident: the Book was revealed by God and there is no question that it is the work of any human being.

(ii) The Qur'ān quite openly and vehemently denounced the deities which the unbelievers worshipped, and urged them to abandon these as they had no share in God's godhead. The unbelievers were also asked to mobilize all whom they wished, including their deities – provided they had any power – to assist them in establishing the falsity of the Prophet's claim by producing a book equal to the Qur'ān. But if at such a crucial stage, their deities fail to come to their aid and do not grant them the power to produce something like the Qur'ān, what then does that prove? Quite obviously, it proves that these so-called deities had neither the power nor even a shred of the attributes necessary for godhead. The fact of their becoming deities was purely the work of a few human beings who had invested such weak, mortal creatures with godhead.

Incidentally, this verse also establishes the fact that in terms of chronological sequence the present *sūrah – Hūd –* was revealed before *Sūrah Yūnus*. For in the present *sūrah,* the unbelievers have been challenged to produce ten *sūrahs* like the Qur'ānic ones. Subsequently, after the unbelievers failed to do so, they were asked in *Sūrah Yūnus* to produce just one *sūrah* like it. (See *Yūnus* 10: 38, n. 46.)

15. What prompted this Qur'ānic remark is the fact that the kind of people who rejected the message of the Qur'ān both in the time of the Prophet (peace be on him) and subsequently have one major characteristic in common – they are all steeped in worldliness. Many of the arguments which they advance in order to reject the Qur'ān are probably after-thoughts, merely rationalized excuses for not accepting the truth. What lies at the root of these people's rejection is the hypothesis that everything other than this world and its gains are worthless, and that everyone should have the fullest opportunity to seize the optimum portion of worldly benefits.

16. Those who keep their attention focused on this world and its benefits will reap worldly benefits in proportion to their efforts. However, since such people have not been concerned with, nor did they direct their efforts to achieving success and well-being in the Hereafter, there is no reason to suppose that their efforts, aimed merely at achieving worldly benefits, will also embrace the benefits of the Hereafter. A person can expect that his action in this world will be of some benefit to him in the Next Life only if he has engaged himself in tasks which are beneficial in the Next Life as well. This can be illustrated by example. A person wants to have a stately mansion to live in and to that end he adopts the means that are ordinarily adopted for its construction. Now, if he has adopted the requisite means he will indeed have a stately mansion. Even if such a person happens to be an unbeliever, this fact will not prevent the mansion from being constructed. However, when such a person breathes his last, he will have to leave behind that mansion and its belongings and will be able to take nothing of it to the Next World. Now, if he has not taken the necessary steps to obtain a mansion in the Next World, he will simply not obtain any such mansion there. Only those who performed deeds which, according to God's Law, would make him deserve a mansion in the Next World will be able to have it.

(17) Can it happen that he who takes his stand on a clear evidence from his Lord,[17] subsequently followed by a witness from Him (in his support),[18] and prior to that the Book of Moses was revealed as a guide and a mercy, (would even he deny the truth in the manner of those who adore the life of this world)? Rather, such men are bound to believe in it.[19] The Fire shall be the promised resort of the groups that disbelieve. So be in no doubt about it for this indeed is the truth from your Lord although most people do not believe.

أَفَمَن كَانَ عَلَىٰ بَيِّنَةٍ مِّن رَّبِّهِۦ وَيَتْلُوهُ
شَاهِدٌ مِّنْهُ وَمِن قَبْلِهِۦ كِتَٰبُ مُوسَىٰٓ
إِمَامًا وَرَحْمَةً ۚ أُو۟لَٰٓئِكَ يُؤْمِنُونَ بِهِۦ ۚ
وَمَن يَكْفُرْ بِهِۦ مِنَ ٱلْأَحْزَابِ فَٱلنَّارُ
مَوْعِدُهُۥ ۚ فَلَا تَكُ فِى مِرْيَةٍ مِّنْهُ ۚ إِنَّهُ ٱلْحَقُّ
مِن رَّبِّكَ وَلَٰكِنَّ أَكْثَرَ ٱلنَّاسِ
لَا يُؤْمِنُونَ ﴿١٧﴾

One might be inclined to say: 'This line of argument at best leads to the conclusion that such a person who cares only for this world, should be denied a mansion in the Next World. But does that also call for consigning him, in the Next World, to Hell-Fire?' On this point the Qur'ān explains on more than one occasion that all those who work in total disregard of the Hereafter necessarily engage in acts which lead them to end up in a heap of Fire in the Next Life rather than in a mansion in Paradise. (See, for instance, *Yūnus* 10, n. 12.)

17. This shows that even apart from revelation, there is ample evidence in man's own self, in the structure of the heavens and the earth, and in the order that prevails in the universe to prove that God is the only creator, master, lord and sovereign of the universe. The evidence referred to above also inclines man to believe that the present life will be followed by another one in which man will be required to render an account of his deeds and wherein he might be requited.

18. The 'witness from Him' is the Qur'ān. The testimony of the natural phenomena combined with that provided by man's own self had already created in man the disposition to affirm the truths mentioned earlier. All that was further reinforced by the Qur'ān which came as reassurance that what he was predisposed to believe in was indeed true.

(18) And who is a greater wrong-doer than he who invents a lie against Allah?[20] Such men will be set forth before their Lord and witnesses will say: 'These are the ones who lied against their Lord. Lo! Allah's curse be upon the wrong-doers;[21] (19) upon those[22] who bar people from the way of Allah, and seek in it crookedness,[23] and disbelieve in the Hereafter. ▶

وَمَنْ أَظْلَمُ مِمَّنِ ٱفْتَرَىٰ عَلَى ٱللَّهِ كَذِبًا
أُو۟لَٰٓئِكَ يُعْرَضُونَ عَلَىٰ رَبِّهِمْ
وَيَقُولُ ٱلْأَشْهَٰدُ هَٰٓؤُلَآءِ ٱلَّذِينَ
كَذَبُوا۟ عَلَىٰ رَبِّهِمْ ۚ أَلَا لَعْنَةُ ٱللَّهِ عَلَى
ٱلظَّٰلِمِينَ ﴿١٨﴾ ٱلَّذِينَ يَصُدُّونَ عَن
سَبِيلِ ٱللَّهِ وَيَبْغُونَهَا عِوَجًا وَهُم
بِٱلْءَاخِرَةِ هُمْ كَٰفِرُونَ ﴿١٩﴾

19. In the present context the verse means that those who are overly infatuated with the allurements of a worldly life will be inclined to reject the message of the Qur'ān. Distinguishable from these are those who take full note of the testimony furnished by their own beings and by the structure and order prevailing in the universe in support of God's unity. This testimony was further reinforced by the heavenly books revealed before the Qur'ān. How could such persons close their eyes to such overwhelming testimony as this and join their voice with those of the unbelievers?

This verse clearly indicates that even before the Qur'ān was revealed, the Prophet (peace be on him) had reached the stage of belief in the Unseen. We have seen in *al-An'ām* (see 6: 75 ff.) the case of Abraham. Before being appointed a Prophet, Abraham (peace be on him) was led by a careful observation of the natural phenomena to knowledge of God's unity. Likewise, the present verse makes it clear that by his reflection, the Prophet (peace be on him), had been led to believe in the Unseen even before the Qur'ān was revealed. Subsequently, when the Qur'ān was revealed it not only confirmed what he had already become inclined to accept, but also provided definite knowledge about it.

20. To invent a lie against God consists of stating that beings other than God also have a share with God in His godhead, that like God they are also entitled to be served and worshipped by God's creatures. Inventing a lie against God also consists of stating that God is not concerned with providing guidance to His creatures, that He did not raise Prophets for that purpose, and that He rather left men free to behave as they pleased. Inventing a lie against God also

(20) They had no power to frustrate Allah's design in the earth,[24] nor did they have any protectors against Allah. Their chastisement will be doubled.[25] They were unable to hear, nor could they see.
(21) They caused utter loss to themselves, and all that they had invented failed them.[26] ▶

أُوْلَٰٓئِكَ لَمْ يَكُونُواْ مُعْجِزِينَ فِي
ٱلْأَرْضِ وَمَا كَانَ لَهُم مِّن دُونِ ٱللَّهِ مِنْ
أَوْلِيَآءَۘ يُضَٰعَفُ لَهُمُ ٱلْعَذَابُۚ مَا كَانُواْ
يَسْتَطِيعُونَ ٱلسَّمْعَ وَمَا كَانُواْ
يُبْصِرُونَ ٢٠ أُوْلَٰٓئِكَ ٱلَّذِينَ خَسِرُوٓاْ
أَنفُسَهُمْ وَضَلَّ عَنْهُم مَّا كَانُواْ
يَفْتَرُونَ ٢١

---

consists of stating that God created human beings by way of jest and sport and that He will not have them render an account to Him, and that He will not requite them for their deeds.

21. Such a proclamation would be made on the Day of Judgement.

22. This is a parenthetical statement. That is, that God's curse will be proclaimed in the Hereafter against those who are guilty of the crimes mentioned.

23. Such persons do not like the Straight Way being expounded to them. They would rather have the Straight Way rendered crooked by altering it under the influence of lust, prejudice, fancy, and superstition. It is only after the way that was once straight has been rendered crooked that they will be willing to accept it.

24. This, again, refers to what will happen in the Next Life.

25. They will suffer punishment for being in error and for misleading others and leaving behind a legacy of error and misguidance for coming generations. (See *Towards Understanding the Qur'ān*, vol. III, *al-A'rāf* 7, n. 30, pp. 23–6 – Ed.)

26. All their conjectures regarding God, the universe and their own selves will prove to be absolutely baseless in the Next Life. Similarly, the notions they entertained about the help and support they would receive from those they considered to be either their deities, or their intercessors with God, or their patrons will prove to be false. Likewise, it will become obvious that all their notions about the After-life were utterly untrue.

(22) Doubtlessly, they shall be the greatest losers in the Hereafter. (23) As for those who believed and acted righteously and dedicated themselves totally to their Lord – they are the people of Paradise, and there they shall abide forever.[27] (24) The example of the two parties is that one is blind and deaf, and the other capable of seeing and hearing. Can the two be equals?[28] Will you, then, not heed?'

(25) (Such were the circumstances) when We sent forth Noah to his people.[29] (He said): 'I have been sent to you to warn you plainly (26) that you may worship none but Allah or else I fear for you the chastisement of a Grievous Day.'[30] ▶

لَا جَرَمَ أَنَّهُمْ فِي الْآخِرَةِ هُمُ
الْأَخْسَرُونَ ﴿٢٢﴾ إِنَّ الَّذِينَ آمَنُوا
وَعَمِلُوا الصَّالِحَاتِ وَأَخْبَتُوا إِلَىٰ رَبِّهِمْ
أُولَٰئِكَ أَصْحَابُ الْجَنَّةِ ۖ هُمْ فِيهَا
خَالِدُونَ ﴿٢٣﴾ ۞ مَثَلُ الْفَرِيقَيْنِ
كَالْأَعْمَىٰ وَالْأَصَمِّ وَالْبَصِيرِ
وَالسَّمِيعِ ۚ هَلْ يَسْتَوِيَانِ مَثَلًا ۚ أَفَلَا
تَذَكَّرُونَ ﴿٢٤﴾ وَلَقَدْ أَرْسَلْنَا نُوحًا إِلَىٰ
قَوْمِهِ إِنِّي لَكُمْ نَذِيرٌ مُبِينٌ ﴿٢٥﴾ أَلَّا
تَعْبُدُوا إِلَّا اللَّهَ ۖ إِنِّي أَخَافُ عَلَيْكُمْ
عَذَابَ يَوْمٍ أَلِيمٍ ﴿٢٦﴾

---

27. This concludes the account about the Hereafter.

28. Can the attitude and ultimate end of both these types of people be the same? Obviously, he who fails to see the right way and ignores the instruction of the guide who directs him to the right way will necessarily stumble and meet with some terrible mishap. However, he who perceives the right way and follows the instructions of his guide will reach his destination, and reach it safely.

The same difference is found between the two parties mentioned here. One of these carefully observes the realities of the universe and pays heed to the teachings of God's Messengers. The other party, however, neither uses their eyes properly to perceive God's signs, nor pays heed to His Messengers. The behaviour of the two parties is, therefore, bound to be different. And when their behaviour is different, there is no reason to believe that their ultimate end will be identical.

(27) The notables among Noah's own people, who had refused to follow him, responded: 'We merely consider you a human being like ourselves.[31] Nor do we find among those who follow you except the lowliest of our folk, the men who follow you without any proper reason.[32] We see nothing in you to suggest that you are any better than us.[33] Rather, we believe you to be liars.' ▶

فَقَالَ ٱلْمَلَأُ ٱلَّذِينَ كَفَرُوا۟ مِن قَوْمِهِۦ مَا نَرَىٰكَ إِلَّا بَشَرًا مِّثْلَنَا وَمَا نَرَىٰكَ ٱتَّبَعَكَ إِلَّا ٱلَّذِينَ هُمْ أَرَاذِلُنَا بَادِىَ ٱلرَّأْىِ وَمَا نَرَىٰ لَكُمْ عَلَيْنَا مِن فَضْلٍۭ بَلْ نَظُنُّكُمْ كَـٰذِبِينَ ﴿٢٧﴾

29. It is pertinent at this stage to bear in mind *Towards Understanding the Qur'ān,* vol. III, *al-A'rāf* 7: 59–64, nn. 47–50, pp. 37–42.

30. Substantially, the same warning was delivered by the Prophet Muḥammad (peace be on him) in the first few verses (viz. 2–3) of this *sūrah.*

31. This is exactly the same absurd objection which the Makkans raised against the Prophet Muḥammad (peace be on him). They found it inconceivable that a mortal like themselves who ate and drank, walked and slept, and who also had a family could be designated a Messenger by God. (See *Yā Sīn* 36, n. 11; *al-Shūrā* 42, n. 41.)

32. Again, it is noteworthy that the same objection raised by Noah's people against him was raised by the Makkans against the Prophet (peace be on him). The objection being that it is only persons of insignificant position who joined the Prophet's (peace be on him) ranks. They, thus, tried to belittle both the Message and the Messenger by highlighting that his followers were either a few raw youths, a bunch of slaves, or a group of feeble-minded and superstitious commoners from the lower rungs of society. (See *Towards Understanding the Qur'ān,* vol. II, *al-An'ām* 6, nn. 34–7, pp. 235–7, and *Yūnus* 10, n. 78, p. 57 above.)

33. The believers claimed that they enjoyed God's favour and mercy, and that those who chose to deviate from their way were subject to God's wrath.

(28) Noah said: 'My people! If I base myself on a clear evidence from my Lord, and I have also been blessed by His mercy[34] to which you have been blind, how can we force it upon you despite your aversion to it? (29) My people! I seek no recompense from you.[35] My recompense is only with Allah. Nor will I drive away those who believe. They are destined to meet their Lord.[36] But I find you to be an ignorant people. ▶

قَالَ يَٰقَوْمِ أَرَءَيْتُمْ إِن كُنتُ عَلَىٰ بَيِّنَةٍ مِّن
رَّبِّي وَءَاتَىٰنِي رَحْمَةً مِّنْ عِندِهِۦ فَعُمِّيَتْ
عَلَيْكُمْ أَنُلْزِمُكُمُوهَا وَأَنتُمْ لَهَا كَٰرِهُونَ
﴿٢٨﴾ وَيَٰقَوْمِ لَآ أَسْـَٔلُكُمْ عَلَيْهِ مَالًا
إِنْ أَجْرِيَ إِلَّا عَلَى ٱللَّهِ ۚ وَمَآ أَنَا۠ بِطَارِدِ
ٱلَّذِينَ ءَامَنُوٓا۟ ۚ إِنَّهُم مُّلَٰقُوا۟ رَبِّهِمْ
وَلَٰكِنِّىٓ أَرَىٰكُمْ قَوْمًا
تَجْهَلُونَ ﴿٢٩﴾

The unbelievers denied this claim. They contended that there was no evidence in support of such a supposition. The unbelievers further argued in opposition to the believers' contention, that it was they, the unbelievers, who enjoyed God's favour. They had riches, political power and influence, and an army of servants to serve them and to carry out their behests. How could it ever be imagined, therefore, that the believers – whose lot was simply miserable – were God's favourites?

34. This amounts to virtually repeating the statement mentioned earlier (see verse 17 and n. 17 ff. above). The statement suggested that the Prophet (peace be on him) had reached the stage of affirming the unity of God as a result of his own reflection. Whereafter, God favoured him by designating him a Prophet and providing him with direct knowledge of the truths about which his heart was already convinced.

This also shows that the Prophets attain belief regarding the realm of the Unseen before they are appointed to the office of prophethood. When they are subsequently designated Prophets, they are endowed with faith in the truths belonging to the realm of the Unseen as a result of direct knowledge of those truths.

35. The Prophet Noah (peace be on him) told his people that he had sincerely counselled his people about what was conducive to their well-being. Noah bore all kinds of hardship and suffering, and all for the well-being of his people. Noah sought to achieve no personal benefit out of his striving to call

(30) My people! Were I to drive the men of faith away, who will protect me from (the chastisement of) Allah? Do you not understand even this much? (31) I do not say to you that I possess Allah's treasures, nor that I have access to the realm beyond the ken of sense-perception, nor do I claim to be an angel.[37] Nor do I say regarding those whom you look upon with disdain that Allah will not bestow any good upon them. Allah knows best what is in their hearts. Were I to say so I would be one of the wrong-doers.'

وَيَٰقَوۡمِ مَن يَنصُرُنِي مِنَ ٱللَّهِ إِن طَرَدتُّهُمۡۚ
أَفَلَا تَذَكَّرُونَ ٣٠ وَلَآ أَقُولُ لَكُمۡ
عِندِي خَزَآئِنُ ٱللَّهِ وَلَآ أَعۡلَمُ ٱلۡغَيۡبَ
وَلَآ أَقُولُ إِنِّي مَلَكٞ وَلَآ أَقُولُ
لِلَّذِينَ تَزۡدَرِيٓ أَعۡيُنُكُمۡ لَن يُؤۡتِيَهُمُ
ٱللَّهُ خَيۡرًاۖ ٱللَّهُ أَعۡلَمُ بِمَا فِيٓ أَنفُسِهِمۡ
إِنِّيٓ إِذٗا لَّمِنَ ٱلظَّٰلِمِينَ ٣١

people to the truth. Noah's sincerity was too transparent to be the subject of any question or dispute. (See *al-Mu'minūn* 23, n. 70; *Yā Sīn* 36, n. 17; *al-Shūrā* 42, n. 41.)

36. The worth of the believers is best known only to their Lord which will become fully evident when they encounter Him on the Day of Judgement. If they indeed are true gems, they will not then become pieces of ordinary rock just because some people in this world had disparagingly thrown them aside. But if, on the contrary, they are indeed nothing but mere pieces of ordinary rock, their Lord has every right to cast them wherever He pleases. (See *Towards Understanding the Qur'ān,* vol. II, *al-An'ām* 6: 52, and *al-Kahf* 18: 28.)

37. This is a rejoinder to the Prophet Noah's opponents. His opponents tried to discredit him by saying that he appeared to them to be merely an ordinary human being just like any one of them. In response to this Noah acknowledges that he is indeed nothing more than a human being, and that he has never claimed to be anything other than that. Hence, any attack on him on the grounds that he was merely a human being was pointless.

Noah (peace be on him), like other Prophets, had claimed no more than what God had intimated to him about the Straight Way comprising right beliefs and

(32) They said: 'O Noah! Surely you have disputed with us and have prolonged your dispute. Now bring upon us the chastisement that you threaten us with; do so, if you are truthful.' (33) Noah said: 'Only Allah will bring it upon you if He so wills, and you will be utterly unable to frustrate that. (34) If I want to give you good advice that will not profit you if Allah Himself has decided to let you go astray.[38] He is your Lord, and to Him will you be returned.'

قَالُواْ يَـٰنُوحُ قَدْ جَـٰدَلْتَنَا فَأَكْثَرْتَ
جِدَٰلَنَا فَأْتِنَا بِمَا تَعِدُنَآ إِن كُنتَ مِنَ
ٱلصَّـٰدِقِينَ ﴿٣٢﴾ قَالَ إِنَّمَا يَأْتِيكُم بِهِ ٱللَّهُ
إِن شَآءَ وَمَآ أَنتُم بِمُعْجِزِينَ ﴿٣٣﴾ وَلَا يَنفَعُكُمْ
نُصْحِىٓ إِنْ أَرَدتُّ أَنْ أَنصَحَ لَكُمْ إِن كَانَ
ٱللَّهُ يُرِيدُ أَن يُغْوِيَكُمْ هُوَ رَبُّكُمْ وَإِلَيْهِ
تُرْجَعُونَ ﴿٣٤﴾

sound principles of behaviour. His people were free to test him in regard to that claim. It was strange, however, that they asked him about a matter which lay beyond the ken of human perception, something which he had never claimed to know. They also made strange demands of him which suggested that he possessed the keys to God's treasures. They even taunted him on the grounds that like other human beings he also ate and drank and walked around.

All this was meaningless for Noah (peace be on him) had never claimed to be an angel and that as such he could dispense with necessary physical and biological requirements. All that Noah (peace be on him) had claimed was that he possessed the knowledge needed to guide human beings in matters of belief, moral conduct, and social behaviour. Now, what sense did it make to ask such a person what gender a cow's calf would be? By what stretch of the imagination can one establish a nexus between the pregnancy of a cow and sound principles of individual and social conduct? (See also *Towards Understanding the Qur'ān*, vol. II, *al-An'ām* 6, nn. 31–2, pp. 234–5.)

38. Such was their obduracy, mischievousness and absolute disregard for righteous behaviour that quite understandably God should decide not to direct them to the right way and instead let them, as they wished, stumble in error. Once God had made such a decision no one's effort to direct them to the right way – not even the Prophet's – could be of any avail.

(35) (O Muḥammad!) Do they say that he himself has forged this message? Tell them: 'If I have forged this, the guilt of it will fall upon me, but I am not responsible for the crimes you are committing.'[39]

أَمْ يَقُولُونَ افْتَرَىٰهُ قُلْ إِنِ افْتَرَيْتُهُۥ فَعَلَىَّ إِجْرَامِى وَأَنَا۠ بَرِىٓءٌ مِّمَّا تُجْرِمُونَ ﴿٣٥﴾

---

39. The context seems to suggest how the opponents reacted to the narration of Noah's story. It seems they would have objected to it on the grounds that the true purpose of narrating Noah's story was to show how it was applicable to the unbelievers. They presumably pointed out that the Prophet (peace be on him) had invented such stories merely to ridicule and disgrace them; that these stories were merely a means whereby he could malign them.

The main theme of the discourse has been interrupted here in order to respond to this objection.

Petty people are apt to misinterpret things. Their mental baseness allows them only to perceive that which is evil and to disregard those aspects which are good. If someone offers a piece of wisdom, or seeks to convey a piece of good advice, or draws the attention of someone to any of his weaknesses, a wise person will benefit from what is said and will reform himself. But a petty person will always be inclined to see something evil in it. Such an attitude will reduce to naught the wisdom or sincere counsel that was offered. Moreover, such a person will continue to adhere to his evil ways. Not only that but he is also likely to attribute some evil motive to the person who had sought to say a word of wisdom or to furnish him with sincere advice.

Even the best advice goes to waste if someone misunderstands it. For it is possible that someone may construe a piece of advice as arising not out of sincere concern for but out of a desire to taunt. In such instances, instead of dispassionately examining his own life with a view to identifying his flaws and weaknesses, this person is likely to feel offended. Such a person will be wont to assume, and will often go about saying, that the advice was actuated by ulterior motives and was meant to insult him. Suppose a reformer mentions, for instructive purposes, what is going on in society. It is possible that some of the things mentioned might also be applicable to a person's case and might seem to allude to some actual flaw or shortcoming in his character. Now, it is quite possible that the reformer did not intend to point an accusing finger at any particular person. Instead, he merely wanted to bring to people's attention the unhealthy attitudes found in society. If the person concerned is wise, he will not enmesh himself with questions about whether the reformer's statement was

(36) It was revealed to Noah that no more of your people, other than those who already believe, will ever come to believe. So do not grieve over their deeds, (37) and build the Ark under Our eyes and Our direction. And do not supplicate Me concerning those who have engaged in wrong-doing. They are doomed to be drowned.[40]

(38) As Noah was building the Ark, whenever the leading men of his nation passed by him, they would scoff at him. He said: 'If you scoff at us, we too scoff at you in like manner. (39) You will come to know who will be struck by a humiliating chastisement, and who will be subjected to an unceasing torment.'[41]

وَأُوحِيَ إِلَىٰ نُوحٍ أَنَّهُۥ لَن يُؤْمِنَ مِن
قَوْمِكَ إِلَّا مَن قَدْ ءَامَنَ فَلَا تَبْتَئِسْ بِمَا
كَانُوا۟ يَفْعَلُونَ ﴿٣٦﴾ وَٱصْنَعِ ٱلْفُلْكَ
بِأَعْيُنِنَا وَوَحْيِنَا وَلَا تُخَٰطِبْنِى فِى
ٱلَّذِينَ ظَلَمُوٓا۟ إِنَّهُم مُّغْرَقُونَ ﴿٣٧﴾
وَيَصْنَعُ ٱلْفُلْكَ وَكُلَّمَا مَرَّ عَلَيْهِ
مَلَأٌ مِّن قَوْمِهِۦ سَخِرُوا۟ مِنْهُ قَالَ إِن
تَسْخَرُوا۟ مِنَّا فَإِنَّا نَسْخَرُ مِنكُمْ كَمَا
تَسْخَرُونَ ﴿٣٨﴾ فَسَوْفَ تَعْلَمُونَ
مَن يَأْتِيهِ عَذَابٌ يُخْزِيهِ وَيَحِلُّ عَلَيْهِ
عَذَابٌ مُّقِيمٌ ﴿٣٩﴾

meant to cast a slur on his character. He will recognize instead the worth of the statement, will seize its instructive aspects, and will make an effort to mend his behaviour accordingly.

However, if a man has a warped mind and is given only to seeing evil intentions in people's actions, he is likely to fling accusations at the reformer. He will go about condemning his statement as a bundle of fabrications concocted with a view to bringing him into disrepute. It is for this reason that the Prophet (peace be on him) was asked to say that if he had fabricated something, he would be responsible for the sin of such a fabrication. This would not, however, absolve others of the guilt and evils they had committed in the past and which they continued to commit.

40. This demonstrates that when a Messenger communicates his Message to his people, they are granted respite from punishment only as long as it

(40) Thus it was until Our command came to pass and the oven boiled over.[42] We said: 'Take into the Ark a pair of every species; and take your own family except those who have already been declared (as unworthy);[43] and also take everyone who believes.'[44] But those who, along with him, had believed were indeed just a few. ▶

حَتَّىٰٓ إِذَا جَآءَ أَمۡرُنَا وَفَارَ ٱلتَّنُّورُ قُلۡنَا
ٱحۡمِلۡ فِيهَا مِن كُلٍّ زَوۡجَيۡنِ
ٱثۡنَيۡنِ وَأَهۡلَكَ إِلَّا مَن سَبَقَ عَلَيۡهِ
ٱلۡقَوۡلُ وَمَنۡ ءَامَنَۚ وَمَآ ءَامَنَ مَعَهُۥٓ
إِلَّا قَلِيلٞ ٤٠

---

remains possible for the social milieu to produce a reasonable number of good people. As soon as that milieu becomes shorn of good people, and none but the iniquitous remain, then the term of respite ends. At this juncture, God's Mercy itself calls for the destruction of these incorrigible rogues lest they also contaminate others. For to show any further leniency to them would amount to perpetrating an injustice on the whole world and on future generations.

41. This fascinating story illustrates how man can be deluded by the appearance of things. When the Prophet Noah (peace be on him) was busy building the Ark on a tract of land far from any sea or river, it must have appeared a very silly thing to do. Noah's people would surely have laughed at him, mocking at the old fellow's apparently senile plan. They may even have called it an adventure of sailing on the Ark across dry land! At that moment it would have simply been inconceivable for anyone to think that the Ark would one day indeed sail on that very tract of land as it became flooded with water. Hence they perhaps went around telling people that if anyone needed proof of Noah's mental derangement, this was now no longer needed.

The same act would, however, have been perceived quite differently by anyone who really knew what was going to happen, who knew that soon enough a ship would indeed be a necessity for anyone who wished to move around. Such a person could only have laughed at the ignorance and stupid complaisance of his people. Noah (peace be on him), who knew these things well, would often have said to himself: 'How stupid are these people! God's chastisement is just about to afflict them, and I have been warning them of this. That moment has all but come and they even see me making an effort to escape the impending chastisement. Is it not strange that they remain totally unperturbed? Not only that, but they look upon me as an utter lunatic.'

This offers a good illustration of two contrasting attitudes. One is based on knowledge of the apparent, one that is grasped by the senses. The other is based on true knowledge, a knowledge of truths that lie beyond the range of the apparent. If one were to be satisfied with what is apparent, one would regard many a thing as sheer folly. Now, if there is someone who knows truths that lie beyond the range of the apparent, that person will consider these apparent follies the very zenith of wisdom. Such a person would indeed consider the flair of smartness displayed by the superficially knowledgeable to be no more than ignorance and stupidity.

42. Commentators on the Qur'ān have offered different explanations of this incident. In our view, the place from which the Flood began was a particular oven. It is from beneath it that a spring of water burst forth. This was followed by both a heavy downpour and by a very large number of springs which gushed forth. *Sūrah al-Qamar* provides relevant information in some detail:

> So We opened the gates of the heaven, with water intermittently pouring forth, and We caused the earth to be cleaved and the springs to flow out everywhere. Then the water (from both the sources – the heaven and the earth) converged to bring about that which had been decreed (*al-Qamar*, 54: 11–12).

In the present verse, the word *tannūr* has been preceded by the article *al*. According to Arabic grammar, this indicates that the reference is to a particular *tannūr* (oven). Thus, it is evident that God had determined that the Flood should commence from a particular oven. As soon as the appointed moment came, and as soon as God so ordained, water burst forth from that oven. Subsequently, it became known as the Flood-Oven.

The fact that God had earmarked a certain oven to serve as the starting-point of the Flood is borne out by *al-Mu'minūn* 23: 27.

43. Information that some members of Noah's family were unbelievers and so were unworthy of God's mercy had already been given. Noah (peace be on him) had also been directed not to provide them with space in the Ark. Presumably these were only two persons. One was Noah's own son; the story of his drowning will be referred to shortly (see verse 43 below). The other was Noah's wife (see *al-Taḥrīm* 66: 15). It is possible that some other members of Noah's family also belonged to this category. Be that as it may, the Qur'ān does not expressly mention any others.

44. This refutes the opinion of those historians and genealogists who trace the ancestry of all human beings to Noah's three sons. This misconception has arisen from the Israelite traditions which suggest that Noah, his three sons and their wives were the only survivors of the Flood. (See *Genesis* 6: 18, 7: 7, p. 1 and 9: 19.) The Qur'ān, however, repeatedly says that apart from Noah's family, at least some other people belonging to his nation – even if only a few – were also saved by God from the Flood. The Qur'ān, therefore, considers the future generations of mankind to have descended not only from Noah, but also

(41) Noah said: 'Embark in it. In the name of Allah is its sailing and its anchorage. My Lord is Ever Forgiving, Most Merciful.'[45]

(42) The Ark sailed along with them amid mountain-like waves. Noah, spotting his son at a distance, called out to him: 'My son, embark with us, and do not be with the unbelievers.' (43) The son replied: 'I will go to a mountain for refuge and it will save me from the water.' Noah said: 'None can save anyone today from the command of Allah except those on whom He may have mercy.' Thereupon a wave swept in between the two and he was drowned.

۞وَقَالَ ٱرۡكَبُواْ فِيهَا بِسۡمِ ٱللَّهِ
مَجۡر۪ىٰهَا وَمُرۡسَىٰهَآۚ إِنَّ رَبِّي لَغَفُورٞ رَّحِيمٞ
(٤١) وَهِيَ تَجۡرِي بِهِمۡ فِي مَوۡجٖ
كَٱلۡجِبَالِ وَنَادَىٰ نُوحٌ ٱبۡنَهُۥ
وَكَانَ فِي مَعۡزِلٖ يَٰبُنَيَّ
ٱرۡكَب مَّعَنَا وَلَا تَكُن مَّعَ
ٱلۡكَٰفِرِينَ (٤٢) قَالَ سَـَٔاوِيٓ إِلَىٰ
جَبَلٖ يَعۡصِمُنِي مِنَ ٱلۡمَآءِۚ قَالَ
لَا عَاصِمَ ٱلۡيَوۡمَ مِنۡ أَمۡرِ ٱللَّهِ إِلَّا مَن
رَّحِمَۚ وَحَالَ بَيۡنَهُمَا ٱلۡمَوۡجُ فَكَانَ
مِنَ ٱلۡمُغۡرَقِينَ (٤٣)

---

from those believers who, under God's directive, were accommodated in the Ark by Noah. It is significant that the Qur'ān mentions post-Flood mankind as the 'offspring of those whom We carried along with Noah' (*al-Isrā'* 17: 3) and the 'offspring of Adam and those whom We carried along with Noah' (*Maryam* 19: 58). It does not refer to them simply as 'the offspring of Noah'.

45. Trust in God is the quintessential characteristic of the believer. True, like any other person, the believer also has recourse to worldly measures. It is, in fact, necessary to use them on account of the laws of nature under which all human beings live and operate. One thing, however, differentiates a believer from a man of the world. A believer, while having recourse to worldly measures, places his reliance on God rather than on the measures he adopts. He is well aware that none of his measures can be of any avail unless they coincide with God's favour and mercy.

(44) And the command was given: 'Earth! Swallow up your water'; and: 'Heaven! Abate!' So the water subsided, the command was fulfilled, and the Ark settled on Mount Judi,[46] and it was said: 'Away with the wrong-doing folk!'	وَقِيلَ يَٰٓأَرْضُ ٱبْلَعِى مَآءَكِ وَيَٰسَمَآءُ أَقْلِعِى وَغِيضَ ٱلْمَآءُ وَقُضِىَ ٱلْأَمْرُ وَٱسْتَوَتْ عَلَى ٱلْجُودِىِّ ۖ وَقِيلَ بُعْدًا لِّلْقَوْمِ ٱلظَّٰلِمِينَ ﴿٤٤﴾

46. Mount Judi is situated to the north-east of the Island of Ibn 'Umar in Kurdistan. According to the Bible, the Ark's resting place was Ararat, which is the name of a particular mountain as well as of a whole range of mountains in Armenia. Ararat, in the sense of a mountain range, extends from the Armenian plateau to southern Kurdistan. The mount called Judi is part of this range and is known even today by the same name.

In ancient historical accounts, Mount Judi is mentioned as the place where the Ark rested. Around 250 B.C., a Babylonian priest, Berasus, wrote a history of his country based on Chaldean traditions. He mentions Judi as the resting-place of Noah's Ark. The history written by Abydenus, a disciple of Aristotle, also corroborates this. Abydenus further remarks that many people in Mesopotamia possessed pieces of the Ark which they used as a charm. They ground those pieces in water and gave the preparation to the sick so as to cure them of their ailments.

In connection with this great incident one is also faced with the question of whether the Flood was universal or whether it was limited to the area inhabited by the people of Noah. This question remains unanswered to this day. Under the influence of Israelite traditions, it is believed that it was a universal Flood (*Genesis* 7: 18–24). The Qur'ān, however, does not explicitly say so. There are several allusions in the Qur'ān which indicate that subsequent generations of mankind are the descendants of those who were saved from the Flood. But that does not necessarily mean that the Flood covered the whole world. For, it is quite plausible that at that point in history the human population was confined only to the area which was overtaken by the Flood, and that those born after the Flood gradually dispersed to other parts of the world.

This view is supported by two things. Firstly, ancient historical traditions, achaeological discoveries and geological data provide evidence that a great flood took place at some period in the distant past in the Tigris-Euphrates region. There is no such evidence for a universal flood. Secondly, traditions about a great flood have been popular among all communities of the world down the ages. Such traditions are found even in the folklore of such distant regions as Australia, America and New Guinea. One may thus conclude that at

LAND OF NOAH'S PEOPLE AND MOUNT JUDI

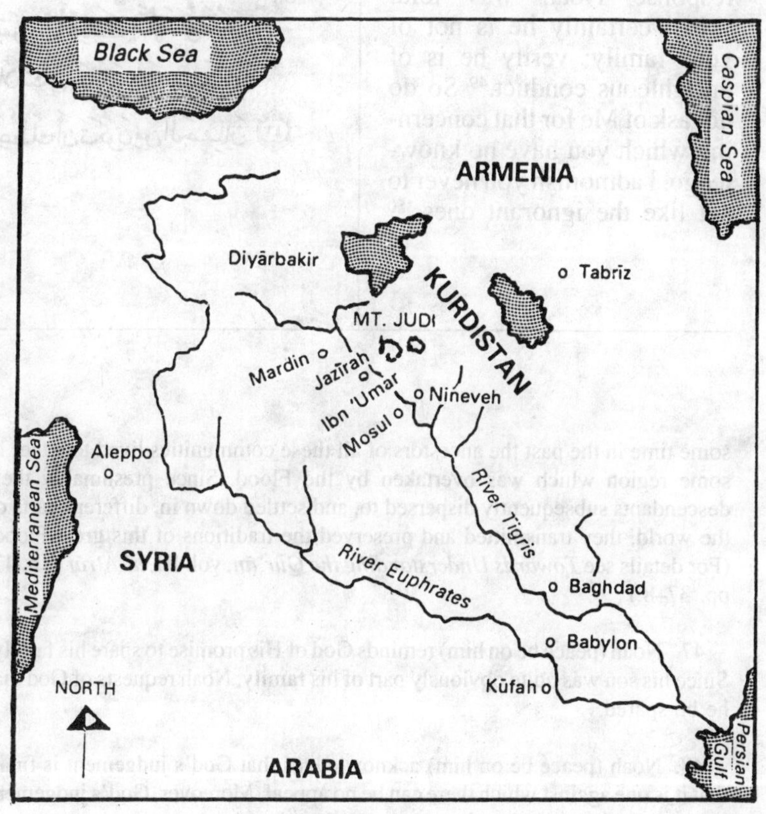

(45) And Noah called out to his Lord, saying: 'My Lord! My son is of my family. Surely Your promise is true,[47] and You are the greatest of those who judge.'[48] (46) In response Noah was told: 'Most certainly he is not of your family; verily he is of unrighteous conduct.[49] So do not ask of Me for that concerning which you have no knowledge. I admonish you never to act like the ignorant ones.'[50]

وَنَادَىٰ نُوحٌ رَّبَّهُۥ فَقَالَ رَبِّ إِنَّ ٱبْنِى
مِنْ أَهْلِى وَإِنَّ وَعْدَكَ ٱلْحَقُّ وَأَنتَ
أَحْكَمُ ٱلْحَٰكِمِينَ ﴿٤٥﴾ قَالَ يَٰنُوحُ إِنَّهُۥ
لَيْسَ مِنْ أَهْلِكَ ۖ إِنَّهُۥ عَمَلٌ غَيْرُ صَٰلِحٍ ۖ
فَلَا تَسْـَٔلْنِ مَا لَيْسَ لَكَ بِهِۦ عِلْمٌ ۖ إِنِّىٓ
أَعِظُكَ أَن تَكُونَ مِنَ ٱلْجَٰهِلِينَ ﴿٤٦﴾

---

some time in the past the ancestors of all these communities lived together in some region which was overtaken by the Flood. Since presumably their descendants subsequently dispersed to, and settled down in, different parts of the world, they transmitted and preserved the traditions of this great Flood. (For details see *Towards Understanding the Qur'ān,* vol. III, *al-A'rāf* 7, n. 47, pp. 37–8.)

47. Noah (peace be on him) reminds God of His promise to spare his family. Since his son was quite obviously part of his family, Noah requests of God that he be spared.

48. Noah (peace be on ḥim) acknowledges that God's judgement is final; that it is one against which there can be no appeal. Moreover, God's judgement is also based on absolute knowledge and perfect justice.

49. The import of this Qur'ānic verse may best be appreciated by analogy to the limbs on a person's body. A limb may become rotten and a physician may decide to remove it by surgical operation. Now, the patient may ask his doctor not to amputate because it is a part of his body. The natural reply of the physician would be that the rotten limb was not truly a part of his body. Such a reply does not amount to denying, in a literal sense, the obvious fact that the limb is a part of that person's body. What such a statement actually means is that a person's body requires sound and healthy limbs rather than those which are rotten. For rotten limbs are not only useless, they are even able to damage

other healthy limbs. In view of the above, it makes sense that that limb be surgically removed.

In a similar way a righteous father may be told that his corrupt son is not a part of his family. The biological fact of his being the son of his father is not being negated here. Rather, it is being said that on a moral plane the son has nothing to do with his father's righteous household.

It is also pertinent to remember the context in which the present pronouncement was made. A judgement was needed in the encounter between faith and unbelief so as to determine who had faith and who was devoid of it. The righteous were to be saved and the evil were to be destroyed. The pronouncement was not intended to suggest that those of a certain stock would be saved while others would be destroyed.

By mentioning Noah's son as 'one of unrighteous conduct', the Qur'ān draws our attention to another significant fact. A worldly person brings up his children and holds them dear for the simple reason that they happen to be his offspring regardless of their conduct. However, for a believer, the main consideration is how his children actually behave. A believer's view of his children is governed by the conception that his children are God's trust placed in his care such that he may bring them up in a manner that allows them to pursue the end for which God has created man. It is possible, however, that in spite of their best efforts parents may not succeed in the proper upbringing of their children and that the latter, when they grow up, fail to obey their Lord. If this happens, parents should realize that all their efforts have been wasted and that there is no reason for them to hold such children dear to their hearts.

The Qur'ān is firm in its suggestion of such an attitude. It is obvious, therefore, that the same holds true for other relatives who are not as close as one's own children. For faith, as we know, is essentially an ideational and moral quality, and people are called believers or men of faith by dint of possessing that quality. It is man's faith which creates affinity between him and all other believers. The essential nexus of this relationship is thus ideational and moral. Those who happen to be a person's kin through blood ties are indeed relatives. If they do not share their faith, however, a believer will fulfil and be required to fulfil only the duties he owes to them on account of the accident of this blood relationship. This relationship, however, is bound to be devoid of the true cordiality and spiritual affinity which characterizes his relationship with believers. And should there be any conflict between belief and unbelief whereby a believer's relatives confront him, the believer is required to treat them exactly as any other unbeliever.

50. God's observation should not give even the slightest misunderstanding that Noah (peace be on him) in any way lacked the true spirit of faith or that his faith was, to any degree, tainted by Ignorance (*Jāhilīyah*). What perhaps one ought to remember, in order to fully appreciate what is being said here is that even Prophets are human. As human beings, it is not always possible even for them to maintain the very high standards of excellence laid down for men of faith. At some psychologically-charged moment even Prophets, despite their

(47) Noah said: 'My Lord! I take refuge with You that I should ask you for that concerning which I have no knowledge. And if You do not forgive me and do not show mercy to me, I shall be among the losers.'[51]

قَالَ رَبِّ إِنِّيٓ أَعُوذُ بِكَ أَنۡ أَسۡـَٔلَكَ مَا لَيۡسَ لِي بِهِۦ عِلۡمٞۖ وَإِلَّا تَغۡفِرۡ لِي وَتَرۡحَمۡنِيٓ أَكُن مِّنَ ٱلۡخَٰسِرِينَ ٤٧

extraordinary spiritual excellence and sublimity, become vulnerable albeit momentarily to human weaknesses. However, as soon as they realize or are made to realize by God that their conduct is falling short of the high standards required of them, they repent. Without the least hesitation or delay, they strive to mend their ways.

In fact there cannot be any better proof of Noah's moral excellence than the present incident mentioned in the Qur'ān. Just consider what had happened. Only a few moments previously Noah's son had drowned before his very eyes, something that would have simply shattered his father's whole being. At such an agonizing moment Noah (peace be on him) was reminded by God that his son had identified himself with falsehood rather than with truth. Noah (peace be on him) was told that this feeling that his son belonged to him merely because he was from his loins was a vestige of *jāhilīyah*. What is significant is that Noah (peace be on him) immediately re-oriented himself and fully adopted the attitude required of him by Islam, doing so despite the fact that the wound that he had sustained was fresh.

51. By relating the story of Noah's son, God has unequivocally and effectively made it clear that His justice is free from all biases, that His judgement is perfect and absolute. The Makkan unbelievers had entertained the illusion that God's wrath would not overtake them no matter how they behaved. They thought so because they happened to be the descendants of Abraham (peace be on him) and the devotees of a number of well-known gods and goddesses. In the past, Jews and Christians also entertained, as they still entertain, illusions of the same kind. In fact, there are also many deviant Muslims who place their reliance on false hopes. They believe that since they are descendants or devotees of some saints, the intercession of those saints will enable them to escape God's justice.

However, the Qur'ān portrays how one of the great Prophets helplessly watches his own flesh and blood drown. In a state of severe emotional agitation, he piteously implores God to forgive his son. In response, God rebukes him. Thus, we see that even a person of a Prophet's ranking failed to salvage an iniquitous son.

(48) It was said: 'Noah! Disembark,[52] with Our peace, and with blessings upon yo. and upon those who are with you. There are also people whom We shall allow to enjoy themselves for a while, and then a painful chastisement from Us shall afflict them.'

(49) We reveal to you these accounts of matters that are beyond the reach of human perception. Neither you nor your people knew about them before this. Be, then, patient. Surely, the good end is for the God-fearing.[53]

(50) And to 'Ād We sent their brother Hūd.[54] He said: 'My people! Serve Allah: you have no god save Him. (In attributing partners to Allah) you have merely been fabricating lies.[55] ▶

قِيلَ يَٰنُوحُ ٱهْبِطْ بِسَلَٰمٍ مِّنَّا وَبَرَكَٰتٍ
عَلَيْكَ وَعَلَىٰٓ أُمَمٍ مِّمَّن مَّعَكَ ۚ وَأُمَمٌ
سَنُمَتِّعُهُمْ ثُمَّ يَمَسُّهُم مِّنَّا عَذَابٌ
أَلِيمٌ ﴿٤٨﴾ تِلْكَ مِنْ أَنۢبَآءِ ٱلْغَيْبِ نُوحِيهَآ
إِلَيْكَ ۖ مَا كُنتَ تَعْلَمُهَآ أَنتَ وَلَا قَوْمُكَ
مِن قَبْلِ هَٰذَا ۖ فَٱصْبِرْ ۖ إِنَّ ٱلْعَٰقِبَةَ
لِلْمُتَّقِينَ ﴿٤٩﴾ وَإِلَىٰ عَادٍ أَخَاهُمْ
هُودًا ۚ قَالَ يَٰقَوْمِ ٱعْبُدُوا۟ ٱللَّهَ مَا
لَكُم مِّنْ إِلَٰهٍ غَيْرُهُۥٓ ۖ إِنْ أَنتُمْ
إِلَّا مُفْتَرُونَ ﴿٥٠﴾

52. Noah (peace be on him) was directed to disembark on the mountain on which the Ark had rested.

53. The Prophet Muḥammad (peace be on him) is consoled by the statement that in the same way that Noah (peace be on him) and his righteous people ultimately succeeded, so will he and his Companions. It is God's law that the opponents of the truth seem to achieve some measure of success in the beginning. But ultimate success is the lot of those who, out of their God-fearing, avoid all erroneous ways while seeking to serve the cause of the truth. The import of the story, therefore, is that the believers should not feel heart-broken by their ephemeral sufferings or the successes of their opponents. Instead, they should persevere, with courage and fortitude, in their struggle for the cause of the truth.

(51) My people! I seek no reward from you for my work. My reward lies only with Him Who created me. Do you not understand anything?[56] (52) My people! Ask your Lord for forgiveness and turn to Him in repentance. He will shower abundant rains upon you from the heaven, and will add strength to your strength.[57] Do not turn away as those given to guilt.'

يَٰقَوْمِ لَآ أَسْـَٔلُكُمْ عَلَيْهِ أَجْرًا ۖ إِنْ
أَجْرِىَ إِلَّا عَلَى ٱلَّذِى فَطَرَنِىٓ ۚ
أَفَلَا تَعْقِلُونَ ﴿٥١﴾ وَيَٰقَوْمِ
ٱسْتَغْفِرُوا۟ رَبَّكُمْ ثُمَّ تُوبُوٓا۟
إِلَيْهِ يُرْسِلِ ٱلسَّمَآءَ عَلَيْكُم
مِّدْرَارًا وَيَزِدْكُمْ قُوَّةً إِلَىٰ
قُوَّتِكُمْ وَلَا تَتَوَلَّوْا۟ مُجْرِمِينَ ﴿٥٢﴾

54. For a detailed account see *Towards Understanding the Qur'ān*, vol. III, *al-A'rāf* 7, nn. 51–6, pp. 42–5.

55. Those whom the Makkan unbelievers associated with God in His divinity actually possessed none of the attributes and powers of God. There was, therefore, no grounds whatsoever for anyone to worship them. Some people had mistakenly taken them as their deities, and looked to those deities to answer their prayers and fulfil their needs.

56. This is a very eloquent statement which also embodies a very weighty argument. The Makkan unbelievers had summarily rejected the Prophet's Message without even seriously considering it. This was indicative of the fact that they did not use their brains. For, had they used them, they would certainly have been impressed by the veracity of the Prophet (peace be on him) and the truth of his teachings. For here was someone who had gone through immense suffering in the course of his calling his people to the truth and in sincerely counselling and admonishing them. Again, it was quite evident from all the Prophet's activities that there was no intention of seeking any benefit for himself or his family. The conclusion was very clear. Such a person must have had a very strong reason to be totally convinced about the truth of his faith. For it is in the cause of his faith that he had renounced all his ease and comfort, eschewed the ambitions of material prosperity, and ventured to undertake the perilous task of challenging the beliefs, customs and ways of life which were so deeply rooted in the history of his people. Such an undertaking naturally exposed him both to the hostility of his own people and to many others.

It is obvious that the teaching of such a person could not have been so flimsy

(53) They said: 'O Hūd! You have not brought to us any clear evidence,[58] and we are not going to forsake our gods merely because you say so. We are not going to believe you. (54) All we can say is that some god of ours has afflicted you with evil.'[59]

قَالُوا۟ يَٰهُودُ مَا جِئْتَنَا بِبَيِّنَةٍ وَمَا
نَحْنُ بِتَارِكِىٓ ءَالِهَتِنَا عَن قَوْلِكَ
وَمَا نَحْنُ لَكَ بِمُؤْمِنِينَ ﴿٥٣﴾ إِن
نَّقُولُ إِلَّا ٱعْتَرَىٰكَ بَعْضُ ءَالِهَتِنَا
بِسُوٓءٍ

and trivial as to be casually cast aside without giving it even a serious thought.

57. This is a reiteration of what was said earlier, 'that you may seek forgiveness of your Lord and turn to Him in repentance whereupon He will grant you a fair enjoyment of life until an appointed term'. (See verse 3 above.) We learn from this that the rise and fall of a nation's fortunes depends on moral factors. For God's rule over the world is based on moral rather than physical laws which are bereft of all distinction between good and evil. The Qur'ān has repeatedly mentioned that when a nation receives God's Message through a Prophet, the fate of that nation depends entirely on how it responds to it. If that nation accepts the Message, God lavishes His bounties and blessings upon it. However, if that nation spurns the Message, it is destroyed.

This is a provision of the moral law according to which God deals with human beings. Another provision of this law is that any nation which, deluded by its worldly prosperity, has recourse to wrong-doing and sin, is doomed to destruction. However, if the people in question while proceeding speedily towards their tragic end, realize their mistake, give up their disobedience of God and sincerely return to His worship and service, their evil end is averted and their term is extended. Not only that but they are also judged to be deserving of reward instead of punishment, and God even ordains that they may attain well-being and ascendancy.

58. The unbelievers contended that Hūd (peace be on him) had no clear evidence to prove that it is God Who had designated him to communicate a message, and that his teachings were true.

59. The unbelievers presumably thought that because of his sacrilegious behaviour towards some saint or deity, Prophet Hūd (peace be on him) had been smitten with madness. Consequently, both words of abuse and stones were hurled at him even though he had once enjoyed much esteem and respect.

Hūd said: 'Indeed I take
Allah as my witness,[60] and
you too to be my witnesses
that I have nothing to do[61] with
your associating with Allah
(55) others than Him in His
divinity. So conspire against
me, all of you, and give me no
respite.[62] (56) I have put
my trust in Allah, Who is my
Lord and your Lord. There is
no moving creature which He
does not hold by its forelock.
Surely, My Lord is on the
straight path.[63] ▶

قَالَ إِنِّيٓ أُشْهِدُ ٱللَّهَ وَٱشْهَدُوٓا۟ أَنِّى بَرِىٓءٌ
مِّمَّا تُشْرِكُونَ ﴿٥٤﴾ مِن دُونِهِۦ ۖ فَكِيدُونِى
جَمِيعًا ثُمَّ لَا تُنظِرُونِ ﴿٥٥﴾ إِنِّى تَوَكَّلْتُ
عَلَى ٱللَّهِ رَبِّى وَرَبِّكُم ۚ مَّا مِن دَآبَّةٍ إِلَّا
هُوَ ءَاخِذٌۢ بِنَاصِيَتِهَآ ۚ إِنَّ رَبِّى عَلَىٰ صِرَٰطٍ
مُّسْتَقِيمٍ ﴿٥٦﴾

---

60. In response to this, Hūd (peace be on him) pointed out that it was true that he had not put forth specific evidence in support of his claim. He contended that rather than bring a set of minor evidence in support of his claim, he had instead brought the weightiest evidence of all – Almighty God Himself. For God and His entire universe bear witness to the truths he enunciated. The same evidence also established that the conceptions entertained by the unbelievers were pure concoctions and lacked even an atom's worth of truth.

61. The unbelievers were adamant. They would not forsake their deities just because Hūd asked them to do so. In response, Prophet Hūd (peace be on him) made it vehemently clear to them that he could not care less for their deities.

62. This is in answer to the unbelievers' contention that Hūd was suffering because he had invited the wrath of their deities upon himself. (Cf. *Yūnus* 10, n. 71.)

63. Whatever God does is absolutely right. All His actions are rightly-directed and sound. None of His actions are arbitrary. He governs the universe, and metes out full justice to all. It is, thus, impossible for someone to follow erroneous doctrines, and to engage in evil-doing and still attain salvation. Nor is it possible that someone who is truthful and righteous will end up a loser.

(57) If you, then, turn away (from the truth), know that I have delivered the message with which I was sent to you. Now my Lord will set up another people in place of you and you shall in no way be able to harm Him.[64] Surely my Lord keeps a watch over everything.'

(58) And when Our command came to pass, We delivered Hūd, together with those who shared his faith, out of special mercy from Us. We delivered them from a woeful chastisement.

(59) Such were 'Ād. They repudiated the signs of their Lord, disobeyed His Messengers,[65] and followed the bidding of every tyrannical enemy of the truth. (60) They were pursued by a curse in this world, and so will they be on the Day of Judgement. Lo! 'Ād disbelieved in the Lord. Lo! ruined are 'Ād, the people of Hūd.

فَإِن تَوَلَّوْا فَقَدْ أَبْلَغْتُكُم مَّا أُرْسِلْتُ بِهِۦٓ
إِلَيْكُمْ ۚ وَيَسْتَخْلِفُ رَبِّى قَوْمًا غَيْرَكُمْ وَلَا
تَضُرُّونَهُۥ شَيْـًٔا ۚ إِنَّ رَبِّى عَلَىٰ كُلِّ شَىْءٍ
حَفِيظٌ ﴿٥٧﴾ وَلَمَّا جَآءَ أَمْرُنَا نَجَّيْنَا
هُودًا وَٱلَّذِينَ ءَامَنُوا۟ مَعَهُۥ بِرَحْمَةٍ
مِّنَّا وَنَجَّيْنَـٰهُم مِّنْ عَذَابٍ غَلِيظٍ ﴿٥٨﴾
وَتِلْكَ عَادٌ ۖ جَحَدُوا۟ بِـَٔايَـٰتِ رَبِّهِمْ
وَعَصَوْا۟ رُسُلَهُۥ وَٱتَّبَعُوٓا۟ أَمْرَ كُلِّ جَبَّارٍ
عَنِيدٍ ﴿٥٩﴾ وَأُتْبِعُوا۟ فِى هَـٰذِهِ ٱلدُّنْيَا لَعْنَةً
وَيَوْمَ ٱلْقِيَـٰمَةِ ۗ أَلَآ إِنَّ عَادًا كَفَرُوا۟ رَبَّهُمْ ۗ
أَلَا بُعْدًا لِّعَادٍ قَوْمِ هُودٍ ﴿٦٠﴾

---

64. This is a rejoinder to the unbelievers' statement that they would in no way forsake their deities and believe in the teachings of Hūd.

65. It is true that only one Messenger (viz. Hūd) had come to them. However, his teachings were the same as those of all the other Messengers who had been raised among different nations and at different times. Hence their rejection of Hūd's message is referred to here as a rejection of all Messengers.

(61) And to Thamūd We sent their brother Ṣāliḥ.[66] He said: 'My people! Serve Allah; you have no god other than Him. He brought you into being out of the earth, and has made you dwell in it.[67] So ask Him to forgive you, and do turn towards Him in repentance.[68] Indeed My Lord is near, responsive to prayers.'[69]

۞ وَإِلَىٰ ثَمُودَ أَخَاهُمْ صَـٰلِحًا ۚ قَالَ يَـٰقَوْمِ ٱعْبُدُوا۟ ٱللَّهَ مَا لَكُم مِّنْ إِلَـٰهٍ غَيْرُهُۥ ۖ هُوَ أَنشَأَكُم مِّنَ ٱلْأَرْضِ وَٱسْتَعْمَرَكُمْ فِيهَا فَٱسْتَغْفِرُوهُ ثُمَّ تُوبُوٓا۟ إِلَيْهِ ۚ إِنَّ رَبِّى قَرِيبٌ مُّجِيبٌ ﴿٦١﴾

66. For further information see *Towards Understanding the Qur'ān*, vol. III, *al-A'rāf* 7, nn. 57–62, pp. 45–8.

67. This substantiates the fact that there is no god other than the One True God; and that He should be the sole object of worship and service. Now, even those who associated others with God in His divinity acknowledged that it is Allah alone Who created them. Using this obvious premise, Prophet Ṣāliḥ (peace be on him) sought to persuade people to affirm that God alone should be worshipped. He emphasized that it is God alone Who had made them into human beings out of the lifeless materials from the earth, and had subsequently settled them on earth. In view of this, who else than God could claim godhead? Likewise, who else could claim that he ought to be served and worshipped?

68. The Thamūd had been guilty of worshipping others besides God. They are now urged to seek God's forgiveness for this grave sin.

69. This verse is aimed at removing a major misconception which had been prevalent among the polytheists. This misconception is in fact one of the major reasons which prompted men to associate others with God in His divinity. One of man's most persistent faults is that he has conceived God to be similar to those worldly rulers who immerse themselves in a life of ease and luxury in their grand palaces. Such rulers are normally far removed from their subjects. To all intents and purposes they are well beyond the direct access of their subjects. The only way for their subjects to reach them is through the auspices of their favourite courtiers. And even if a subject succeeds in conveying his pleadings through a courtier, these rulers are often too arrogant to directly

(62) They said: 'O Ṣāliḥ! Until now you were one of those among us on whom we placed great hopes.[70] Now, would you forbid us to worship what our forefathers were wont to worship?[71] Indeed we are in disquieting doubt about what you are calling us to.'[72]

قَالُوا يَـٰصَـٰلِحُ قَدْ كُنتَ فِينَا مَرْجُوًّا
قَبْلَ هَـٰذَآ ۖ أَتَنْهَىٰنَآ أَن نَّعْبُدَ
مَا يَعْبُدُ ءَابَآؤُنَا وَإِنَّنَا لَفِى شَكٍّ
مِّمَّا تَدْعُونَآ إِلَيْهِ مُرِيبٍ ﴿٦٢﴾

---

respond to such pleadings. This is one aspect of the function of a courtier – to communicate to a ruler the pleadings of his subjects, and also to communicate to the subjects the response of the ruler.

Since God was often conceived in the image of such worldly rulers many people fell prey to the false belief that God is well above the reach of ordinary human beings. This belief spread further because many clever people found it quite profitable to propagate such a notion. No wonder many people felt God could only be approached through powerful intermediaries and intercessors. The only way that a person's prayer could reach God and be answered by Him was to approach Him through one of the holy men. It was, therefore, considered necessary to grease the palm of the religious functionaries who supposedly enjoyed the privilege of conveying a man's offerings and prayers to the One on high.

This misconception gave birth to a pantheon of small and large deities and intercessors who are supposed to act as intermediaries between man and God. This misconception has given rise to institutionalized priesthood, according to which no ritual, whether relating to birth or death, can be performed without the active participation of the priests.

Prophet Ṣāliḥ (peace be on him) strikes at the root of this ignorant system, and totally demolishes its intellectual infrastructure. This he does by emphasizing two facts: that God is extremely close to His creatures and that He answers their prayers. Thus he refutes many misconceptions about God: that He is far away, altogether withdrawn from human beings, and that He does not answer their prayers if they are to directly approach Him. God, no doubt, is transcendent, and yet He is extremely close to every person. Everyone will find Him just beside himself. Everyone can whisper to Him the innermost desires of his heart. Everyone can address his prayers to God both in public and in private, by verbally expressing those prayers or addressing them to Him without so much as uttering a single word. Moreover, God answers the prayers of all His creatures directly. The fact is that God's court with all its majesty is just around everyone's corner, so close to one's threshold, and always open to all. How silly it is, therefore, for people to search for those intercessors who they think will help them approach God. (See also *Towards Understanding the Qur'ān,* vol. I, *al-Baqarah* 2, n. 188.)

70. The people of Ṣāliḥ (peace be on him) centred many expectations around him. On account of his wisdom, intelligence, maturity, and dignified personality they expected Ṣāliḥ to rise to great heights. They also believed that he would not only achieve personal greatness and prosperity, but would also assist his people in their bid to excel against other tribes and nations in terms of worldly benefits. However, no sooner had Ṣāliḥ begun to teach his people that they are obligated to exclusively worship and serve the One True God and pay due heed to the Hereafter than they became altogether disenchanted with him.

It may be recalled that the predicament of the Makkan unbelievers was no different from that of the people of Ṣāliḥ (peace be on him). The Makkans also recognized that Muḥammad (peace be on him) was a person of outstanding qualities. They were confident that he would grow into a very successful merchant and that they would also benefit from his trading acumen. But then they found that the Prophet (peace be on him), contrary to their expectations, began to invite them to serve and worship the One True God. He also began to urge them to pay heed to the Next Life and to observe moral excellence. They were instantly disappointed and became totally averse to him. They even began to give vent to the idea that the Prophet (peace be on him) who for so long had been a perfectly normal person, was now seized by some strange mental disease. In their view it was because of this mental derailment that he had ruined his own life and also threw cold water on the hopes and expectations of his people.

71. This was the main reason which the unbelievers advanced to support their view, the rationale they offered for the worship of the deities in which they believed. The simple reason was, as stated here and elsewhere in the Qur'ān, that their ancestors had also worshipped them!

This brings into sharp relief the fundamental difference between the rationale offered by Islam and that offered by *jāhilīyah*. Ṣāliḥ (peace be on him) had said that none but God deserves to be worshipped. He argued that since God had created human beings and had enabled them to settle on earth, they, therefore, ought to worship Him. The unbelievers responded by saying that their deities also deserved to be worshipped, indeed had been worshipped by their ancestors and so they could not just forsake them. In other words, they proclaimed their commitment to follow in the footsteps of their ancestors even if those ancestors had been altogether ignorant and stupid.

72. The Qur'ān does not specify the 'disquieting doubt' to which the unbelievers were subjected. The reason for this is that although all of them had doubts, the doubt entertained by each was different. It may even be said that whenever people are asked to accept the truth, all those who believe in one kind

(63) Ṣāliḥ said: 'My people! What do you think? If I had a clear evidence from my Lord, and then He also bestowed His mercy upon me, who will rescue me from the punishment of Allah if I still disobey Him? You can only make me lose even more.[73] (64) My people! This she-camel of Allah is a sign for you. So let her pasture on Allah's earth, and do not hurt her or else some chastisement – which is near at hand – should overtake you.'

قَالَ يَٰقَوْمِ أَرَءَيْتُمْ إِن كُنتُ عَلَىٰ
بَيِّنَةٍ مِّن رَّبِّى وَءَاتَىٰنِى مِنْهُ رَحْمَةً
فَمَن يَنصُرُنِى مِنَ ٱللَّهِ إِنْ عَصَيْتُهُۥ
فَمَا تَزِيدُونَنِى غَيْرَ تَخْسِيرٍ ﴿٦٣﴾ وَيَٰقَوْمِ
هَٰذِهِۦ نَاقَةُ ٱللَّهِ لَكُمْ ءَايَةً
فَذَرُوهَا تَأْكُلْ فِىٓ أَرْضِ ٱللَّهِ وَلَا
تَمَسُّوهَا بِسُوٓءٍ فَيَأْخُذَكُمْ عَذَابٌ
قَرِيبٌ ﴿٦٤﴾

---

of falsehood or the other feel disturbed. The complacent faith which they had before they became acquainted with the truth is simply gone, and a 'disquieting doubt' creeps in and begins to agitate them. Although each of them may feel this differently, an amount of disquiet is nevertheless common to all unbelievers.

Before the unbelievers were invited to the truth, they may never have felt the need to critically examine their position. But after the call to the truth has been made such an attitude can no longer persist. This is so because the trenchant criticism of *jāhilīyah* made by the Prophet of the day together with his weighty arguments in support of his teachings is bound to have its effect. Moreover, his lofty morals, his firmness, his forbearance, his grace and dignity, his straightforward and honest ways, and his wisdom and sagacity create a certain respect for him even among his staunchest enemies. Not only that but the people concerned cannot help but notice that the best elements in the society of the day are continually drawn to the call of the truth. They also observe that as a result of embracing the truth the lives of these people are perceptibly transformed. Taken together, all these factors agitate the minds of those who wish to cling to and even promote the old *jāhilīyah* even after the truth has been made known to them.

73. Prophet Ṣāliḥ (peace be on him) makes it clear to his people that if he were to follow the advice which they offered him, it would virtually lead to his perdition. Were Ṣāliḥ (peace be on him) to act contrary to his conscience and in

(65) But they slaughtered
her. Thereupon Ṣāliḥ warned
them: 'Enjoy yourselves in
your homes for a maximum of
three days. This is a promise
which shall not be belied.'

(66) Then, when Our com-
mand came to pass, We saved
Ṣāliḥ and those who shared his
faith through Our special
mercy, from the disgrace of
that day.[74] Truly Your Lord is
All-Strong, All-Mighty. (67)
And the Blast overtook those
who were wont to do wrong,
and then they lay lifeless in
their homes (68) as though
they had never lived there
before.

Oh, verily the Thamūd
denied their Lord! Oh, the
Thamūd were destroyed.

فَعَقَرُوهَا فَقَالَ تَمَتَّعُواْ فِي دَارِكُمْ
ثَلَٰثَةَ أَيَّامٍۖ ذَٰلِكَ وَعْدٌ غَيْرُ مَكْذُوبٍ
٦٥ فَلَمَّا جَآءَ أَمْرُنَا نَجَّيْنَا صَٰلِحًا
وَٱلَّذِينَ ءَامَنُواْ مَعَهُۥ بِرَحْمَةٍ مِّنَّا
وَمِنْ خِزْيِ يَوْمِئِذٍۚ إِنَّ رَبَّكَ هُوَ ٱلْقَوِيُّ
ٱلْعَزِيزُ ٦٦ وَأَخَذَ ٱلَّذِينَ ظَلَمُواْ
ٱلصَّيْحَةُ فَأَصْبَحُواْ فِي دِيَٰرِهِمْ
جَٰثِمِينَ ٦٧ كَأَن لَّمْ يَغْنَوْاْ فِيهَآۗ
أَلَآ إِنَّ ثَمُودَاْ كَفَرُواْ رَبَّهُمْۗ
أَلَا بُعْدًا لِّثَمُودَ ٦٨

opposition to the knowledge and guidance intimated to him by God, he would be liable to God's punishment, and his people would be helpless in their efforts to rescue him from that punishment. Moreover, Ṣāliḥ (peace be on him) was not an ordinary person but a Prophet. This made his dereliction in the sight of God even more grave. For, God would take him to task on the grounds that although he had been encumbered with the duty to direct his people to the right way, he had consciously led them to error.

74. The folk traditions of the Sinaitic Peninsula indicate that when a severe punishment afflicted the Thamūd, Ṣāliḥ (peace be on him) migrated to Sinai. Hence, close to the Mount of Moses there is a hillock called Nabī Ṣāliḥ. These traditions make one believe that it is here that Prophet Ṣāliḥ (peace be on him) lived.

(69) Indeed Our messengers came to Abraham, bearing glad tidings. They greeted him with 'peace', and Abraham answered back to them 'peace', and hurriedly brought to them a roasted calf.[75] (70) When he perceived that their hands could not reach it, he mistrusted them, and felt afraid of them.[76] They said: 'Do not be afraid. We have been sent to the people of Lot.'[77] ▶

وَلَقَدْ جَآءَتْ رُسُلُنَآ إِبْرَٰهِيمَ
بِٱلْبُشْرَىٰ قَالُوا۟ سَلَٰمًا قَالَ
سَلَٰمٌ فَمَا لَبِثَ أَن جَآءَ بِعِجْلٍ
حَنِيذٍ ﴿٦٩﴾ فَلَمَّا رَءَآ أَيْدِيَهُمْ لَا
تَصِلُ إِلَيْهِ نَكِرَهُمْ وَأَوْجَسَ
مِنْهُمْ خِيفَةً قَالُوا۟ لَا تَخَفْ إِنَّآ
أُرْسِلْنَآ إِلَىٰ قَوْمِ لُوطٍ ﴿٧٠﴾

75. This shows that the angels visited Prophet Abraham (peace be on him) in human form and that initially they did not disclose their identity. Prophet Abraham (peace be on him), therefore, thought that they were strangers, and immediately arranged a good meal for them.

76. Some commentators on the Qur'ān are of the view that when the guests hesitated to take food Prophet Abraham (peace be on him) felt suspicious about their intentions. He even became apprehensive that they had come with some hostile design. For, in Arabia when someone declines the food offered to him by way of hospitality, this gives rise to the fear that he has not come as a guest but rather with subversive purposes. The very next verse, however, does not lend any support to this view.

77. The words as well as the tone of the verse suggest that as soon as Abraham (peace be on him) noticed that his guests were disinclined to eat, he realized that they were angels. Since angels appear in human form only in very exceptional circumstances, what terrified Abraham (peace be on him) was the possibility that the angels may have been sent to inflict punishment on account of any lapses that he himself, his family, or his people may have committed. Had Abraham (peace be on him) not been sure about the identity of his guests – as some Qur'ān-commentators believe – they would have said: 'Do not fear, we are angels sent by your Lord.' However, they did not say so. They rather tried to allay Abraham's fears by saying: 'Do not be afraid, we have been sent to the people of Lot.' It is, thus, clear that Abraham had become aware of their true identity. What caused Abraham (peace be on him) to worry was the idea that the angels had been sent to his people, that his people were about to suffer a

(71) And Abraham's wife
was standing by and on hearing this she laughed.[78] And
We gave her the good news of
(the birth of) Isaac, and after
Isaac, of Jacob.[79] (72) She
said: 'Woe is me![80] Shall I
bear a child now that I am an
old woman and my husband is
well advanced in years.[81] This
is indeed strange!' (73)
They said: 'Do you wonder at
Allah's decree?[82] Allah's
mercy and His blessings be
upon you, O people of the
house. Surely, He is Praiseworthy, Glorious.'

وَٱمْرَأَتُهُۥ قَآئِمَةٌ فَضَحِكَتْ فَبَشَّرْنَـٰهَا
بِإِسْحَـٰقَ وَمِن وَرَآءِ إِسْحَـٰقَ يَعْقُوبَ ﴿٧١﴾
قَالَتْ يَـٰوَيْلَتَىٰٓ ءَأَلِدُ وَأَنَا۠ عَجُوزٌ وَهَـٰذَا
بَعْلِى شَيْخًا ۖ إِنَّ هَـٰذَا لَشَىْءٌ عَجِيبٌ
﴿٧٢﴾ قَالُوٓا۟ أَتَعْجَبِينَ مِنْ أَمْرِ ٱللَّهِ ۖ رَحْمَتُ
ٱللَّهِ وَبَرَكَـٰتُهُۥ عَلَيْكُمْ أَهْلَ ٱلْبَيْتِ ۚ إِنَّهُۥ
حَمِيدٌ مَّجِيدٌ ﴿٧٣﴾

---

severe chastisement. However, he was soon to feel relieved that the angels had been sent to the people of Lot rather than to his own. So there was no reason to fear that his own people would soon suffer destruction.

78. According to this verse, the whole of Abraham's family was worried about the visit of the angels in human form. From sheer anxiety Abraham's wife also came out. However, when she came to know that the coming of the angels did not forebode any evil, she was reassured and became joyful.

79. The angels gave the glad tidings of the birth of Isaac to Sarah rather than to Abraham. For Abraham (peace be on him) already had a son called Ishmael, born of his first wife Hagar. At that time Sarah was without any issue, and for this reason she felt sad. When the angels gave her the glad tidings they foretold her not only of the birth of Isaac, but also of her grandson, Jacob. It is needless to say, perhaps, that both of them – Isaac and Jacob – became Messengers of great standing.

80. This expression does not, in any way, suggest that Sarah, instead of feeling happy, considered this prediction the foreboding of a calamity. In point of fact the expression is an exclamation to which women, in particular, resort to in a state of wonder and amazement. Thus, what is intended is not what the

(74) Thus when fear had left Abraham and the good news had been conveyed to him, he began to dispute with Us concerning the people of Lot.[83] (75) Surely Abraham was forbearing, tender-hearted and oft-turning to Allah. (76) Thereupon (Our angels) said to him: 'O Abraham! Desist from this, for indeed your Lord's command has come; and a chastisement which cannot be averted[84] is about to befall them.'

فَلَمَّا ذَهَبَ عَنْ إِبْرَٰهِيمَ ٱلرَّوْعُ وَجَآءَتْهُ
ٱلْبُشْرَىٰ يُجَٰدِلُنَا فِى قَوْمِ لُوطٍ ٧٤
إِنَّ إِبْرَٰهِيمَ لَحَلِيمٌ أَوَّٰهٌ مُّنِيبٌ ٧٥
يَٰٓإِبْرَٰهِيمُ أَعْرِضْ عَنْ هَٰذَآ إِنَّهُۥ قَدْ جَآءَ
أَمْرُ رَبِّكَ وَإِنَّهُمْ ءَاتِيهِمْ عَذَابٌ غَيْرُ
مَرْدُودٍ ٧٦

words literally suggest; the purpose is merely to express a sense of wonder.

81. According to the Bible, Abraham was one hundred years and Sarah ninety years old at that time.

82. Ordinarily, it is uncommon for women to bear children at such an advanced age. However, such a thing is not at all beyond the range of God's power. And since the tiding had been conveyed at the instance of God, there was no reason why a staunch believer such as Sarah should feel astonished, let alone entertain any doubts about it.

83. The word 'dispute' here expresses the nexus of affection and endearment between Abraham (peace be on him) and God. Perusal of this verse brings to one's mind Abraham's persistent pleading to God that He may spare Lot's people His chastisement. To this God replied that since they were totally devoid of all good and had exceeded all reasonable limits, they did not deserve any leniency. Yet Abraham (peace be on him) continued to plead for them and presumably submitted that if there was even the least bit of good left in them, their chastisement be deferred so that this good may come to the fore.

It is interesting to note that the Bible also recounts this 'dispute' between God and Abraham. However, the Qur'ānic account, though brief, is much more meaningful, and significant. (Cf. *Genesis* 18: 23–32.)

84. The mention of Abraham's story as a preamble to the story of the people of Lot may appear somewhat out of tune with the purpose for which the events of the past are being narrated here. However, to better appreciate this, two things should be borne in mind. Firstly, that the immediate addressees of the Qur'ān were the Quraysh. The Quraysh, since they were the descendants of Abraham (peace be on him), were the custodians of the Ka'bah – the shrine of God. For the same reason, they also had a predominant influence over the religious, moral, cultural and political life of Arabia. The Quraysh believed that since they were the offspring of a Prophet who enjoyed God's favour, they would never be punished by God. They felt sure that Abraham (peace be on him) would intercede effectively with God on their behalf.

The Qur'ān strikes a powerful blow to the Makkans' misconceptions. They are told, in the first instance, the story of the Prophet Noah (peace be on him) in graphic detail: how he watched his own son drown and how he distressfully prayed to God to show mercy to him. And yet, as we know, Noah's prayer was to no avail. Not only was Noah's prayer not granted, he was even rebuked for praying on behalf of his unrighteous son.

Noah's story is followed by a narration of Abraham's story. Abraham (peace be on him) enjoys, on the one hand, the innumerable blessings of God. He is also addressed by God in terms which are clearly indicative of God's special love and affection for him. On the other hand, when Abraham interferes in a manner that amounted to compromising justice with regard to an evil-doing nation, God sets his intercession aside.

The second thing that ought to be borne in mind is that the present discourse emphasizes to the Quraysh that God's law of retribution has always been operative in history. The Quraysh had become altogether oblivious of that law and were no longer afraid of it. The Qur'ān, therefore, drew their attention to its constant manifestation in human history, including the traces of its operation in their immediate surroundings.

Their attention was also drawn to Abraham (peace be on him) who had migrated for the sake of the truth and had settled down in an alien land. Apparently, he had no power or resources at his disposal. Nonetheless, God rewarded him for his righteousness. He also caused Abraham's wife to deliver a child when she had reached the age of barrenness and when Abraham himself had also reached an advanced age. This child was Isaac (peace be on him) who was to become the father of another Prophet, Jacob (peace be on them). The progeny of Isaac and Jacob are known as the Children of Israel. They were indeed a great people who retained, for centuries, their ascendancy in the region – Palestine and Syria – where Abraham (peace be on him) had first set his foot as an uprooted, homeless refugee.

Distinguishable from the Israelites were the people of Lot. They remained immersed in their evil deeds and continued to bask in the warmth of their prosperity. They had no idea at all that on account of this iniquity they would be overtaken by God's punishment in the near future. Hence, whenever the Prophet Lot (peace be on him) attempted to admonish them, they scornfully brushed his counsel aside. However, the same day on which it was decided to

(77) And when Our messengers came to Lot,[85] he was perturbed by their coming and felt troubled on their account, and said: 'This is a distressing day.'[86] (78) And his people came to him rushing. Before this they were wont to commit evil deeds. Lot said: 'My people! Here are my daughters; they are purer for you.[87] Have fear of Allah and do not disgrace me concerning my guests. Is there not even one right-minded person in your midst?' ▶

وَلَمَّا جَآءَتْ رُسُلُنَا لُوطًا سِيٓءَ بِهِمْ
وَضَاقَ بِهِمْ ذَرْعًا وَقَالَ هَٰذَا يَوْمٌ
عَصِيبٌ ﴿٧٧﴾ وَجَآءَهُۥ قَوْمُهُۥ يُهْرَعُونَ
إِلَيْهِ وَمِن قَبْلُ كَانُوا۟ يَعْمَلُونَ
ٱلسَّيِّـَٔاتِ ۚ قَالَ يَٰقَوْمِ هَٰٓؤُلَآءِ بَنَاتِى
هُنَّ أَطْهَرُ لَكُمْ ۖ فَٱتَّقُوا۟ ٱللَّهَ وَلَا
تُخْزُونِ فِى ضَيْفِىٓ ۖ أَلَيْسَ مِنكُمْ
رَجُلٌ رَّشِيدٌ ﴿٧٨﴾

---

exalt the progeny of Abraham (peace be on him) into a very outstanding nation, it was also decided to annihilate the people of Lot who had become exceedingly wicked. So thorough was the destruction to which they were subjected that to-day there exists no trace of their habitation.

85. For details see *Towards Understanding the Qur'ān*, vol. III, *al-A'rāf* 7, nn. 63–8, pp. 49–53 – Ed.

86. What seems to be evident from the story as related in the Qur'ān is that the angels had come to Lot (peace be on him) in the form of handsome young boys. It also seems that Lot (peace be on him) was unaware that they were angels. He also felt quite disturbed, therefore, at the sight of the visiting young boys. His reaction was natural in view of the known degeneration and unabashed perversity prevalent among his people.

87. It is possible that Lot (peace be on him) used the word 'daughters' to refer to the totality of females in his nation as such. For a Messenger is indeed like a father to his people, and all the females of that nation are to him like his own daughters. It is also possible that when Lot used the word 'daughters' he meant his own daughters. Whatever is the correct interpretation, one should not misunderstand the statement and think it an invitation for Lot's people to indulge in illegitimate sex. For the very next part of his remark, viz. 'they are purer for you', excludes all justification for such a misunderstanding.

The whole thrust of Lot's statement was that if they wished to satisfy their

(79) They said: 'Surely you
already know that we have
nothing to do with your
daughters.[88] You also know
well what we want.' (80)
He said: 'Would that I had the
strength to set you straight, or
could seek refuge in some
powerful support.' (81)
Thereupon the angels said: 'O
Lot! We indeed are messengers of your Lord. And your
people will in no way be able
to hurt you. So depart with
your family in a part of the
night and let no one of you
turn around[89] excepting your
wife (who shall not go); for
what will befall them shall
also befall her.[90] In the morning their promised hour will
come. Is not the morning
near?'

قَالُوا لَقَدْ عَلِمْتَ مَا لَنَا فِي بَنَاتِكَ مِنْ حَقٍّ
وَإِنَّكَ لَتَعْلَمُ مَا نُرِيدُ ﴿٧٩﴾ قَالَ لَوْ أَنَّ لِي
بِكُمْ قُوَّةً أَوْ آوِي إِلَىٰ رُكْنٍ شَدِيدٍ
﴿٨٠﴾ قَالُوا يَا لُوطُ إِنَّا رُسُلُ رَبِّكَ لَن
يَصِلُوا إِلَيْكَ فَأَسْرِ بِأَهْلِكَ بِقِطْعٍ
مِّنَ اللَّيْلِ وَلَا يَلْتَفِتْ مِنكُمْ أَحَدٌ
إِلَّا امْرَأَتَكَ إِنَّهُ مُصِيبُهَا مَا أَصَابَهُمْ
إِنَّ مَوْعِدَهُمُ الصُّبْحُ أَلَيْسَ الصُّبْحُ
بِقَرِيبٍ ﴿٨١﴾

sex-urge, they should do so in the natural and legitimate manner as laid down by God. Lot (peace be on him) wished to underscore the fact that the natural and legitimate means of sexual satisfaction were readily available as there was no dearth of women in their society.

88. This Qur'ānic statement vividly portrays the moral degradation and perversity of those people. They had brazenly deviated from the natural way of satisfying their sexual desires and had adopted instead an altogether perverse and filthy way. What was even more heinous was that their interest had become confined only to those perverse forms of sexual gratification which had come into vogue in their society. This perversity had reached such a point where they felt no shame in stating that they were not interested at all in what was universally held to be the natural and legitimate way of sexual satisfaction.

This is the lowest conceivable depth of moral degeneration and perversity. Such a case is very different from that of a person who might commit a sin in a moment of weakness when he is overwhelmed by his passions, but has not

(82) And when Our command came to pass, We turned the town upside down, and rained on it stones of baked clay, one on another,[91] (83) marked from your Lord.[92] Nor is the punishment far off from the wrong-doers.[93]

فَلَمَّا جَآءَ أَمۡرُنَا جَعَلۡنَا عَٰلِيَهَا سَافِلَهَا وَأَمۡطَرۡنَا عَلَيۡهَا حِجَارَةً مِّن سِجِّيلٍ مَّنضُودٍ ﴿٨٢﴾ مُّسَوَّمَةً عِندَ رَبِّكَ ۖ وَمَا هِيَ مِنَ ٱلظَّٰلِمِينَ بِبَعِيدٍ ﴿٨٣﴾

ceased to distinguish good from evil. For it is quite possible for such a person to mend his ways.

But even if he does not mend his ways, he may, at the most, be considered a man who has lapsed into evil ways. But a person who becomes so thoroughly perverse that his interest is confined only to what is forbidden and sinful, and who believes that all that is right and permissible is simply not meant for him, is altogether a different situation. Such a person is not only wicked, but has sunk so low that he cannot be truly considered a human being. Such a person is a worm that thrives only on filth and finds all that is clean and pure totally disagreeable. Were such a worm to be found in the house of someone who loves cleanliness, he would use insecticide to get rid of it at the first available opportunity! Such being the case, how is it conceivable that God, the Lord of this universe, can allow such worms to concentrate and become strong at any given place or time?

89. The warning implied in directing Lot (peace be on him) and his household to depart at their earliest was loud and clear. They were told not to tarry behind in the region which had been marked for total destruction.

90. This is the third instructive event related in this *sūrah*. The purpose of relating it is to underscore the fact that family connections with, and the intercession of, people of high spiritual standing can be of no avail in rescuing a people from the punishment they invite upon themselves by their evil deeds.

91. This scourge probably took the form of a severe earthquake combined with volcanic eruptions. The earthquake turned their dwellings upside down and by means of a volcanic eruption they were subjected to a severe rain of stones. The expression 'stones of baked clay' perhaps refers to the stones formed by the underground heat and lava in volcanic regions. The signs of this volcanic eruption can be noticed almost everywhere in the region south and east of the Dead Sea even today.

(84) And to (the people of)
Midian We sent their brother
Shu'ayb.[94] He said: 'My people! Serve Allah; you have no
god other than Him. And do
not diminish the measure and
weight. Indeed I see that you
are prospering now, but I fear
for you the chastisement of an
encompassing day in the
future. (85) My people!
Give full measure and weight
with justice, do not diminish
the goods of others, and do not
go about creating corruption
in the land. (86) The gains
that Allah lets you retain are
better for you, if you indeed
believe. In any case, I have not
been appointed a keeper over
you.'[95]

۞ وَإِلَىٰ مَدْيَنَ أَخَاهُمْ شُعَيْبًا قَالَ
يَٰقَوْمِ ٱعْبُدُوا۟ ٱللَّهَ مَا لَكُم
مِّنْ إِلَٰهٍ غَيْرُهُۥ وَلَا تَنقُصُوا۟
ٱلْمِكْيَالَ وَٱلْمِيزَانَ إِنِّىٓ
أَرَىٰكُم بِخَيْرٍ وَإِنِّىٓ أَخَافُ
عَلَيْكُمْ عَذَابَ يَوْمٍ مُّحِيطٍ
﴿٨٤﴾ وَيَٰقَوْمِ أَوْفُوا۟ ٱلْمِكْيَالَ
وَٱلْمِيزَانَ بِٱلْقِسْطِ وَلَا تَبْخَسُوا۟
ٱلنَّاسَ أَشْيَآءَهُمْ وَلَا تَعْثَوْا۟ فِى
ٱلْأَرْضِ مُفْسِدِينَ ﴿٨٥﴾ بَقِيَّتُ ٱللَّهِ
خَيْرٌ لَّكُمْ إِن كُنتُم مُّؤْمِنِينَ وَمَآ
أَنَا۠ عَلَيْكُم بِحَفِيظٍ ﴿٨٦﴾

---

92. This implies that each stone had been earmarked for a specific act of destruction.

93. The moral of the story is that those who engage in acts of transgression should not delude themselves into believing that they are safe from God's punishment. For, if the people of Prophet Lot (peace be on him) could be overtaken by a severe chastisement, so can they. For none can overwhelm God or frustrate His plan: neither the people of Lot nor any other.

94. For details see *Towards Understanding the Qur'ān*, vol. III, *al-A'rāf* 7, nn. 69–75, pp. 53–7.

95. Shu'ayb (peace be on him) made it clear to his people that he had no power to compel them to adopt one kind of behaviour or another. His task was merely that of a sincere adviser. All he could do was to admonish and warn them. It was up to them either to pay heed to that advice or to disregard it. What really mattered was that one day all human beings will be mustered by God to

(87) They replied: 'O Shu'ayb! Does your Prayer enjoin upon you[96] that we should forsake the deities whom our forefathers worshipped, or that we should give up using our wealth as we please?[97] Do you fancy that you, and only you, are forbearing and right-directed?'

قَالُواْ يَٰشُعَيْبُ أَصَلَوٰتُكَ تَأْمُرُكَ أَن نَّتْرُكَ مَا يَعْبُدُ ءَابَآؤُنَآ أَوْ أَن نَّفْعَلَ فِيٓ أَمْوَٰلِنَا مَا نَشَٰٓؤُاْ إِنَّكَ لَأَنتَ ٱلْحَلِيمُ ٱلرَّشِيدُ ﴿٨٧﴾

render an account of their deeds. It is this – the rendering of an account before God – that people should truly fear. It matters little whether they care for Shu'ayb or not. What really matters is whether they have any fear of standing before God's judgement. If they do fear this, it is essential that they give up the iniquity in which they are engrossed.

96. This, in fact, is a taunting remark. Remarks which are expressive of the same spirit are heard today among every group of people who are heedless of God and who are engrossed in sin and evil. Prayer is obviously the first and the most obvious symbol of man's religious orientation. That orientation is not simply considered a dangerous disease, but the most dangerous one by irreligious people. Hence, Prayer is looked upon by these people as a manifestation of mental derailment rather than what it actually is – an act of worship.

Irreligious people are also aware that those who become religiously committed are not content merely with self-reform. Such people are wont to go a step further and strive to reform others. Not only that, but it even becomes difficult for such people to refrain from criticizing attitudes opposed to religion and morality. Hence, irreligious people feel jittery because they fear that Prayer is not simply performed as a religious ritual but that it is the precursor of endless sermonizing on religion and morality. In addition, it may even lead to scathing criticisms of every aspect of social life. It is for this reason that Prayer is often singled out for every kind of taunt and reproach. Moreover, if those who observe Prayer criticize the evils rampant in their society and urge people to act righteously, this inspires opponents of religion to direct every possible invective against Prayer and to lash out at it as the source of every conceivable evil.

97. This is a full-blooded expression of the world-view of Ignorance *(Jāhilīyah)* as distinguished from that of Islam. The Islamic view is that all

(88) Shu'ayb said: 'My people! What do you think? If I stand on clear evidence from my Lord, and He has also provided me a handsome provision from Himself[98] – (should I be ungrateful to Him and share your error and iniquity?) Nor do I desire to act contrary to what I admonish you.[99] I desire nothing but to set things right as far as I can. My succour is only with Allah. In Him have I put my trust, and to Him do I always turn. ▶

قَالَ يَٰقَوْمِ أَرَءَيْتُمْ إِن كُنتُ عَلَىٰ
بَيِّنَةٍ مِّن رَّبِّي وَرَزَقَنِي مِنْهُ رِزْقًا
حَسَنًا وَمَا أُرِيدُ أَنْ أُخَالِفَكُمْ إِلَىٰ
مَا أَنْهَىٰكُمْ عَنْهُ إِنْ أُرِيدُ
إِلَّا ٱلْإِصْلَٰحَ مَا ٱسْتَطَعْتُ وَمَا
تَوْفِيقِيٓ إِلَّا بِٱللَّهِ عَلَيْهِ تَوَكَّلْتُ وَإِلَيْهِ
أُنِيبُ ﴿٨٨﴾

worship except the worship of God is erroneous. It is erroneous because worshipping any other than the One True God is supported by nothing – neither reason, knowledge, nor revelation. Moreover, God should not only be worshipped in the limited sphere of life called 'religion'. God's worship should extend to all aspects of life – social, cultural, economic and political. For all that man has in the world belongs only to God. Man, therefore, has no right to consider any aspect of his life to be independent of God's guidance.

The contrary of this is *Jāhilīyah*. According to this view, man ought to observe the customs and usages he inherits from his ancestors, and he ought to do so merely because they come down from the past. This world-view considers religion to be confined to the domain of ritual; the ritual of worship. As for the ordinary affairs of worldly life, man ought to act as he pleases.

It is thus quite clear that there is nothing so 'modern' about the tendency of driving a wedge between the religious and secular spheres of life. For some three and a half thousand years ago the nation of Shu'ayb was as emphatically insistent on bifurcating life into two water-tight compartments – the secular and the religious – as Westerners and their Eastern disciples of our time are wont to do. There seems little justification, therefore, to characterize the attitude of the present-day secularists as something altogether novel, as an attitude that has emerged in modern times as a result of the cumulative intellectual progress of mankind. Far from it, the new-fangled ideology which is being played up everywhere for its freshness and newness is, in fact, the same stale, old-fashioned obscurantism which characterized *Jāhilīyah* several thousand years ago. Likewise, the Islamic defiance of, and opposition to, *Jāhilīyah* is also a perennial reality of human history.

98. 'Provision' in this context has two connotations. It might signify, in the first place, the provision of knowledge of the truth communicated by God to someone. Secondly, it might also signify, as it commonly does, the provision of the means bestowed by God on His creatures in order that they may be able to live.

Were we to understand this word in the first sense, the verse substantially repeats the same point that has been expressed earlier in this *sūrah* through the Prophets Muḥammad, Noah and Ṣāliḥ (peace be on them). Common to their statements is their affirmation that they found the signs of the truth in their own beings and in the universe around them. Those signs were corroborated by direct knowledge of the truth intimated to them by God. (See verses 17, 28 and 63 above – Ed.) Hence it was not possible for them to join their people in their errors of belief and in their acts of wickedness.

However, if the word is taken in the latter sense, it amounts to a response to the sarcastic remark hurled at Shu'ayb: 'Do you fancy that you, and only you, are forbearing and right-directed?' (See verse 87 above.) It is noteworthy that the answer to this most bitter and caustic query is couched in exceedingly moderate and dispassionate words. The answer amounts to telling his opponents that if his Lord had granted Shu'ayb knowledge of reality and also a livelihood that is pure and lawful, how could their sarcastic remarks change the fact that Shu'ayb had received God's favours? Also, in view of the favours which God had lavished upon Shu'ayb, how could it be appropriate for him to act ungratefully towards God by legitimizing their erroneous beliefs and acts of corruption?

99. Shu'ayb pointed out to his detractors that they could measure his integrity by only one thing: whether he practised what he preached. Had he forbidden others from visiting false deities, and then had become the custodian of some such shrine, people would have been justified in reproaching him for inconsistency and self-contradiction. They could have rightly criticized him for preaching something and practising its opposite. Had he asked them to abstain from unlawful earnings and had himself resorted to dishonest practices they would have been perfectly justified in accusing him of talking of honesty merely to build up a good image of himself and then exploiting it for his personal ends.

It was clear, however, that Shu'ayb could be accused of nothing like that. It was crystal clear that he had stayed well away from all those vices which he asked others to abstain from. He had no stains on him of which he wanted others to remain free. Shu'ayb also practised all those acts of goodness to which he invited others. All this was sufficient to establish that Shu'ayb was fully sincere about his mission.

(89) My people! Let not your opposition to me lead you to guilt that would bring upon you the chastisement that struck earlier the people of Noah, and the people of Hūd, and the people of Ṣāliḥ. And the land of the people of Lot is not far from you![100] (90) Seek the forgiveness of your Lord and turn to Him in repentance. Surely my Lord is Ever Merciful, Most Loving.'[101]

(91) They said: 'O Shu'ayb! We do not understand much of what you say.[102] Indeed we see you weak in our midst. Were it not for your kinsmen, we would surely have stoned you for you have no strength to overpower us.'[103]

وَيَٰقَوْمِ لَا يَجْرِمَنَّكُمْ شِقَاقِىٓ أَن
يُصِيبَكُم مِّثْلُ مَآ أَصَابَ قَوْمَ نُوحٍ
أَوْ قَوْمَ هُودٍ أَوْ قَوْمَ صَٰلِحٍ وَمَا قَوْمُ لُوطٍ
مِّنكُم بِبَعِيدٍ ﴿٨٩﴾ وَٱسْتَغْفِرُوا۟
رَبَّكُمْ ثُمَّ تُوبُوٓا۟ إِلَيْهِ إِنَّ رَبِّى
رَحِيمٌ وَدُودٌ ﴿٩٠﴾ قَالُوا۟ يَٰشُعَيْبُ
مَا نَفْقَهُ كَثِيرًا مِّمَّا تَقُولُ وَإِنَّا لَنَرَىٰكَ
فِينَا ضَعِيفًا وَلَوْلَا رَهْطُكَ لَرَجَمْنَٰكَ
وَمَآ أَنتَ عَلَيْنَا بِعَزِيزٍ ﴿٩١﴾

100. Shu'ayb reminded his people of the story of the people of Lot (peace be on him). This tragic episode took place not far from where the people of Shu'ayb lived. In addition, it was no more than six or seven centuries previously that the people of Lot were utterly destroyed.

101. God is neither callous nor merciless. He has no enmity towards His own creatures. It cannot even be conceived that God would want to punish people just for the fun of it. It is only when people exceed all reasonable limits and exercise no restraint in their wickedness that God punishes them, and then only reluctantly. He is so prone to forgiveness that no matter how sinful a person may have become, God's mercy encompasses him if only he sincerely repents and turns to God. For God's love and compassion for His creatures is simply immense.

The Prophet (peace be on him) fully illustrated this by two examples. One is that of a man who had a camel carrying his food and water provisions. The camel strays away in a dreary desert. The person continues to search for the

(92) Shuʻayb said: 'My people! Are my kinsmen mightier with you than Allah that you (hold the kinsmen in awe while) you cast Allah behind your back? Surely my Lord encompasses all what you do. (93) My people! Go on working according to your way and I will keep working (according to mine). Soon you will come to know who will be afflicted by a humiliating chastisement, and who is proved a liar. And watch, I shall also watch with you.'

قَالَ يَٰقَوْمِ أَرَهْطِىٓ أَعَزُّ عَلَيْكُم مِّنَ
ٱللَّهِ وَٱتَّخَذْتُمُوهُ وَرَآءَكُمْ ظِهْرِيًّا ۖ إِنَّ
رَبِّى بِمَا تَعْمَلُونَ مُحِيطٌ ﴿٩٢﴾ وَيَٰقَوْمِ
ٱعْمَلُوا۟ عَلَىٰ مَكَانَتِكُمْ إِنِّى عَٰمِلٌ ۖ
سَوْفَ تَعْلَمُونَ مَن يَأْتِيهِ عَذَابٌ
يُخْزِيهِ وَمَنْ هُوَ كَٰذِبٌ ۖ
وَٱرْتَقِبُوٓا۟ إِنِّى مَعَكُمْ رَقِيبٌ ﴿٩٣﴾

---

camel until he retires under the shade of a tree in utter despair. Then, suddenly, he finds the camel standing right in front of him. When a sinner repents and turns to God, He is even more joyous than the owner of the camel who suddenly finds his lost beast in a moment of total despair. (See Muslim, *al-Tawbah, Bāb fī al-Ḥadd 'alá al-Tawbah,* traditions 1–8.)

The second example is perhaps even more moving. 'Umar narrated that once a few prisoners of war were brought to the Prophet (peace be on him). One of them was a woman whose infant child had been left behind. Her motherly compassion overwhelmed her to such an extent that she would grab any baby she could lay her hands on, would clasp him to her bosom, and start suckling him. When the Prophet (peace be on him) saw that woman in such a state of mind he asked the Companions whether they thought she would cast her children into fire. The Companions replied in the negative. They said that rather than throw her children into a fire, she would make every possible effort lest they slide into it. The Prophet (peace be on him) added: 'God is even more merciful to His servants than this woman is to her child.' (Muslim, *al-Tawbah, Bāb Sa'at Raḥmat Allāh* – Ed.)

A little reflection may help one appreciate that it is God Who has created compassion in the hearts of parents for their children. Had God not created this compassion for children, their parents may, in fact, have been quite inimical to them. For a child is indeed one of the greatest causes of parents' discomfort and annoyance. If one remembers that it is God Who planted love and compassion for children in the hearts of parents it is quite easy to grasp the extent of God's love and compassion for His creatures.

(94) And when Our command came to pass, We delivered Shu'ayb and those who shared his faith, through Our mercy, and the Blast seized those who were engaged in wrong-doing, so they lay lifeless in their homes (95) as though they had never dwelt in them before.

Lo! Away with (the people of) Midian, even as the Thamūd were done away with!

وَلَمَّا جَآءَ أَمْرُنَا نَجَّيْنَا شُعَيْبًا وَٱلَّذِينَ
ءَامَنُوا۟ مَعَهُۥ بِرَحْمَةٍ مِّنَّا وَأَخَذَتِ ٱلَّذِينَ
ظَلَمُوا۟ ٱلصَّيْحَةُ فَأَصْبَحُوا۟ فِى دِيَٰرِهِمْ
جَٰثِمِينَ ﴿٩٤﴾ كَأَن لَّمْ يَغْنَوْا۟ فِيهَآ ۗ أَلَا
بُعْدًا لِّمَدْيَنَ كَمَا بَعِدَتْ ثَمُودُ ﴿٩٥﴾

---

102. When Shu'ayb's people stated that they did not understand much of what Shu'ayb said, they did not say so because Shu'ayb (peace be on him) spoke in some foreign language, or because he talked in an ambiguous or complicated manner. On the contrary, Shu'ayb's teaching was quite clear and simple and was conveyed to his people in a language they fully understood – their own. The difficulty in understanding Shu'ayb's teaching arose from the fact that his people had become simply too perverse to grasp it.

It is always the case that when some people become fully seized by their prejudice, are overpowered by their lusts, or begin to move vehemently in one particular intellectual direction, they hardly have the patience to give ear to any idea which is different from their own. But even if they were to listen to any unfamiliar idea, it would only sound to them as gibberish, as something coming to them from some other planet.

103. It should be borne in mind that exactly the same situation that had obtained in the past among the people of Shu'ayb also obtained in Makka at the time these verses were revealed. The Quraysh were seething with enmity towards Prophet Muḥammad (peace be on him) and wanted to put an end to his life in much the same way as Shu'ayb's people were inimical to him. The only reason which prevented the Quraysh from violently laying their hands on the Prophet (peace be on him) was that his clan, Hāshim, stood firmly behind him.

Thus, the story of Shu'ayb in relation to his people was exactly the same as that of Prophet Muḥammad (peace be on him) in relation to the Quraysh. The

(96) And indeed We sent Moses with Our signs and with a clear authority (97) to Pharaoh and his nobles. But they obeyed the command of Pharaoh even though Pharaoh's command was not rightly-directed. (98) He shall stand at the head of his people on the Day of Resurrection, and will bring them down to the Fire.[104] What a wretched destination to be led to! (99) They were pursued by a curse in this world and so will they be on the Day of Resurrection. What an evil reward will they receive!

وَلَقَدْ أَرْسَلْنَا مُوسَىٰ بِـَٔايَـٰتِنَا وَسُلْطَـٰنٍ
مُّبِينٍ ﴿٩٦﴾ إِلَىٰ فِرْعَوْنَ وَمَلَإِي۟هِۦ
فَٱتَّبَعُوٓا۟ أَمْرَ فِرْعَوْنَ ۖ وَمَآ أَمْرُ فِرْعَوْنَ
بِرَشِيدٍ ﴿٩٧﴾ يَقْدُمُ قَوْمَهُۥ يَوْمَ ٱلْقِيَـٰمَةِ
فَأَوْرَدَهُمُ ٱلنَّارَ ۖ وَبِئْسَ ٱلْوِرْدُ
ٱلْمَوْرُودُ ﴿٩٨﴾ وَأُتْبِعُوا۟ فِى هَـٰذِهِۦ
لَعْنَةً وَيَوْمَ ٱلْقِيَـٰمَةِ ۚ بِئْسَ ٱلرِّفْدُ
ٱلْمَرْفُودُ ﴿٩٩﴾

---

story of Shu'ayb is narrated here precisely because of the obvious resemblance it bears to the predicament of Prophet Muḥammad (peace be on him).

Soon we will also come across (see verse 93) a very instructive statement of Shu'ayb's in response to the harsh expression of hostility (see verse 91). The implication is quite clear. The same statement would be addressed by Muḥammad (peace be on him) to his own unbelieving people.

104. It clearly emerges from this verse as well as from other verses of the Qur'ān that those who lead a nation or a group of people in the present world will also be their leaders on the Day of Resurrection. If the leaders had directed their people to truth, virtue and righteousness their followers will gather under their banner on the Day of Resurrection and will march to Paradise under their leadership. On the other hand, if these leaders called their people to erroneous beliefs, to immorality, or to false ways of conduct, they will continue to follow them even on the Day of Resurrection and until they end up in Hell. This seems evident from the remark made by the Prophet (peace be on him) about Imr al-Qays: 'Imr al-Qays will bear the standard of the poets of *Jāhilīyah* to the Fire.' (Aḥmad ibn Ḥanbal, *Musnad,* vol. 2, p. 228 – Ed.)

Now everyone can visualize what kind of procession both these would be, each pressing on to their destined goal. There would be the procession of those who had been misled by their so-called leaders. On that Day they would be

(100) That is an account of some towns which We recount to you. Of them some are still standing and some have been mown down. (101) We did not wrong them; it is rather they who wronged themselves. And when the command of your Lord came to pass, the gods besides Allah whom they had called upon, did not avail them in the least. They added nothing to them except ruin.

(102) Such is the seizing of your Lord that when He does seize the towns immersed in wrong-doing, His seizing is painful, terrible. (103) Surely in that is a sign for him who fears the chastisement of the Hereafter.[105] That will be a Day when all men shall be mustered together; that will be a Day when whatever happens shall be witnessed by all. (104) Nor shall We withhold it except till an appointed term.▶

ذَٰلِكَ مِنْ أَنۢبَآءِ ٱلْقُرَىٰ نَقُصُّهُۥ عَلَيْكَ
مِنْهَا قَآئِمٌ وَحَصِيدٌ ﴿١٠٠﴾ وَمَا
ظَلَمْنَـٰهُمْ وَلَـٰكِن ظَلَمُوٓا۟ أَنفُسَهُمْ فَمَآ
أَغْنَتْ عَنْهُمْ ءَالِهَتُهُمُ ٱلَّتِى يَدْعُونَ
مِن دُونِ ٱللَّهِ مِن شَىْءٍ لَّمَّا جَآءَ أَمْرُ رَبِّكَ
وَمَا زَادُوهُمْ غَيْرَ تَتْبِيبٍ ﴿١٠١﴾ وَكَذَٰلِكَ
أَخْذُ رَبِّكَ إِذَآ أَخَذَ ٱلْقُرَىٰ وَهِىَ ظَـٰلِمَةٌ
إِنَّ أَخْذَهُۥٓ أَلِيمٌ شَدِيدٌ ﴿١٠٢﴾ إِنَّ فِى ذَٰلِكَ
لَءَايَةً لِّمَنْ خَافَ عَذَابَ ٱلْـَٔاخِرَةِ ذَٰلِكَ
يَوْمٌ مَّجْمُوعٌ لَّهُ ٱلنَّاسُ وَذَٰلِكَ يَوْمٌ
مَّشْهُودٌ ﴿١٠٣﴾ وَمَا نُؤَخِّرُهُۥٓ إِلَّا
لِأَجَلٍ مَّعْدُودٍ ﴿١٠٤﴾

fully conscious of the dangerous end to which they would be in due course dragged. They would, therefore, quite naturally look upon those leaders as the ones responsible for all their suffering and misfortune. In the front line of the procession would be the so-called leaders and behind them would be throngs of their followers hurling abuses and curses at them. In sharp contrast, will be the other procession, the one led by those whose leadership made their followers merit entry into Paradise. With this blissful end in view, the followers will joyously press ahead, lavishing prayers and grateful tributes on their leaders.

105. In such incidents of history there are instructive signs for all people. Only a little reflection will make them realize that the punishment of the unrighteous is inevitable and that the information provided by the Prophets (peace be on them) in this respect is absolutely true. These signs can also help men have some idea of how horrible the Day of Judgement will be. This realization is likely to create in man's heart a fear which will direct him to righteous behaviour.

One may well ask, what are the signs in human history which indicate that there is an After-life, one in which people are liable to suffer punishment? These signs can easily be appreciated by those who do not consider history to consist merely of a series of unrelated events and who are inclined to reflect over the underlying logic of those events and so derive some conclusion from them. What is most conspicuous in the long record of history is the constantly recurring phenomenon of the rise and fall of nations. Moreover, this rise and fall seems to be tied up with certain moral factors. The way in which certain nations have encountered significant falls and have suffered destruction clearly indicates that man, in this universe, is under a dispensation in which blind physical laws do not predominate. Instead, under that dispensation a moral law is also in operation. The result is that the nations which maintain a given minimum level of adherence to moral principles are rewarded. Those who slide below that minimum level of adherence to moral principles, are granted a temporary respite. However, once a nation falls perceptibly below that minimum level, it meets its tragic end and is made a lesson of for future generations. The occurrence and repetition of these events at regular intervals leaves no doubt whatsoever that retribution is a permanent feature, a fully-fledged law that operates in human history.

Moreover, were one to carefully reflect upon the different forms of punishment which visited these different nations of the world, one would also realize that those punishments only partially accord with the requirements of justice and retribution. Were total justice to be meted out, it would be necessary to do a great deal more. For the punishments which struck the nations of the world in the past, struck only those generations which lived at the time when the punishment visited them. But there are generations of men who sowed the wind of wickedness but disappeared when that wind developed into a whirlwind. The consequences of their evil deeds were faced by the generations that followed after them. It is obvious in this case that the real culprits escaped retribution.

Now, if we are able to grasp the inner workings of this universe by our study of history, this should lead us to the conclusion that the unfulfilled requirements of justice call for a new order of existence to be brought into being. It is only then that those transgressors and wrong-doers who escaped divine punishment in the worldly life can be duly punished and their punishment will be much more severe than that suffered by the evil-doers in the world. (See *Towards Understanding the Qur'ān*, vol. III, *al-A'rāf* 7, n. 30, pp. 23–6 and vol. IV, *Yūnus* 10, n. 10, p. 9.)

(105) And when the appointed Day comes, no one shall even dare to speak except by the leave of Allah.[106] Then some will be declared wretched, others blessed. (106) As for the wretched, they shall be in the Fire, and in it they shall sigh and groan. (107) They shall abide in it as long as the heavens and the earth endure,[107] unless your Lord may will otherwise. Surely your Lord does whatsoever He wills.[108] (108) And as for those who are blessed, they shall abide in the Garden as long as the heavens and the earth endure, unless your Lord may will otherwise.[109] They shall enjoy an unceasing gift.

يَوْمَ يَأْتِ لَا تَكَلَّمُ نَفْسٌ إِلَّا بِإِذْنِهِۦ
فَمِنْهُمْ شَقِيٌّ وَسَعِيدٌ ﴿١٠٥﴾ فَأَمَّا ٱلَّذِينَ
شَقُوا۟ فَفِى ٱلنَّارِ لَهُمْ فِيهَا زَفِيرٌ وَشَهِيقٌ
﴿١٠٦﴾ خَـٰلِدِينَ فِيهَا مَا دَامَتِ ٱلسَّمَـٰوَٰتُ
وَٱلْأَرْضُ إِلَّا مَا شَآءَ رَبُّكَ إِنَّ رَبَّكَ فَعَّالٌ
لِّمَا يُرِيدُ ﴿١٠٧﴾ ۞ وَأَمَّا ٱلَّذِينَ سُعِدُوا۟
فَفِى ٱلْجَنَّةِ خَـٰلِدِينَ فِيهَا مَا دَامَتِ
ٱلسَّمَـٰوَٰتُ وَٱلْأَرْضُ إِلَّا مَا شَآءَ رَبُّكَ
عَطَآءً غَيْرَ مَجْذُوذٍ ﴿١٠٨﴾

---

106. Some people entertain the misconception that their saintly patrons will intercede on their behalf and obtain salvation for them on the Day of Resurrection. They believe that some of the saints will simply stage a sit-in protest before God, and will thus virtually extract from Him a pardon for their devotees. All this, of course, is sheer nonsense. For in God's majestic court, everyone – howsoever great they may otherwise be, including angels – will be in a state of spellbinding awe. At that awe-inspiring moment – the Day of Judgement – none will even dare speak until God Himself permits him to do so.

There are of course many in this world who make offerings at the altars of many beside God in the belief that they will simply have an overwhelming influence with God. Many people continue to commit misdeeds in the hope that the intercession of such beings will bring about their rescue. Such people will face utter disappointment on that Day.

107. There are two possible interpretations for the words, 'as long as the heavens and the earth endure'. One possibility is that they refer to the heavens

(109) [O Prophet!] Have no doubt about what they worship. For they worship what their fathers worshipped before.[110] And (yet) We shall grant them their due portion in full, diminishing of it nothing.

فَلَا تَكُ فِي مِرْيَةٍ مِّمَّا يَعْبُدُ هَٰٓؤُلَآءِ مَا يَعْبُدُونَ إِلَّا كَمَا يَعْبُدُ ءَابَآؤُهُم مِّن قَبْلُ وَإِنَّا لَمُوَفُّوهُمْ نَصِيبَهُمْ غَيْرَ مَنقُوصٍ ﴿١٠٩﴾

and the earth of the Next World. The other possibility is that they have been used figuratively to convey the idea of perpetuity. One thing, however, is quite certain: these words do not refer to the present heavens and earth, because the Qur'ān makes it quite clear that these would be totally transformed on the Last Day. (See *Ibrāhīm* 14: 48 – Ed.) As for the events being referred to in the present verse, they quite obviously belong to the Next Life.

108. There is no power other than God's that can prevent the sinners from suffering eternal punishment. However, God may Himself will that someone may be spared His unending punishment. He may also decide to pardon such a person after he has been made to suffer a period of punishment in the After-life. In such cases, God certainly has both the authority and the power to do that. For if there is any law, it is God Who has made it, and hence that law can set no limit upon His power and authority.

109. A person's permanent stay in Paradise is equally not contingent upon some higher law that would compel God to facilitate this. On the contrary, people will be able to stay there permanently only by dint of God's grace and mercy. If God were to act otherwise, He obviously has both the power and the authority to do so.

110. This does not mean that the Prophet (peace be on him) entertained any 'doubts' concerning the deities whom the unbelievers associated with God in His divinity. Though this verse is ostensibly addressed to the Prophet (peace be on him), it is really aimed at conveying a message to the people of Makka. The thrust of the verse is that no sensible person should entertain the notion that those who worship false gods and pray to them have any plausible grounds for doing so and for expecting some benefit from such worship.

The fact of the matter is that the worship of false deities and the offerings, sacrifices and invocations addressed to them were supported neither by knowledge, careful observation, nor any scientific experimentation. The only basis for such worship was blind imitation of their ancestors. The same shrines

(110) And We certainly gave Moses the Book before, and there arose disagreements about it (even as there are disagreements now about the Book revealed to you).[111] Had it not been for a decree that had already gone forth from your Lord, the matter would have long been decided between them.[112] Indeed they are in a disquieting doubt about it. (111) Surely your Lord will recompense all to the full for their deeds. For indeed He is well aware of all what they do.▶

وَلَقَدْ ءَاتَيْنَا مُوسَى ٱلْكِتَٰبَ
فَٱخْتُلِفَ فِيهِ وَلَوْلَا كَلِمَةٌ سَبَقَتْ
مِن رَّبِّكَ لَقُضِىَ بَيْنَهُمْ وَإِنَّهُمْ لَفِى
شَكٍّ مِّنْهُ مُرِيبٍ ﴿١١٠﴾ وَإِنَّ كُلًّا لَّمَّا
لَيُوَفِّيَنَّهُمْ رَبُّكَ أَعْمَٰلَهُمْ إِنَّهُۥ بِمَا
يَعْمَلُونَ خَبِيرٌ ﴿١١١﴾

---

found amongst today's polytheists were also found among several past nations of the world. The same miraculous feats which are popular today were equally popular in the past among other nations. However, when God's punishment seized those nations which worshipped false deities, they were utterly destroyed. Their shrines proved altogether unavailing.

111. If people launch scurrilous attacks on the Qur'ān, this is not altogether novel. The same happened before. When Moses (peace be on him) was granted the scripture, people raised a variety of objections against it. The Prophet Muḥammad (peace be on him) should not, therefore, feel disheartened that his people rejected the teachings of the Qur'ān despite their lucidity.

112. This is being said in order to comfort the Prophet (peace be on him) and his Companions. They are being asked to be patient and not to seek a hasty judgement from God concerning those who differ about the Qur'ān. For God will soon come forth with His judgement. He has determined that this judgement will neither come a moment before, nor a moment after the expiry of the term. It is true human beings wish God's judgement to come hastily. As for God, He never judges hastily.

(112) So remain, (O Muḥammad), you and those who have returned with you (to the fold of faith and obedience from unbelief and rebellion) steadfast (in adhering to the straight way) as you were commanded. And do not exceed the limits of (service to Allah). For certainly He is aware of all what you do. (113) And do not incline towards the wrong-doers lest the Fire might seize you and you will have none as your protector against Allah; and then you will not be helped from anywhere. (114) And establish the Prayer at the two ends of the day and in the first hours of the night.[113] Indeed the good deeds drive away the evil deeds. This is a Reminder to those who are mindful of Allah.[114] (115) And be patient; for indeed Allah never lets the reward of those who do good go to waste.

فَاسْتَقِمْ كَمَآ أُمِرْتَ وَمَن تَابَ مَعَكَ
وَلَا تَطْغَوْا۟ إِنَّهُۥ بِمَا تَعْمَلُونَ بَصِيرٌ
﴿١١٢﴾ وَلَا تَرْكَنُوٓا۟ إِلَى ٱلَّذِينَ ظَلَمُوا۟
فَتَمَسَّكُمُ ٱلنَّارُ وَمَا لَكُم مِّن
دُونِ ٱللَّهِ مِنْ أَوْلِيَآءَ ثُمَّ
لَا تُنصَرُونَ ﴿١١٣﴾ وَأَقِمِ ٱلصَّلَوٰةَ
طَرَفَىِ ٱلنَّهَارِ وَزُلَفًا مِّنَ ٱلَّيْلِ إِنَّ
ٱلْحَسَنَٰتِ يُذْهِبْنَ ٱلسَّيِّـَٔاتِ ذَٰلِكَ
ذِكْرَىٰ لِلذَّٰكِرِينَ ﴿١١٤﴾ وَٱصْبِرْ فَإِنَّ
ٱللَّهَ لَا يُضِيعُ أَجْرَ ٱلْمُحْسِنِينَ ﴿١١٥﴾

113. The 'two ends of the day' refer to the morning and the sunset. Similarly, the 'first hours of the night' refer to the time of the *'Ishā'* Prayer. We thus learn that this Qur'ānic verse dates back to the time when the five daily Prayers had as yet not been prescribed. The Prophet's ascension took place at a later time than the revelation of these verses and it is then that the five daily Prayers were prescribed. (For further explanation see *al-Isrā'* 17, n. 95; *Ṭā Hā* 20: 111; and *al-Rūm* 30: 124.)

(116) Why were there not, out of the generations that passed away before you, righteous men who would forbid others from causing corruption on the earth? And if such were there, they were only a few whom We had saved from those generations, or else the wrong-doers kept pursuing the ease and comfort which had been conferred upon them, thus losing themselves in sinfulness. (117) And your Lord is not such as would wrongfully destroy human habitations while their inhabitants are righteous.[115] ▶

فَلَوْلَا كَانَ مِنَ ٱلْقُرُونِ مِن قَبْلِكُمْ
أُوْلُواْ بَقِيَّةٍ يَنْهَوْنَ عَنِ ٱلْفَسَادِ فِى
ٱلْأَرْضِ إِلَّا قَلِيلًا مِّمَّنْ أَنجَيْنَا
مِنْهُمْ وَٱتَّبَعَ ٱلَّذِينَ ظَلَمُواْ
مَآ أُتْرِفُواْ فِيهِ وَكَانُواْ مُجْرِمِينَ
١١٦ وَمَا كَانَ رَبُّكَ لِيُهْلِكَ
ٱلْقُرَىٰ بِظُلْمٍ وَأَهْلُهَا
مُصْلِحُونَ ١١٧

114. The Qur'ān informs the believers of the best way to drive away the evils which are rampant in the world and how to obliterate the wrongs perpetuated by the inveterate enemies of Islam. It counsels the believers to become increasingly righteous. For the righteousness of the believers will ultimately overwhelm evil and corruption. Now, since Prayers constantly remind people of God, they are the best means of making people righteous. The power that the believers receive from Prayer will not only enable them to repulse the onslaught of the organized forces of evil, but also to establish a righteous and benevolent order in the world. (For further elaboration see *al-'Ankabūt* 29, nn. 77–9.)

115. These verses bring out, in a significantly instructive manner, the real factors which caused the destruction of those nations whose history has been narrated earlier (see verse 36 ff. above). Reviewing that history, the Qur'ān points out the single common denominator of all those nations which met their doom in the past. All those nations had formerly been favoured with God's blessings. But drunk with affluence, they resorted to mischief on earth. Their collective conscience was also completely vitiated. The result was that no righteous person was left among them to prevent them from committing evils. And if any such person did exist, their number was either too small, or their voice too feeble to prevent evils from predominating. This situation eventually

(118) Had your Lord so
willed, He would surely have
made mankind one commun-
ity. But as things stand, now
they will not cease to differ
among themselves and to
follow erroneous ways (119)
except for those on whom
your Lord has mercy. And it is
for this (exercise of freedom
of choice) that He has created
them.[116] And the word of your
Lord was fulfilled: 'Indeed I
will fill the Hell, with men and
jinn, altogether.'

وَلَوۡ شَآءَ رَبُّكَ لَجَعَلَ ٱلنَّاسَ أُمَّةٗ وَٰحِدَةٗۖ
وَلَا يَزَالُونَ مُخۡتَلِفِينَ ﴿١١٨﴾ إِلَّا مَن
رَّحِمَ رَبُّكَۚ وَلِذَٰلِكَ خَلَقَهُمۡۗ وَتَمَّتۡ
كَلِمَةُ رَبِّكَ لَأَمۡلَأَنَّ جَهَنَّمَ مِنَ
ٱلۡجِنَّةِ وَٱلنَّاسِ أَجۡمَعِينَ ﴿١١٩﴾

invited God's wrath upon them. Had they not been so evil, there was no reason why God should punish them. After all, He bears no such grudge against His creatures that would prompt Him to punish people even when they act righteously.

The above statement is intended to underscore three points. Firstly, that it is imperative that there should always be a good number of righteous people in every society; those who would invite people to righteousness and prevent them from evil. For God likes to see that there is righteousness in the world. And if God does tolerate the existence of evil in human society, He does so since the potential for righteousness continues to exist in that society. But such tolerance endures only as long as that potential remains. However, if the condition of a community deteriorates, rendering it altogether devoid of good people, or if the good people in that community become an insignificant minority, too weak to prevent it from proceeding along its evil ways, then God's chastisement begins to loom large over it. That much can be said for sure. However, it is difficult to say with any precision when God's chastisement will actually smite that community and destroy it.

Secondly, a community that is prepared to put up with everything except a group of righteous people in its midst – people that call men to do good and forbid them from doing evil – is certainly destined for self-destruction. The attitude of that community clearly shows that it cherishes all that would lead to its destruction, and that it is intolerant of all that would ensure its survival.

Thirdly, God's final decision whether to punish a community or not depends on the extent to which that community is possessed of the elements that would

(120) (O Muḥammad!) We narrate these anecdotes of Messengers to you that We may strengthen through them your heart. In these anecdotes come to you the truth, and an exhortation, and a reminder for the believers. (121) As for those who are bent on not believing, tell them: 'Work according to your way and we are working according to our way. (122) And do wait for the end of things; we too are waiting. (123) All that is hidden in the heavens and the earth lies within the power of Allah. To Him are all matters referred for judgement. So do serve Him, and place in Him all your trust. Your Lord is not heedless of what you do.'[117]

وَكُلًّا نَّقُصُّ عَلَيْكَ مِنْ أَنۢبَآءِ ٱلرُّسُلِ مَا
نُثَبِّتُ بِهِۦ فُؤَادَكَ ۚ وَجَآءَكَ فِى هَٰذِهِ
ٱلْحَقُّ وَمَوْعِظَةٌ وَذِكْرَىٰ لِلْمُؤْمِنِينَ
﴿١٢٠﴾ وَقُل لِّلَّذِينَ لَا يُؤْمِنُونَ ٱعْمَلُوا۟ عَلَىٰ
مَكَانَتِكُمْ إِنَّا عَٰمِلُونَ ﴿١٢١﴾ وَٱنتَظِرُوٓا۟
إِنَّا مُنتَظِرُونَ ﴿١٢٢﴾ وَلِلَّهِ غَيْبُ ٱلسَّمَٰوَٰتِ
وَٱلْأَرْضِ وَإِلَيْهِ يُرْجَعُ ٱلْأَمْرُ كُلُّهُۥ
فَٱعْبُدْهُ وَتَوَكَّلْ عَلَيْهِ ۚ وَمَا رَبُّكَ
بِغَٰفِلٍ عَمَّا تَعْمَلُونَ ﴿١٢٣﴾

---

enable it to respond to the call of truth. If it has such people in good numbers that would suffice to extirpate evil and establish a righteous order, such a community is spared the kind of chastisement which embraces whole communities and totally destroys them. If it is subjected to some partial rather than an all-embracing chastisement, the purpose of it is to enable its righteous elements to mend their ways.

It is possible, however, that in spite of continued efforts, the community will be unable to throw up a sufficient number of good people needed to bring about its reform. It is also possible that the community will demonstrate by its action that it is full of corrupt people and altogether bereft of virtuous ones. The community, in such a case, has obviously become a heap of coal in which no diamonds are left. When such a stage is reached God causes a fire to erupt, a fire that reduces this heap of coal to a heap of ashes. (For further elaboration see *al-Dhāriyāt* 51, n. 34.)

116. This is being said in order to remove misconceptions which are often put forward under the appellation 'fate'.

The explanation of the destruction of those ancient nations mentioned above is liable to give rise to serious objections. For, in the context of the above explanation it might be pointed out that the non-existence of righteous persons in a nation, or their existence in very small numbers, depends entirely on God's will. If such is the case, how can any blame be directed at those nations? For, after all, why did God not create a large number of good people in those nations?

In the course of clarifying this misconception, it is pointed out here that God's will with regard to human beings does not consist of binding them to follow an inalterable course of conduct in the manner of plants, animals and other similar living beings who, as we know, have no choice except to follow the course determined for them either by the laws of nature or their instincts. Had such been the case, there would be no point in inviting human beings to believe, to raise Prophets, to reveal scriptures. All human beings would have been born as ones who would believe and submit to God's command. However, it was God's will regarding man that he should be granted free will and be vested with the power to follow the ways of his choice. It was God's will that the ways leading both to Paradise and Hell should remain open to him, and that everyone be provided with the opportunity to make a choice between them. Thus, whatever one is able to acquire is the fruit of his own labour.

Now, the very scheme of man's creation consists of granting him free will and providing the opportunity to choose between belief and unbelief. In such a case it is simply inconceivable that a nation would wilfully decide to go astray and God compel it to righteousness. If a nation decides to set up a system that produces rogues who try to excel one another in their evil, wrong-doing and sin, how can God forcibly direct them, by means of His direct interference, to the course of righteousness? Such an interference is simply not a part of God's scheme of things. Members of a community become good or bad as a result of the measures taken by that nation itself. But a time may come when a community immerses itself so deeply in evil that no sizeable group of good people are left in it to champion righteousness. Alternatively, the social system of that community may be so geared as to leave no room for reform. When such a stage is reached, God simply lets that community proceed to the tragic end that it has chosen for itself.

Those nations which deserve God's mercy are possessed of altogether different characteristics. Such nations abound in persons who respond to the call of righteousness. Moreover, their social values make it possible for righteous people to carry on their efforts to bring about reform. (For further elaboration see *Towards Understanding the Qur'ān,* vol. II, *al-An'ām* 6, n. 24, pp. 228–9.)

117. God is cognizant of all that is being done by the two parties engaged in the encounter between belief and unbelief. It is simply inconceivable that there should be chaos and disorder in God's realm. For God's realm is not the realm of a negligent, heedless sovereign who is unaware of what is going on. However, since God is Wise and Forbearing, He does not resort to punishing

people hastily. However, justice is eventually meted out and those who deserve punishment are ultimately punished. Thus, all those who are engaged in the effort to bring about reform, should feel reassured that their efforts will not be wasted.

On the other hand, there are also those who are engaged in making and perpetuating mischief, who have focused all their efforts on brutally persecuting reformers and suppressing their reform efforts. Such people should know that all their evil deeds are known to God, and that they will be made to pay very dearly for these misdeeds.

Sūrah 12

Yūsuf

(Joseph)

(Makkan Period)

Period of Revelation

Upon examination of the contents of this *sūrah,* it would appear that it was probably revealed in the last phase of the Prophet's life in Makka. At that time the Quraysh were considering ways of how to get over the threat posed by the Prophet (peace be on him): whether to kill, or banish, or imprison him.

At the same time, probably at the instigation of the Jews, some of the Makkans tried to test whether the Prophet (peace be on him) derived his knowledge from on high or not. To this end they asked him: what caused the Israelites to migrate to Egypt? They asked this question because the Arabs were unfamiliar with the story; there was no trace of it in their historical traditions. More importantly, the Prophet (peace be on him) had not referred to it before.

The Makkans, therefore, thought that there were only two possibilities. One, that the Prophet (peace be on him) would answer the question but would fail to answer it in detail. The other possibility was that under one pretext or the other, he would try to defer answering the question so as to gain time. They also thought that the Prophet (peace be on him) would subsequently solicit help from some of the Jews and this would inevitably and completely expose him. It would then become clear to all that he had no access to the Divine source of knowledge.

But the result of the test was quite contrary to their expectations. For God enabled the Prophet (peace be on him) to narrate the whole story of

Joseph then and there. Not only that but the story was wholly applicable to the contemporary situation of the Quraysh. It showed that the Quraysh were playing the role of Joseph's brothers.

Main Objectives of the Sūrah

The story was revealed to achieve two main objectives. Firstly, in order to provide proof that would establish Muḥammad's claim to be a Prophet. It was also significant that the evidence which was being provided was proof asked for by the opponents themselves rather than proof which was volunteered by the Prophet (peace be on him). Thus, it was possible to establish, by the test which the Prophet's opponents had themselves proposed, that his source of knowledge was revelation rather than hearsay. This purpose is spelled out firstly in verses 3 and 7, and quite forcefully again in verses 102–3.

The second purpose in revealing this *sūrah* was to highlight the close resemblance of Prophet Joseph's and his brothers' story, with the situation then pertaining in Makka. The resemblance was so close that the very narration of Joseph's story amounted to a reminder to the Quraysh that their attitude towards the Prophet (peace be on him) was similar to that of Joseph's brothers. Now, Joseph's brothers failed to defeat God's plan. Instead, they lay humbled at the feet of their brother, a brother whom once they had callously cast into a pit. The implication being that the Quraysh will meet a similar end; their machinations against God's plan will be reduced to naught. A time will come when the Quraysh, in the manner of Joseph's brothers, will also be forced to beg for the mercy of the same brother whom they were once bent on annihilating. This purpose has also been set forth in the very opening part of this *sūrah* (see verse 7) where it has been said: 'Verily in the story of Joseph and his brothers there are many signs for those who inquire (about the truth).'

By linking the story of Prophet Joseph (peace be on him) to the encounter between Prophet Muḥammad (peace be on him) and the Quraysh, the Qur'ān virtually prophesied what was going to happen. The events which unfolded during the ten years following the revelation of this *sūrah,* represent the fulfilment of that prophesy.

One year and a half or two years after the revelation of this *sūrah* the Quraysh hatched a conspiracy against the Prophet (peace be on him). They did so in a manner reminiscent of the conspiracy of Joseph's brothers. Like Joseph's brothers, the Quraysh attempted to assassinate the Prophet (peace be on him). To ensure the security of his life he was forced to migrate from Makka. Then again, during his exile, the Prophet (peace be on him) was able to gain ascendancy and power in a manner that reminds one of Joseph (peace be on him). What happened to the Makkans on the occasion of the conquest of Makka was exactly the same as had befallen Joseph's brothers on their last appearance before him in the capital of Egypt. Joseph's brothers begged him to show them mercy. In a pitiable predicament they stood before Joseph (peace be on him), imploring: 'So give us corn in full measure and give it to us in charity. Allah rewards those who are charitable' (*Yūsuf* 12: 88). Although Joseph (peace be on him) had the power to avenge himself, he pardoned them, saying: 'No blame lies with you today. May Allah forgive you. He is the Most Merciful of all those who are merciful' (*Yūsuf* 12: 92).

After the conquest of Makka, the vanquished Quraysh also stood humbled before Prophet Muḥammad (peace be on him). The Prophet (peace be on him) also had full power to avenge himself. Instead, he inquired of them: 'How am I going to treat you?' They replied: 'You are a magnanimous brother and the son of a magnanimous brother.' To this the Prophet replied: 'I say to you what Joseph said to his brothers: "No blame lies with you today. May Allah forgive you. He is the most Merciful of all those who are merciful." You may go, all of you are free.' (Al-Wāqidī, *al-Maghāzī*, vol. 2, p. 835 – Ed.)

Main Themes

The two subjects mentioned above constitute the main themes of the *ah*. However, like other stories in the Qur'ān, the present story has not been narrated either for the sake of story-telling, nor just for the recording of historical facts. Instead, the story has been used as a means to effectively communicate the basic message of the Qur'ān.

This story also brings into sharp relief the fact that the religion of Prophets Abraham, Isaac, Jacob and Joseph (peace be on them) was the same as preached by Prophet Muḥammad (peace be on him). Those Prophets had earlier invited people to exactly the same basic teachings to which Prophet Muḥammad (peace be on him) invited people in his time.

Through this story the Qur'ān highlights the conduct of Prophets Jacob and Joseph (peace be on them), showing how it contrasts with the character and conduct of Joseph's brothers, of the members of the trading caravan, of the wife of the chief official (*'azīz*), of the upper-class ladies and ruling coterie of Egypt. These contrasting images automatically raise certain questions in the minds of those who notice the difference. For they see, on the one hand, the ideal characters which develop out of belief that one should surrender to the Will of God and have a strong faith in one's accountability in the Hereafter. On the other hand, they see the characters of an altogether different kind, characters moulded by unbelief and ignorance, by excessive worldliness and lack of any concern for God and the Hereafter. Once acquainted with these contrasting traits, everyone is able to ask his conscience: 'Which of these two models is to my liking.'

Through Joseph (peace be on him), the Qur'ān also drives home another profound truth. It underscores that whatever God wills to happen, does indeed come to happen. By his own scheming man can neither succeed in defeating God's plan, nor alter it. In fact, very often man works to execute some of his plans and everything seems to proceed satisfactorily, leading him to believe that he has succeeded in striking his target. But if the plan is not in accord with God's plan, he eventually discovers that all his efforts have been in vain, and that he has, in fact, implemented God's plan rather than his own.

What has been said above is well illustrated by Joseph's story. Joseph's brothers believed that he was the major impediment in the fulfilment of their ambitions. It is for this reason that they cast him into a pit. When that was done, they believed that they had removed that impediment from their way, once and for all. But what actually happened was that they were instrumental in placing Joseph on the first rung of the ladder which would take him to the great heights of eminence which God had destined for him. Furthermore, their behaviour earned them, in the end, utter humiliation and embarrassment. For instead of visiting Joseph (peace be on him) – their brother – in an honourable way, they were compelled by force of circumstance to humble themselves before him and seek pittance from him. Likewise the wife of the Egyptian chief sought to take her revenge on Joseph (peace be on him) by means of his imprisonment. But as future events showed, her action paved the way for Joseph's rise to power and glory. As for her own self, she subsequently had to suffer the embarrassment of publicly confessing her perfidy. By her action she deprived herself of the honour and prestige that she might have enjoyed as the godmother of the ruler of Egypt.

These are not isolated incidents. History is replete with instances which bear out that no one can bring into disgrace anyone upon whom God wants to bestow honour. For God turns the tables against those who plan to humiliate someone whom He wills to honour. The result is that the efforts of such a person's opponents only contribute to his rise and success. As for those who devise hostile schemes, they receive only humiliation and disgrace. Likewise, when God decides to bring about someone's downfall, nothing can sustain him. All attempts to rescue such a person end in failure, and those who engage in such attempts face utter humiliation.

If someone fully grasps this, he will also realize that he should not transgress the bounds laid down by God's Law while pursuing his objectives or devising strategies for that purpose. As for success and failure, they lie solely in God's Hand. However, one who has recourse to fair means to achieve right purposes will at least be spared disgrace and humiliation. On the contrary, those who resort to crooked means to achieve unrighteous purposes, are bound, in any case, to be humiliated in the Next Life, and are even liable to suffer degradation in the present world.

Another lesson to be learned from this story is that man ought to rely on God and ought to turn to Him alone. If those engaged in struggling for the cause of the truth remembered this lesson when faced with severe opposition, they would find much-needed comfort and solace. Moreover, they would no longer feel overawed by the seemingly menacing strategies of their opponents. Thanks to their reliance on God, and their disposition to leave the results of their efforts to Him, they would be able to continue their striving and fulfil their duty.

The greatest lesson of this story, however, is that a true believer, one whose conduct conforms to Islamic ideals and who is also possessed of wisdom is able to conquer a whole country by force of his moral character alone. This is well illustrated by the life of Joseph (peace be on him). A helpless, resourceless youth at the tender age of seventeen, he was sold into slavery in a totally strange land. Joseph's unenviable predicament cannot be exaggerated since we know how miserable was the lot of slaves at that time. What is more, Joseph (peace be on him) was imprisoned for an indefinite period in connection with an offence allegedly involving moral turpitude. From such depths of humiliation Joseph (peace be on him) rose, by dint of his faith and moral excellence, to the great eminence that we all know, and eventually held sway over the whole of Egypt.

Historical and Geographical Context

For a better understanding of this story, let us bear in mind the historical and geographical circumstances prevailing at that time. Joseph was a son of Jacob, a grandson of Isaac, and great-grandson of Abraham (peace be on them all). According to the Biblical account, which is implicitly endorsed by the Qur'ān, Jacob had twelve sons from his four wives. Joseph (peace be on him) and his younger brother Benjamin were born of one wife and the other ten were born of others.

Jacob (peace be on him) was settled in the valley of Hebron, presently called al-Khalīl, in Palestine. Both Isaac and Abraham (peace be on them) had lived there before him. Moreover, Jacob (peace be on him) had some of his property in Shechem, presently known as Nablus.

If we were to accept the findings of Biblical scholars, Joseph (peace be on him) was born in 1906 B.C. The incident mentioned in the present *sūrah* – his dream followed by his being cast into a pit – took place around the year 1890 B.C. At that time Joseph was seventeen years old. As to the pit into which he was thrown, it was situated, according to Biblical and Talmudic traditions, near Dothan to the north of Shechem. The caravan that rescued him from the pit was travelling from Gilead (Transjordan) *en route* to Egypt. The ruins of Gilead can still be seen to the east of the river Jordan in the valley of Elbas.

The 15th dynasty of Hyksos kings ruled Egypt at that time. They were of Arabian descent. Having moved from Palestine and Syria in 3000 B.C. to Egypt, they had seized power in Egypt. Both Arab historians and the commentators of the Qur'ān refer to them as 'Amālīq (Amalekites). This accords with the recent findings of Egyptologists. In Egypt, their position was that of alien invaders who established themselves owing to internal dissensions obtaining in that country. This accounts for why Joseph (peace be on him) rose to political power in their regime. It also accounts for why the Israelites were subsequently and warmly welcomed in Egypt, were settled in the most fertile parts, and became highly influential there. All this is explained in terms of the racial affinity pertaining between them and the alien rulers of Egypt.

The Hyksos continued to rule over Egypt till the end of the fifteenth century B.C. However, during this period, political power actually rested with the Israelites. The Qur'ān refers to God's favour upon them: 'when He raised Prophets amongst you and appointed you the rulers' (*al-Mā'idah* 5: 20). Later on, a massive national uprising took place and led to the overthrow of the Hyksos regime and the banishment of 250,000 Amalekites from Egypt. The Hyksos were replaced by a highly bigoted Coptic dynasty which virtually obliterated every remnant of the Amalekite period. The rulers of this dynasty also embarked upon a brutal oppression of the Israelites the details of which have been mentioned in the Qur'ān in connection with the story of Prophet Moses (peace be on him). (See, for instance, *al-Baqarah* 2: 49 – Ed.)

A study of this period of Egyptian history reveals that the Hyksos did not at any point recognize the Egyptian pantheon of gods and goddesses. They had, instead, brought their own from Syria. They even tried to introduce and popularize their faith in Egypt. This explains why the Qur'ān does not refer to the Egyptian sovereign contemporaneous with Joseph as Pharaoh, basically, because the word 'Pharaoh' had a religious connotation while the Amalekites did not subscribe to Egyptian religious beliefs and practices. The Bible, however, mistakenly refers to them as Pharaohs. Probably the compilers of the Bible believed indiscriminately that all Egyptian rulers were Pharaohs.

MAP RELATING TO THE STORY OF PROPHET JOSEPH

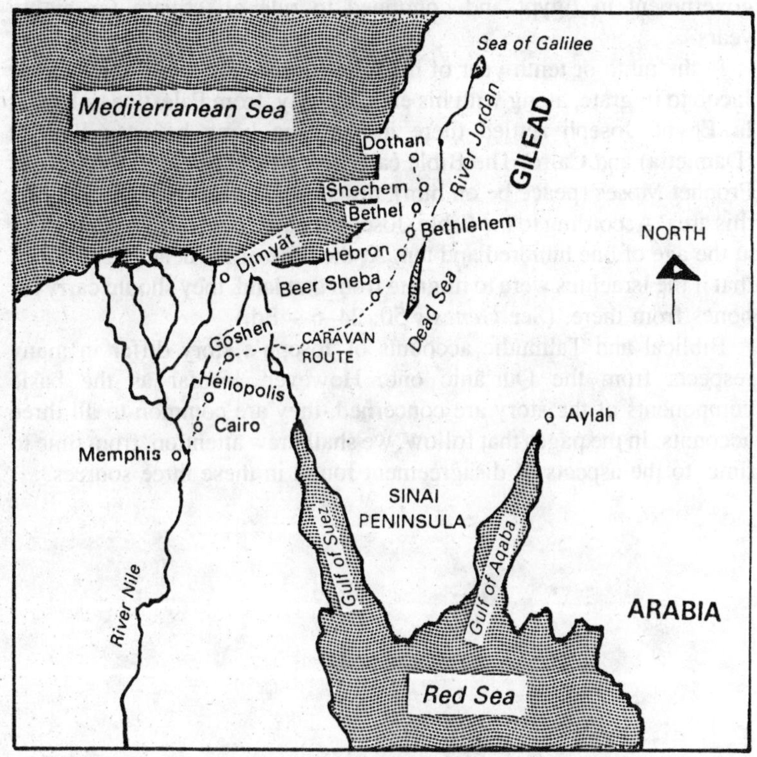

Explanation

1. Dothan is the place where, according to the Old Testament, the brothers of Prophet Joseph 'cast him into a pit'. (Genesis 37: 24.)

2. Shechem is where Prophet Joseph had his ancestral piece of land. It is now called Nablus.

3. Hebron is the place where Prophet Joseph lived. It is now called al-Khalil.

4. Memphis was the capital of ancient Egypt. It is now called Minif.

5. Goshen is where Prophet Joseph settled his father and brothers in Egypt. (Genesis 47: 6, 11.)

Modern scholars who have studied the Bible and Egyptian history from a comparative perspective believe that the king of the Hyksos dynasty, Apophis, was a contemporary of Joseph (peace be on him). Memphis was then the capital of Egypt. Today its ruins are to be found some fourteen miles to the south of Cairo. Joseph arrived there when he was about seventeen or eighteen years of age. He remained in the house of the Egyptian chief official for two to three years and then spent some eight to nine years in prison. At the age of thirty he took control of the government in Egypt and continued to rule effectively for eighty years.

In the ninth or tenth year of his rule, Joseph sent word to his father Jacob to migrate, along with his entire family, from Palestine to Egypt. In Egypt, Joseph settled there in the area lying between Dimyāt (Damietta) and Cairo. The Bible calls this area Goshen. In the time of Prophet Moses (peace be on him), descendants of Joseph still lived in this area. According to the Bible, Joseph (peace be on him) passed away at the age of one hundred and ten. At the time of his death he enjoined that if the Israelites were to migrate from that land, they should carry his bones from there. (See *Genesis* 50: 24–6 – Ed.)

Biblical and Talmudic accounts of Joseph's story differ in many respects from the Qur'ānic one. However, insofar as the basic components of the story are concerned, they are common to all three accounts. In the pages that follow, we shall draw attention, from time to time, to the aspects of disagreement found in these three sources.

In the name of Allah, the Merciful, the Compassionate.

(1) *Alif. Lām. Rā.* These are the verses of a Book that clearly expounds the truth. (2) We have revealed it as a Recitation[1] in Arabic that you [the people of Arabia] – may fully understand.[2] (3) (O Muḥammad!) By revealing the Qur'ān to you We narrate to you in the best manner* the stories of the past although before this narration you were utterly unaware of them.[3]

1. The word 'Qur'ān' is a derivative of the Arabic verb *qara'a* meaning 'to read'. When a verb is used as a noun, it signifies something that embodies that meaning *par excellence*. For example, if we were to call someone 'bravery' rather than 'brave', it would mean that we wish to stress that he and bravery are identical. Hence, the appellation 'Qur'ān' with reference to a book suggests that it is something that is meant to be read or recited over and over again by all – elite and commoners alike.

2. This does not mean that the Qur'ān is specifically addressed to Arabs. The real purpose of the statement is to emphasize to those among whom the Prophet (peace be on him) preached, that the Qur'ān was revealed in Arabic, their own language. That being the case, the Arabs could not therefore shield themselves behind the excuse that they could not fully appreciate its message. The Qur'ān is also characterized by its inimitable features which testify to its Divine provenance. These features could also not escape the attention of those who were native speakers of Arabic.

Some people are inclined to deny the universal character of the Qur'ānic message. In order to prove their point, they are wont to pick upon statements such as the present one. They contend on that basis that the Qur'ān is

*The expression *'aḥsan al-qaṣaṣ'* in the verse has generally been considered to mean 'best stories' – Ed.

(4) Call to mind when Joseph said to his father: 'My father! I saw [in a dream] eleven stars and the sun and the moon: I saw them prostrating themselves before me.' (5) His father said: 'My son! Do not relate your dream to your brothers lest they hatch a plot to harm you.[4] Indeed Satan is man's open enemy.

إِذْ قَالَ يُوسُفُ لِأَبِيهِ يَٰٓأَبَتِ إِنِّي رَأَيْتُ
أَحَدَ عَشَرَ كَوْكَبًا وَٱلشَّمْسَ وَٱلْقَمَرَ
رَأَيْتُهُمْ لِي سَٰجِدِينَ ﴿٤﴾ قَالَ يَٰبُنَيَّ
لَا تَقْصُصْ رُءْيَاكَ عَلَىٰٓ إِخْوَتِكَ
فَيَكِيدُوا۟ لَكَ كَيْدًا ۖ إِنَّ ٱلشَّيْطَٰنَ
لِلْإِنسَٰنِ عَدُوٌّ مُّبِينٌ ﴿٥﴾

exclusively addressed to Arabs and is meant for none other. This is a very superficial statement, however, which shows very little understanding. For, any universal message will have to be expressed in some language of the world. Also, he who has to propagate that message no doubt prefers to start with his own people such that it can firstly be fully understood and secondly, spread onwards; a purpose that can be best achieved by presenting it in that people's language. This is the only natural way for any message or movement to spread and be universalized.

3. As indicated in the introductory remarks, in their bid to expose the falsity of the Prophet (peace be on him) some of the Makkan unbelievers tried to put him to a test. Presumably at the instigation of a few Jews they aimed to surprise the Prophet (peace be on him) by abruptly asking him why the Israelites had migrated to Egypt (see p. 1 ff.). It is because of this background that the Qur'ānic narration of this chapter of Israeli history was prefaced by the statement: '(O Muḥammad!) By revealing the Qur'ān to you we narrate to you in the best manner the stories of the past although before this narration you were utterly unaware of them' (verse 3).

Although this sentence is apparently addressed to the Prophet (peace be on him), it is in fact meant for his opponents who were not convinced that he had acquired his knowledge through revelation.

4. This is a reference to Joseph's ten brothers who were born of his stepmothers. Jacob (peace be on him) was well aware that the stepbrothers were jealous of Joseph. He was also aware that the brothers, lacking the scruples of righteous people, would not hesitate to use any means, howsoever vile, to achieve their selfish aims. Jacob (peace be on him), therefore, thought it necessary to warn Joseph (peace be on him) about them. As for Joseph's

(6) (As you have seen in the dream), so will your Lord choose you[5] (for His task) and will impart to you the comprehension of the deeper meaning of things[6] and will bestow the full measure of His favour upon you and upon the House of Jacob even as He earlier bestowed it in full measure upon your forefathers, Abraham and Isaac. Surely your Lord is All-Knowing, Wise.'[7]

وَكَذَٰلِكَ يَجْتَبِيكَ رَبُّكَ وَيُعَلِّمُكَ مِن
تَأْوِيلِ ٱلْأَحَادِيثِ وَيُتِمُّ نِعْمَتَهُۥ عَلَيْكَ
وَعَلَىٰٓ ءَالِ يَعْقُوبَ كَمَآ أَتَمَّهَا عَلَىٰٓ أَبَوَيْكَ
مِن قَبْلُ إِبْرَٰهِيمَ وَإِسْحَٰقَ ۚ إِنَّ رَبَّكَ عَلِيمٌ
حَكِيمٌ ۝٦

dream, its meaning was clear. Jacob was the sun; his wife, the stepmother of Joseph, was the moon; and his eleven sons were the eleven stars.

5. The word 'choosing' here signifies the choice of someone for the bestowal of prophethood.

6. The Qur'ānic expression *ta'wīl al-aḥādīth* does not simply signify explanation of the true meaning of dreams, as people are wont to believe. What it really signifies is that God would bless Joseph with the capacity to grasp complicated matters, to understand the nature of things.

7. Biblical and Talmudic accounts vary from the Qur'ānic statement made here. According to the Bible, when Joseph related his dream to Jacob he rebuked him, saying: 'What is this dream that you have dreamed? Shall I and your mother and your brothers indeed come to bow ourselves to the ground before you?' (*Genesis* 37: 10 – Ed.) However, if one reflects a little, one can easily appreciate that the Qur'ānic account is in greater harmony with Jacob's character as a Prophet than the Biblical one. Joseph had simply recounted his dream. He had not expressed any wish or desire of his own. If the dream was true – and Jacob interpreted it on the assumption that the dream was true – it could be taken to indicate that God had decreed that Joseph would rise to great heights. In that event, how can any good-natured person, let alone a Prophet, feel offended at such a dream and rebuke one who had had such a dream? Is it conceivable that any good-natured father, instead of feeling happy at the thought of his son's rise to eminence, would be incensed at it?

(7) Verily in the story of Joseph and his brothers there are many signs for those who inquire (about the truth). (8) And call to mind when the brothers of Joseph conferred together and said: 'Surely Joseph and his brother[8] are dearer to our father than we are, although we are a group of so many. Our father is clearly mistaken.[9] ▶

۞ لَّقَدْ كَانَ فِي يُوسُفَ وَإِخْوَتِهِۦٓ
ءَايَٰتٌ لِّلسَّآئِلِينَ ﴿٧﴾ إِذْ قَالُوا۟
لَيُوسُفُ وَأَخُوهُ أَحَبُّ إِلَىٰٓ أَبِينَا
مِنَّا وَنَحْنُ عُصْبَةٌ إِنَّ أَبَانَا لَفِى
ضَلَٰلٍ مُّبِينٍ ﴿٨﴾

8. This refers to Benjamin, Joseph's true brother, who was younger than him by a few years. His mother had passed away at the time of his birth. This explains why Jacob cared more for these two sons. Moreover, out of all his sons it was in Joseph alone that Jacob saw clear indications of righteousness and piety. Moreover, the statement made by Jacob upon hearing of Joseph's dream also indicates that he was well aware of Joseph's extraordinary potential.

On the other hand, the character of the ten stepbrothers was sharply at variance with that of Joseph as is evident from subsequent events. How, then, can it be conceived that a righteous person such as Jacob would be happy with such corrupt sons? Curiously enough, one of the reasons for Joseph's brothers' jealousy as mentioned in the Bible reflects very poorly on Joseph's character. According to the Bible, Joseph 'brought an ill report' of his brothers to his father (*Genesis* 37: 2 – Ed.), which would make one presume that it was one of the reasons for their hatred for him.

9. For a better understanding of this statement, one should bear in mind the material conditions of nomadic, tribal societies. Such a society is usually devoid of an organized state, and generally consists of a number of independent tribes that live side by side. In such a society, a man's strength depends entirely on the number of his supporters, and these consist of his sons, grandsons, brothers, and nephews. These members of the family are extremely important since a person depends only upon them in the event of an attack upon his person, property or honour. Under such circumstances, a person is naturally inclined to hold his youthful sons dearer than the women or children of his household for it is the former who bear the brunt of any fighting with the enemy. When the ten stepbrothers noticed that Jacob gave Joseph – who was

(9) So either kill Joseph or cast him into some distant land so that your father's attention may become exclusively yours. And after so doing become righteous.'[10] (10) Thereupon one of them said: 'Do not kill Joseph, but if you are bent upon doing something, cast him down to the bottom of some dark pit, perhaps some caravan passing by will take him out of it.' (11) After so deciding they said to their father: 'Why is it that you do not trust us regarding Joseph although we are his true well-wishers?[11] ▶

ٱقۡتُلُواْ يُوسُفَ أَوِ ٱطۡرَحُوهُ أَرۡضٗا يَخۡلُ
لَكُمۡ وَجۡهُ أَبِيكُمۡ وَتَكُونُواْ مِنۢ بَعۡدِهِۦ
قَوۡمٗا صَٰلِحِينَ ٩ قَالَ قَآئِلٞ مِّنۡهُمۡ
لَا تَقۡتُلُواْ يُوسُفَ وَأَلۡقُوهُ فِي غَيَٰبَتِ
ٱلۡجُبِّ يَلۡتَقِطۡهُ بَعۡضُ ٱلسَّيَّارَةِ إِن
كُنتُمۡ فَٰعِلِينَ ١٠ قَالُواْ يَٰٓأَبَانَا
مَا لَكَ لَا تَأۡمَ۬نَّا عَلَىٰ يُوسُفَ وَإِنَّا لَهُۥ
لَنَٰصِحُونَ ١١

---

still small and they were grown up and strong – greater affection, they thought that their father had become senile.

10. This statement reflects the psychological make-up of those who, even when they vigorously pursue their desires, still make an effort to maintain some relationship with faith and righteousness. Such people seem to have a peculiar way of conciliating between their responses to the demands of righteousness on the one hand, and of self-indulgence on the other. When they are under strong pressure from their lusts, they go ahead and commit an evil act, keeping the demands of faith temporarily in abeyance. However, as soon as they feel pangs of guilt, they try to assuage their conscience, assuring it that what they had committed was merely an ephemeral act of sinning; that this sin was inevitable as only thus could an important purpose be achieved. They further assure their conscience that it will not be long before they repent and revert to their original righteousness.

11. The Qur'ānic narrative on this point is different both from that of the Bible and the Talmud. The Biblical version mentions that Joseph's brothers had gone towards Shechem to graze their cattle. In their absence, it was Jacob himself who sent Joseph to look for them. (*Genesis* 37: 12–16 – Ed.) This, however, seems highly improbable. For Jacob knew well that his other sons

(12) Send him out with us tomorrow that he may enjoy himself and play while we will be there, standing guard over him.' (13) Their father answered: 'It grieves me indeed that you should take him with you for I fear that some wolf might eat him while you are negligent of him.' (14) They said: 'Should a wolf eat him, despite the presence of our strong group, we would indeed be a worthless lot!' (15) So when they went away with Joseph and decided to cast him in the bottom of the dark pit, We revealed to Joseph: 'Surely a time will come when you will remind them of their deed. They know nothing about the consequence of what they are doing.'[12] ▶

أَرْسِلْهُ مَعَنَا غَدًا يَرْتَعْ وَيَلْعَبْ
وَإِنَّا لَهُۥ لَحَٰفِظُونَ ﴿١٢﴾ قَالَ إِنِّى
لَيَحْزُنُنِىٓ أَن تَذْهَبُوا۟ بِهِۦ وَأَخَافُ
أَن يَأْكُلَهُ ٱلذِّئْبُ وَأَنتُمْ عَنْهُ
غَٰفِلُونَ ﴿١٣﴾ قَالُوا۟ لَئِنْ أَكَلَهُ
ٱلذِّئْبُ وَنَحْنُ عُصْبَةٌ إِنَّآ إِذًا
لَّخَٰسِرُونَ ﴿١٤﴾ فَلَمَّا ذَهَبُوا۟ بِهِۦ
وَأَجْمَعُوٓا۟ أَن يَجْعَلُوهُ فِى غَيَٰبَتِ
ٱلْجُبِّ وَأَوْحَيْنَآ إِلَيْهِ لَتُنَبِّئَنَّهُم
بِأَمْرِهِمْ هَٰذَا وَهُمْ لَا يَشْعُرُونَ ﴿١٥﴾

were highly jealous of Joseph. So why would Jacob have sent Joseph on such a perilous mission? Given the circumstances of the case, the Qur'ānic account appears more plausible.

12. We have translated the Qur'ānic words وَهُمْ لَا يَشْعُرُونَ as follows: 'they know nothing about the consequence of what they are doing'. The Qur'ānic expression here may be interpreted in three ways, and each of the three interpretations seems to fit the situation. One interpretation suggests that God comforted Joseph by means of revelation and that his brothers were unaware that he had received such a revelation. The second meaning could be that Joseph would one day make his brothers realize their mistakes in circumstances which for the moment were out of the range of their imaginations. The third meaning could be that Joseph's brothers were doing something out of sheer ignorance, without realizing its possible consequences.

(16) At nightfall they came to their father weeping (17) and said: 'Father! We went racing with one another and left Joseph behind with our things, and then a wolf came and ate him. We know that you will not believe us howsoever truthful we might be.' (18) And they brought Joseph's shirt, stained with false blood. Seeing this their father exclaimed: 'Nay (this is not true); rather your evil souls have made it easy for you to commit a heinous act. So I will bear this patiently, and in good grace.[13] It is Allah's help alone that I seek against your fabrication.'[14]

وَجَآءُوٓ أَبَاهُمْ عِشَآءً يَبْكُونَ ﴿١٦﴾
قَالُوا۟ يَٰٓأَبَانَآ إِنَّا ذَهَبْنَا نَسْتَبِقُ
وَتَرَكْنَا يُوسُفَ عِندَ مَتَٰعِنَا
فَأَكَلَهُ ٱلذِّئْبُ ۖ وَمَآ أَنتَ بِمُؤْمِنٍ
لَّنَا وَلَوْ كُنَّا صَٰدِقِينَ ﴿١٧﴾ وَجَآءُو
عَلَىٰ قَمِيصِهِۦ بِدَمٍ كَذِبٍ ۚ قَالَ بَلْ سَوَّلَتْ
لَكُمْ أَنفُسُكُمْ أَمْرًا ۖ فَصَبْرٌ جَمِيلٌ ۖ
وَٱللَّهُ ٱلْمُسْتَعَانُ عَلَىٰ مَا تَصِفُونَ ﴿١٨﴾

The Bible and Talmud do not mention that God comforted Joseph by His words. Instead, the Talmud says that when Joseph was thrown into the pit he cried profusely and made impatient pleas to his brothers. On the contrary, if one goes through the Qur'ānic account there emerges an altogether different image. This account portrays the life-history of a young man who had the potential to become – as indeed he later did become – one of the major figures of human history. This is also in sharp contrast with the Talmudic version. That version mentions that in a desert a few bedouin threw a young boy into a pit. This is followed by a portrayal of Joseph's actions in which there is nothing that would distinguish him from any other boy in that situation.

13. The text has the words صَبْرٌ جَمِيلٌ . Literally that may be translated as 'gracious patience'. This signifies a patience which is devoid of complaint, of piteous entreaties, of frothing and fuming; a patience which consists of enduring suffering with calm and dignity.

14. The image of Jacob that emerges from accounts of the story in both the Bible and the Talmud is also run of the mill. According to the Bible, on hearing

(19) And a caravan came, and they sent their water-drawer to draw water. As he let down his bucket in the well he (observed Joseph) and cried out: 'This is good news. There is a boy.' They concealed him, considering him as part of their merchandise, while Allah was well aware of what they did. (20) Later they sold him for a paltry sum – just a few dirhams;[15] they did not care to obtain a higher price.

وَجَآءَتْ سَيَّارَةٌ فَأَرْسَلُوا۟ وَارِدَهُمْ فَأَدْلَىٰ
دَلْوَهُۥ قَالَ يَٰبُشْرَىٰ هَٰذَا غُلَٰمٌ وَأَسَرُّوهُ
بِضَٰعَةً وَٱللَّهُ عَلِيمٌۢ بِمَا يَعْمَلُونَ
﴿١٩﴾ وَشَرَوْهُ بِثَمَنٍۭ بَخْسٍ دَرَٰهِمَ
مَعْدُودَةٍ وَكَانُوا۟ فِيهِ مِنَ
ٱلزَّٰهِدِينَ ﴿٢٠﴾

the news of the grievous incident, Jacob rent his garments, put sackcloth upon his loins, and mourned for his son many days (*Genesis* 37: 34). Likewise, the Talmud mentions that Jacob abandoned himself to grief and lay with his face to the ground refusing to be comforted and cried: 'Yes, this was the shirt of my son' and he mourned for many years.

This description makes Jacob look like any ordinary person. However, in the Qur'ānic version Jacob stands out head and shoulders above ordinary humans. He appears as an embodiment of forbearance and patience. Nor does he lose his poise on hearing the shocking news about his son. Moreover, thanks to his unusual intelligence, when Joseph's stepbrothers come forth with a made-up story, Jacob saw through the whole matter. He instantly grasped that his jealous sons had fabricated the account. Despite the grievous nature of the incident, Jacob maintains his grace and dignity, patiently endures what has befallen him, and places his full faith in God (see verses 7–18 – Ed.).

15. What seems to have happened was that Joseph's brothers cast him into a pit and then left him. Thereafter, a caravan passing by rescued Joseph, taking him to Egypt where they sold him. The Bible, however, mentions that Joseph's brothers later came across a caravan of Ishmaelites. They sought to take Joseph out of the pit and sell him to the caravan only to discover that Midianite traders had already taken Joseph from the pit and sold him to the Ishmaelites for twenty shekels of silver. Later, the compilers of the Bible conveniently forgot the fact that, according to their own account, Joseph had already been sold to the Ishmaelites. It is strange, therefore, to note that later on it is mentioned that

(21) The man from Egypt[16] who bought him said to his wife:[17] 'Take good care of him, possibly he might be of benefit to us or we might adopt him as a son.'[18] Thus We found a way for Joseph to become established in that land and in order that We might teach him to comprehend the deeper meaning of things.[19] Allah has full power to implement His design although most people do not know that. (22) And when Joseph reached the age of maturity, We granted him judgement and knowledge.[20] Thus do We reward those who do good.

وَقَالَ ٱلَّذِى ٱشْتَرَىٰهُ مِن مِّصْرَ
لِٱمْرَأَتِهِۦٓ أَكْرِمِى مَثْوَىٰهُ عَسَىٰٓ
أَن يَنفَعَنَآ أَوْ نَتَّخِذَهُۥ وَلَدًا ۚ
وَكَذَٰلِكَ مَكَّنَّا لِيُوسُفَ فِى
ٱلْأَرْضِ وَلِنُعَلِّمَهُۥ مِن تَأْوِيلِ
ٱلْأَحَادِيثِ ۚ وَٱللَّهُ غَالِبٌ عَلَىٰٓ
أَمْرِهِۦ وَلَٰكِنَّ أَكْثَرَ ٱلنَّاسِ
لَا يَعْلَمُونَ ﴿٢١﴾ وَلَمَّا بَلَغَ
أَشُدَّهُۥٓ ءَاتَيْنَٰهُ حُكْمًا وَعِلْمًا ۚ
وَكَذَٰلِكَ نَجْزِى ٱلْمُحْسِنِينَ ﴿٢٢﴾

Joseph was sold in Egypt by the same Midianite traders. (For a full account see *Genesis* 37: 25–8 and 36.)

In sharp contrast to this is the Talmudic account which says that the Midianite traders took Joseph out of the pit and enslaved him. Subsequently, on discovering this, Joseph's brothers remonstrated with them. After they had paid twenty shekels of silver to his brothers, they stopped quarrelling. Then they sold Joseph to the Ishmaelites also for twenty shekels of silver and they later sold him in Egypt. This has given rise to the popular tradition among Muslims that Joseph's brothers sold Joseph. It must be clarified, however, that the Qur'ān does not bear this out.

16. The Bible refers to this person as Potiphar. At a later point in the Qur'ān he is mentioned as *'azīz* (see verses 30 and 51). It is significant that the same title *'azīz* has elsewhere been used in the Qur'ān for Joseph (see verse 78).

This shows that the person mentioned here was the holder of a highly important title or the incumbent of some highly important office. For *'azīz* literally means one possessed of irresistible power. Biblical and Talmudic accounts describe this person as an officer of the royal bodyguard. Ibn Jarīr al-Ṭabarī, on the authority of 'Abd Allāh ibn 'Abbās, describes him as one in charge of the royal treasury. (See al-Ṭabarī's comments on verse 21 in his *Commentary* – Ed.)

17. The Talmud names her as Zelicha. This is the basis for the popularity of this name in Muslim folklore. However, the belief that Joseph later married the same woman – a belief which has become a part of popular Muslim tradition – has no basis in authoritative Islamic sources. In fact, no statement to that effect is found either in the Qur'ān or in Israelite historical traditions. Above all, it is altogether unbecoming of a Prophet to marry a woman whose moral corruption was directly known to him. The Qur'ān, as we know, lays down the following principle concerning matrimonial relationships: 'Impure women are for impure men, and impure men are for impure women, pure women are for pure men and pure men are for pure women' (*al-Nūr* 24: 26).

18. The Talmud states that at that time Joseph was eighteen years old. When Potiphar saw Joseph he was greatly impressed by his features. He felt sure that Joseph was not a born slave but came from a noble lineage, who had somehow fallen on bad days. Hence, when Potiphar was buying Joseph, he told the traders that he did not look like a slave. He even expressed the suspicion that the traders might have stolen him from somewhere.

This explains why Potiphar did not treat Joseph as a slave. Instead, he put him in charge of his house and all his properties. The Bible says: 'So he left all he had in Joseph's charge; and having him he had no concern for anything but the food which he ate' (*Genesis* 39: 6).

19. Joseph had been brought up as a shepherd in a semi-nomadic milieu. There was no organized state at that time in Canaan and northern Arabia. Nor had culture and civilization made any significant headway in that region. A number of independent tribes lived there and they migrated from one part to the other. Apart from those migratory tribes, a few other tribes had also settled down in certain areas where they had established small states.

As to their lifestyle, it would seem to have resembled that of the Pathan tribes in the free tribal area adjacent to the North West Frontier Province of Pakistan. Thanks to Joseph's upbringing in such a milieu, he possessed the virtues characteristic of a bedouin tribal life. Moreover, he had also inherited the spirit of godliness and religious piety.

God wanted to entrust Joseph with the mission of Prophet in Egypt, at that time the most advanced country. However, the qualities, experience, vision and insight needed to carry out such a task could hardly have been developed in his nomadic surroundings. God, therefore, placed Joseph in the house of an Egyptian high official.

Observing Joseph's exceptional qualities and talents, the official concerned put him in charge of his house and all his properties. Thus, Joseph had the opportunity to develop his potentialities to the full. In addition, the experience of handling the properties of this official gave Joseph the necessary expertise

(23) And it so happened that the lady in whose house Joseph was living, sought to tempt him to herself, and one day bolting the doors she said: 'Come on now!' Joseph answered: 'May Allah grant me refuge! My Lord has provided an honourable abode for me (so how can I do something so evil?). Such wrong-doers never prosper.'[21] ▶

وَرَٰوَدَتْهُ ٱلَّتِى هُوَ فِى بَيْتِهَا عَن نَّفْسِهِۦ وَغَلَّقَتِ ٱلْأَبْوَٰبَ وَقَالَتْ هَيْتَ لَكَ ۚ قَالَ مَعَاذَ ٱللَّهِ ۖ إِنَّهُۥ رَبِّىٓ أَحْسَنَ مَثْوَاىَ ۖ إِنَّهُۥ لَا يُفْلِحُ ٱلظَّٰلِمُونَ ﴿٢٣﴾

that would later help him in administering a vast kingdom. The above verse alludes to that.

20. The Qur'ān often uses such an expression to signify the conferment of prophethood. As to the expression, 'judgement', it refers both to the capacity and the authority to judge. Hence, the statement that God granted someone 'judgement' suggests that God equipped him with the capacity to make sound judgements relating to human affairs and also conferred upon him the requisite authority to do so. As for 'knowledge', this refers to that special knowledge of the truth which is directly intimated to Prophets by means of revelation.

21. The translators as well as the commentators of the Qur'ān interpret the expression 'my lord' as referring to the person in whose employment Joseph worked at that time. In other words, Joseph said that he could not betray his 'lord' – i.e. the chief who had treated him so well. What this meant is that in view of the official's kindness to Joseph, his indulgence in illegitimate sex with the wife of the chief was absolutely out of the question.

Personally speaking, I do not agree with the interpretation that the word *rabbī* ('my lord') refers to the official. It is true that from the viewpoint of Arabic usage, such an interpretation is admissible. For the expression *rabbī* is also used to signify human masters. However, it seems altogether unbecoming of a Prophet that he would abstain from a sin out of consideration for some human being rather than out of consideration for God.

If we turn to the Qur'ān, there is not a single instance in which a Prophet would have called anyone other than God his *rabbī* ('lord'). Moreover, in verses 41, 42 and 50 of this very *sūrah*, Joseph underscores the basic difference between his own faith and the faith of the Egyptians. The difference consists of the following. Whereas the One True God alone is the Lord of Joseph, the

(24) And she advanced towards him, and had Joseph not perceived a sign from his Lord he too would have advanced towards her.[22] Thus was Joseph shown a sign from his Lord that We might avert from him all evil and indecency,[23] for indeed he was one of Our chosen servants. ▶

وَلَقَدْ هَمَّتْ بِهِۦ وَهَمَّ بِهَا لَوْلَآ أَن رَّءَا بُرْهَٰنَ رَبِّهِۦ كَذَٰلِكَ لِنَصْرِفَ عَنْهُ ٱلسُّوٓءَ وَٱلْفَحْشَآءَ إِنَّهُۥ مِنْ عِبَادِنَا ٱلْمُخْلَصِينَ ﴿٢٤﴾

Egyptians had taken human beings to be their lords. (See verses 39–40 – Ed.) Thus, there is strong reason to consider the expression used by Joseph as meaning God. Now, since there is a good basis for such an interpretation, there is no reason to prefer an interpretation that is inconsistent with the station of a Prophet.

22. The word *burhān* denotes an argument or proof. *'Burhān'* from the Lord signifies the argument inspired by God to arouse Joseph's conscience and convince him that it is not at all appropriate for him to accept the woman's invitation to illegitimate enjoyment. Now, what was the 'argument' to which reference has been made in the present verse? That argument has already been mentioned in the previous verse: 'My Lord has provided an honourable abode for me (so how can I do something so evil?). Such wrongdoers never prosper' (*Yūsuf* 12: 23). This was the argument which dissuaded Joseph in such a tempting circumstance and in the very prime of his youth from committing the sin to which he was invited.

Moreover, the Qur'ān also states that Joseph too would have advanced towards her had he not perceived the *burhān* from his Lord (see verse 24). This throws full light on the infallibility of Prophets. The doctrine of the infallibility of Prophets does not mean that they are devoid of predisposition towards sin. What infallibility of the Prophets means is that even though Prophets have the potential to commit sin, even though they possess all human characteristics – feelings, passions and desires – their nature is so righteous and they are so God-fearing that they never consciously intend to do so. This is so because they are endowed with such powerful arguments from their Lord that they are not carried away by their lusts. And even if a Prophet succumbs to any weakness – and then only inadvertently – God immediately sends a revelation which enables him to mend his behaviour. This is a special arrangement that has been made by God with regard to Prophets. The reason being that if a Prophet deviates even slightly from the right way, this encourages others to become engrossed in a variety of sins.

(25) Then both of them rushed to the door, each seeking to get ahead of the other, and she tore Joseph's shirt from behind. Then both of them found the husband of the lady at the door. Seeing him she said: 'What should be the punishment of him who has foul designs on your wife except that he should be imprisoned or subjected to painful chastisement?' (26) Joseph said: 'It is she who was trying to tempt me to herself.' And a witness belonging to her own household testified (on ground of circumstantial evidence):[24] 'If his shirt is torn from the front, then she is telling the truth and he is a liar. (27) But if his shirt is torn from behind, then she has lied, and he is truthful.'[25] ►

وَٱسْتَبَقَا ٱلْبَابَ وَقَدَّتْ قَمِيصَهُۥ مِن
دُبُرٍ وَأَلْفَيَا سَيِّدَهَا لَدَا ٱلْبَابِ ۚ قَالَتْ
مَا جَزَآءُ مَنْ أَرَادَ بِأَهْلِكَ سُوٓءًا إِلَّآ أَن
يُسْجَنَ أَوْ عَذَابٌ أَلِيمٌ ﴿٢٥﴾ قَالَ هِىَ
رَٰوَدَتْنِى عَن نَّفْسِى ۚ وَشَهِدَ شَاهِدٌ
مِّنْ أَهْلِهَآ إِن كَانَ قَمِيصُهُۥ قُدَّ
مِن قُبُلٍ فَصَدَقَتْ وَهُوَ مِنَ ٱلْكَٰذِبِينَ
﴿٢٦﴾ وَإِن كَانَ قَمِيصُهُۥ قُدَّ مِن دُبُرٍ
فَكَذَبَتْ وَهُوَ مِنَ ٱلصَّٰدِقِينَ ﴿٢٧﴾

23. The Qur'ānic statement: 'Thus it happened so that We might avert from him all evil and indecency' (verse 24), may be interpreted in two ways. The first interpretation is that Joseph perceived an argument from his Lord and refrained from committing the sin under God's direction and because of His succour. This was because God wanted to keep Joseph, to whom He had entrusted prophethood, free from every evil and indecency.

There is also another interpretation of the verse, one that seems more profound. According to this view, the situation in which Joseph was placed was in fact an important part of his moral training. In order to enable Joseph to attain the highest degree of spiritual purity and excellence, it was an essential part of God's plan to test him and so expose him to such temptation. In this test, Joseph was required to marshal his will-power and piety to the optimum so as to subdue his sensual desires once and for all.

In order to appreciate this particular mode of training, one should remember the moral conditions pertaining to Egyptian society at that time. In this *sūrah* (see verse 23 ff.), we have a glimpse of these conditions. We know from the Qur'ān (see verse 30 ff.) that sexual licentiousness was almost as rampant in the Egyptian society of those days, and particularly among the upper class, as it is among contemporary Westerners or those non-Westerners who mimic their ways.

Thus we note that Joseph was required to carry out his mission – the mission of a Prophet – among a people who were immersed in moral corruption. In addition, Joseph had to carry out his prophetic mission not in the capacity of an ordinary person, but in the capacity of a ruler. We also know the extent to which the upper-class ladies of Egypt were infatuated with Joseph even though they believed him to be a slave. It is not difficult to imagine, therefore, the extent to which those ladies would have gone in order to seduce such an attractive young man after he had become ruler of Egypt. God enabled Joseph to successfully pass through this test and to further develop his firmness of character. It also became clear to the ladies of Egypt – dissolute though they were – that their amorous gestures to Joseph were of no avail.

24. The situation that comes to mind seems to be the following. The chief official *('azīz)* seems to have been accompanied by someone who was a relative of his wife. This relative would have thus come to know of the incident and heard the two parties exchanging charges of guilt. Now, it so happened that besides Joseph and the official's wife there was no other first-hand witness of the incident. Thus, it was not possible to ask anyone else to testify.

The only course left, therefore, was to decide the case on grounds of circumstantial evidence. In some traditions it has been claimed that the statement mentioned in the verse was made by an infant baby who lay in his cradle. God had especially granted him the faculty of speech in order that he might make his deposition. (See al-Qurṭubī's comments on verse 26 in his *Commentary* – Ed.)

It must, however, be noted that this tradition is not supported by any reliable chain of transmission. Moreover, the infant's ability would seem to suggest something miraculous. Furthermore, the circumstantial evidence to which the person in question has referred also seems quite reasonable. Were we to consider his suggestion, it would become quite evident that he was intelligent, mature and experienced, and was able quickly to get to the heart of the matter. It would not be surprising if he was a judge or magistrate. It is interesting to note that this story about the evidence of an infant mentioned by Qur'ān-commentators is derived from Jewish traditions. (See Paul Isaac Hershon, *Talmudic Miscellany,* London, 1880, p. 256.)

25. The whole point of this statement is that if the shirt was rent from the front, it indicated that Joseph had taken the initiative in advancing towards the lady and that the latter had resisted his amorous advances. However, if Joseph's shirt was rent from the back, that showed the opposite, viz. that it was

(28) So when the husband saw Joseph's shirt torn from behind he exclaimed: 'Surely, this is one of the tricks of you women; your tricks are indeed great. (29) Joseph, disregard this. And you – woman – ask forgiveness for your sin, for indeed it is you who has been at fault.'[25a]

فَلَمَّا رَءَا قَمِيصَهُۥ قُدَّ مِن دُبُرٍ قَالَ إِنَّهُۥ
مِن كَيْدِكُنَّ إِنَّ كَيْدَكُنَّ عَظِيمٌ ﴿٢٨﴾
يُوسُفُ أَعْرِضْ عَنْ هَٰذَا وَٱسْتَغْفِرِى
لِذَنۢبِكِ إِنَّكِ كُنتِ مِنَ
ٱلْخَاطِـِٔينَ ﴿٢٩﴾

the lady who had made the advances while Joseph had tried to run away from her. This statement also contains a subtle suggestion which needs to be pointed out. The fact that only Joseph's shirt was mentioned implies that there were no traces of any violence on the body or dress of the lady. Had Joseph been guilty of making any advances, traces of his violent advances would clearly have been visible.

25(a). The Biblical account of the incident is quite clumsy. It reads as follows:

> . . . she caught him by his garment, saying, 'Lie with me'. But he left his garment in her hand, and fled and got out of the house. And when she saw that he had left his garment in her hand, and had fled out of the house, she called to the men of her household and said to them: 'See, he has brought among us a Hebrew to insult us; he came in to me to lie with me, and I cried out with a loud voice; and when he heard that I lifted up my voice and cried, he left his garment with me, and fled and got out of the house.' Then she laid up his garment by her until his master came home, and she told him the same story, saying, 'The Hebrew servant, whom you have brought among us, came in to me to insult me; but as soon as I lifted up my voice and cried, he left his garment with me and fled out of the house.'
>
> When his master heard the words which his wife spoke to him, 'This is the way your servant treated me', his anger kindled. And Joseph's master took him and put him into the prison, the place where the king's prisoners were confined . . . (*Genesis* 39: 12–20).

In sum, this highly improbable report suggests that Joseph was dressed in such a garment that would fall away as soon as Zelicha laid her hands on it. As for Joseph, leaving his garment behind, he ran away, probably stark naked.

(30) And some ladies in the city began to say: 'The chief's wife, violently in love with her houseboy, is out to tempt him. We think she is totally mistaken.' (31) Hearing of their sly talk the chief's wife sent for those ladies, and arranged for them a banquet, and got ready couches,[26] and gave each guest a knife. Then, while they were cutting and eating the fruit, she signalled Joseph: 'Come out to them.' When the ladies saw him they were so struck with admiration that they cut their hands, exclaiming: 'Allah preserve us. This is no mortal human. This is nothing but a noble angel!' ►

۞ وَقَالَ نِسْوَةٌ فِي ٱلْمَدِينَةِ ٱمْرَأَتُ
ٱلْعَزِيزِ تُرَٰوِدُ فَتَىٰهَا عَن نَّفْسِهِۦ قَدْ
شَغَفَهَا حُبًّا إِنَّا لَنَرَىٰهَا فِي ضَلَٰلٍ
مُّبِينٍ ﴿٣٠﴾ فَلَمَّا سَمِعَتْ بِمَكْرِهِنَّ
أَرْسَلَتْ إِلَيْهِنَّ وَأَعْتَدَتْ لَهُنَّ مُتَّكَـًٔا
وَءَاتَتْ كُلَّ وَٰحِدَةٍ مِّنْهُنَّ سِكِّينًا
وَقَالَتِ ٱخْرُجْ عَلَيْهِنَّ فَلَمَّا رَأَيْنَهُۥٓ أَكْبَرْنَهُۥ
وَقَطَّعْنَ أَيْدِيَهُنَّ وَقُلْنَ حَٰشَ لِلَّهِ مَا هَٰذَا
بَشَرًا إِنْ هَٰذَآ إِلَّا مَلَكٌ كَرِيمٌ ﴿٣١﴾

Thus Joseph's garment remained in possession of the lady, providing undeniable proof of his guilt. In such circumstances, no sensible person would believe that Joseph was not guilty.

So much for the Biblical account. Now let us turn to the Talmudic version. According to the Talmud, on hearing the complaint from his wife, Potiphar had Joseph severely whipped. Then he lodged a case against him in the court. However, when the judges looked at Joseph's garment, they concluded that the woman was at fault for it was rent from the back and not from the front. Even a little reflection makes it evident that the Qur'ānic version is much more plausible than the Talmudic one. For who on earth could believe that such an influential dignitary would take to court a case which would bring him into disrepute by highlighting that his wife was molested by his own slave.

This is one of the most obvious differences between the Qur'ānic and Israelite accounts of Joseph's story. This difference proves beyond any shadow of doubt the absurdity of the Orientalists' allegation that the Prophet (peace be on him) had taken over the stories of the Prophets from the Israelites. On the contrary, the fact is that it is the Qur'ān which purged the Israelite stories of their demeaning errors. The world is indeed indebted to the Qur'ān for having

(32) She said: 'So now you see! This is the one regarding whom you reproached me. Indeed I tried to tempt him to myself but he held back. And if he does not follow my order, he will certainly be imprisoned and humiliated.'[27] (33) Joseph said: 'My Lord! I prefer imprisonment to what they ask me to do. And if You do not avert from me the guile of these women, I will succumb to their attraction and lapse into ignorance.'[28] ▶

قَالَتْ فَذَٰلِكُنَّ ٱلَّذِى لُمْتُنَّنِى فِيهِ ۖ وَلَقَدْ
رَٰوَدتُّهُۥ عَن نَّفْسِهِۦ فَٱسْتَعْصَمَ ۖ وَلَئِن لَّمْ
يَفْعَلْ مَآ ءَامُرُهُۥ لَيُسْجَنَنَّ وَلَيَكُونًا مِّنَ
ٱلصَّٰغِرِينَ ﴿٣٢﴾ قَالَ رَبِّ ٱلسِّجْنُ أَحَبُّ
إِلَىَّ مِمَّا يَدْعُونَنِىٓ إِلَيْهِ ۖ وَإِلَّا تَصْرِفْ
عَنِّى كَيْدَهُنَّ أَصْبُ إِلَيْهِنَّ وَأَكُن مِّنَ
ٱلْجَٰهِلِينَ ﴿٣٣﴾

provided the true version of those stories and thus restored the correct image of the Prophets.

26. This refers to the banquet where the guests were lying on couches. Egyptian archaeological monuments also bear out that in such parties couches were used.

The Bible makes no mention of this banquet. However, the Talmud mentions it though its account differs significantly from that in the Qur'ān. The Talmudic narrative is totally bereft of the vividness, the underlying spirit, the naturalness and the moral tenor of the Qur'ānic narrative.

27. This gives some idea of the moral degeneration of the upper classes of Egyptian society. Obviously, the guests invited to the banquet of the official's wife would have been upper-class ladies. Now, the official's wife presented before them the attractive young man with whom she was passionately in love. By so doing she tried to make the ladies realize why she could not help falling madly in love with such a handsome youth. It is significant that those ladies fully agreed that the young man was overwhelmingly attractive, and that it was quite understandable why any woman would have had such a crush on him. It is significant that the hostess felt no reluctance in brazenly declaring that if Joseph did not respond to her amorous advances, she would have him cast into prison and suffer humiliation.

All this goes to show that there is nothing so new about the promiscuity

(34) Thereupon his Lord granted his prayer, and averted their guile from him.[29] Surely He alone is All-Hearing, All-Knowing.

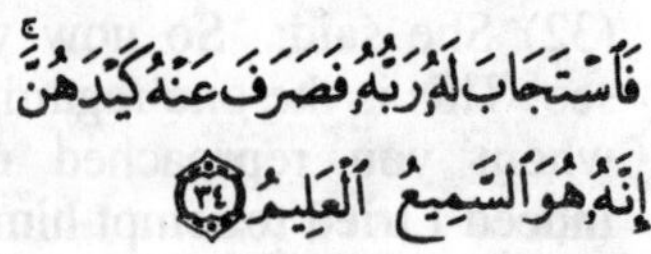

which characterizes the social life of Europe and America today. Centuries ago more or less the same situation obtained in Egypt as it obtains in our 'enlightened' times.

28. These verses recapture the situation in which Joseph found himself. He appears as a handsome young man about nineteen or twenty years old. Having come to Egypt after spending the early part of his life in a bedouin milieu, Joseph was physically attractive and appeared to be full of youth and vigour. After having passed through the adversities of poverty, banishment and forced slavery, by a quirk of fate Joseph came to the house of a highly influential person, a representative of the most civilized empire of the world in those days. In this new environment, Joseph first encounters the amorous advances of the lady of the house. As the news of his comeliness spread through the capital, upper-class ladies of the town also fell for him.

All alone, Joseph vigilantly resists temptation at almost every step. Every possible effort is made to arouse his passions and to destroy the foundations of his righteous character. Wherever he goes he encounters temptation and seduction in their most alluring forms. At the slightest show of inclination on Joseph's part, those ladies were willing to do all that lay in their power to pander to his lust. Joseph faced this difficult situation all day and all night. Were he to suffer a momentary lapse, he would have entered any of the innumerable portals of sin that stood ajar, waiting to receive him. Placed in such a situation this God-fearing youth overcomes all Satanic temptations with astounding success.

What is all the more amazing is that despite such exceptional restraint, such remarkable resistance to temptation, there is no trace of pride in Joseph. He never boasts that by dint of his righteousness he was able to overcome the temptations which faced him. He never displays any feeling of self-adulation. He never brags at remaining firm in the face of the temptation. On the contrary, Joseph is highly conscious of his human susceptibility. He admits the possibility that unless God graciously assists him, he might at some point fall prey to any temptation. He humbly implores God, therefore, to help him and to rescue him from those temptations.

This was in fact the most sensitive stage in Joseph's training. The qualities of honesty, trustworthiness, chastity, truthfulness, fairness, self-discipline,

(35) Then it occurred to them to cast Joseph into prison for a while even though they had seen clear signs (of Joseph's innocence and of the evil ways of their ladies).[30]

(36) And with Joseph[31] two other slaves[32] entered the prison. One of them said: 'I saw myself pressing wine in a dream'; and the other said: 'I saw myself carrying bread on my head of which the birds were eating.' Both said: 'Tell us what is its interpretation; for we consider you to be one of those who do good.'[33]

ثُمَّ بَدَا لَهُم مِّنۢ بَعْدِ مَا رَأَوُا ٱلْآيَٰتِ
لَيَسْجُنُنَّهُۥ حَتَّىٰ حِينٍ ﴿٣٥﴾ وَدَخَلَ
مَعَهُ ٱلسِّجْنَ فَتَيَانِ قَالَ أَحَدُهُمَآ
إِنِّىٓ أَرَىٰنِىٓ أَعْصِرُ خَمْرًا وَقَالَ ٱلْآخَرُ
إِنِّىٓ أَرَىٰنِىٓ أَحْمِلُ فَوْقَ رَأْسِى خُبْزًا
تَأْكُلُ ٱلطَّيْرُ مِنْهُ نَبِّئْنَا بِتَأْوِيلِهِۦٓ إِنَّا
نَرَىٰكَ مِنَ ٱلْمُحْسِنِينَ ﴿٣٦﴾

---

moderation, and mental poise and balance which lay dormant in his personality were all fully mobilized. Joseph himself was unaware of those qualities. However, when he was put to the test, they all came to the fore. Joseph, thus, became aware of the qualities he possessed and began to know to what use he could put them.

29. Averting 'the guile of these women' refers to God's investing Joseph with a firm character which enabled him to frustrate their guile. This also means that it is because of Divine Providence that Joseph suffered imprisonment. This, as we shall see, proved to be a blessing in disguise.

30. The imprisonment of Joseph under such circumstances amounted, on the one hand, to his moral victory. On the other hand, it amounted to the defeat of the Egyptian élite. Joseph was now no longer an unknown person. Everyone in the capital had now become familiar with his name. Most of the ladies of the Egyptian upper-class had fallen for him. The ruling classes grasped the gravity of the problem posed by Joseph's overwhelming attractiveness, a problem which menaced their family lives. They thought it prudent that such a person be put behind bars.

Obviously, a person who was so extraordinarily attractive could not have remained unknown to others. It was natural that he would have become the talk

(37) Joseph said: 'I will inform you about the interpretation of the dreams before the arrival of the food that is sent to you. This knowledge is part of what I have been taught by my Lord. I have renounced the way of those who do not believe in Allah, and who deny the Hereafter, (38) and I have adopted the way of my forefathers – Abraham and Isaac and Jacob. It is not for us to associate any with Allah in His divinity. It is out of Allah's grace upon us and upon mankind (that He did not require of us to serve any beside Allah) and yet most people do not give thanks. (39) Fellow-prisoners! Is it better that there be diverse lords, or just Allah, the One, the Irresistible? ▶

قَالَ لَا يَأْتِيكُمَا طَعَامٌ تُرْزَقَانِهِۦٓ إِلَّا
نَبَّأْتُكُمَا بِتَأْوِيلِهِۦ قَبْلَ أَن يَأْتِيَكُمَا
ذَٰلِكُمَا مِمَّا عَلَّمَنِى رَبِّىٓ ۚ إِنِّى تَرَكْتُ
مِلَّةَ قَوْمٍ لَّا يُؤْمِنُونَ بِٱللَّهِ وَهُم
بِٱلْءَاخِرَةِ هُمْ كَٰفِرُونَ ﴿٣٧﴾
وَٱتَّبَعْتُ مِلَّةَ ءَابَآءِىٓ إِبْرَٰهِيمَ
وَإِسْحَٰقَ وَيَعْقُوبَ ۚ مَا كَانَ لَنَآ أَن
نُّشْرِكَ بِٱللَّهِ مِن شَىْءٍ ۚ ذَٰلِكَ مِن
فَضْلِ ٱللَّهِ عَلَيْنَا وَعَلَى ٱلنَّاسِ وَلَٰكِنَّ
أَكْثَرَ ٱلنَّاسِ لَا يَشْكُرُونَ ﴿٣٨﴾
يَٰصَىٰحِبَىِ ٱلسِّجْنِ ءَأَرْبَابٌ
مُّتَفَرِّقُونَ خَيْرٌ أَمِ ٱللَّهُ ٱلْوَٰحِدُ
ٱلْقَهَّارُ ﴿٣٩﴾

of the day in every household. People would also have come to know that Joseph was not just a physically attractive youth. He was also possessed of nobility, firmness of character and elegance of behaviour. People would also have become aware that Joseph had not been imprisoned because he was a criminal. They fully knew that it was easier for the ruling classes to consign Joseph, despite his innocence, to suffer imprisonment than to keep their women within the bounds of decent behaviour. It is for this reason that they afterwards decided to consign him to prison.

This also shows that sending innocent persons to prison in disregard of the due process of justice and without caring to establish their guilt or innocence is one of the accepted practices of rulers from olden days. In this regard, the evil forces of today are no better than those of four thousand years ago.

The only difference perhaps is that the rulers in those days did not pay lip-service to 'democracy' while the rulers of today never tire of that. Even

(40) Those whom you serve beside Him are merely idle names that you and your fathers have fabricated, without Allah sending down any sanction for them. All authority to govern rests only with Allah. He has commanded that you serve none but Him. This is the right way of life, though most people are altogether unaware. ▶

مَا تَعْبُدُونَ مِن دُونِهِۦٓ إِلَّآ أَسْمَآءً سَمَّيْتُمُوهَآ أَنتُمْ وَءَابَآؤُكُم مَّآ أَنزَلَ ٱللَّهُ بِهَا مِن سُلْطَٰنٍ ۚ إِنِ ٱلْحُكْمُ إِلَّا لِلَّهِ ۚ أَمَرَ أَلَّا تَعْبُدُوٓا۟ إِلَّآ إِيَّاهُ ۚ ذَٰلِكَ ٱلدِّينُ ٱلْقَيِّمُ وَلَٰكِنَّ أَكْثَرَ ٱلنَّاسِ لَا يَعْلَمُونَ ﴿٤٠﴾

---

today they indulge in acts of lawlessness to achieve their ends. Whenever they are in need of a legal cover for their excesses, they know how to hammer out a piece of legislation geared to that end. The evil forces of the past committed wrongs against others in a clumsy manner. The evil forces of today also resort to excesses against others. However, when they do so they try to convince others that the persons concerned posed a threat to the whole nation rather than just to them. The evil ones of the past were simply oppressors. The evil ones of today, in addition to being so, are also liars and devoid of all sense of shame.

31. At the time of his imprisonment Joseph was barely twenty or twenty-one years old. According to the Talmud, when Joseph assumed the reins of Egypt, after being released from prison, he was thirty years old. The Qur'ān says that Joseph remained in prison for a few years. The actual word used in the Qur'ān is *biḍ'*, which denotes a maximum period of ten years.

32. According to the Bible, one of the two slaves who entered the prison along with Joseph, was the chief butler of the Egyptian king and the other was his chief baker. (*Genesis* 40: 1–3 – Ed.) According to the Talmud, the Egyptian king had sent them to prison for he had found some grit in the bread and a fly in the wine which were served at a banquet.

33. This gives some idea of how highly Joseph was regarded in the prison. The incidents related earlier also show why the two prisoners approached Joseph for an interpretation of their dreams. This also explains why they told him: 'We consider you to be one of those who do good' (verse 36). Everyone both inside and outside the prison knew well that Joseph was not a criminal. On the contrary, he was known as a virtuous person. He was exposed to the most

(41) Fellow-prisoners! [This is the interpretation of your dreams]: one of you will serve wine to his lord [the king of Egypt]. As for the other, he will be crucified and birds will eat of his head. The question concerning what you asked has thus been decided.'[34]

يَٰصَٰحِبَيِ ٱلسِّجۡنِ أَمَّآ أَحَدُكُمَا فَيَسۡقِي رَبَّهُۥ خَمۡرٗاۖ وَأَمَّا ٱلۡأٓخَرُ فَيُصۡلَبُ فَتَأۡكُلُ ٱلطَّيۡرُ مِن رَّأۡسِهِۦۚ قُضِيَ ٱلۡأَمۡرُ ٱلَّذِي فِيهِ تَسۡتَفۡتِيَانِ ﴿٤١﴾

seductive temptations to which any person can be exposed, but he had stood firm. No wonder he began to be looked upon as the most virtuous person in the whole land. He stood head and shoulders above all, including the religious leaders. As a result, not only the prisoners but also the prison authorities held Joseph in high esteem. The Bible, therefore, makes this observation:

> And the keeper of the prison committed to Joseph's care all the prisoners who were in the prison; and whatever was done there he was the doer of it; the keeper of the prison paid no heed to anything that was in Joseph's care (*Genesis* 39: 22–3).

34. This discourse by Joseph, which is at the very heart of the story, stands out as one of the best expositions of monotheism in the Qur'ān. Strangely enough, this finds no place in the Bible and the Talmud which represent Joseph as no more than a pious and wise person. The Qur'ān, however, also highlights those features of his conduct which are passed over in silence in both those sources. It underscores his prophetic mission and indicates he had embarked upon it while still in prison.

Joseph's discourse is far too important to be passed over superficially. It provides a wealth of significant points which should be given serious consideration.

(1) This is the first occasion where we find Joseph (peace be on him) preaching the true faith. In the biographical information about Joseph provided by the Qur'ān prior to this incident, we have some idea about the moral excellence which characterized Joseph's life from the very beginning. However, prior to this discourse, we do not come across any instance of religious preaching of the kind found here.

This indicates that the early stages of his life were of a preparatory nature, and were designed to develop in him the capacities that would enable him to undertake his mission as a Prophet.

In short, we learn that prophethood was conferred upon Joseph during the period of his imprisonment. The present discourse is the first sustained statement that he makes in that capacity.

(2) It is again for the first time that Joseph (peace be on him) publicly discloses his true identity. So far he had calmly and patiently endured the adversities which befell him. His life even before this oration was quite an eventful one. He was made a captive, was brought to Egypt, was sold to the Egyptian chief, and was then imprisoned. On none of these occasions did Joseph disclose his true identity. At no point did he identify that he was the grandson of Abraham and Isaac and the son of Jacob. His parents and grandparents were no ordinary mortals. The members of the caravan, both Midianite and Ishmaelite, knew this family very well. The Egyptians too were not unfamiliar with his forefathers, at least not with Abraham. The reference to Abraham, Jacob and Isaac in Joseph's present discourse implies that all of them were very well known in Egypt.

It is also significant that Joseph had never invoked the name of his parents and grandparents to extricate himself from the dire straits in which he found himself during the preceding four or five years. Presumably he realized that he had to endure hardships so that he might develop the qualities required to play the role which God had decided to entrust him with.

When Joseph started his religious preaching, it became necessary for him to emphasize that he was not presenting a new religious faith. On the contrary, he claimed to be a part of that universal movement of monotheism whose earlier exponents were Abraham, Isaac and Jacob (peace be on them). This point had to be made. For anyone who stands for the truth never lays claim to novelty. He rather declares, at the very outset, that he is concerned with inviting people to the eternal truth which has been presented throughout the ages by its exponents.

(3) The manner in which Joseph (peace be on him) availed himself of the opportunity offered by his imprisonment and his interaction with his fellow prisoners provides an important lesson. It tells how exponents of the true faith should act with wisdom and prudence in preaching the truth. The occasion for preaching the faith in Joseph's case was provided by fellow prisoners who narrated their dreams to him. They also expressed their esteem for Joseph (peace be on him) and asked him to interpret their dreams and Joseph promised to do so. However, he said that he would only do so after informing them of the sources of his knowledge on which he would depend for the interpretation of the dreams. Thus, he found a good reason to present his message before them.

From this we learn that if someone is really keen to preach the truth and also has wisdom, he can make use of a hundred different opportunities and direct the subject of the conversation to his basic message. Conversely, if someone is devoid of the burning desire to serve his cause and preach his message, he will never to able to make use of the opportunities that present themselves. A truly committed person is always on the lookout for every possible opportunity, and he avails himself of it whenever any such opportunity arises.

There is a world of difference, however, between a prudent person who wisely uses the opportunities to preach his message and the stupid preacher who does so clumsily in disregard of time and place, and tries to force his ideas upon people. Such preachers are often also quarrelsome and obnoxious with the result that they create revulsion against the teachings they seek to preach.

(4) From this we also learn the right way of presenting the message of faith. Joseph (peace be on him) did not start by presenting detailed rules and regulations. He first introduced the fundamental point which distinguishes the way of truth from that of falsehood. Joseph, therefore, clearly explained the basic difference between monotheism and polytheism. Moreover, he explained this difference in such simple and reasonable terms that no one with common sense could have helped but appreciate it.

The analogy which Joseph (peace be on him) used to elucidate his message had a special appeal for the people around him because they had experienced slavery themselves. They, therefore, knew well what is better for people: to serve one master or several masters. This analogy would have enabled them to recognize that which is better: serving the Lord of the universe or serving His creatures.

It is also significant that Joseph (peace be on him) did not clumsily ask people to abandon their faith and embrace his. Rather, he told them in moving terms that God, by ordaining that His servants should serve none but Him, had done them a great favour. It is astonishing that people are still not thankful to Him for this favour. They continue to invent their gods and to worship them.

Joseph also criticizes the religious doctrines of his audience. But his criticism is couched in reasonable terms and contains nothing that would hurt their susceptibilities. He simply tells them that those whom they had taken as their deities and whom they considered to have control over power, wealth, health, and other blessings from God, were merely empty names. They have no power to provide anything. The only true Lord and Master was God Whom they also recognized as the Creator and Lord of the universe. They were, however, oblivious of the fact that the Lord and Creator of the universe had not sanctioned godhead for any of the deities they worshipped. God has exclusive power to rule over His creation, and He has commanded that men may not worship any other than Him.

(5) The discourse also indicates how Joseph spent his eight-year term in prison. Some people assume that since the Qur'ān mentions only one of Joseph's speeches that he invited people to the true faith on only one occasion. Such an assumption seems altogether improper. For, to think

(42) And Joseph said to the one of the two prisoners who he knew would be set free: 'Mention me in your lord's presence.' But Satan caused him to forget mentioning this to his lord [the king of Egypt] and so Joseph languished in prison for several years.[35]

وَقَالَ لِلَّذِى ظَنَّ أَنَّهُۥ نَاجٍ مِّنْهُمَا
ٱذْكُرْنِى عِندَ رَبِّكَ فَأَنسَىٰهُ
ٱلشَّيْطَٰنُ ذِكْرَ رَبِّهِۦ فَلَبِثَ فِى
ٱلسِّجْنِ بِضْعَ سِنِينَ ﴿٤٢﴾

so would amount to charging a Prophet with dereliction of duty. Apart from that, Joseph's keenness to call people to the true faith is evident from the incident just mentioned. Two of his fellow prisoners had asked him to interpret their dreams. Joseph made use of this opportunity to preach the faith. In view of the above, how can it even be conceived that such a person would have spent his eight long years in prison without making any effort to preach his message.

35. This Qur'ānic statement فَأَنسَاهُ الشَّيْطَانُ ذِكْرَ رَبِّهِ has been interpreted by some Qur'ān-commentators to mean that Satan caused Joseph to become negligent in remembering God, his Lord, and asked a creature of God to secure his release by bringing his case to the attention of his master (that is, the Egyptian king). It was for this reason that God punished Joseph and why he languished in prison for several years. (See al-Qurṭubī's comments on the present verse – Ed.)

However, such an interpretation is absolutely wrong. The correct interpretation, in our view, is the one offered by Mujāhid and Muḥammad ibn Isḥāq among the scholars of the early period, and by Ibn Kathīr among the scholars of a relatively later period. According to their interpretation, the pronoun refers to the person who, in Joseph's view, was about to be set free. Hence, what the verse means is that Satan caused this person to forget mentioning the case of Joseph to his lord. A tradition is also related in this connection which says that the Prophet (peace be on him) said: 'Had Joseph (peace be on him) not made the statement that he did, he would not have languished in the prison for several years'.

One may, however, ask: What is the degree of authenticity of this tradition? According to Ibn Kathīr, every chain of transmission in the tradition is 'weak'. In some of its versions, the report has been attributed to the Prophet (peace be on him). In others, Sufyān ibn Wakī' and Ibrāhīm ibn Yazīd are the transmitters of these traditions and both of them are unreliable. In other

(43) And once the king[36] said: 'I have dreamt that there are seven fat cows and seven lean cows are devouring them, and there are seven fresh green ears of corn and seven others dry and withered. My nobles! Tell me what is the interpretation of this dream, if you are well-versed in the interpretation of dreams.'[37] (44) They said: 'These are confused dreams, and we do not know the interpretation of such dreams.'

(45) Then of the two prisoners, the one who had been set free, now remembered, after the lapse of a long period, what Joseph had said. He said: 'I will tell you the interpretation of this dream; just send me (to Joseph in prison).'[38]

وَقَالَ ٱلۡمَلِكُ إِنِّيٓ أَرَىٰ سَبۡعَ بَقَرَٰتٖ
سِمَانٖ يَأۡكُلُهُنَّ سَبۡعٌ عِجَافٞ
وَسَبۡعَ سُنۢبُلَٰتٍ خُضۡرٖ وَأُخَرَ
يَابِسَٰتٖۖ يَٰٓأَيُّهَا ٱلۡمَلَأُ أَفۡتُونِي فِي
رُءۡيَٰيَ إِن كُنتُمۡ لِلرُّءۡيَا تَعۡبُرُونَ
٤٣ قَالُوٓاْ أَضۡغَٰثُ أَحۡلَٰمٖۖ وَمَا
نَحۡنُ بِتَأۡوِيلِ ٱلۡأَحۡلَٰمِ بِعَٰلِمِينَ ٤٤
وَقَالَ ٱلَّذِي نَجَا مِنۡهُمَا وَٱدَّكَرَ بَعۡدَ
أُمَّةٍ أَنَا۠ أُنَبِّئُكُم بِتَأۡوِيلِهِۦ
فَأَرۡسِلُونِ ٤٥

---

versions, the tradition is *mursal*, and in such matters *mursal* traditions* are not taken into account. (See Ibn Kathīr's comments on this verse – Ed.)

The tradition is also implausible on grounds of common sense. For it does not stand to reason that the efforts of a person who was subjected to injustice and oppression would be considered an act of forgetting God and be regarded as inconsistent with having trust in Him.

36. Omitting a few years of Joseph's life in prison, the thread of the narrative is picked up again. It is connected with the stage which marks the worldly rise of Joseph.

******Mursal* **traditions are those in which a Successor narrates a report about or from the Prophet (peace be on him) without referring to any Companion – Ed.**

(46) Then he went to Joseph and said to him: 'Joseph, O truthfulness incarnate,[39] tell me the true meaning of the dream in which seven fat cows are devoured by seven lean ones; and there are seven green ears of corn and seven others dry and withered so that I may return to the people and they may learn.'[40] ▶

يُوسُفُ أَيُّهَا ٱلصِّدِّيقُ أَفْتِنَا فِي سَبْعِ
بَقَرَٰتٍ سِمَانٍ يَأْكُلُهُنَّ سَبْعٌ
عِجَافٌ وَسَبْعِ سُنۢبُلَٰتٍ خُضْرٍ
وَأُخَرَ يَابِسَٰتٍ لَّعَلِّيٓ أَرْجِعُ إِلَى ٱلنَّاسِ
لَعَلَّهُمْ يَعْلَمُونَ ﴿٤٦﴾

37. According to the Bible and the Talmud, the king was greatly disturbed by his dreams. By a public declaration he invited all the wise men and magicians of his realm and placed the matter before them. (For the Biblical account see *Genesis* 41: 1 ff.)

38. The Qur'ānic account here is quite brief. The Bible and the Talmud, however, mention some details – details which conform to common sense. According to the information made available by the Bible and Talmud, the chief butler provided relevant information about Joseph to the king. The butler also mentioned that Joseph had rightly interpreted his own dream as well as the dreams of his fellow prisoners during the period of their imprisonment. (See *Genesis* 41: 9 ff.) He also sought the king's permission to go and see Joseph and ask him the true meaning of the king's dreams.

39. In Arabic usage the word *ṣiddīq,* which occurs in this verse, denotes the highest degree of truthfulness and veracity. The use of the word shows how deeply that person had been influenced by Joseph's character. The impression seems to have been a very profound one since it endured for a very long time. (For further elucidated meaning of the term see *Towards Understanding the Qur'ān,* vol. II, *al-Nisā'* 4, n. 99, p. 57.)

40. One of the two prisoners asked Joseph to interpret the dream in order that his true worth might be recognized and so that it might also be realized that a big mistake had been committed by having a person of his standing imprisoned. This, he thought, would also enable him to fulfil the promise he had made to Joseph in prison (see verse 42).

(47) Joseph said: 'You shall cultivate consecutively for seven years. Leave in the ear all that you have harvested except the little out of which you may eat. (48) Then there will follow seven years of great hardship in which you will eat up all you have stored earlier, except the little that you may set aside. (49) Then there will come a year when people will be helped by plenty of rain and they will press (grapes).'[41]

(50) The king said: 'Bring this man to me.' But when the royal messenger came to Joseph he said:[42] 'Go back to your master and ask him about the case of the women who had cut their hands. Surely my Lord has full knowledge of their guile.'[43] ▶

قَالَ تَزْرَعُونَ سَبْعَ سِنِينَ دَأَبًا فَمَا
حَصَدتُّمْ فَذَرُوهُ فِي سُنۢبُلِهِۦٓ إِلَّا
قَلِيلًا مِّمَّا تَأْكُلُونَ ﴿٤٧﴾ ثُمَّ يَأْتِي مِنۢ
بَعْدِ ذَٰلِكَ سَبْعٌ شِدَادٌ يَأْكُلْنَ مَا
قَدَّمْتُمْ لَهُنَّ إِلَّا قَلِيلًا مِّمَّا تُحْصِنُونَ
﴿٤٨﴾ ثُمَّ يَأْتِي مِنۢ بَعْدِ ذَٰلِكَ عَامٌ فِيهِ
يُغَاثُ ٱلنَّاسُ وَفِيهِ يَعْصِرُونَ ﴿٤٩﴾
وَقَالَ ٱلْمَلِكُ ٱئْتُونِي بِهِۦ فَلَمَّا جَآءَهُ
ٱلرَّسُولُ قَالَ ٱرْجِعْ إِلَىٰ رَبِّكَ
فَسْـَٔلْهُ مَا بَالُ ٱلنِّسْوَةِ ٱلَّتِي
قَطَّعْنَ أَيْدِيَهُنَّ إِنَّ رَبِّي بِكَيْدِهِنَّ
عَلِيمٌ ﴿٥٠﴾

41. The actual word *(ya'ṣirūn)* used in the Qur'ān literally means 'they press out or squeeze out' something (e.g. grapes, olives, etc.). The mention of pressing suggests the verdure and prosperity which would follow the famine as a result of rainfall and the rise in the water-level of the Nile. When the land would receive enough rainfall, there would be a luxuriant growth of oil seeds and fruits, both juicy and dry. Also the cattle would yield more milk as a result of the good quality fodder available to them.

Joseph did not confine himself to interpreting the king's dream. He also suggested to him to take precautionary measures against famine during the years of prosperity, the steps that ought to be taken to store the grain. Moreover, Joseph foretold that the days of famine would be followed by those of prosperity. He prophesied this even though there was no hint of it in the king's dream.

42. The narration from this point on till the king's meeting with Joseph constitutes an important part of the Qur'ānic account of the story. However, these events go altogether unmentioned in the Bible and the Talmud. According to the Biblical version:

> Then Pharaoh sent and called Joseph, and they brought him hastily out of the dungeon; and when he had shaved himself and changed his clothes, he came in before Pharaoh. And Pharaoh said to Joseph, 'I have had a dream, and there is no one who can interpret it; and I have heard it said of you that when you hear a dream you can interpret it.' (*Genesis* 41: 14–15 – Ed.)

The Talmudic account is even more degrading. According to it, the king ordered that Joseph be brought before him. He commanded his officers to be careful not to frighten the young man lest he may misinterpret the dream. So the king's servants brought forth Joseph from his dungeon and shaved him, clothed him in a new dress and presented him before the king. The king was seated upon his throne, and the glitter of gold and precious stones which adorned the throne dazzled Joseph's eyes. Now, there was a seven-step stair to the throne. The custom in Egypt was that a prince or noble who held audience with the king, ascended to the sixth step and addressed the king from there. But when an ordinary private citizen was called into the king's presence, the king descended to the third step and addressed him from there. In accordance with this custom Joseph stood and saluted the king by bowing. The king descended to the third step and talked to Joseph. (H. Polano, *The Talmudic Selections*, pp. 87–8.)

This is the Israelite image of a Prophet as great as Joseph. As we shall note, the image is quite unedifying. In sharp contrast to that is the image of Joseph that emerges from the Qur'ānic account of the story. One is struck by the grace and dignity characterizing Joseph's personality, especially the dignified portrayal of his attitude to the suggestion of his release from prison, and the manner of his meeting with the king. People may exercise their common sense and decide which of the two images is more consistent with and closer to one expected of a Prophet.

One more point is of significance. If Joseph was truly as degraded a character as the Talmud would have us believe, it does not make sense that the Egyptian king would have entrusted to him control over his whole dominion. In a civilized country one is elevated to such a high position only if one has established one's mental and moral standing. Thus, the Qur'ānic account seems considerably more plausible and consistent with reason and common sense than the Biblical and Talmudic ones.

43. Joseph pointed out that as far as his Lord – God – was concerned, He fully knew him to be innocent. He stressed, however, that before his release, their lord – the king of Egypt – should also thoroughly ascertain what had occasioned his imprisonment. For Joseph did not want to be released under circumstances that would warrant the continuance of any stigma on his

(51) Thereupon the king asked the women:[44] 'What happened when you sought to tempt Joseph?' They said: 'Allah forbid! We found no evil in him.' The chief's wife said: 'Now the truth has come to light. It was I who sought to tempt him. He is indeed truthful.'[45]

قَالَ مَا خَطْبُكُنَّ إِذْ رَٰوَدتُّنَّ يُوسُفَ
عَن نَّفْسِهِۦ ۚ قُلْنَ حَٰشَ لِلَّهِ مَا
عَلِمْنَا عَلَيْهِ مِن سُوٓءٍ ۚ قَالَتِ ٱمْرَأَتُ
ٱلْعَزِيزِ ٱلْـَٰٔنَ حَصْحَصَ ٱلْحَقُّ أَنَا۠
رَٰوَدتُّهُۥ عَن نَّفْسِهِۦ وَإِنَّهُۥ لَمِنَ
ٱلصَّٰدِقِينَ ﴿٥١﴾

character. Hence, before Joseph was freed, it was necessary to establish beyond doubt that he was absolutely innocent. For it was not Joseph who had committed any offence. The real culprits were the high officials of the state. It is they who had made him unjustly suffer imprisonment, despite the purity of his character. Ironically, he was imprisoned on the grounds of his alleged moral corruption of which their own ladies were guilty.

The way Joseph makes this demand clearly suggests that the Egyptian king knew well about the whole incident which had taken place in the banquet hall of the Egyptian chief's wife. The incident seems to have been so well known that it was enough to merely allude to it.

Moreover, while asking that the king might inquire about the incident, Joseph refers only to the ladies present in the banquet to the exclusion of the chief's wife. This is further proof of his dignified character. For although the chief's wife had attempted to harm him, her husband had been very kind to Joseph. He acted, therefore, with unusual sensitivity and circumspection lest his name and honour were subjected to any slur.

44. So far as this query is concerned, it is possible that the ladies might have been brought to the palace where they were asked to answer this question. Another possibility is that the king might have sent some reliable messenger to each of those ladies who might have put this question singly to each of them.

45. It can well be imagined how these pieces of evidence would have revived the incident that had taken place some eight or nine years earlier. It would have once again brought into full prominence the personality of Joseph who had languished in the oblivion of prison for several years. It would also have established the moral authority of Joseph both among the Egyptian élite and the general public.

(52) Joseph said:[46] 'I did this so that he [i.e. the chief] may know that I did not betray him in his absence, and that Allah does not allow the design of the treacherous to succeed. (53) I do not seek to acquit myself; for surely one's self prompts one to evil except him to whom my Lord may show mercy. Verily my Lord is Ever Forgiving, Most Merciful.'

ذَٰلِكَ لِيَعْلَمَ أَنِّي لَمْ أَخُنْهُ بِالْغَيْبِ وَأَنَّ
اللَّهَ لَا يَهْدِي كَيْدَ الْخَائِنِينَ ﴿٥٢﴾
۞ وَمَا أُبَرِّئُ نَفْسِي إِنَّ النَّفْسَ
لَأَمَّارَةٌ بِالسُّوءِ إِلَّا مَا رَحِمَ
رَبِّي إِنَّ رَبِّي غَفُورٌ رَحِيمٌ ﴿٥٣﴾

We have already noted that the Bible and the Talmud mention that the king made a public declaration through which he invited all the wise men and magicians of his realm. The men so assembled failed to interpret the king's dream and the dream was interpreted by Joseph. (See n. 37 above and *Genesis* 41: 1 ff. – Ed.)

This incident would have made Joseph the centre of everyone's attention. Moreover, when the king summoned Joseph to the court, instead of rushing out of the prison, he sent back the king's envoy with the request that his case may first be examined so that it be known whether he was guilty or innocent.

It is possible that such an attitude may have created, in the minds of some people, the suspicion that Joseph was perhaps overly ambitious and vain. They would have wondered at his not rushing out of prison as soon as the king had asked him to come out of it. However, people would subsequently have come to know that Joseph had set some preconditions for his release and for meeting the king. This would also have aroused curiosity among the people concerning the result of the inquiry that Joseph had proposed.

Naturally some time after that the findings of the inquiry would have become known. This would certainly have aroused among the general public deep admiration for Joseph's righteousness and purity of character. No one could have ignored the fact that those very persons who had once collaborated in having Joseph imprisoned now testified to his moral excellence.

If one remembers the situation obtaining at that time, it is amply clear that the circumstances were propitious for Joseph's rise to the highest positions of authority. It is, therefore, not surprising that in his meeting with the king Joseph asked him to entrust to him the financial affairs of the kingdom. The readiness with which the king appointed him to this position becomes quite understandable if we consider the moral prestige that Joseph then enjoyed in Egypt. Had his prestige rested merely with the fact that a prisoner had rightly interpreted the king's dream, Joseph could have expected, at the most, some reward from the king and his release from prison. It is quite unreasonable to assume that the mere ability to interpret dreams would have prompted Joseph to ask the king: 'Place me in charge of the treasures of the land' (see verse 55). Nor is it feasible that the king's recognition of his ability to interpret dreams would have prompted him to place the treasures of Egypt in Joseph's hands.

46. Probably this remark would have been made by Joseph after he was informed of the findings of the inquiry while he was still in prison. Some Qur'ān-commentators, including such outstanding ones as Ibn Taymīyah and Ibn Kathīr, consider this not to be a remark made by Joseph, but one by the chief's wife. The argument they put forward in support of this opinion is that it occurs in close sequence to the earlier remark by the chief's wife. It is also pointed out that there does not occur any word in between that would indicate that the statement of the chief's wife comes to an end with إِنَّهُ لَمِنَ الصَّادِقِينَ ('He is indeed truthful'), and whatever follows thereafter is the statement of Joseph.

They hold that if there is a two-part statement it would ordinarily be regarded as the statement of one person unless there is some strong reason to hold the contrary view. Such a view could be held, for instance, if there is explicit ascription of a part of the statement to another person. However, if there is no explicit statement to that effect, then there must be some circumstantial reason for believing that one part of the statement was made by one person, and another part by someone else. For it would only then be possible to distinguish between the statements of two persons. Since the above passage provides no such indication, it should be assumed that the whole passage starting from أَلْآنَ حَصْحَصَ الْحَقُّ ('Now the truth has come to light') right up to the end of verse 53 is that of the chief's wife.

It is indeed surprising that even a perceptive scholar such as Ibn Taymīyah should have overlooked the most important clue as to who made a statement. Now, let us consider the first sentence in verse 51, (viz. 'Now the truth has come to light. It was I who sought to tempt him. He is indeed truthful'). This undoubtedly befits the chief's wife. That statement, however, is followed by another which has quite a different tenor: 'I did this so that he may know that I did not betray him in his absence, and that Allah does not allow the design of the treacherous to succeed. I do not seek to acquit myself; for surely one's self prompts one's evil except him to whom my Lord may show mercy. Verily my Lord is Ever Forgiving, Most Merciful.' It is crystal clear that such a statement is altogether out of tune with the tenor and character of the chief's wife. The content of the statement is sufficient to prove that it was made by Joseph rather than by the chief's wife. Clearly, the virtues of righteousness, magnanimity, modesty and God-consciousness which underlie the statement are not at all in harmony with the character of the woman who had earlier tried to seduce Joseph, shamelessly saying to him: 'Come on now'. (See verse 23 above.)

(54) The king said: 'Bring him to me. I will choose him for my own service.'

So when Joseph spoke to him the king said: 'You are now one of established position, fully-trusted by us.'[47] (55) Joseph said: 'Place me in charge of the treasures of the land. I am a good keeper and know my task well.'[47a]

وَقَالَ ٱلْمَلِكُ ٱئْتُونِى بِهِۦٓ أَسْتَخْلِصْهُ لِنَفْسِى ۖ فَلَمَّا كَلَّمَهُۥ قَالَ إِنَّكَ ٱلْيَوْمَ لَدَيْنَا مَكِينٌ أَمِينٌ ﴿٥٤﴾ قَالَ ٱجْعَلْنِى عَلَىٰ خَزَآئِنِ ٱلْأَرْضِ ۖ إِنِّى حَفِيظٌ عَلِيمٌ ﴿٥٥﴾

We also know the other remarks made by the chief's wife, such as: 'On seeing her husband she said: ''What should be the punishment of him who has foul designs on your wife?'' ' (verse 25). Not only that but, she had also brazenly declared: 'If he does not follow my order, he will certainly be imprisoned and humiliated' (verse 32). But the remark under discussion is of quite a different nature. Such a statement could have been made only by one who had earlier made remarks such as the following: 'My Lord has provided an honourable abode for me (so how can I do something so evil?') (verse 23) and 'My Lord! I prefer imprisonment to what they ask me to do. And if you do not avert from me the guile of these women, I will succumb to their attraction and lapse into ignorance' (verse 33).

In sum, no sensible person can believe that such a noble and lofty statement was made by the chief's wife rather than by Joseph unless there is a clear indication to the effect that the chief's wife had undergone a basic change of manner and character; regrettably there is no indication to that effect.

47. This statement by the king clearly indicates that he considered Joseph worthy of every position of responsibility.

47(a). In light of the clarifications made earlier, it is evident that the present statement by Joseph was not at all in the nature of an ambitious job-hunter applying to the king for a government post at the first available opportunity. This statement was in fact the last in a series of efforts made by Joseph to push open the door to the desired transformation of the entire system. Thus, this marked the culmination of Joseph's rise to moral authority which had proceeded apace for a period of ten to twelve years.

The time was thus quite ripe and all that Joseph had to do was to push gently, and the door to the desired transformation would be flung open. For Joseph had come a long way. He had successfully faced a series of tests and trials. Also, things had happened in such a manner that everyone in Egypt, from the king down to the paupers, had become fully acquainted with Joseph. In the course of the tests to which he was put he had fully established that he was perceptibly above his contemporaries in such qualities as trustworthiness, truthfulness, forbearance. self-restraint, magnanimity, intelligence and far-sightedness. These qualities in his personality were too manifest to be denied by anybody. Everyone in Egypt bore witness to Joseph's superb character. Thus Joseph had in fact won the hearts and minds of all including the Egyptian king.

Joseph's remark that he was a good keeper and knew his task well was not merely a claim. It was an established fact which everyone recognized. The only thing that needed to be done, therefore, was that Joseph should express his readiness to accept the reins of power. Nothing more was required than that Joseph should communicate his readiness to assume power. For the king and his council were already convinced that he was the most appropriate person to administer Egypt. This requirement was completed by the above statement.

No sooner had Joseph expressed his readiness to assume governmental responsibility than the council happily agreed to hand over power to him. All this goes to prove that the situation had become fully ripe for Joseph to seize power and there was no resistance to it from any quarter. (According to the Talmud, the decision to hand over power to Joseph was not made by the king alone. It was rather a unanimous decision by the royal council.)

Now, what was the nature and extent of the power that Joseph sought and which was entrusted to him? Those who are not fully familiar with Joseph's true story tend to interpret the expression 'treasures of the land' quite literally. They tend to assume that Joseph was perhaps appointed as the treasury or revenue officer, or minister of finance, or minister of food.

However, in light of the Qur'ānic, Biblical and Talmudic accounts of the story, there is no disagreement on the point that Joseph was handed total control (in Roman terminology, dictator) of the Egyptian empire. He enjoyed absolute authority over the affairs of Egypt. According to the Qur'ān, when Jacob reached Egypt, Joseph was seated on his throne so that he 'raised his parent to the throne beside himself' (verse 100). This clearly indicates the extent of his authority. The Qur'ān also recounts Joseph's remark to the effect that: 'My Lord! You have bestowed dominion on me' (verse 101). Likewise, the officials describe Joseph's cup as the king's cup (see verse 72). Referring to Joseph's rule over Egypt, the Qur'ān describes it: 'Thus did we establish Joseph in the land and he had the authority to settle wherever he pleased' (verse 56).

As to the Biblical version, it also confirms that Joseph wielded total authority. The Bible mentions that Pharaoh said to Joseph:

> Since God has shown you all this, there is none so discreet and wise as you are; you shall be over my house, and all my people shall order themselves

> as you command; only as regards the throne will I be greater than you. Behold, I have set you over all the land of Egypt . . . Moreover Pharaoh said to Joseph, I am Pharaoh and without your consent no man shall lift up hand or foot in all the land of Egypt. And Pharaoh called Joseph's name Zephenath-paneah (*Genesis* 41: 39–45).

The Talmudic version presents the same picture. It identifies that when Joseph's brothers returned to their father, they told him the following:

> The king of Egypt is a mighty potentate; over his people he is supreme: upon his word they go out and upon his word they come in; his word governs, and the voice of his master Pharaoh is not required.

Now let us turn to the other question as to why Joseph sought such power? Did he offer his services to an un-Islamic government, indicating his readiness to administer it in accordance with its un-Islamic laws? Or did he instead intend to shape the cultural, moral and political system according to Islamic principles after assuming power? This question has been best answered in al-Zamakhsharī's Commentary on the Qur'ān, *al-Kashshāf,* in these words:

> When Joseph said: 'Place me in charge of the treasures of the land' (verse 55 above), what he really wanted was to make God's commands operate, to establish the truth, and promote justice. He wanted to achieve the necessary authority for accomplishing the task for which Messengers are raised. He did not demand power out of any love for it or out of love for the world. Since he knew well that no one else could accomplish such a task, he presented himself for that. (See al-Zamakhsharī's comments on verse 55.)

As a matter of fact were this line of questioning to be pursued seriously, it would give rise to another question which is even more important and fundamental. The question is: 'Was Joseph a Prophet or not?' If he was a Prophet, then it must be asked: 'Does the Qur'ānic concept of prophethood warrant that a Prophet should offer his services for administering the affairs of an un-Islamic system in accordance with its ungodly laws?' In fact this question gives rise to an even more sensitive question: 'Was Joseph at all a truthful person?'

Now, if we believe that Joseph was truthful, that raises still another question: 'How can we reconcile Joseph's truthfulness with the fact that he invited people to something quite different from that?' For we know that Joseph had launched his Prophetic mission during his imprisonment by putting forth the question: 'Is it better that there be diverse lords, or Allah, the One, the Irresistible?' (see verse 39 above). We also know that Joseph had also repeatedly told the people that their ruler was one of those whom they had falsely taken as lords.

Moreover, Joseph had also clearly expressed the idea, which was a basic

(56) Thus did We invest Joseph with the authority in that he had the authority to settle wherever he pleased.[48] We bestow favour, out of Our Mercy, on whomsoever We please, and We do not cause the reward of those who do good to go to waste. (57) Surely the reward of the Hereafter is better for those who believe and act in a God-fearing way.[49]

وَكَذَٰلِكَ مَكَّنَّا لِيُوسُفَ فِي ٱلْأَرْضِ يَتَبَوَّأُ مِنْهَا حَيْثُ يَشَآءُ نُصِيبُ بِرَحْمَتِنَا مَن نَّشَآءُ وَلَا نُضِيعُ أَجْرَ ٱلْمُحْسِنِينَ ﴿٥٦﴾ وَلَأَجْرُ ٱلْآخِرَةِ خَيْرٌ لِّلَّذِينَ ءَامَنُوا۟ وَكَانُوا۟ يَتَّقُونَ ﴿٥٧﴾

ingredient of his message, that sovereignty belongs only to the One True God (see verse 40 above). Now, were we to accept that as soon as the opportunity offered itself Joseph sought and became a part of the system of government which was led by the Egyptian king and which operated on the premise that sovereignty belongs to the king rather than God, that would be totally inconsistent with all that he had taught.

The fact is that the above interpretation of the verse by scholars during a period of Muslim decline betrays the mentality displayed at some stage of Jewish history and is characterized by the Jews. When the Jews fell prey to degeneration, they found it too difficult to rise to the heights displayed by the noble characters from their ancestry. Instead, they almost brought down their great ancestors, including Prophets, to their own level so that they might rationalize their own degeneracy. They wished to serve un-Islamic regimes. When they wished to so degrade themselves, they felt embarrassed by the heights to which the exponents of Islam had reached in the past. In order to overcome their embarrassment and to relieve their conscience of any guilt, they brought down a very noble Prophet – Joseph – to the degrading level of serving an un-Islamic system of government.

The Jews did so even though Joseph's life offers the lesson that even a single righteous believer suffices to bring about an Islamic revolution by dint of his character and wisdom. Joseph's life also illustrates that a believer's moral strength – provided he knows how to use it well – can enable him, even without recourse to arms, to conquer a whole country, even an empire.

48. This means that now that Egypt was under his control, he could call every part of it his own. Joseph could go without any let or hindrance to any

(58) And Joseph's brothers came to Egypt and presented themselves before him.[50] He recognized them, but they did not know him.[51] (59) And when he had prepared for them their provisions, Joseph said: 'Bring to me your other brother from your father. Do you not see that I give full measure and am most hospitable? (60) If you do not bring him to me, you shall have no corn from me; and do not even attempt to come close to me.'[52] (61) They said: 'We will surely try to prevail over our father to send him. Be sure we shall do so.' (62) And Joseph said to his servants: 'Put surreptitiously in their packs the goods they had given in exchange for corn.' Joseph did so expecting that they would find it when they returned home. Feeling grateful for this generosity, they might be inclined to return to him.

وَجَآءَ إِخْوَةُ يُوسُفَ فَدَخَلُوا۟ عَلَيْهِ
فَعَرَفَهُمْ وَهُمْ لَهُۥ مُنكِرُونَ ﴿٥٨﴾ وَلَمَّا
جَهَّزَهُم بِجَهَازِهِمْ قَالَ ٱئْتُونِى بِأَخٍ
لَّكُم مِّنْ أَبِيكُمْ ۚ أَلَا تَرَوْنَ أَنِّىٓ أُوفِى
ٱلْكَيْلَ وَأَنَا۠ خَيْرُ ٱلْمُنزِلِينَ ﴿٥٩﴾ فَإِن لَّمْ
تَأْتُونِى بِهِۦ فَلَا كَيْلَ لَكُمْ عِندِى
وَلَا تَقْرَبُونِ ﴿٦٠﴾ قَالُوا۟ سَنُرَٰوِدُ عَنْهُ
أَبَاهُ وَإِنَّا لَفَٰعِلُونَ ﴿٦١﴾ وَقَالَ لِفِتْيَٰنِهِ
ٱجْعَلُوا۟ بِضَٰعَتَهُمْ فِى رِحَالِهِمْ لَعَلَّهُمْ
يَعْرِفُونَهَآ إِذَا ٱنقَلَبُوٓا۟ إِلَىٰٓ أَهْلِهِمْ
لَعَلَّهُمْ يَرْجِعُونَ ﴿٦٢﴾

---

part of Egypt that he wanted. The above verse, thus, describes the total sway, the all-pervasive authority Joseph held over Egypt.

Early commentators of the Qur'ān have understood this verse in this way. For instance, Ibn Jarīr al-Ṭabarī, citing Ibn Zayd, has explained this verse to mean that God had put Joseph in charge of everything in Egypt. Joseph was free to do whatever he wished since the whole land was under his control. Such was his authority that had he wanted, he could even have placed himself above Pharaoh. Al-Ṭabarī also quotes a statement from Mujāhid, one of the earliest

(63) When they returned to their father they said: 'Father! We have been denied further supply of corn. So send with us our brother that we may bring the supplies. We shall be responsible for his protection.' (64) The father said: 'Shall I trust you with regard to him as I trusted you earlier with regard to his brother? Allah is the Best One for protection and is the Most Merciful.' (65) And when they opened their things they found that their goods had been given back to them. Thereupon they cried: 'Father! What else would we desire? Look, even our goods have been given back to us, so we shall go now and bring supplies for our family, protect our brother, and bring another camel-load of corn. That additional supply will be easily secured.' ▶

فَلَمَّا رَجَعُوٓا إِلَىٰٓ أَبِيهِمْ قَالُوا يَٰٓأَبَانَا
مُنِعَ مِنَّا ٱلْكَيْلُ فَأَرْسِلْ مَعَنَآ
أَخَانَا نَكْتَلْ وَإِنَّا لَهُۥ لَحَٰفِظُونَ
(٦٣) قَالَ هَلْ ءَامَنُكُمْ عَلَيْهِ إِلَّا كَمَآ
أَمِنتُكُمْ عَلَىٰٓ أَخِيهِ مِن قَبْلُ فَٱللَّهُ خَيْرٌ
حَٰفِظًا وَهُوَ أَرْحَمُ ٱلرَّٰحِمِينَ (٦٤) وَلَمَّا
فَتَحُوا مَتَٰعَهُمْ وَجَدُوا بِضَٰعَتَهُمْ
رُدَّتْ إِلَيْهِمْ قَالُوا يَٰٓأَبَانَا مَا نَبْغِى
هَٰذِهِۦ بِضَٰعَتُنَا رُدَّتْ إِلَيْنَا وَنَمِيرُ
أَهْلَنَا وَنَحْفَظُ أَخَانَا وَنَزْدَادُ كَيْلَ
بَعِيرٍ ذَٰلِكَ كَيْلٌ يَسِيرٌ (٦٥)

leading Qur'ān-commentators, that the Egyptian king had embraced Islam at the hand of Joseph. (See al-Ṭabarī's comments on verse 56 – Ed.)

49. This is to warn people from assuming that worldly power and authority constitute the true reward of righteousness. The best reward of righteous conduct – and one which a believer must aim at – is what God will bestow on him in the Next Life.

50. Once again the events of some seven or eight years have been skipped over and the narration has been resumed at the point which describes the migration of the Israelites to Egypt and the first clues that Jacob (peace be on him) received concerning his missing son. The events of the intervening period

which have been omitted refer to the period in which, according to Joseph's interpretation of the dream, there would first be seven years of prosperity in Egypt. During this period Joseph took all the precautionary measures which he had suggested to the king at the time he interpreted the dream.

This was followed by a famine and the famine was not confined to Egypt. It also spread to neighbouring countries, namely Syria, Palestine, Transjordan and northern Arabia. Thanks to the wise measures adopted by Joseph, only one country – Egypt – had plenty of grain despite the severe famine conditions which prevailed in the region. This compelled people in neighbouring countries to turn to Egypt, soliciting it to provide them with grain. It was this need to purchase grain which occasioned Joseph's brothers to travel from Palestine to Egypt. Presumably, Joseph had banned foreigners from carrying grain without special permission from the government, and beyond a certain measure. Hence when Joseph's brothers tried to purchase grain they would have been faced with the need to obtain permission from the government. It is for this reason that they had to appear before Joseph.

51. That Joseph's brothers did not recognize him came as no surprise to him. For at the time they had cast him into the pit, Joseph was only seventeen years old. Now, he was around thirty-eight. During such a long period everyone changes a great deal. Moreover, it could never have occurred to Joseph's brothers that their brother, whom they had thrown into a pit, would have become the all-powerful ruler of such a great country as Egypt.

52. In view of the brevity of the narration one may find it difficult to grasp why, despite Joseph's desire not to reveal his identity to his brothers, he insisted his step-brothers bring Benjamin along on their next visit.

A little reflection, however, should clarify the point. It will be recalled that food rationing was in force in Egypt at that time and each individual was entitled to a specified quantity of grain and no more. As we know, the ten brothers had come with the purpose of obtaining grain, and would naturally have asked for a share on behalf of their father and their eleventh brother. This presumably provided Joseph with reasonable enough grounds to make his point. He could possibly have accepted there was a valid reason for their father not to come to Egypt, for he was old and blind but there was no such reason in respect of their brother. Joseph might even have expressed the suspicion that they were perhaps trying to obtain additional supplies of grain under fictitious names, and that they may illegally try to sell the grain they had obtained for their family at some extortionate price. In response, Joseph's brothers might have explained their family circumstances. They might even have said that their brother was a step-brother, and that for certain reasons their father was unwilling to send him along with them. In reply, Joseph might have said that trusting their word he would permit them to receive the full supply of grain on this occasion. but if they failed to bring their step-brother the next time, they would receive no grain at all.

On the one hand, Joseph warned them. On the other hand, he tried to win

(66) Their father said: 'I shall never send him with you until you give me a solemn promise in the name of Allah that you will bring him back to me, unless you yourselves are surrounded.' Then when they had given him their solemn promise, he said: 'Allah watches over what we have said.' (67) And he enjoined them: 'My sons! Do not enter the city by one gate; rather enter it by different gates.[53] I can be of no help to you against Allah. Allah's command alone prevails. In Him have I put my trust and in Him should all those who have faith put their trust.' ▶

قَالَ لَنْ أُرْسِلَهُۥ مَعَكُمْ حَتَّىٰ تُؤْتُونِ
مَوْثِقًا مِّنَ ٱللَّهِ لَتَأْتُنَّنِى بِهِۦٓ إِلَّآ أَن يُحَاطَ
بِكُمْ فَلَمَّآ ءَاتَوْهُ مَوْثِقَهُمْ قَالَ ٱللَّهُ عَلَىٰ
مَا نَقُولُ وَكِيلٌ ﴿٦٦﴾ وَقَالَ يَٰبَنِىَّ لَا تَدْخُلُوا۟
مِنۢ بَابٍ وَٰحِدٍ وَٱدْخُلُوا۟ مِنْ أَبْوَٰبٍ
مُّتَفَرِّقَةٍ وَمَآ أُغْنِى عَنكُم مِّنَ ٱللَّهِ
مِن شَىْءٍ إِنِ ٱلْحُكْمُ إِلَّا لِلَّهِ عَلَيْهِ
تَوَكَّلْتُ وَعَلَيْهِ فَلْيَتَوَكَّلِ
ٱلْمُتَوَكِّلُونَ ﴿٦٧﴾

---

over their hearts by doing them a favour and entertaining them. All this is understandable since Joseph (peace be on him) would have been very keen to meet his brother Benjamin again and to become acquainted with the welfare of his family.

All this is simple enough, a matter easily understood. On reflection, the whole affair is so plain and natural that one need give no credence whatsoever to the exaggerated version of the story we find in the Bible (see *Genesis* 42–3).

53. This shows how Jacob, who had already gone through the bitter experience of sending Joseph with his step-brothers, might have felt about sending Benjamin with them. Although Jacob had full trust in God and also displayed the utmost patience, he was, after all, a human being. It is natural that a host of suspicions would have crossed his mind. It is also natural that occasionally he would have shivered at the possibility that he might never see Benjamin again. He, therefore, spared no effort in taking precautionary measures.

The precautionary measure suggested by Jacob – that the eleven brothers

(68) And it so happened that when they entered the city (by many gates) as their father had directed them, this precautionary measure proved ineffective against Allah's will. There was an uneasiness in Jacob's soul which he so tried to remove. Surely he was possessed of knowledge owing to the knowledge We bestowed upon him. But most people do not know the truth of the matter.[54]

وَلَمَّا دَخَلُوا۟ مِنْ حَيْثُ أَمَرَهُمْ أَبُوهُم مَّا كَانَ يُغْنِى عَنْهُم مِّنَ ٱللَّهِ مِن شَىْءٍ إِلَّا حَاجَةً فِى نَفْسِ يَعْقُوبَ قَضَىٰهَا ۚ وَإِنَّهُۥ لَذُو عِلْمٍ لِّمَا عَلَّمْنَٰهُ وَلَٰكِنَّ أَكْثَرَ ٱلنَّاسِ لَا يَعْلَمُونَ ﴿٦٨﴾

---

should not enter the Egyptian capital by the same gate – can be appreciated when one considers the political conditions of the day. For Joseph's brothers hailed from the independent tribal areas adjacent to Egypt. It is likely, therefore, that the Egyptians might have looked upon them suspiciously. (Witness the suspicions entertained by the British about the residents of the free tribal areas neighbouring the North Western Frontier Province during the Raj.) Jacob might have feared that if his sons entered in a group during a period of famine, they would be mistaken for wild tribesmen looking for loot and plunder. In the previous verse, too, Jacob's remark that 'unless you yourselves are surrounded' (verse 66) seems to indicate his apprehension was of a political nature.

54. Jacob's statements show how one should combine and maintain an even balance between one's worldly means and the full trust that one ought to have in God. Such a perfect balance was possible only because of the knowledge which God had bestowed on Jacob out of His grace and mercy. Jacob took all possible measures required by common sense and dictated by experience. It is also for this reason that he reminded his sons of their unbecoming behaviour towards Joseph and warned them not to repeat it; he made them solemnly swear in the name of God that they would protect their step-brother Benjamin. Moreover, in view of the political conditions then prevailing, he ordered them to adopt all measures that would prevent them from being 'surrounded' by others.

On the other hand, Joseph was fully conscious of the fact as suggested by his remark (see verse 68) that no matter what precautionary measures human

(69) When they presented themselves before Joseph, he took his brother aside to himself and said: 'Verily I am your own brother Joseph; so do not grieve over the manner they have treated you.'[55]

(70) Then, while Joseph was having their provisions loaded, he put his drinking-cup in his brother's saddle-bag.[56] And then a herald cried: 'Travellers, you are thieves.'[57] (71) Turning back they asked: 'What have you lost?' (72) The officials said: 'We have lost the king's cup.' (And their chief added): 'He who brings it shall have a camel-load of provisions, I guarantee that.'

وَلَمَّا دَخَلُوا۟ عَلَىٰ يُوسُفَ ءَاوَىٰٓ
إِلَيْهِ أَخَاهُ ۖ قَالَ إِنِّىٓ أَنَا۠ أَخُوكَ فَلَا
تَبْتَئِسْ بِمَا كَانُوا۟ يَعْمَلُونَ ﴿٦٩﴾
فَلَمَّا جَهَّزَهُم بِجَهَازِهِمْ جَعَلَ
ٱلسِّقَايَةَ فِى رَحْلِ أَخِيهِ ثُمَّ أَذَّنَ مُؤَذِّنٌ
أَيَّتُهَا ٱلْعِيرُ إِنَّكُمْ لَسَٰرِقُونَ ﴿٧٠﴾
قَالُوا۟ وَأَقْبَلُوا۟ عَلَيْهِم مَّاذَا
تَفْقِدُونَ ﴿٧١﴾ قَالُوا۟ نَفْقِدُ
صُوَاعَ ٱلْمَلِكِ وَلِمَن جَآءَ بِهِۦ
حِمْلُ بَعِيرٍ وَأَنَا۠ بِهِۦ زَعِيمٌ ﴿٧٢﴾

---

beings might take, nothing prevails against God's will. Hence, man should be clear in his mind that there is no security except God's. Man should, therefore, place his true reliance on Him rather than on worldly measures.

Such a balance in thought and deed can be maintained only by a person who has full knowledge of the truth. Such a person knows the requirement of God's laws: that man should work and strive for something for which he has a natural predisposition. At the same time, he is quite aware that the power that really counts is God's. While a believer strives as others do, he nevertheless knows that without the support of God man's effort is absolutely useless.

Sadly, this fact is known only to a very few. For most people are totally dependent on their own efforts and become oblivious to the fact that man must have trust in God and remember that God's will alone prevails. On the other hand, there are those who indolently leave things to God; they disregard the fact that alongside their trust in God, they are also required to work.

55. This little sentence encapsulates all that transpired between the two real brothers at their reunion after a lapse of some twenty-one to twenty-two years. During this meeting, Joseph would have told Benjamin of all the situations he

(73) They said: 'By Allah, you certainly know that we did not come to act corruptly in this land, nor are we those who steal.' (74) The officials said: 'If you are lying, what will be the penalty for him who has stolen?' ▶

قَالُواْ تَٱللَّهِ لَقَدْ عَلِمْتُم مَّا جِئْنَا
لِنُفْسِدَ فِي ٱلْأَرْضِ وَمَا كُنَّا سَٰرِقِينَ
﴿٧٣﴾ قَالُواْ فَمَا جَزَٰٓؤُهُۥٓ إِن كُنتُمْ
كَٰذِبِينَ ﴿٧٤﴾

---

found himself in prior to having reached his present stage of power and renown. Benjamin would have told Joseph of the maltreatment meted out to him by his step-brothers. Joseph would also have comforted Benjamin, saying that from now onwards he would stay with him and that he would not allow him to return with his cruel step-brothers. It is quite likely that at this point the two brothers would have jointly worked out a plan that would enable Benjamin to remain behind in Egypt. The two brothers did not, however, wish to disclose this plan as Joseph (peace be on him) wanted certain things to stay concealed at least for a while.

56. Apparently, Joseph himself devised the scheme whereby his drinking cup be put in Benjamin's saddle-bag. This was done with Benjamin's full knowledge and consent as is evident from the preceding verse. For, had Joseph simply issued a public order preventing Benjamin from returning, he would have been forced to reveal his true identity. This was unwise at that stage. Hence, the two brothers would have discussed how to achieve their desired purpose.

Doubtlessly the scheme which they devised was bound to bring Benjamin's reputation under a temporary cloud as he would be implicated in a case of theft. However, it would not be difficult to subsequently remove such a misunderstanding. For, at a date mutually agreed upon by the two brothers, they could reveal the undisclosed part of the whole story and, thus, remove the stigma of moral turpitude from his brother.

57. Neither the present verse nor the ones that follow provide any hint whatsoever to support the belief that Joseph (peace be on him) had taken his servants into his confidence regarding this matter and directed them to level a false charge of theft against the caravan. The incident seems to have been no more than that the drinking cup was surreptitiously put in Benjamin's saddle-bag. Later on, the government officials would have concluded that someone from the caravan had committed the theft.

(75) They replied: 'He in whose saddlebag the cup is found, he himself shall be its recompense.' Thus do We punish the wrong-doers.'[58] (76) Then Joseph began searching their bags before searching his own brother's bag. Then he brought forth the drinking-cup from his brother's bag. Thus did We contrive to support Joseph.[59] He had no right, according to the religion of the king [i.e. the law of Egypt] to take his brother, unless Allah so willed.[60] We exalt whomsoever We will over others by several degrees. And above all those who know is the One Who truly knows.

قَالُوا۟ جَزَٰٓؤُهُۥ مَن وُجِدَ فِى رَحْلِهِۦ فَهُوَ
جَزَٰٓؤُهُۥ ۚ كَذَٰلِكَ نَجْزِى ٱلظَّٰلِمِينَ
﴿٧٥﴾ فَبَدَأَ بِأَوْعِيَتِهِمْ قَبْلَ وِعَآءِ
أَخِيهِ ثُمَّ ٱسْتَخْرَجَهَا مِن وِعَآءِ
أَخِيهِ ۚ كَذَٰلِكَ كِدْنَا لِيُوسُفَ ۖ
مَا كَانَ لِيَأْخُذَ أَخَاهُ فِى دِينِ
ٱلْمَلِكِ إِلَّآ أَن يَشَآءَ ٱللَّهُ ۚ نَرْفَعُ
دَرَجَٰتٍ مَّن نَّشَآءُ ۗ وَفَوْقَ كُلِّ
ذِى عِلْمٍ عَلِيمٌ ﴿٧٦﴾

58. It must be remembered that since Joseph's brothers belonged to the Abrahamic family, the relevant law which they referred to was the Abrahamic law. According to that law, a thief had to be handed over to the person whose property he had stolen.

59. It is worth casting a glance at the whole series of events and then considering which specific device was directly inspired by God in support of Joseph. Obviously, Joseph himself suggested putting the drinking-cup in Benjamin's saddle-bag. In normal circumstances, the servants would have detained all members of the caravan suspecting that any one of them might have stolen Joseph's cup. What, then, constitutes the step which was part of God's own plan?

A careful study of the relevant verses brings out one fact very clearly – that the servants asked the suspected culprits to state the punishment for theft. In response, they mentioned the punishment laid down by Abrahamic law. This served two purposes. Firstly, it enabled Joseph to act according to Abrahamic law. Secondly, it enabled Joseph to detain Benjamin rather than to send him to prison.

60. It was unbecoming of Joseph, as a Prophet, to follow Egyptian law in a matter that related to him personally. The scheme which had been devised to retain his brother presented one problem. Joseph could have detained his brother but in order to do so it would have been necessary to have recourse to Egyptian penal law. This was unbecoming of a Prophet who had taken authority into his own hands in order to replace man-made laws with those of God.

Had God so willed, He could have let Joseph – a Prophet – commit this mistake. However, God did not do so. Thus, thanks to God's inspiration, a way out of the difficulty was found. An inquiry was addressed to Joseph's brothers. What punishment was laid down for a thief? In response, they mentioned the relevant provision of Abrahamic law. This was quite pertinent since Joseph's brothers were not subjects of the Egyptian state. Instead, they came from another territory which was independent. They were quite prepared, in accordance with the provisions of their law, to hand over a member of their group to the authorities that he may be punished for his crime. Hence, there was no need for Joseph to have recourse to Egyptian penal laws.

In this way God bestowed His favour upon Joseph and demonstrated His infinitely superior knowledge. What could be a greater means of exalting Joseph's position than this? When out of human weakness, Joseph was on the verge of committing an error God planned from on high and found a way to prevent this from happening. Such an exalted status is conferred only on those who prove their mettle after successfully going through a series of tests. Now, although Joseph (peace be on him) was quite knowledgeable and acted wisely, there was nevertheless a gap in the plan he had devised. That gap was filled by the One Whose knowledge surpasses the knowledge of every knower.

There are some points relating to the incident which deserve some explanation:

(1) Usually translators and commentators on the Qur'ān consider the verse to mean the following: 'Joseph could not have apprehended his brother according to the law of the land'. The Qur'ānic expression مَا كَانَ لِيَأْخُذَ أَخَاهُ is interpreted to mean that Joseph 'did not have the authority to apprehend his brother', rather than that it was 'inappropriate and unbecoming of Joseph' to do so. Such an understanding of the verse is wrong both from the point of view of Arabic idiom and Qur'ānic usage. For the Arabic usage مَا كَانَ لَهُ means 'it is not proper for him'. There are many instances of this usage in the Qur'ān to support this sense:

(a) 'It is not befitting to the majesty of Allah that He should take a son' (*Maryam* 19: 35).

(b) 'It is not proper for us to associate any with Allah in His divinity' (*Yūsuf* 12: 38).

(c) 'Allah is not going to disclose to you what is hidden in the realm beyond the reach of perception' (*Āl 'Imrān* 3: 179).

(d) 'And Allah will never leave your faith to waste' (*al-Baqarah* 2: 143).

(e) 'It is not Allah who wrongs them' (*al-Tawbah* 9: 70).

(f) 'Allah will not let the believers stay in the state they are' (*Āl 'Imrān* 3: 179).

(g) 'It is not for a believer to slay another believer' (*al-Nisā'* 4: 92).

In view of the above instances of Qur'ānic usage, the verse under discussion as usually interpreted by Qur'ān-commentators, makes no sense. For, what would prevent Joseph from arresting a thief under the king's law? In fact, there has never been any state on earth which prevented the arrest of a thief.

(2) By using the expression *dīn al-malik* to signify 'royal law', God has Himself indicated the meaning of the word (*dīn*). For it is quite evident that God's Messengers are raised to implement and enforce *dīn Allāh* ('the law of God') rather than 'the law of the king'. However, if it was not possible, due to adverse circumstances, to replace the king's law by God's law, it was at least unbecoming of a messenger to follow the king's law in a matter that related to his own self.

Thus, Joseph's decision not to punish his brother in accordance with the king's law was not based on the grounds that it was not possible for him to do so under the king's law. Rather, the only reason was that, being a Messenger of God, it was not appropriate for Joseph to follow the king's law instead of God's law in matters relating to himself.

(3) By using the term *dīn* to denote 'the law of the land', God has indicated the wide-ranging jurisdiction of *dīn*. This strikes at the very root of the concept of *dīn* or religion – which is perceived, according to ordinary parlance, to be concerned merely with adherence to a set of religious belief and rituals, of adhering to certain forms of worshipping the One True God.

Were one to accept such a narrow conception, religion would be able to say nothing worthwhile about man's societal life, about politics, civilization, economy, justice, legislation and such other facets of man's worldly life. Or, if religion has anything to say about such matters, it would merely be of a recommendatory nature. According to such a view, if people follow the guidelines provided by religion, all well and good. But if they do not, and instead follow man-made laws, then there is nothing objectionable about this.

This patently erroneous concept of religion, which has been popular among Muslims for quite some time, largely accounts for why Muslims have become negligent in their duty of establishing an Islamic order of life. As a result, they have become reconciled to live under a way of life based on *Jāhilīyah*. Not only that but some Muslims, in our time, have even come to believe that it is the *sunnah* of a Prophet (viz. Joseph) to administer a system of life based on *Jāhilīyah*. Such ideas have made Muslims ready to become cogs in the machinery of an un-Islamic government, willing to bend their efforts to operate it efficiently.

Such an attitude, according to the present verse, is altogether wrong. Instead we are told that the law on which society is based and which governs the affairs of the state is as much a part of *dīn* (religion) as prayer. This is further borne out by such Qur'ānic verses as: 'The true religion with Allah is Islam' (*Āl 'Imrān* 3: 18). 'And whoever seeks a way other than this way of Islam, will find that it will not be accepted from him' (*Āl 'Imrān* 3: 85).

These verses require that believers should totally submit themselves to *dīn*. And *dīn*, apart from prescribing Prayer and Fasting, also lays down laws relevant for operating the social system and the administration of a country. The Qur'ān, as we have noted above, stipulates that if Muslims deviate from Islam whether in matters of worship or of social organization, such an attitude is unacceptable to God.

(4) It should also be pointed out, in light of the above verse, that at that time 'the law of the king' rather than the 'law of God' operated in Egypt. Now, since Joseph had political control over Egypt, the conclusion is that Joseph enforced the 'law of the king' rather than the 'law of God'. It might even be argued that Joseph's adherence to Abrahamic law rather than to the royal law of Egypt in a matter relating to himself makes little difference. For it is evident that it is according to man-made laws that cases were judged in Egypt during his period of rule.

Such a view might seem quite weighty at first sight, but those who look at the matter a little more carefully will be able to put things into perspective. It is true that Joseph (peace be on him) was designated to give effect to the laws of God. In fact this was at the heart of his mission as a Prophet and his basic task as a ruler. All this is quite evident.

It should be remembered, however, that the system operating in any country does not change overnight. Suppose a group of people who sincerely wish to establish the Islamic order of life gain total control over the affairs of a country. It would nevertheless take several years before those people succeeded in changing the social, economic, political, judicial, and legal system of that country. During the transitional period they would be forced to retain existing laws until such time as their proposed changes make some significant headway.

It should also be remembered that Prophet Muḥammad (peace be on him) took some nine to ten years (after the *Hijrah*) to bring about total change in Arabia. During the transitional period people continued to drink wine, followed the inheritance laws of the *Jāhilīyah* period, and engaged in business transactions which were not at all in conformity with the principles of Islam.

(77) They said: 'No wonder that he steals for a brother of his stole before.'[61] But Joseph kept his reaction to himself without disclosing the truth to them. He merely said (to himself): 'You are an evil lot. Allah knows well the truth of the accusation that you are making against me (to my face).'

قَالُوٓا۟ إِن يَسْرِقْ فَقَدْ سَرَقَ أَخٌ لَّهُۥ مِن قَبْلُ ۚ فَأَسَرَّهَا يُوسُفُ فِى نَفْسِهِۦ وَلَمْ يُبْدِهَا لَهُمْ ۚ قَالَ أَنتُمْ شَرٌّ مَّكَانًا ۖ وَٱللَّهُ أَعْلَمُ بِمَا تَصِفُونَ ﴿٧٧﴾

Likewise, Islamic civil and criminal laws did not begin to fully operate from the very first day. So, if during the first eight or nine years of Joseph's rule, the old laws of the Egyptian state remained in operation, it is not at all surprising. This does not in any way warrant the idea that God's Messenger was designated to put into effect laws made by men rather than by God.

A further question might also be raised. If it was appropriate for Egyptian royal law to be in force in the whole country, why was it inappropriate for Joseph (peace be on him) to follow that law in his personal life? This matter can perhaps be fully understood if we remember the method of Prophet Muḥammad (peace be on him).

It is well known that during the first few years of Prophet Muḥammad's rule when a great many Islamic laws had not been promulgated, people drank wine but the Prophet certainly did not indulge in it. Likewise, people carried on transactions involving interest but the Prophet (peace be on him) never engaged in any such transaction. Other Muslims continued to indulge in several practices relating to marriage such as *mut'ah* (temporary marriage) and the combining of two sisters in wedlock all of which were later prohibited. It is significant, however, that while others indulged in these practices the Prophet (peace be on him) always abstained from them.

This shows that there is a difference between a Prophet's gradual enforcement of Islamic law owing to compulsions of a practical nature, and to following the ways of *Jāhilīyah* during the period of transition. Ordinary believers are condoned during the transitional phase, but it is certainly unbecoming of a Messenger of God to engage in practices which he had been designated to obliterate.

61. Joseph's brothers made this remark to overcome their embarrassment. They had said earlier that they were not thieves. But when they came to know that the stolen cup had been recovered from the saddle-bag of their brother,

(78) They said: 'O powerful chief [*al-'azīz*]![62] His father is an age-stricken man, (and in order that he may not suffer) seize one of us in his stead. We indeed consider you an excellent person.' (79) Joseph said: 'Allah forbid that we should seize any except him with whom we found our good.[63] Were we to do so, we would surely be one of the wrong-doers.'

قَالُوا يَٰٓأَيُّهَا ٱلْعَزِيزُ إِنَّ لَهُۥٓ أَبًا شَيْخًا
كَبِيرًا فَخُذْ أَحَدَنَا مَكَانَهُۥٓ إِنَّا
نَرَىٰكَ مِنَ ٱلْمُحْسِنِينَ ﴿٧٨﴾ قَالَ
مَعَاذَ ٱللَّهِ أَن نَّأْخُذَ إِلَّا مَن
وَجَدْنَا مَتَٰعَنَا عِندَهُۥٓ إِنَّآ
إِذًا لَّظَٰلِمُونَ ﴿٧٩﴾

Benjamin, they invented a lie and dissociated themselves from him. They even made a scandalous statement about Benjamin's brother, Joseph. This only shows the kind of treatment they were capable of meting out to Benjamin had he not enjoyed Joseph's protection. This also demonstrates why both Benjamin and Joseph preferred that Benjamin not join the ten brothers on their return journey.

62. In the above verse the title *'azīz* (literally the 'powerful one') has been used for Joseph. In view of this usage, some Qur'ān-commentators are of the opinion that Joseph was appointed to the same office that had been held earlier by Zelicha's husband. Some have even gone further towards the fantastic with the stories they have weaved. In these stories, it is claimed that since the former *'azīz* had died, Joseph was appointed to his office; that by dint of a miracle Zelicha's youth was restored, and that the Egyptian king joined Joseph and Zelicha in wedlock. To crown it all, these writers even claimed to know what transpired between Joseph and Zelicha on their wedding night.

It is obvious such stories are nothing more than fiction. We have already noted that the word *'azīz* was not the specific appellation of any particular office. (See n. 16, above – Ed.) It was used in the sense of 'incumbent of power'. This expression, in Egypt, was synonymous with the honorific words used for incumbents of power in different languages. Whatever word might have been used for incumbents of power in the Egyptian language at that time has been denoted in the Qur'ān by the Arabic word *'azīz*.

Now so far as Zelicha's marriage with Joseph is concerned, the only basis for it is the Biblical and Talmudic account of Joseph's story. In that account Joseph has been mentioned as having married Asenath, the daughter of

(80) Then, when they had despaired of Joseph they went to a corner and counselled together. The eldest of them said: 'Do you not know that your father has taken a solemn promise from you in the name of Allah, and you failed in your duty towards Joseph? So I will not depart from this land until my father permits me, or Allah pronounces His judgement in my favour. He is the best of those who judge.

فَلَمَّا اسْتَيْـَٔسُوا مِنْهُ خَلَصُوا نَجِيًّا
قَالَ كَبِيرُهُمْ أَلَمْ تَعْلَمُوٓا أَنَّ
أَبَاكُمْ قَدْ أَخَذَ عَلَيْكُم مَّوْثِقًا مِّنَ
اللَّهِ وَمِن قَبْلُ مَا فَرَّطتُمْ فِي يُوسُفَ
فَلَنْ أَبْرَحَ الْأَرْضَ حَتَّىٰ يَأْذَنَ لِيٓ أَبِيٓ
أَوْ يَحْكُمَ اللَّهُ لِي وَهُوَ خَيْرُ
الْحَاكِمِينَ ﴿٨٠﴾

Potophra. (*Genesis* 41: 45 – Ed.) Now the name of Zelicha's husband was Potiphar. Such diverse fragments of information reached Qur'ān-commentators from a variety of Israelite sources. Quite a bit of this material was derived from oral accounts. It is not surprising, therefore, that Potophra was confused with Potiphar. Again, the word 'daughter' changed into 'wife' and it was easily imagined that the wife could be none other than Zelicha. And Zelicha could have been married to Joseph only if her husband had died. Potiphar was, therefore, assumed to have died. Thus, the whole romantic legend of 'Joseph and Zelicha' came into being.

63. Joseph's circumspection is noteworthy. When the cup was found in Benjamin's saddle-bag, Joseph did not charge him with stealing. Joseph, according to the Qur'ān, used the expression 'with whom we found our good' (see verse 79). In Islamic terminology, such an expression is termed as *tawriyah*. The term denotes 'covering up' or 'concealing' some fact. One may resort to *tawriyah* in a situation when there remains no other alternative to save a victim from his oppressor, or to ward off a serious mischief other than resorting to a statement or device which conceals the true facts. Faced with a difficult situation such as the one mentioned above, a pious person would refrain from lying, but he might well resort to an ambiguous statement or to a device aimed at concealing facts so as to ward off wrongs. Such an action is quite permissible from both the religious and moral viewpoints, provided the motive for the action is to ward off some serious evil rather than to reap some benefit.

Now let us consider how in this particular instance Joseph fulfilled all the conditions of a permissible *tawriyah*. First, he put the drinking cup in

(81) So go back to your father and tell him: "Father! Your son has certainly been guilty of stealing. We did not see him stealing but testify according to what we know; and obviously we had no power to keep watch over what is beyond the reach of perception. (82) You may inquire of the dwellers of the city where we were, and of the people of the caravan with whom we travelled. We are altogether truthful in what we say." '

(83) The father heard the narration and said: '(All that is untrue). But your souls have made it easy for you to engage in a heinous act.[64] So, I will be graciously patient even at this. Allah may well bring them all back to me. He is All-Knowing, All-Wise.' ▶

ٱرْجِعُوٓا۟ إِلَىٰٓ أَبِيكُمْ فَقُولُوا۟ يَٰٓأَبَانَآ
إِنَّ ٱبْنَكَ سَرَقَ وَمَا شَهِدْنَآ
إِلَّا بِمَا عَلِمْنَا وَمَا كُنَّا لِلْغَيْبِ
حَٰفِظِينَ ﴿٨١﴾ وَسْـَٔلِ ٱلْقَرْيَةَ ٱلَّتِى
كُنَّا فِيهَا وَٱلْعِيرَ ٱلَّتِىٓ أَقْبَلْنَا فِيهَا ۖ
وَإِنَّا لَصَٰدِقُونَ ﴿٨٢﴾ قَالَ بَلْ
سَوَّلَتْ لَكُمْ أَنفُسُكُمْ أَمْرًا ۖ فَصَبْرٌ
جَمِيلٌ ۖ عَسَى ٱللَّهُ أَن يَأْتِيَنِى بِهِمْ
جَمِيعًا ۚ إِنَّهُۥ هُوَ ٱلْعَلِيمُ
ٱلْحَكِيمُ ﴿٨٣﴾

Benjamin's saddle-bag with the latter's full consent. He did not, however, direct the servants to charge Benjamin with stealing. When the servants charged the brothers with theft, Joseph simply stood up and without uttering a word searched their belongings. Subsequently, when Joseph's brothers requested him to detain any of them in place of Benjamin, he simply responded by saying that they themselves had suggested that only the person with whom the stolen good was found should be detained. Now since the cup was found in Benjamin's saddle-bag he could be detained. For, how could anyone else be detained?

Instances of such *tawriyah* are also found in the military campaigns of the Prophet (peace be on him). There is no valid reason, therefore, to find fault with the practice of *tawriyah* in the manner described above.

(84) Then he turned his back to them, and said: 'O my grief for Joseph!' His eyes whitened with grief and he was choked up with sorrow trying to suppress his grief. (85) The sons said: 'By Allah! You will continue to remember Joseph until you will either consume yourself with grief, or will die.' (86) He said: 'I will address my sorrow and grief only to Allah, and I know about Allah what you do not know. (87) My sons! Go and try to find out about Joseph and his brother and do not despair of the mercy of Allah. Verily only the unbelievers despair of Allah's mercy.'

(88) On going to Egypt they presented themselves to Joseph and said to him: 'O chief! We and our family are struck with distress and have brought only a paltry sum. So give us corn in full measure, and give it to us in charity.[65] Allah rewards those who are charitable.' ▶

وَتَوَلَّىٰ عَنْهُمْ وَقَالَ يَٰٓأَسَفَىٰ عَلَىٰ يُوسُفَ
وَٱبْيَضَّتْ عَيْنَاهُ مِنَ ٱلْحُزْنِ فَهُوَ
كَظِيمٌ ﴿٨٤﴾ قَالُوا۟ تَٱللَّهِ تَفْتَؤُا۟
تَذْكُرُ يُوسُفَ حَتَّىٰ تَكُونَ حَرَضًا
أَوْ تَكُونَ مِنَ ٱلْهَٰلِكِينَ ﴿٨٥﴾
قَالَ إِنَّمَآ أَشْكُوا۟ بَثِّى وَحُزْنِىٓ إِلَى ٱللَّهِ
وَأَعْلَمُ مِنَ ٱللَّهِ مَا لَا تَعْلَمُونَ
﴿٨٦﴾ يَٰبَنِىَّ ٱذْهَبُوا۟ فَتَحَسَّسُوا۟ مِن
يُوسُفَ وَأَخِيهِ وَلَا تَا۟يْـَٔسُوا۟ مِن
رَّوْحِ ٱللَّهِ ۖ إِنَّهُۥ لَا يَا۟يْـَٔسُ مِن رَّوْحِ ٱللَّهِ
إِلَّا ٱلْقَوْمُ ٱلْكَٰفِرُونَ ﴿٨٧﴾ فَلَمَّا
دَخَلُوا۟ عَلَيْهِ قَالُوا۟ يَٰٓأَيُّهَا ٱلْعَزِيزُ
مَسَّنَا وَأَهْلَنَا ٱلضُّرُّ وَجِئْنَا بِبِضَٰعَةٍ
مُّزْجَىٰةٍ فَأَوْفِ لَنَا ٱلْكَيْلَ وَتَصَدَّقْ
عَلَيْنَآ ۖ إِنَّ ٱللَّهَ يَجْزِى
ٱلْمُتَصَدِّقِينَ ﴿٨٨﴾

---

64. Jacob said that it was not at all difficult for his sons to accuse Benjamin – whose character and conduct he knew to be excellent – of stealing a cup. Such behaviour on their part did not surprise him. For in the past, they had deliberately caused their brother Joseph to be lost. Not only that, they had felt no compunction in bringing back his shirt with false blood-stains in order to

(89) When Joseph heard this (he could not hold himself and said): 'Do you remember what you did to Joseph and his brother when you were ignorant?' (90) They exclaimed: 'Are you indeed Joseph?' He said: 'Yes, I am Joseph and this is my brother. Allah has surely been gracious to us. Indeed whoever fears Allah and remains patient, Allah does not allow the reward of such people to go to waste.' (91) They said: 'We swear by Allah! Indeed Allah has chosen you in preference to us and we were truly guilty.' (92) He replied: 'No blame lies with you today. May Allah forgive you. He is the Most Merciful of all those who are merciful. (93) Take this shirt of mine and throw it over my father's face. He will regain his sight. And bring to me all your family.'

قَالَ هَلْ عَلِمْتُم مَّا فَعَلْتُم بِيُوسُفَ
وَأَخِيهِ إِذْ أَنتُمْ جَٰهِلُونَ ﴿٨٩﴾
قَالُوٓا۟ أَءِنَّكَ لَأَنتَ يُوسُفُ قَالَ
أَنَا۠ يُوسُفُ وَهَٰذَآ أَخِى قَدْ مَنَّ
ٱللَّهُ عَلَيْنَآ إِنَّهُۥ مَن يَتَّقِ وَيَصْبِرْ
فَإِنَّ ٱللَّهَ لَا يُضِيعُ أَجْرَ
ٱلْمُحْسِنِينَ ﴿٩٠﴾ قَالُوا۟ تَٱللَّهِ لَقَدْ
ءَاثَرَكَ ٱللَّهُ عَلَيْنَا وَإِن كُنَّا
لَخَٰطِـِٔينَ ﴿٩١﴾ قَالَ لَا تَثْرِيبَ
عَلَيْكُمُ ٱلْيَوْمَ يَغْفِرُ ٱللَّهُ لَكُمْ وَهُوَ
أَرْحَمُ ٱلرَّٰحِمِينَ ﴿٩٢﴾
ٱذْهَبُوا۟ بِقَمِيصِى هَٰذَا فَأَلْقُوهُ
عَلَىٰ وَجْهِ أَبِى يَأْتِ بَصِيرًا وَأْتُونِى
بِأَهْلِكُمْ أَجْمَعِينَ ﴿٩٣﴾

---

reinforce their claim that Joseph had been eaten by a wolf. And now they were telling Jacob, with equal ease of conscience, that Benjamin had committed a theft.

65. They told Joseph that whatever he would grant them would be charity. For the trivial amount they offered as a price for the large amount of grain given to them was far from adequate.

(94) And as the caravan set out (from Egypt), their father said (in Canaan): 'Indeed I smell the fragrance of Joseph.[66] I say so although you may think that I am doting.' (95) They said: 'Surely you are still in your same old "craze".'[67]

(96) And when the bearer of good news came he threw Joseph's shirt over Jacob's face, whereupon he regained his sight, and said: 'Did I not tell you that I know from Allah what you do not know?'

وَلَمَّا فَصَلَتِ ٱلْعِيرُ قَالَ أَبُوهُمْ
إِنِّي لَأَجِدُ رِيحَ يُوسُفَ لَوْلَآ أَن
تُفَنِّدُونِ ﴿٩٤﴾ قَالُواْ تَٱللَّهِ إِنَّكَ لَفِي
ضَلَٰلِكَ ٱلْقَدِيمِ ﴿٩٥﴾ فَلَمَّآ أَن
جَآءَ ٱلْبَشِيرُ أَلْقَىٰهُ عَلَىٰ وَجْهِهِۦ فَٱرْتَدَّ
بَصِيرًا قَالَ أَلَمْ أَقُل لَّكُمْ إِنِّيٓ أَعْلَمُ
مِنَ ٱللَّهِ مَا لَا تَعْلَمُونَ ﴿٩٦﴾

66. This indicates the extraordinary faculties possessed by the Prophets. The caravan had just set out from Egypt, carrying Joseph's shirt. And yet, even though Jacob was hundreds of miles away, he could smell its fragrance. From this we also learn that these faculties were not their personal acquisitions. They were special endowments bestowed upon the Prophets by God. Whenever God so wills, He enables the Prophets to mobilize those faculties and to do so to the extent that He pleases. We know that Joseph had been in Egypt for years and yet Jacob had never smelled his fragrance. But suddenly, when God so willed, it became possible for him to smell the fragrance of Joseph's shirt even though it was far away.

It is also interesting to note the difference between the Qur'ānic and Israelite images of Jacob. The Qur'ān portrays Jacob with all the glory of a Prophet. On the contrary, the Israelite sources portray him as hardly different from an ordinary bedouin. According to the Bible:

> And they [i.e. the sons] told him: 'Joseph is still alive, and he is ruler over all the land of Egypt.' And his heart fainted, for he did not believe them and when he saw the wagons which Joseph had sent to carry him, the spirit of their father Jacob revived . . . (*Genesis* 45: 26–7).

67. It is evident from the above verse that except for Joseph none of the brothers truly valued his father. Jacob himself had despaired of his sons because of their moral degeneracy. Jacob's mission and message had

(97) They said: 'Father! Pray for the forgiveness of our sins; we were truly guilty.' (98) He said: 'I shall pray to my Lord for your forgiveness, for He, and indeed He alone, is Ever Forgiving, Most Merciful.'

(99) And when they went to Joseph,[68] he took his parents aside[69] and said (to the members of his family): 'Enter the city now, and if Allah wills, you shall be secure.'

قَالُواْ يَـٰٓأَبَانَا ٱسۡتَغۡفِرۡ لَنَا ذُنُوبَنَآ إِنَّا كُنَّا
خَـٰطِـِٔينَ ﴿٩٧﴾ قَالَ سَوۡفَ أَسۡتَغۡفِرُ
لَكُمۡ رَبِّيٓۖ إِنَّهُۥ هُوَ ٱلۡغَفُورُ ٱلرَّحِيمُ
﴿٩٨﴾ فَلَمَّا دَخَلُواْ عَلَىٰ يُوسُفَ ءَاوَىٰٓ
إِلَيۡهِ أَبَوَيۡهِ وَقَالَ ٱدۡخُلُواْ مِصۡرَ إِن
شَآءَ ٱللَّهُ ءَامِنِينَ ﴿٩٩﴾

---

enlightened those outside his household. But members of his own family scarcely held him in any esteem. Such instances are quite common in history. Many great men have received no appreciation from their compatriots.

68. According to the Bible, the members of Jacob's family who migrated to Egypt at that time were sixty-seven in number. This number does not include Jacob's daughters-in-law. Jacob was then one hundred and thirty years old and subsequently lived in Egypt for another seventeen years.

One may wonder about one thing. When the Israelites first entered Egypt their number, including Joseph, was only sixty-eight. But after some five hundred years, when they migrated from Egypt, their numbers had swelled to hundreds of thousands. According to the Bible, when Moses conducted a census in the Sinai desert after just one year, the number of combatant males was 603,550. Using this figure as our basis, their total number at the time must have been at least two million. Is it physically possible that a group of sixty-eight people could grow into two million within a span of just five hundred years?

If we were to suppose that the total population of Egypt at that time was twenty million – which would be a highly exaggerated figure – the Israelites would form just one tenth of it. Is it possible for a family to multiply in such great numbers by normal reproduction? Reflection on this question leads us to another important fact; it is simply impossible for a family to multiply so profusely in just five hundred years.

However, the Israelites were the progeny of Messengers of God. Their leader, Joseph, who had paved the way for their settlement in Egypt, was himself a Messenger. For between four and five centuries the Israelites held total sway over Egypt. During this period, they must have preached their religion. As a result, those Egyptians who had embraced Islam would have become distinct from non-Muslim Egyptians and in the course of time assimilated into the Israeli way of life.

As a consequence, the local unbelieving Egyptians would have treated the converted Egyptians as aliens in the same manner as the Hindus of India treated the Muslims of Indian origin. The appellation 'Israeli' would have been applied to those converts in the manner that the term 'Muhammadan' is often applied to all non-Arab Muslims. Moreover, owing to the close religious, social and matrimonial relationships with the Israelites, those Egyptians who converted to Islam would have become distinct from their non-Muslim Egyptian compatriots and in the course of time would have been identified with the Israelites. This accounts for the fact that when an upsurge of nationalist feeling took place in Egypt, it was not only the original Israelites but also the converted Egyptians which were subjected to severe oppression. Later on, when the original Israelites migrated from Egypt, these converts migrated with them.

Our conclusion on the subject is corroborated by several Biblical statements. For example, in a passage in *Exodus* where the departure of the Israelites from Egypt has been described, it is remarked, 'a mixed multitude went up also with them . . .' (*Exodus* 12: 38). The following statement also has the same import: 'Now the rabble that was among them had a strong craving . . .' (*Numbers* 11: 4). Thus, in the Commandments revealed to Moses we find the following statement:

> For the assembly, there shall be one state for you and for the stranger who sojourns with you, a perpetual statute throughout your generations; as you are, so shall the sojourner be before the Lord. One law and one ordinance shall be for you and for the stranger who sojourns with you, (*Numbers* 15: 15–16).
>
> But the person who does anything with a high hand, whether he is native or sojourner, reviles the Lord, and that person shall be cut off from among his people, (*Numbers* 15: 30).
>
> And I charged your judges at that time, 'hear the cases between your brethren, and judge righteously between a man and his brother or the alien that is with him', (*Deuteronomy* 1: 16).

It is difficult, however, to determine the exact term used in the Scriptures for non-Israelites for which the terms 'strangers' and 'aliens' were subsequently used.

69. According to the Talmud, 'when Joseph learned that his father was upon the way, he gathered together his friends and officers, and soldiers of the realm, attired in rich garments . . . and formed a great company to meet Prophet

(100) And after they had entered the city, Joseph raised his parents to the throne beside himself, and they (involuntarily) fell down in prostration before him.[70] Joseph said: 'Father! This is the fulfilment of the vision I had before – one that My Lord has caused to come true. He was kind to me when He rescued me from the prison, and brought you from the desert after Satan had stirred discord between me and my brothers. Certainly my Lord is subtle in the fulfilment of His will; He is All-Knowing, All-Wise.' ►

وَرَفَعَ أَبَوَيْهِ عَلَى ٱلْعَرْشِ وَخَرُّوا۟ لَهُۥ
سُجَّدًا وَقَالَ يَٰٓأَبَتِ هَٰذَا تَأْوِيلُ رُءْيَٰىَ
مِن قَبْلُ قَدْ جَعَلَهَا رَبِّى حَقًّا وَقَدْ أَحْسَنَ
بِىٓ إِذْ أَخْرَجَنِى مِنَ ٱلسِّجْنِ وَجَآءَ بِكُم
مِّنَ ٱلْبَدْوِ مِنۢ بَعْدِ أَن نَّزَغَ ٱلشَّيْطَٰنُ
بَيْنِى وَبَيْنَ إِخْوَتِىٓ إِنَّ رَبِّى لَطِيفٌ
لِّمَا يَشَآءُ إِنَّهُۥ هُوَ ٱلْعَلِيمُ ٱلْحَكِيمُ ١٠٠

Jacob on the way and escort him to Egypt. Music and gladness filled the land, and all the people, the women and the children assembled on the house tops to view the magnificent display'. (H. Polano, *The Talmudic Selections,* p. 111.)

70. The use of the term *'sajdah'* (prostration) in the above verse has given rise to considerable misconception. This misconception reached such heights that some people interpreted the verse to justify prostration before kings and saints, calling it 'prostration of greeting' or 'prostration of respect' as distinguished from 'prostration of worship'.

Since in Islam prostration is associated with worship, some scholars resorted to an altogether novel explanation. They contended that it was only the prostration of worship, provided it was directed to any other than God, which was prohibited in the earlier versions of Divine Law. As for prostration which did not signify any worship, it was permissible even in respect of persons other than God. They claimed that it is only in the *Sharī'ah* of Prophet Muḥammad (peace be on him) that all forms of prostration directed to anyone other than God are forbidden.

What lies at the core of all this confusion is the word *sajdah* (prostration) as used in the verse. It has been taken in the technical sense in which it has come to be used in Islam as meaning putting one's feet, knees and forehead on the ground. However, the true meaning of *sajdah* is 'to bow' and in the above verse the word has been used exactly in that sense. Bowing as a form of respect was in vogue in ancient cultures. The practice is still in vogue in some countries of the world. When people wish to thank or welcome, or even receive someone, they are wont to put their hands on their chest and bow a little. The act, called bowing in English, is expressed in Arabic by the word *sajdah.* Numerous references to this bowing are found in the Bible signifying that it was an established form of paying respect to others. The Arabic version of the Bible uses exactly the same expression with reference to Abraham's reception of three persons approaching his tent.

فَلمّا نَظَرَ رَكَضَ لاستِقْبالِهِمْ مِنْ بَابَ الخَيْمَةِ وَسَجَدَ الى الأَرْضِ (تكوين: ١٨ـ٢٣)

In the English version of the Bible too we find references to bowing as a sign of respect. For instance, after mentioning that a piece of land was donated as a burying place for Sarah, Prophet Abraham expressed his thankfulness in the following manner: 'Abraham rose and bowed to the Hittites, the people of the land' (*Genesis* 23: 7). To cite another example: 'Then Abraham bowed down before the people of the land' (*Genesis* 23: 12). Numerous references to this practice are found in the Bible which establishes beyond doubt that the act concerned did not mean prostration in the sense in which *sajdah* is used as a technical Islamic term.

Some people, who have studied the question superficially, have contended that in the different versions of the Divine Law prior to the advent of Prophet Muḥammad (peace be on him) it was permissible to prostrate before others than the One True God. Such a statement is utterly devoid of all justification. For if prostration is taken in the technical sense that it denotes in Islam, it has never been lawful to offer it to anyone other than God. According to the Bible, during the Babylonian captivity of the Israelites, King Ahasuerus advanced Haman and set him above all the princes who were with him: 'And all the king's servants who were at the king's gate bowed down and did obeisance to Haman; for the king had so commanded concerning him. But Mordecai did not bow down or do obeisance' (*Esther* 3: 2). This was because the Israelites were not supposed to do so. The following details of this incident found in the Talmud are significant.

The servants of the King said to Mordecai: 'Why will thou refuse to bow before Haman, transgressing thus the wishes of the King? Do we not bow before him?' 'Ye are foolish' answered Mordecai, 'aye wanting in reason. Listen to me. Shall a mortal, who must return to dust, be glorified? Shall I bow down before one born of woman whose days are short? When he is small he cries and weeps as a child: when he grows older sorrow and sighing are his portion; his days are full of wrath and anger and at the end he returns to dust. Shall I bow to one like him? No, I prostrate myself before the Eternal God, who lives for ever. To Him the great Creator and Ruler of the Universe, and to no other will I bow'. (H. Polano, *The Talmudic Selections*, p. 172.)

This speech was made some one thousand years before the revelation of the

(101) My Lord! You have bestowed dominion upon me and have taught me to comprehend the depths of things. O Creator of heavens and the earth! You are my Guardian in this world and in the Hereafter. Cause me to die in submission to You, and join me, in the end, with the righteous.'[71]

۞ رَبِّ قَدْ ءَاتَيْتَنِى مِنَ ٱلْمُلْكِ
وَعَلَّمْتَنِى مِن تَأْوِيلِ ٱلْأَحَادِيثِ ۚ فَاطِرَ
ٱلسَّمَٰوَٰتِ وَٱلْأَرْضِ أَنتَ وَلِىِّۦ فِى
ٱلدُّنْيَا وَٱلْءَاخِرَةِ ۖ تَوَفَّنِى مُسْلِمًا
وَأَلْحِقْنِى بِٱلصَّٰلِحِينَ ﴿١٠١﴾

Qur'ān by a believing Israelite. It does not suggest in any way that it was permissible to prostrate before anyone other than God.

71. These utterances by Joseph (peace be on him) present before us the image of a true man of faith, of a paragon of moral excellence. A person coming from a family of nomadic shepherds, a victim of the conspiracies of his own brothers, Joseph reaches the height of worldly glory by successfully going through the vicissitudes of fortune. The famine-stricken members of his family, including his jealous brothers who had wanted to kill him, are now solely dependent on him. All of them stand before him in abject humiliation.

Such an opportunity is generally used by people to boast of their achievements and to reproach and insult those who had earlier been unkind to them. However, this truly God-conscious person behaves in an entirely different manner. Rather than take pride in his rise to eminence, he fully acknowledges God's favour which helped him to rise to such an exalted position. He does not reproach the members of his family who had been conspicuously unkind to him in his childhood. On the contrary, he thanks God Who has enabled him to be reunited with them after a long time.

In addition, Joseph does not utter a single word of complaint against his jealous brothers. He does not even mention their misdeeds. Ascribing their deeds to Satan's prompting, he simply says that it was Satan who had 'stirred discord between me and my brothers' (verse 100). Instead of dwelling on his brothers' misconduct, Joseph makes the best use of the incident, saying that it was God Who contrived his rise to glory. In other words, what Satan had prompted his brothers to do was a part of divine dispensation, something that turned out to be to his own good. In the end, summing up all this in a few words, Joseph once again submits to God in thanksgiving for bestowing on him

(102) (O Muḥammad!) This is some news from the unseen that We reveal to you for you were not present with them when Joseph's brothers jointly resolved on a plot. (103) And most of the people, howsoever you might so desire, are not going to believe.[72] (104) You do not seek from them any recompense for your service. This is merely an admonition to all mankind.[73]

ذَٰلِكَ مِنْ أَنۢبَآءِ ٱلْغَيْبِ نُوحِيهِ إِلَيْكَ
وَمَا كُنتَ لَدَيْهِمْ إِذْ أَجْمَعُوٓا۟ أَمْرَهُمْ وَهُمْ
يَمْكُرُونَ ﴿١٠٢﴾ وَمَآ أَكْثَرُ ٱلنَّاسِ
وَلَوْ حَرَصْتَ بِمُؤْمِنِينَ ﴿١٠٣﴾
وَمَا تَسْـَٔلُهُمْ عَلَيْهِ مِنْ أَجْرٍ إِنْ هُوَ
إِلَّا ذِكْرٌ لِّلْعَٰلَمِينَ ﴿١٠٤﴾

---

kingdom and wisdom, of having rescued him from prison, for having placed him at the helm of the largest state in the world.

Finally, Joseph makes a moving prayer to God, asking Him to hold him fast in submission to Him and to join him with the righteous when he dies. This is indeed an example of the most noble and perfect conduct conceivable in a righteous person.

To one's utter astonishment, this highly significant speech by Joseph finds no place in either the Bible or the Talmud. These books abound in detail concerning trivial matters. However, they are usually devoid of things that have moral value or shed light on the mission of the Prophets or their basic teachings. These books scarcely provide the materials from which one may learn any important lesson.

As we conclude this story, it is worth reminding the readers that the Qur'ānic account of Joseph's story is an independent account, not a rearrangement of the Biblical and Talmudic accounts. A comparative study of Joseph's story in these three sources makes it quite apparent that on several important points, the Qur'ānic account significantly differs from the other two sources. In several cases, the Qur'ān elaborates the information found in the Bible and the Talmud. It also omits some of the details mentioned in the Bible. Moreover, the Qur'ān refutes the Bible and the Talmud on some important matters relating to the story. It, thus, leaves no grounds for the charge that Prophet Muḥammad (peace be on him) took over this story from the Israelites.

72. This refers to the stubbornness of the unbelievers. On the one hand, after careful deliberation and mutual consultation, they decided to put a number of

(105) How many are the signs in the heavens and the earth[74] which people pass by without giving any heed![75] (106) And most of them do not believe in Allah except when they associate others with Him.[76] ▶

وَكَأَيِّن مِّنْ ءَايَةٍ فِى ٱلسَّمَٰوَٰتِ
وَٱلْأَرْضِ يَمُرُّونَ عَلَيْهَا وَهُمْ عَنْهَا
مُعْرِضُونَ ﴿١٠٥﴾ وَمَا يُؤْمِنُ أَكْثَرُهُم
بِٱللَّهِ إِلَّا وَهُم مُّشْرِكُونَ ﴿١٠٦﴾

---

questions to the Prophet (peace be on him) so as to test the truth of his claim to prophethood. When the Prophet (peace be on him) successfully responded to their demands it was naturally expected that they would no longer persist in their denial of the truth and would no longer cast any doubt on the divine origin of the Qur'ān. God, however, tells Prophet Muḥammad (peace be on him) that the unbelievers would still act unreasonably and would find one pretext after another for their denial of the Prophet (peace be on him). They did not disbelieve because they had failed to have access to the arguments that would convince them regarding his prophethood. That was not the case at all. They simply did not want to believe in the Prophet (peace be on him) and hence any reasonable discussion with them was out of the question.

The purpose of this clarification was not to remove any misgiving that the Prophet (peace be on him) might have had. Though the statement here is apparently addressed to the Prophet (peace be on him), it is in fact directed to the unbelievers and its purpose is to warn them against their obduracy. They had tried to put the Prophet (peace be on him) to the test by suddenly demanding that he tell them something about the migration of the Israelites to Egypt if his claim to prophethood was true. In response, the whole of Joseph's story was related to them there and then.

In conclusion, it was remarked that now it was for those stubborn people to judge for themselves whether they had any justification whatsoever for putting the Prophet (peace be on him) to any further test. If they had been sincere in testing him, then they should have welcomed the truth which had become apparent in response to their query. However, the unbelievers were still adamant in denying the truth even after it had become manifest.

73. In addition to the warning given in the preceding verse, the present verse also carries a subtle note of warning, wherein the element of admonition is more conspicuous than the reproach.

Even though the verse is apparently addressed to the Prophet (peace be on him), it is meant, in fact, for the unbelievers. They are being asked to think and to see for themselves how unjustified they were in their adamance. Had the

Prophet (peace be on him) been carrying out his mission to fulfil his own personal ends, the believers would be justified in rejecting his message. However, they could see for themselves that he was an absolutely selfless person who was working for their good. The Prophet (peace be on him) could not have gained anything for himself out of the reform for which he was striving. Therefore, there was no point in their adamant rejection of him. There was no reason why a person should have prejudice against someone who was inviting them to their common good. The unbelievers were, therefore, well advised to pay heed to what the Prophet (peace be on him) taught and to do so with an open mind. After that it was up to them to accept his teachings if they were convinced, or to reject them if they were not.

74. The story of Joseph which began with the opening verse of this *sūrah* concludes here. Had the purpose been merely to tell a tale, this should have marked the end of the *sūrah*. But the Qur'ān narrates stories in order to instruct and educate. Hence, the opportunity to bring home the true message or lesson of a story is never missed. The story of Joseph was narrated to people at their own asking. This accounts for the attention with which they listened to the story. Hence, after the actual story ended, the basic message of the Qur'ān was succinctly conveyed.

75. This verse aims at arousing people from their apathy to God's signs spread throughout the universe. For everything in the heavens and the earth is not only an object of existence, but also a sign that points to the reality. All those who observe different things as though they were merely objects of existence, fail to observe them in a manner becoming of human beings. Their observation is rather one characteristic of brutes. Were one to observe a tree or a mountain and see nothing beyond them, one would be engaging in an activity common to both animals and human beings. Animals also know the uses to which they can put those natural objects. What distinguishes man from animals in this respect is that man has been endowed with senses as well as with a rational mind. It does not behove man, therefore, to just observe things and exert himself to merely knowing how he could make use of them. Man is rather expected to go beyond observation and embark, by dint of his rational faculty, on a quest for reality. In his quest, he will be helped by the natural phenomena which in fact are signs of that reality.

Unfortunately, even if natural phenomena can successfully attract the attention of many people, these people still have no curiosity for the reality. They suffer from a state of apathy which leads them to all kinds of erroneous ideas and doctrines. Such people virtually shut their minds to the message of the Prophets. Had they not done so, it would not have been difficult at all for them to appreciate that Message and benefit from the guidance provided by the Prophets.

76. That is the natural consequence of the apathy and heedlessness mentioned in the previous verse. As people become blind to the landmarks,

(107) Do they, then, feel secure that no overwhelming chastisement would visit them, nor the Hour suddenly come upon them without their even perceiving it.[77] (108) Tell them plainly: 'This is my way: I call you to Allah, on the basis of clear perception – both I and those who follow me. Allah – glory be to Him – is free of every imperfection.[78] I have nothing to do with those who associate others with Allah in His divinity.'

أَفَأَمِنُوٓا۟ أَن تَأْتِيَهُمْ غَٰشِيَةٌ مِّنْ عَذَابِ
ٱللَّهِ أَوْ تَأْتِيَهُمُ ٱلسَّاعَةُ بَغْتَةً وَهُمْ
لَا يَشْعُرُونَ ﴿١٠٧﴾ قُلْ هَٰذِهِۦ سَبِيلِىٓ
أَدْعُوٓا۟ إِلَى ٱللَّهِ ۚ عَلَىٰ بَصِيرَةٍ أَنَا۠ وَمَنِ
ٱتَّبَعَنِى ۖ وَسُبْحَٰنَ ٱللَّهِ وَمَآ أَنَا۠ مِنَ
ٱلْمُشْرِكِينَ ﴿١٠٨﴾

---

they go off the right track and get lost. Despite this, only a few are totally misdirected, in the sense that they go so far as to deny God as their Creator and Provider. Most people affirm the existence of God but associate others with Him. Their misunderstanding consists in believing that there are others as well who have a share in God's attributes, power, and authority, and also in God's rightful claims against His creatures. Men could have escaped such false doctrines if they had just reflected over the numerous signs across the universe which unmistakably point to God's unity.

77. This question is intended to shake people out of their complacency, to jolt them into abandoning their carefree attitude to life. Such an attitude is born of an inner feeling that a long life remains ahead of them, that they will continue to enjoy a secure life for a long time. Thanks to this action, people tend to put off concern for the ultimate end of life. This is obviously an erroneous attitude for no one knows exactly what the span of his life will be. Death can suddenly seize anyone at any moment. Who is not aware that man has no prescience of what will happen at the next moment?

Thus there is no justification for putting off matters. The basic problems of life must be faced without delay. Man should give serious thought as to the way he ought to go. And if a person decides to follow one way or another, he should carefully consider – and again without delay – if there are sufficient reasons to believe that the way he has chosen is the right one. He should also consider whether the natural phenomena also provide any evidence to support the rightness of the way he has chosen. Further, he should look at the historical

(109) The Messengers whom We raised before you (O Muḥammad!) and to whom We sent down revelations, were only human beings, and were from among those living in earthly habitations. Have these people not travelled in the earth that they may observe the end of their predecessors? Certainly the abode of the Hereafter is much better for those (who accepted the call of the Messengers and) acted in a God-fearing manner. Will you still not act with good sense?[79] ▶

وَمَآ أَرۡسَلۡنَا مِن قَبۡلِكَ إِلَّا رِجَالٗا
نُّوحِيٓ إِلَيۡهِم مِّنۡ أَهۡلِ ٱلۡقُرَىٰٓۗ أَفَلَمۡ
يَسِيرُواْ فِي ٱلۡأَرۡضِ فَيَنظُرُواْ
كَيۡفَ كَانَ عَٰقِبَةُ ٱلَّذِينَ مِن
قَبۡلِهِمۡۗ وَلَدَارُ ٱلۡأٓخِرَةِ خَيۡرٞ
لِّلَّذِينَ ٱتَّقَوۡاْۚ أَفَلَا تَعۡقِلُونَ ١٠٩

record of man and examine the consequences that ensued from following the way of his choice in the past.

78. God is certainly free from any imperfections attributed to Him. Here reference has been made to the imperfections attributed to God by polytheists. Such ascriptions to God are a natural corollary of polytheistic beliefs.

79. This Qur'ānic exhortation sums up a number of points and issues. Let us attempt an elaboration of what the Qur'ān here seeks to convey.

The unbelievers pay no attention to the Prophet's message. This is because they find it quite unusual that one morning someone from among them, who grew up before their very eyes, should have been appointed God's Messenger. The Qur'ān points out, however, that this was not a unique event in human history. For even before the advent of Prophet Muḥammad (peace be on him) God had raised many Prophets and they too were human beings. Nor did it ever happen that a stranger appeared among a people and claimed to be God's Messenger. All those who were raised to bring about reform among the people of a given place belonged to that place, such as Jesus, Moses, Abraham and Noah (peace be on them).

Now it was for the unbelievers to consider the end of the people who did not accept the Prophet's messages of reform and kept running after their baseless fancies and unbridled lusts. In the course of their trade journeys the Makkans

(110) (It also happened with the earlier Messengers that for long they preached and people paid no heed) until the Messengers despaired of their people, and the people also believed that they had been told lies (by the Messengers), and then suddenly Our help came to the Messengers. And when such an occasion comes We rescue whom We will; as for the guilty, Our chastisement cannot be averted from them.

(111) Certainly in the stories of the bygone people there is a lesson for men of understanding. What is being narrated in the Qur'ān is no fabrication; it is rather confirmation of the Books that preceded it, and a detailed exposition of everything,[80] and a guidance and mercy for men of faith.

حَتَّىٰٓ إِذَا ٱسۡتَيۡـَٔسَ ٱلرُّسُلُ وَظَنُّوٓاْ
أَنَّهُمۡ قَدۡ كُذِبُواْ جَآءَهُمۡ نَصۡرُنَا
فَنُجِّيَ مَن نَّشَآءُۖ وَلَا يُرَدُّ بَأۡسُنَا عَنِ
ٱلۡقَوۡمِ ٱلۡمُجۡرِمِينَ ١١٠ لَقَدۡ كَانَ
فِي قَصَصِهِمۡ عِبۡرَةٞ لِّأُوْلِي ٱلۡأَلۡبَٰبِۗ
مَا كَانَ حَدِيثٗا يُفۡتَرَىٰ وَلَٰكِن
تَصۡدِيقَ ٱلَّذِي بَيۡنَ يَدَيۡهِ وَتَفۡصِيلَ
كُلِّ شَيۡءٖ وَهُدٗى وَرَحۡمَةٗ لِّقَوۡمٖ
يُؤۡمِنُونَ ١١١

---

used to pass by the ruined houses of 'Ād, Thamūd, Midian, and the people of Lot. Was there a lesson that they could learn? The ruins were not only reminders of the tragic end of those peoples in this world; they also betokened a far worse end in the Next Life. In contrast, those who mend their ways and become righteous will not only enjoy a felicitous life in this world, but will be even better off in the Next.

80. 'A detailed exposition of everything' refers to a detailed exposition of all that is necessary for man's guidance. This does not encompass everything in a literal sense. Some people misunderstand the purpose of this verse and consider 'everything' to include even such matters as detailed knowledge of forestry, medicine, mathematics and all other branches of learning.

Sūrah 13

al-Ra'd

(Thunder)

(Makkan Period)

Title

The title of this *sūrah* is derived from verse 13 which states that *al-ra'd* (thunder) 'celebrates Allah's praise and holiness; and the angels, too, for awe of Him'. It is obvious that the choice of *al-Ra'd* (thunder) for the title of the *sūrah* does not signify that the *sūrah* discusses the phenomenon of thunder. Here, as elsewhere, the title mainly serves the purpose of distinguishing one *sūrah* from another.

Period of Revelation

A perusal of verses 27 ff. and 38 ff. indicates that the *sūrah* was revealed around the same period when *Sūrahs Yūnus, Hūd* and *al-A'rāf* were revealed. In other words, the present *sūrah* was revealed in the last period of the Prophet's life in Makka.

The contents of the *sūrah* clearly indicate that the Prophet (peace be on him) had by then spent quite a long time inviting people to Islam. During this period his enemies resorted to a wide variety of stratagems both to hurt him and to frustrate his mission. As a result of this continued hostility, the situation had become so grave that the Muslims wished that some miracle were performed that would enable their compatriots to perceive and embrace the truth. In this context, God explains to the Muslims that He does not direct people to the right way in that manner. He also explains that if God allows the unbelievers to go their own way for a while, leaving them unpunished, this does not warrant Muslims losing heart and throwing up their hands in despair. Verse 31 of the *sūrah* suggests that the unbelievers had continuously rejected the truth out of their sheer adamance and that they had reached such a stage of obstinacy that even if the dead rose from their graves and spoke to them, they would still have found some pretext to evade acceptance of the truth.

All these bits and pieces of internal evidence suggest that the *sūrah* must have been revealed in the last phase of the Makkan period of the Prophet's life.

Subject Matter

The opening verse of the *sūrah* sets out its theme. It unequivocally declares that the teaching of Muḥammad (peace be on him) is the truth and those who do not believe in it are clearly in error. This theme permeates the whole *sūrah*. In a variety of ways the discourse focuses on showing the truth of Islam's major doctrines, God's unity, the Hereafter, and prophethood. The moral and spiritual benefits accruing from belief in these truths are explained and the disadvantages which ensue from rejecting them are also set out in detail. The *sūrah* also demonstrates that unbelief is tantamount to sheer stupidity and ignorance.

The purpose of the discourse is not confined to merely pursuing people intellectually. It also aims to create in people the impulse to embrace the truth. The invitation to the truth has not simply been made on the basis of logical reasoning and argumentation. An appeal to the hearts of people is also made and in a variety of ways. They are warned about God's severe chastisement if they reject the truth, and are promised rich rewards if they believe in the truth and act righteously. Earnest appeals emanating from sympathy and compassionate concern are made to people to give up their obduracy and embrace the true faith.

In the course of the discourse, the objections against Islam that were commonly made by its opponents are refuted without specifically mentioning any of them. Similarly, the doubts that people themselves entertained or which the opponents of Islam put in their minds regarding Islam are removed. Special attention is also paid to men of faith. A word of consolation and encouragement is offered to them for after a prolonged period of strenuous struggle they were on the verge of exhaustion and had begun to look for Divine intervention and support.

In the name of Allah, the Merciful, the Compassionate.

(1) *Alif. Lām. Mīm. Rā.* These are the verses of the Divine Book. Whatever has been revealed to you from your Lord is the truth, and yet most (of your) people do not believe.[1]

(2) It is Allah Who has raised the heavens without any supports that you could see,[2] and then He established Himself on the Throne (of Dominion).[3] ▶

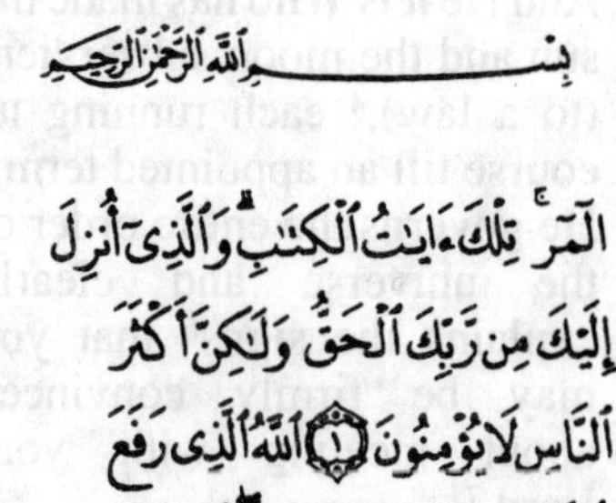

1. This constitutes the introduction of the *sūrah*. Addressing Prophet Muḥammad (peace be on him) God makes it quite clear that the majority of his people are disinclined towards his teaching. However, their aversion to it does not detract from the fact that his teaching is a revelation from God and as such constitutes the truth.

This brief introduction is followed by the main discourse which consists of explaining to the unbelievers why the Prophet's teaching is true, and why its rejection is altogether erroneous.

In order to fully appreciate the discourse, it should be remembered that at that time the teaching of the Prophet (peace be on him) was mainly comprised of the following three elements. First, that godhead in its entirety rests with the One True God, and hence He alone deserves to be served and worshipped. Second, that the present life will inevitably be followed by the Hereafter in which all will have to render an account of their deeds. Third, that the Prophet (peace be on him) is the Messenger of God, and that all that he teaches is from God and not from himself. It is precisely these basic teachings which the unbelievers refused to accept. However, a variety of persuasive means were employed to explain these truths and to remove any doubts and misconceptions that the people might entertain about them.

2. In other words, the heavens were raised without anything perceptible to support them. There is nothing tangible in space which holds the virtually infinite number of heavenly bodies together. Nevertheless, there is a force – an

And He it is Who has made the sun and the moon subservient (to a law),[4] each running its course till an appointed term.[5] He governs the entire order of the universe and clearly explains the signs[6] that you may be firmly convinced about meeting with your Lord.[7]

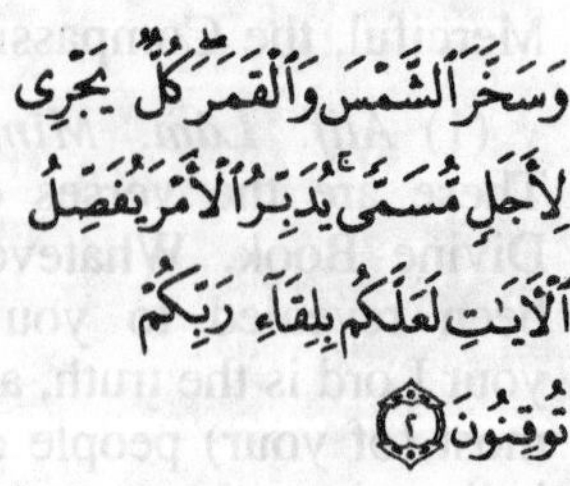

imperceptible one – which keeps each heavenly body exactly where it belongs and regulates its orbit. This force also prevents these immense bodies from colliding with the earth or with each other.

3. For further details see *Towards Understanding the Qur'ān,* vol. III, *al-A'rāf* 7, n. 41, pp. 33–4. It suffices to state here that the Qur'ānic verses which mention that God established Himself on the Throne (see *al-A'rāf* 7: 54; *Yūnus* 10: 3; *Ṭā Hā* 20: 5, etc. – Ed.) are meant to emphasize that God not only created the universe but also holds total sway over it. The cosmos is neither a self-operating, automated workshop as a group of ignoramuses is wont to fancy. Nor is it a theatre consisting of a myriad of deities as another group of inept people is inclined to believe. The cosmos is a well-organized, superbly ordered system which is fully under the control of its Creator.

4. It should also be remembered that the Qur'ān addresses itself to a people who did not deny the existence of God. Nor did they deny that He alone created the universe and that it is He alone Who raised the canopy of the heavens, and made the sun and the moon subservient to a law. In view of the fact that even the polytheists accepted this, it was altogether unnecessary to marshal any evidence or present any argument to prove that God alone created the heavens and the earth and yoked the sun and the moon to follow a set of cosmic laws. Hence, rather than do that the facts which were accepted by all are mentioned in order to build an argument upon them. The argument is that since none other than God rules over the universe, none other than Him deserves to be served and worshipped.

At this stage the following question might be posed: How can such an argument carry any weight with those who believe neither in the existence of God, nor in His being the only One Who created and rules over the universe? The fact is that the argument which has been presented to establish the unity of God is equally relevant to establish God's existence. The whole argument for

God's unity is based on the premise that the universe constitutes one integrated system, which is subject to a colossal body of laws. These laws clearly point to the existence of an all-pervasive power, a wisdom immune from every imperfection, a knowledge free of every error. It is obvious that such a system can operate only if it is subject to the will of no more than one being who effectively controls it. It is no less obvious that such a well-ordered system cannot operate if there is none to operate it. How can there be an order without there being someone who established it? How can there be a law without a sovereign to enforce it? How can there be wisdom without there being someone who embodies it? How can there be knowledge without a knower? Above all, how can one even conceive of creation without a creator? To think, therefore, that this vast universe, which is so perfectly ordered, could have come into being on its own, or that such order could emerge in it without there being anyone's will behind it, is either rank irrationality or incurable obduracy.

5. The system regulating the universe testifies to the fact that an all-pervasive power controls it and that an immense wisdom permeates it. Moreover, everything in the universe indicates that nothing in it is everlasting. Everything has a term and that it vanishes with the expiry of that term. This applies not only to the component parts of the universe but also to the universe as a whole. The structure of the universe clearly indicates that it will not last for ever. A moment has definitely been set for it to come to an end. When that moment comes, the present world will vanish into non-existence and will be replaced by another one. Hence, there is no reasonable ground to think that the Resurrection will not come.

6. There are many signs which indicate that the information about the ultimate truths provided by the Prophet (peace be on him) is indeed fully reliable. If one looks around with open eyes there are innumerable signs spread across the heavens and the earth which testify to the truths which the Qur'ān invites men to accept.

7. Now, the evidence of the natural phenomena in support of the truth that God alone is the creator and sovereign of the universe is all too evident. However, the idea that the natural phenomena also provide evidence as to the soundness of the Prophet's teaching that man is accountable before his Lord, and that he will receive reward and punishment in the Hereafter are subtle. Hence, this aspect of the evidence of natural phenomena is spelled out.

The natural phenomena testify to the Hereafter in two ways. First, when we consider the structure of the heavens and the earth and the subjection of heavenly bodies to a system, we are convinced of God's immense power. For it is by dint of His power that God created the heavens and the earth and ensured the regularity of their movement along their orbits. If we remember this, it is easy to appreciate that He certainly also has the power to bring back to life all men after their death.

(3) He it is Who has spread out the earth and has placed in it firm mountains and has caused the rivers to flow. He has made every fruit in pairs, two and two, and He it is Who causes the night to cover the day.[8] Surely there are signs in these for those who reflect.	وَهُوَ ٱلَّذِى مَدَّ ٱلْأَرْضَ وَجَعَلَ فِيهَا رَوَٰسِىَ وَأَنْهَٰرًا وَمِن كُلِّ ٱلثَّمَرَٰتِ جَعَلَ فِيهَا زَوْجَيْنِ ٱثْنَيْنِ يُغْشِى ٱلَّيْلَ ٱلنَّهَارَ إِنَّ فِى ذَٰلِكَ لَءَايَٰتٍ لِّقَوْمٍ يَتَفَكَّرُونَ ③

Second, the order that seems to prevail in the heavens also proves that the Creator is absolutely wise. Now, it seems quite inconceivable that God Who created man, Who endowed him with reason and understanding, granted him free-will, and enabled him to exercise control over innumerable things on the earth, would not call him to account. It is inconceivable that such an All-Wise God will not reward those who do good, and punish those who commit evil. It simply cannot be imagined that He would not take to task the wrong-doers and recompense those who were wronged.

Now, it is possible for a foolish and insensitive worldly ruler to leave the affairs of the state totally to his officials, utterly neglecting his responsibilities and immersing himself in the pleasures of life. However, such a thing is simply inconceivable with regard to the All-Knowing and All-Wise God.

Thus, an observation of the heavens leads one to believe that not only is the Next Life possible, but that it is inevitable.

8. After drawing attention to heavenly bodies, reference is made to the earth. Once again, there is a myriad of signs here which point to God's power and wisdom. The signs of God's power and wisdom on earth – like His signs in the heavens – provide strong evidence in support of God's unity and an After-life.

The arguments adduced in this context may be succinctly stated as follows:

(1) The close connection between the earth and the heavenly bodies in general, and the sun and the moon in particular is quite evident. It is also evident that there is a close link between the earth's creatures and the countless mountains and rivers. All these provide clear proof of the fact that these objects have neither been created nor are they governed by different gods. For, had that been so, it would be inconceivable that there should come to be that perfect harmony and accord which we find

(4) And on the earth there are many tracts of land neighbouring each other.[9] There are on it vineyards, and sown fields, and date palms: some growing in clusters from one root, some standing alone.[10] They are irrigated by the same water, and yet We make some excel others in taste. Surely there are signs in these for a people who use their reason.[11]

وَفِي ٱلْأَرْضِ قِطَعٌ مُّتَجَٰوِرَٰتٌ
وَجَنَّٰتٌ مِّنْ أَعْنَٰبٍ وَزَرْعٌ وَنَخِيلٌ
صِنْوَانٌ وَغَيْرُ صِنْوَانٍ يُسْقَىٰ بِمَآءٍ
وَٰحِدٍ وَنُفَضِّلُ بَعْضَهَا عَلَىٰ بَعْضٍ
فِي ٱلْأُكُلِ إِنَّ فِي ذَٰلِكَ لَأَيَٰتٍ
لِّقَوْمٍ يَعْقِلُونَ ﴿٤﴾

---

between them; and that even if such a harmony and accord would have come to be at a given moment, it would not have lasted for long. Nor would it have been possible to chalk out a unified plan for the creation and regulation of the universe. Nor would it have been possible to contrive a system in which the different elements of the universe are so elaborately inter-dependent and so perfectly inter-related that all things right from the earth to the heavens constitute a harmonious system which never allows for any conflict or friction.

(2) As we know, this vast spherical body – the earth – lies suspended in space. We also find on it a large number of enormous mountains from which huge rivers spring. On the surface of the earth countless trees grow and bear fruit. The earth also witnesses the astonishing cycle of day and night which proceeds with absolute regularity. All these are proof of the boundless power of God Who created everything. It is sheer folly to think that such an All-Powerful Being would lack the power to restore human beings to life after their death.

(3) An intelligent person can hardly fail to notice the structure of the earth, the presence of the mountains on its surface, the flow of rivers which originate from those mountains, the fact that all species of fruit produce two kinds of fruit, and the regular cycle of day and night. Nor can he fail to perceive the underlying wisdom of, and the innumerable advantages inherent in, the whole scheme of things which encompass the universe – facts which testify that God Who devised that scheme is possessed of absolute wisdom. The phenomena mentioned above also proves that the earth is not ruled by a force devoid of will, nor by one who treats it

merely as a plaything. Everything on the earth manifests the wisdom of an All-Wise Being, and that too at its zenith.

Now, if there is someone who even after observing and reflecting over all this still believes that after creating man and providing him with endless opportunities to act, God would simply reduce him to dust, leaving him unrequited for his deeds, then he must certainly be a fool.

9. God has caused the various regions of the world to differ from one another despite their contiguity. These regions differ in many respects – in their configuration, in their colour, in their component elements, in their characteristics, properties and potentialities, in the produce which they yield and in the chemical and mineral deposits which are hidden under their surface. The variation and diversity thus found abounds in wisdom and leads to countless benefits. Let us disregard for a moment the benefits inherent in this diversity in respect of other species of creation and simply consider the benefits which accrue to human beings. In this regard it will be noted that there is a very close correspondence between the diverse interests and purposes of man and the diversity which characterizes the different regions of the world. The result of all this is manifest in the growth and efflorescence of human culture and civilization.

It would be bold and impetuous for anyone to brand all this as the outcome of mere coincidence. On the contrary, common sense suggests that all this indubitably represents the careful and benevolent planning of the All-Wise Creator.

10. Some date palm trees have just one trunk whereas others have two or more stems from the same root.

11. In the first place, this verse points to the signs of God's unity, power and wisdom in the universe. However, it also subtly hints at another truth – that no part of the universe is characterized by a dull and drab sameness. It is the same earth and yet each tract of it differs from the other in colour, configuration, and properties. Likewise, while the earth is the same, and the same water is used for irrigation, yet different grains and fruits grow. Not only do we see that the fruit of the same tree differs even though they belong to the same species – differ from each other in shape, size and other features. Also, from the same root two different stems rise, each with its distinct characteristics.

Anyone who reflects over these diversities will have no difficulty in understanding the differences in temperaments, predilections and attitudes of his fellow beings. As we shall see later in the same *sūrah* (see verse 27 ff.), had God so willed, He would have made all men alike. However, the underlying wisdom of the creation of the universe does not call for absolute sameness. It rather calls for diversity and variety. Had everyone been similar, the alluring attractions of the world would have been rendered meaningless.

(5) And were you to wonder, then wondrous indeed is the saying of those who say: 'What! After we have been reduced to the dust, shall we be created afresh?' They are the ones who disbelieved in their Lord;[12] they are the ones who shall have shackles around their necks. They shall be the inmates of the Fire,[13] wherein they will abide for ever.

۞ وَإِن تَعْجَبْ فَعَجَبٌ قَوْلُهُمْ أَءِذَا
كُنَّا تُرَٰبًا أَءِنَّا لَفِى خَلْقٍ جَدِيدٍ ۗ أُو۟لَٰٓئِكَ
ٱلَّذِينَ كَفَرُوا۟ بِرَبِّهِمْ ۖ وَأُو۟لَٰٓئِكَ
ٱلْأَغْلَٰلُ فِىٓ أَعْنَاقِهِمْ ۖ وَأُو۟لَٰٓئِكَ
أَصْحَٰبُ ٱلنَّارِ ۖ هُمْ فِيهَا خَٰلِدُونَ ٥

(6) They challenge you to hasten the coming of evil upon them before the coming of any good,[14] although people who followed a like course before had met with exemplary punishment (from Allah). Verily your Lord is forgiving to men despite all their wrong-doing. Verily your Lord is also severe in retribution.

وَيَسْتَعْجِلُونَكَ بِٱلسَّيِّئَةِ قَبْلَ
ٱلْحَسَنَةِ وَقَدْ خَلَتْ مِن قَبْلِهِمُ
ٱلْمَثُلَٰتُ ۗ وَإِنَّ رَبَّكَ لَذُو مَغْفِرَةٍ
لِّلنَّاسِ عَلَىٰ ظُلْمِهِمْ ۖ وَإِنَّ رَبَّكَ
لَشَدِيدُ ٱلْعِقَابِ ٦

12. The unbelievers' denial of the After-life amounts to denying God, denying His power, and denying His wisdom. For they do not simply call into question that men will be resurrected. Implicit in their rejection of the After-life is the idea that God either lacks the power to create human beings afresh, or the wisdom to recognize the need to do so.

13. The Qur'ānic statement that, 'they are the ones who shall have shackles around their necks', means that they are prisoners of their ignorance and obduracy, prisoners of their lusts, prisoners of uncritical adherence to their ancestral ways. It is because of all this that they have become incapable of thinking independently. They are too strongly bound by their prejudices to appreciate that the Hereafter is inevitable. They continue to deny it despite the fact that reason and common sense require that the present life be followed by another.

(7) Those who refused to believe in you say: 'Why has no [miraculous] sign been sent down upon him from his Lord?'[15] You are only a warner, and every people has its guide.[16]

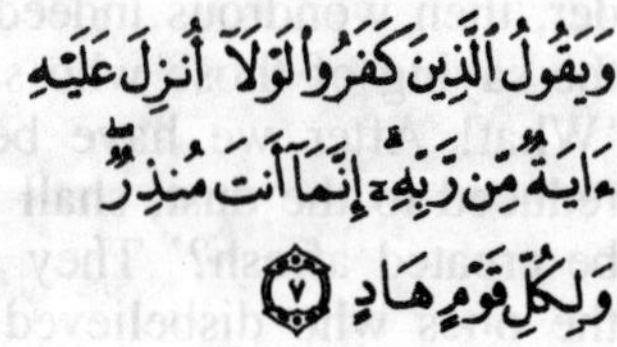

14. The unbelievers of Makka used to say to the Prophet (peace be on him) that if he was indeed a true Messenger, why did God's scourge not strike them. They expressed their amazement at the fact that they were not chastised although the Prophet (peace be on him) had warned them that if they rejected God's Message, a dreadful punishment would seize them. Sometimes they would even say in a challenging tone: 'Our Lord! Hasten to us our sentence even before the Day of Accounting' (*Ṣād* 38: 16). On other occasions they would say: 'O Allah! If this indeed be the truth from You, then rain down stones upon us from heaven, or bring upon us a painful chastisement.' (See *Towards Understanding the Qur'ān*, vol. III, *al-Anfāl* 8: 32, and n. 26, p. 150 – Ed.)

The present verse is a rejoinder to the unbelievers' impudent remarks. It is simply foolish that instead of asking for felicity some people should implore God to bring upon them His chastisement. But this was precisely what the unbelievers did. On the other hand, instead of punishing them instantly, God granted them a reprieve so that they may be given the opportunity to reform themselves. It is astonishing that the people concerned neither appreciated God's leniency nor gave thanks to Him for it. Ironically, instead of availing themselves of the reprieve to mend their ways, they asked God to expeditiously terminate that reprieve and so chastise them.

15. The expression '[miraculous] sign' here signifies the sign that would persuade the unbelievers to have faith in Muḥammad (peace be on him) as God's Messenger. Such was their mentality that they were not willing to appreciate the truth of the Prophet's teaching even though they found that it was supported by weighty arguments and persuasive proofs. They were also not prepared to consider the excellence of the Prophet's character as a strong testimony in support of the truth of his teaching. Nor were they prepared to take into account the full significance of the moral transformation which the Prophet's teaching had brought about in the lives of his Companions. Nor did they pay any heed to the weighty arguments set out in the Qur'ān which showed the hollowness of their polytheistic beliefs and the glaring errors of the superstitions to which they subscribed. They turned a blind eye to all these and

(8) Allah knows what every female bears; and what the wombs fall short of (in gestation), and what they may add.[17] With Him everything is in fixed measure. (9) He knows both what is hidden and what is manifest. He is the Supreme One, the Most High.

ٱللَّهُ يَعْلَمُ مَا تَحْمِلُ كُلُّ أُنثَىٰ وَمَا
تَغِيضُ ٱلْأَرْحَامُ وَمَا تَزْدَادُ
وَكُلُّ شَىْءٍ عِندَهُۥ بِمِقْدَارٍ ﴿٨﴾
عَٰلِمُ ٱلْغَيْبِ وَٱلشَّهَٰدَةِ ٱلْكَبِيرُ
ٱلْمُتَعَالِ ﴿٩﴾

insisted that they would believe only if they could come across a miracle that would indisputably prove that the Prophet's claim to Prophethood was true.

16. This pithy statement is God's response to the unbelievers' demand for a miracle. The statement, however, was not directly addressed to them but to the Prophet (peace be on him). He is told that he should not be overly concerned with the question as to which kind of miraculous sign would persuade the unbelievers to believe. For it is not his task to satisfy everybody. His task is simply to arouse those people steeped in ignorance and apathy and to vehemently warn them against the dire consequences to which their evil ways would lead them. God had appointed guides in different ages and among different peoples and had asked them to shoulder this same task now entrusted to Prophet Muḥammad (peace be on him). Once the Prophet (peace be on him) has delivered his message, everyone is free either to act wisely and follow that message, or to remain steeped in heedlessness and apathy and so disregard it.

Thus God dismisses the demand of the unbelievers for a miracle. He then informs them in forceful terms that they live in the realm of an All-Knowing and Just God Who fully knows all His creatures from their inception and maintains a vigil over them throughout the full duration of their lives. Moreover, when He requites His creatures, He requites them with absolute justice, His decisions being in consideration of their merits. Above all, He is an All-Powerful God and hence the decisions He makes are entirely His for there is no power in the heavens or on the earth which can influence His judgement.

(10) It is all the same for Him whether any of you says a thing secretly, or says it loudly, and whether one hides oneself in the darkness of night, or struts about in broad daylight. (11) There are guardians over everyone, both before him and behind him, who guard him by Allah's command.[18] Verily Allah does not change a people's condition unless they change their inner selves. And when Allah decides to make a people suffer punishment, no one can avert it. Nor can any be of help to such a people against Allah.[19]

سَوَآءٌ مِّنكُم مَّنْ أَسَرَّ ٱلْقَوْلَ وَمَن
جَهَرَ بِهِۦ وَمَنْ هُوَ مُسْتَخْفٍۭ بِٱلَّيْلِ
وَسَارِبٌۢ بِٱلنَّهَارِ ﴿١٠﴾ لَهُۥ مُعَقِّبَٰتٌ مِّنۢ
بَيْنِ يَدَيْهِ وَمِنْ خَلْفِهِۦ يَحْفَظُونَهُۥ مِنْ
أَمْرِ ٱللَّهِ ۗ إِنَّ ٱللَّهَ لَا يُغَيِّرُ مَا بِقَوْمٍ
حَتَّىٰ يُغَيِّرُوا۟ مَا بِأَنفُسِهِمْ ۗ وَإِذَآ أَرَادَ ٱللَّهُ
بِقَوْمٍ سُوٓءًا فَلَا مَرَدَّ لَهُۥ ۚ وَمَا لَهُم مِّن
دُونِهِۦ مِن وَالٍ ﴿١١﴾

17. This means that while a child is in his mother's womb, God – and He alone – watches over the development of that child in every respect. He oversees the increase or decrease in each of its limbs, endowments and capacities.

18. God directly watches over everyone and is well aware of everyone's deeds and movements. Not only that, but the angels appointed by Him also remain with everyone throughout their lives and record all their actions. This truth has been emphasized with a view to warning those who fancy that they are free to lead the kind of life they wish to, and that they are not accountable to anyone. Such people court their own disaster.

19. People are told in plain words not to entertain the illusion that any saint or *jinn* or angel is powerful enough to rescue people from God's chastisement. Such patrons that they may choose will be utterly unable in the Next Life, despite the bribe of homages and offerings received from their devotees, to be of any effective help to them.

(12) He it is Who causes you to see lightning that inspires you with both fear and hope, and He it is Who whips up heavy clouds. (13) The thunder celebrates His praise and holiness,[20] and the angels, too, for awe of Him.[21] He hurls thunderbolts, striking with them whom He wills the while they are engaged in disputation concerning Allah. He is Mighty in His contriving.[22]

هُوَ ٱلَّذِي يُرِيكُمُ ٱلۡبَرۡقَ خَوۡفٗا
وَطَمَعٗا وَيُنشِئُ ٱلسَّحَابَ ٱلثِّقَالَ
١٢ وَيُسَبِّحُ ٱلرَّعۡدُ بِحَمۡدِهِۦ
وَٱلۡمَلَٰٓئِكَةُ مِنۡ خِيفَتِهِۦ وَيُرۡسِلُ
ٱلصَّوَٰعِقَ فَيُصِيبُ بِهَا مَن يَشَآءُ
وَهُمۡ يُجَٰدِلُونَ فِي ٱللَّهِ وَهُوَ شَدِيدُ
ٱلۡمِحَالِ ١٣

20. The thunder of the clouds shows that it is God Who causes winds to blow, vapours to rise, heavy clouds to accumulate, the lightning to flash, and the clouds to bring about the downpour which provides His creatures with water. All this shows that God's wisdom and power are absolute; that He is perfect and free from all defect; that none shares with Him in His godhead. For those who are not appreciative of their distinct humanity and thus look upon the thunder in the manner of brutes hold that thunder is no more than a deafening sound from the clouds. But those who have ears that are capable of heeding the truth realize that thunder proclaims God's unity.

21. The statement that the angels celebrate God's praise for awe of Him has been made for a definite reason. The reason is that polytheists, throughout the ages, have taken angels as deities, as objects of worship, thinking that they share godhead with God. Refuting this mistaken belief, the Qur'ān says that they are not God's partners in His sovereignty. If anything, they are His obedient servants who hold God in awe and celebrate His praise and holiness.

22. God has innumerable devices which He can use against anyone He pleases. He can even punish people by means which they will be unable to anticipate even a moment before it comes to pass. Who could consider such people, who arbitrarily blurt out all kinds of nonsense about the All-Powerful Being, to be wise?

(14) To Him alone should all prayer be addressed,[23] for those to whom they do address their prayers beside Him are altogether powerless to respond to them. The example of praying to any other than Allah is that of a man who stretches out his hands to water, asking it to reach his mouth, although water has no power to reach his mouth. The prayers of the unbelievers are a sheer waste! (15) All that is in the heavens and the earth prostrates itself, whether willingly or by force,[24] before Allah; and so do their shadows in the morning and in the evening.[25]

لَهُۥ دَعْوَةُ ٱلْحَقِّ ۖ وَٱلَّذِينَ يَدْعُونَ مِن دُونِهِۦ
لَا يَسْتَجِيبُونَ لَهُم بِشَىْءٍ إِلَّا كَبَـٰسِطِ
كَفَّيْهِ إِلَى ٱلْمَآءِ لِيَبْلُغَ فَاهُ وَمَا هُوَ بِبَـٰلِغِهِۦ ۚ
وَمَا دُعَآءُ ٱلْكَـٰفِرِينَ إِلَّا فِى ضَلَـٰلٍ ﴿١٤﴾
وَلِلَّهِ يَسْجُدُ مَن فِى ٱلسَّمَـٰوَٰتِ وَٱلْأَرْضِ
طَوْعًا وَكَرْهًا وَظِلَـٰلُهُم بِٱلْغُدُوِّ
وَٱلْـَٔاصَالِ ﴿١٥﴾

23. To 'address all prayer to God' signifies one's calling upon God to come to one's aid. People ought to do so because the power needed to fulfil man's purposes and to remove his difficulties and distresses lies with God alone. Hence, it is quite appropriate to address all prayers to Him, and to Him alone.

24. Prostration refers to bowing down in obeisance, to carrying out a command, and to lowering oneself in submission to someone. In this sense, every creature of God in the heavens and the earth is in a state of prostration before God. The laws of God are such that no creature is capable of deviating even a hair's breath from His providential will. In fact both the believer and the unbeliever submit to the natural laws devised by God. The difference between the two is that while the believer submits out of volition, the unbeliever submits out of compulsion for it is beyond his power to do otherwise.

25. The prostration of shadows before God refers to the falling of the shadows on the earth: to the west, in the morning, and in the afternoon to the east. This symbolizes the subjection of those objects to God's will and command.

(16) Ask them: 'Who is the Lord of the heavens and the earth?' Say: 'Allah.'[26] Tell them: 'Have you taken beside Him as your patrons those who do not have the power to benefit or to hurt even themselves?' Say: 'Can the blind and the seeing be deemed equals?[27] Or can light and darkness be deemed equals?[28] If that is not so, then have those whom they associate with Allah in His divinity ever created anything like what Allah did so that the question of creation has become dubious to them?'[29] Say: 'Allah is the creator of everything. He is the One, the Irresistible.'[30]

قُلْ مَن رَّبُّ ٱلسَّمَٰوَٰتِ وَٱلْأَرْضِ قُلِ ٱللَّهُ قُلْ
أَفَٱتَّخَذْتُم مِّن دُونِهِۦٓ أَوْلِيَآءَ لَا يَمْلِكُونَ
لِأَنفُسِهِمْ نَفْعًا وَلَا ضَرًّا قُلْ هَلْ يَسْتَوِى
ٱلْأَعْمَىٰ وَٱلْبَصِيرُ أَمْ هَلْ تَسْتَوِى
ٱلظُّلُمَٰتُ وَٱلنُّورُ أَمْ جَعَلُوا۟ لِلَّهِ شُرَكَآءَ
خَلَقُوا۟ كَخَلْقِهِۦ فَتَشَٰبَهَ ٱلْخَلْقُ عَلَيْهِمْ قُلِ
ٱللَّهُ خَٰلِقُ كُلِّ شَىْءٍ وَهُوَ ٱلْوَٰحِدُ
ٱلْقَهَّٰرُ ١٦

---

26. It should be clear that even the unbelievers were convinced that God is the Lord of the heavens and the earth. Hence, when they were asked: 'Who is the Lord of the heavens and the earth?' they could not have said that God is not the Lord of the heavens and the earth. For to say that would be contrary to their own belief. However, when the Prophet (peace be on him) put that question to them, they evaded saying unequivocally that God is the Lord of the heavens and the earth. They were equivocal in their reply because a clear statement to the effect that God is the Lord of the heavens and the earth would necessitate affirmation of monotheism. They would then be left with no reasonable ground to cling to polytheism.

Sensing the weakness of their position, the unbelievers kept quiet. It is for this very reason that the Qur'ān directs the Prophet (peace be on him) on several occasions to put such questions to the unbelievers: Who is the Creator of the heavens and the earth? Who is the Lord of the universe? Who provides sustenance to all? Further, after having put those questions, the Prophet (peace be on him) is directed to come forth with the response – that Allah is the Creator and Lord of the universe Who provides sustenance to all. The logical corollary of that statement is – and this has also been explicated in the Qur'ān –

that since Allah is the Creator, Lord and Sustainer, there are no grounds for man serving or worshipping anyone other than Him.

27. The word 'blind' in the verse has been used to refer to those who even while they observe the natural phenomena are nevertheless blind to the signs of God's unity in them. The 'seeing ones' are those who not only observe the natural phenomena but who also appreciate that every particle of the universe and every leaf of the trees provide a wealth of knowledge about God. The question posed here amounts to telling the unbelievers that if they are mentally blind, this does not mean that those who see should also behave like them. How is it possible that those who clearly perceive the truth should stumble in darkness as do the blind?

28. The word 'light' here obviously refers to the light of true knowledge which belonged to the Prophet (peace be on him) and his followers. As for 'darkness', it stands for the ignorance in which the unbelievers were stumbling. Through the present query the unbelievers are told that those who are blessed with light can never agree to part with it and so do not wander about in darkness as do the unbelievers. If light had no meaning for the unbelievers, that was their business. But there are also those who not only have light but also know the difference between light and darkness. How is it possible that those, who are able to see their way in life by dint of the broad daylight in which they live, would agree to distance themselves from light and so revert to darkness?

29. The point that is being made here is that quite evidently God alone has created the universe and all that there is in it. There is no ambiguity in the matter making it difficult for people to decide which objects were created by God and which were created by others. Had there been any such ambiguity there would at least have been some basis for polytheism. The fact, however, is that even polytheists admit that their deities created absolutely nothing. So, what justification is there in believing that false deities have a share either in the power or rights of God?

30. The Qur'ānic expression *qahhār* means one who has the power to command and to keep all in a state of subservience. That God alone is the Creator of all persons and things was acknowledged by everyone, including the polytheists. Once a rational being affirms that God is the Creator, he is also bound to affirm that God is 'the One, the Irresistible'. Naturally, the Creator is bound to be unique since everything and everybody has been created by Him. What justification is there, then, to associate anyone or anything with the Creator in His attributes, powers and rights?

Likewise, God is bound to be Irresistible. For to be in a state of subjection to, and under the control of, the Creator is innate in the very nature of everything and everyone created by God. For if the Creator does not have absolute power, He will be unable to create. Hence, anyone who accepts God to be the Creator

(17) Allah sends down water from the heavens and the river-beds flow, each according to its measure, and the torrent carries along a swelling scum.[31] And likewise, from that metal which they smelt in the fire to make ornaments and utensils, there arises scum like it.[32] Thus does Allah depict truth and falsehood. As for the scum, it passes away as dross; but that which benefits mankind abides on the earth. Thus does Allah explain (the truth) through examples.

أَنزَلَ مِنَ ٱلسَّمَآءِ مَآءً فَسَالَتْ أَوْدِيَةٌۢ
بِقَدَرِهَا فَٱحْتَمَلَ ٱلسَّيْلُ زَبَدًا رَّابِيًاۚ
وَمِمَّا يُوقِدُونَ عَلَيْهِ فِى ٱلنَّارِ ٱبْتِغَآءَ حِلْيَةٍ
أَوْ مَتَٰعٍ زَبَدٌ مِّثْلُهُۥۚ كَذَٰلِكَ يَضْرِبُ ٱللَّهُ ٱلْحَقَّ
وَٱلْبَٰطِلَۚ فَأَمَّا ٱلزَّبَدُ فَيَذْهَبُ جُفَآءًۖ
وَأَمَّا مَا يَنفَعُ ٱلنَّاسَ فَيَمْكُثُ فِى ٱلْأَرْضِۚ
كَذَٰلِكَ يَضْرِبُ ٱللَّهُ ٱلْأَمْثَالَ ﴿١٧﴾

of all cannot deny two rational and logical corollaries of that belief – (a) that God is One, and (b) that He is Irresistible. It is, therefore, an act of rank irrationality that anyone should consider someone other than the Creator to be the object of his worship. It is equally irrational that rather than pray in distress to the Creator Who is possessed of absolute power, one should pray to a creature who is shorn of that power.

31. This parable is about the knowledge granted to the Prophet (peace be on him) through revelation. This knowledge has been likened to 'water from heaven'. As for men of faith, they have been likened to 'river-beds'. They are filled with rainfall, each according to its capacity, whereafter they flow. The tumultuous campaign of opposition against Islam mounted by its enemies has been likened to the 'swelling scum' which appears on the surface of flood water.

32. A furnace is heated up in order to purge a metal of its impurities. In so doing, impurities appear on the surface and momentarily it appears as if there is nothing else.

(18) There is good reward for those who respond to the call of their Lord. And those who do not respond to their Lord, (a time will come when) they shall offer all they have – even if they have all the riches of the world and the like of it besides – to redeem themselves (from the chastisement of Allah).[33] They will be subjected to a severe reckoning[34] and Hell shall be their refuge. And what a wretched resting place it is!

لِلَّذِينَ ٱسْتَجَابُوا۟ لِرَبِّهِمُ ٱلْحُسْنَىٰ ۚ
وَٱلَّذِينَ لَمْ يَسْتَجِيبُوا۟ لَهُۥ لَوْ أَنَّ
لَهُم مَّا فِى ٱلْأَرْضِ جَمِيعًا وَمِثْلَهُۥ مَعَهُۥ
لَٱفْتَدَوْا۟ بِهِۦٓ ۚ أُو۟لَٰٓئِكَ لَهُمْ سُوٓءُ
ٱلْحِسَابِ وَمَأْوَىٰهُمْ جَهَنَّمُ ۖ وَبِئْسَ
ٱلْمِهَادُ ﴿١٨﴾

---

33. Those who do not accept the call of the Prophets will be subjected to severe chastisement. Such will be the severity of this chastisement that people would be quite willing to part with all their riches to rescue themselves from it.

34. The 'severe reckoning' of a person would mean one in which none of the omissions or mistakes committed by him are forgiven, nor any misdeed allowed to go unpunished.

The Qur'ān tells us that those who rebelled against God would be subjected to such reckoning. In contrast, those who were faithful to God and had submitted themselves to Him will have an 'easy reckoning'. In view of the good deeds of such persons, their lapses will be overlooked. In deference to their overall record, many of their omissions will be forgiven. This point has been further elaborated in a tradition in Abū Dā'ūd on the authority of 'Ā'ishah. 'Ā'ishah says: 'I said, O Messenger of Allah! For me the most terrifying verse of the book of Allah is the one which says: "Whoever does evil shall reap its consequence" (*al-Nisā'* 4: 123).' To this the Prophet replied: 'O 'Ā'ishah! Don't you know that any inconvenience which an obedient servant of God suffers in this life, so much so that even if he is pricked by a thorn, Allah reckons it as an atonement for some of his sins. Thus his account is cleared during his worldly life. As for those who will be subjected to reckoning in the Hereafter, they will inevitably be punished'. 'Ā'ishah said: 'If that is so, then what is meant by the verse: "Then he who is given his record in his right hand, will be subjected to an easy reckoning" (*al-Inshiqāq* 84: 7–8).' The Prophet

(19) He who knows that the Book which has been sent to you from your Lord is the truth, is he like him who is blind to that truth?[35] It is only men of understanding who take heed:[36] (20) those who fulfil their covenant with Allah and do not break their compact after firmly confirming it;[37] (21) who join together the ties which Allah has bidden to be joined;[38] who fear their Lord and dread lest they are subjected to severe reckoning; (22) who are steadfast in seeking the good pleasure of their Lord;[39] who establish Prayer and spend both secretly and openly out of the wealth We have provided them, and who ward off evil with good.[40] ▶

۞ أَفَمَن يَعْلَمُ أَنَّمَآ أُنزِلَ إِلَيْكَ مِن رَّبِّكَ ٱلْحَقُّ
كَمَنْ هُوَ أَعْمَىٰٓ ۚ إِنَّمَا يَتَذَكَّرُ أُو۟لُوا۟ ٱلْأَلْبَٰبِ
﴿١٩﴾ ٱلَّذِينَ يُوفُونَ بِعَهْدِ ٱللَّهِ وَلَا يَنقُضُونَ
ٱلْمِيثَٰقَ ﴿٢٠﴾ وَٱلَّذِينَ يَصِلُونَ مَآ أَمَرَ ٱللَّهُ
بِهِۦٓ أَن يُوصَلَ وَيَخْشَوْنَ رَبَّهُمْ
وَيَخَافُونَ سُوٓءَ ٱلْحِسَابِ ﴿٢١﴾ وَٱلَّذِينَ
صَبَرُوا۟ ٱبْتِغَآءَ وَجْهِ رَبِّهِمْ وَأَقَامُوا۟
ٱلصَّلَوٰةَ وَأَنفَقُوا۟ مِمَّا رَزَقْنَٰهُمْ سِرًّا
وَعَلَانِيَةً وَيَدْرَءُونَ بِٱلْحَسَنَةِ ٱلسَّيِّئَةَ

(peace be on him) said: 'That means that his whole record of deeds will be presented before God. However, one who is subjected to reckoning, will amount to his undoing.' (Cf. Abū Dā'ūd, *K. al-Janā'iz, 'Bāb 'Iyādat al-Nisā'*, where substantively the same point has been emphasized, even though there are some slight differences in the text of the tradition in the different works of *Ḥadīth* – Ed.)

The matter can perhaps best be understood by the analogy of a master and a servant. If the servant is faithful, the master will be inclined to connive at his minor faults. In fact, in view of the great services the servant may have rendered his master, the latter is likely even to overlook his major faults. However, the master's attitude will be altogether different if there are reasons for him to feel convinced that the servant has been treacherous towards him or has wilfully committed a breach of trust. In such cases, he will be inclined to disregard any services he may have rendered in the past, and will presumably take cognizance of all his offences – both major and minor.

35. Obviously the two cannot be alike. Their attitudes in this world were different, and so will be their end in the Hereafter.

36. Those who accept the teachings of God and respond positively to the call of His Messenger are not mentally blind. On the contrary, they are a group of intelligent and perceptive people. As a result, they are characterized by certain outstanding qualities in the life of the world and theirs will be a blissful end in the Next Life. (For this see verses 20–4 below – Ed.)

37. Here reference is made to the primordial covenant which God asked man to make – that he will serve only Him. (For further elaboration of this covenant see *Towards Understanding the Qur'ān*, vol. III, *al-A'rāf* 7, nn. 134–5, pp. 97–101.)

Every human being is bound by this covenant. The message of this covenant is innate in human nature. The covenant binds man as soon as he is born both as a result of God's act of creation and the nurturing and sustenance provided by Him. It cannot be denied that man's sustenance comes from God. Nor can it be denied that man avails himself of the faculties bestowed upon and the resources granted to him by God. These very facts automatically bind man to the covenant mentioned above, and bind him in a life-long commitment. No sensible person who has any sense of gratitude for all the good done to him by God will wilfully break this covenant. All that can happen is an occasional lapse here or another there, and that too undeliberately.

38. The word 'ties' here refers to all social and cultural relationships between human beings. As we know, it is only when these relationships are sound and healthy that man's social life can be truly successful.

39. These are the people who restrain their desires and control their passions and predilections. Such people are not lured by the prospect of material benefits and of the pleasures attendant upon disobedience of God. Instead, they obey God and cheerfully bear all losses and sufferings resulting from it. Thus, steadfastness or patience is the very core of a true believer's life. With his eyes focused on God's good pleasure and the abiding reward of the Hereafter, the believer exercises self-restraint, resolutely encountering the temptation to commit sins.

40. Instead of engaging in evil, the believers ward off evil with good. If they are wronged by others, they do not subject the latter to wrong in return. Even when others lie against them, they still tell the truth about them. No matter how dishonest others might have been in their dealings with them, they remain honest. The conduct of the believers has been aptly portrayed in the following saying of the Prophet (peace be on him): 'Do not follow the ways of others, saying: "If others do good, we will also do good to them; but if others wrong us, we will also wrong them." Discipline yourself to a principle. If people do good to you, do good to them; and if they mistreat you, [still] refrain from being

Theirs shall be the ultimate abode (23) – the Everlasting Gardens: which they shall enter and so shall the righteous from among their fathers, and their spouses, and their offspring who acted righteously. And angels shall enter unto them from every gate, and say: (24) 'Peace be upon you.[41] You merit this reward for your patience.' How excellent is the ultimate abode! ▶

أُوْلَٰٓئِكَ لَهُمْ عُقْبَى ٱلدَّارِ ﴿٢٢﴾ جَنَّٰتُ عَدْنٍ
يَدْخُلُونَهَا وَمَن صَلَحَ مِنْ ءَابَآئِهِمْ وَأَزْوَٰجِهِمْ
وَذُرِّيَّٰتِهِمْ ۖ وَٱلْمَلَٰٓئِكَةُ يَدْخُلُونَ عَلَيْهِم مِّن
كُلِّ بَابٍ ﴿٢٣﴾ سَلَٰمٌ عَلَيْكُم بِمَا صَبَرْتُمْ ۚ
فَنِعْمَ عُقْبَى ٱلدَّارِ ﴿٢٤﴾

unjust.' (See al-Tirmidhī, *Abwāb al-Birr wa al-Ṣilah, 'Bāb Mā Jā' fī al-Iḥsān wa al-'Afw* – Ed.)

Of similar import is the tradition in which the Prophet (peace be on him) mentions that his Lord had enjoined nine commands. Four of those commands are as follows: 'That I should speak with justice in anger and happiness; that I should render the right of him who deprives me; that I should give him who denies me; that I should forgive him who wrongs me.'* Another tradition expresses the same idea in another saying of the Prophet (peace be on him): 'Do not betray him who betrays you.' (Al-Tirmidhī, *Abwāb al-Buyū', 'Bāb Mā Jā' fī al-Nahy li al-Muslim an yadfa' ilá al-khamr yabī'uh lah'* – Ed.) 'Umar has also said something to the same effect: 'The best way to punish someone who has not behaved towards you in a God-fearing manner is that you behave with him in a God-fearing way.'

41. This does not simply mean that angels will come from all directions to greet them, wishing them peace. It also means that angels will convey the glad tidings to the believers that they had come to an abode where they shall forever enjoy peace. They will be secure against every calamity and suffering, against every toil, fear and danger. (For details see *al-Ḥijr* 15, n. 29 below.)

*The tradition is not traceable in the major collections of authentic traditions. For the text of the tradition see Ibn al-Athīr, *Jāmi' al-Uṣūl*, 12 vols., Cairo, 1949–1955, vol. 12, p. 316 – Ed.

(25) As for those who break the covenant of Allah after firmly confirming it, who cut asunder the ties that Allah has commanded to be joined, and who create corruption in the land: Allah's curse shall be upon them and theirs shall be a wretched abode (in the Hereafter).

(26) Allah enlarges the provision of whomsoever He wills and grants others in strict measure.[42] They exult in the life of the world, although compared with the Hereafter, the life of the world is no more than temporary enjoyment.

وَٱلَّذِينَ يَنقُضُونَ عَهْدَ ٱللَّهِ مِنۢ بَعْدِ
مِيثَٰقِهِۦ وَيَقْطَعُونَ مَآ أَمَرَ ٱللَّهُ بِهِۦٓ
أَن يُوصَلَ وَيُفْسِدُونَ فِى ٱلْأَرْضِ
أُو۟لَٰٓئِكَ لَهُمُ ٱللَّعْنَةُ وَلَهُمْ سُوٓءُ ٱلدَّارِ
﴿٢٥﴾ ٱللَّهُ يَبْسُطُ ٱلرِّزْقَ لِمَن يَشَآءُ
وَيَقْدِرُ وَفَرِحُوا۟ بِٱلْحَيَوٰةِ ٱلدُّنْيَا
وَمَا ٱلْحَيَوٰةُ ٱلدُّنْيَا فِى ٱلْءَاخِرَةِ إِلَّا
مَتَٰعٌ ﴿٢٦﴾

42. The background of the verse is that steeped in ignorance, the Makkan unbelievers did not determine the worth of people in consideration of their belief and action. Instead, they judged the excellence of people on the basis of their richness or poverty. They entertained the delusion that anyone who receives means of worldly well-being in abundance is in God's favour, no matter how deeply immersed he may be in doctrinal error or moral corruption. On the contrary, anyone who is subjected to miserable conditions of living is disliked by God no matter how righteous he may be. It is for this reason that the unbelievers considered the chiefs of the Quraysh superior to the poverty-stricken Companions of the Prophet (peace be on him). They held up the prosperity of the chiefs as evidence of God's support of them. In order to remove the misunderstanding, the law governing the distribution of worldly provisions is explained. It is clarified that God's decision to grant worldly riches is based on a whole host of considerations and the extent of a person's material fortune is not necessarily the basic indicator of a person's moral worth in the sight of God. The true basis on which one should judge who is a better person than another is whether he embraces the true world-view and acts righteously or not. As for the utterly ignorant, they use a very simple criterion by which they judge people – who is rich and who is poor.

(27) Those who have rejected the (message of Muhammad) say: 'Why has no sign been sent down upon him from his Lord?'[43] Tell them: 'Allah lets go astray those whom He wills, and guides to Himself those who turn to Him.'[44] (28) Such are the ones who believe (in the message of the Prophet) and whose hearts find rest in the remembrance of Allah. Surely in Allah's remembrance do hearts find rest. (29) So those who believe (in the message of the truth) and do good are destined for happiness and a blissful end.

وَيَقُولُ ٱلَّذِينَ كَفَرُوا۟ لَوْلَآ أُنزِلَ عَلَيْهِ ءَايَةٌ
مِّن رَّبِّهِۦ ۚ قُلْ إِنَّ ٱللَّهَ يُضِلُّ مَن يَشَآءُ
وَيَهْدِىٓ إِلَيْهِ مَنْ أَنَابَ ﴿٢٧﴾ ٱلَّذِينَ ءَامَنُوا۟
وَتَطْمَئِنُّ قُلُوبُهُم بِذِكْرِ ٱللَّهِ ۗ أَلَا
بِذِكْرِ ٱللَّهِ تَطْمَئِنُّ ٱلْقُلُوبُ ﴿٢٨﴾
ٱلَّذِينَ ءَامَنُوا۟ وَعَمِلُوا۟ ٱلصَّـٰلِحَـٰتِ
طُوبَىٰ لَهُمْ وَحُسْنُ مَـَٔابٍ ﴿٢٩﴾

43. This question has already been answered in verse 7 above and that should be kept in view here. Virtually the same objection has been mentioned here. However, here it is refuted in a different way.

44. God does not forcibly direct to the right way those who, instead of turning to God for guidance, defiantly turn away from Him. God allows such people to stumble in the deviant ways of their choice. The same factors which direct those who seek God's guidance to the right way are allowed to become the factors of misguidance in respect of those who seek error. Such persons are unable to benefit from the light which, rather than illuminating their path, merely serves to dazzle their vision. This is what is meant by saying that: 'Allah lets go astray those whom He wills.'

The Qur'ānic rejoinder to the unbelievers' demand for a miraculous sign is surpassing in its eloquence. For as we know, the unbelievers used to ask the Prophet (peace be on him) to produce some miraculous sign. They claimed that only after some such sign had been shown to them would they be convinced of the truth of his claim. Such people are being told that if they failed to find the right way, it is not because there were no signs pointing to it. Their failure was the result of their not being keen enough to be led to the right way. There are

(30) Thus have We sent you as a Messenger[45] to a community before which many other communities have passed away that you may recite to them whatever We have revealed to you. And yet they deny the Lord of Mercy.[46] Say to them: 'He is my Lord, there is no god but Him. In Him I have placed all my trust and to Him I shall return.'

(31) And what would have happened were a Qur'ān to be revealed wherewith mountains could be set in motion, or the earth cleft, or the dead made to speak?[47] ▶

كَذَٰلِكَ أَرْسَلْنَٰكَ فِىٓ أُمَّةٍ قَدْ خَلَتْ
مِن قَبْلِهَآ أُمَمٌ لِّتَتْلُوَا۟ عَلَيْهِمُ ٱلَّذِىٓ
أَوْحَيْنَآ إِلَيْكَ وَهُمْ يَكْفُرُونَ
بِٱلرَّحْمَٰنِ ۚ قُلْ هُوَ رَبِّى لَآ إِلَٰهَ إِلَّا
هُوَ عَلَيْهِ تَوَكَّلْتُ وَإِلَيْهِ مَتَابِ
٣٠ وَلَوْ أَنَّ قُرْءَانًا سُيِّرَتْ بِهِ
ٱلْجِبَالُ أَوْ قُطِّعَتْ بِهِ ٱلْأَرْضُ
أَوْ كُلِّمَ بِهِ ٱلْمَوْتَىٰ ۗ

signs galore. They are spread all around them. And yet, they are led by none of those signs to God for they are not interested in being directed to His Way. In such instances, how can any sign be of any avail to them? As for those who earnestly seek the way of God, there is no dearth of signs for them. Such people observe those signs and are directed to the right way.

45. That is to say that the Prophet (peace be on him) was sent without any signs of the kind which the unbelievers had clamoured for.

46. This is an indictment of the unbelievers. They have definitely turned away from devotion to God; they associate others with God in His attributes and powers and rights; they offer thanks to others than God for the bounties bestowed upon them by God alone.

47. In order to appreciate this verse it is important to bear in mind that it is in fact addressed to the Muslims rather than to the unbelievers. When the Muslims repeatedly came across the unbelievers' demand for miraculous signs, they anxiously desired that some miraculous sign – one that would persuade the unbelievers to believe – should indeed be shown to them. Moreover, the believers noticed that since such signs were not in evidence,

(To show such signs is not at all difficult for) everything rests entirely with Allah.[48] So, do men of faith (still look forward to such a sign in response to the demand of the unbelievers and) not despair as a result of knowing that had Allah so willed, He could have guided all to the truth.[49] Misfortune continues to afflict the unbelievers on account of their misdeeds, or to befall on locations close to their habitation. This will continue until Allah's promise (of chastisement) is fulfilled. Surely Allah does not go back upon His promise. (32) Surely the Messengers before you were ridiculed, but I always initially granted respite to those who disbelieved, and then I seized them (with chastisement). Then, how awesome was My chastisement!

بَلْ لِّلَّهِ ٱلْأَمْرُ جَمِيعًا أَفَلَمْ يَاْيْـَٔسِ
ٱلَّذِينَ ءَامَنُوٓا۟ أَن لَّوْ يَشَآءُ ٱللَّهُ
لَهَدَى ٱلنَّاسَ جَمِيعًا وَلَا يَزَالُ
ٱلَّذِينَ كَفَرُوا۟ تُصِيبُهُم بِمَا صَنَعُوا۟
قَارِعَةٌ أَوْ تَحُلُّ قَرِيبًا مِّن دَارِهِمْ
حَتَّىٰ يَأْتِيَ وَعْدُ ٱللَّهِ إِنَّ ٱللَّهَ
لَا يُخْلِفُ ٱلْمِيعَادَ ﴿٣١﴾ وَلَقَدِ
ٱسْتُهْزِئَ بِرُسُلٍ مِّن قَبْلِكَ
فَأَمْلَيْتُ لِلَّذِينَ كَفَرُوا۟ ثُمَّ
أَخَذْتُهُمْ فَكَيْفَ كَانَ
عِقَابِ ﴿٣٢﴾

despite the demand for them, the unbelievers had an opportunity to stir up doubts about the truth of the Prophet's message. This increased their anxiety.

In the present verse the Muslims are being asked if they were really convinced that had such miraculous signs been shown, the unbelievers would have embraced the true faith? Did they entertain the illusion that the unbelievers were all but ready to believe and the only thing that was lacking was a miraculous sign? Such a view is altogether erroneous and simplistic. For the unbelievers were a myopic lot who had failed to observe the light of the truth in the teachings of the Qur'ān, in the natural phenomena spread all across the universe, in the exemplary life of the Prophet (peace be on him), and in the

(33) Then, is it in regard to Him Who watches over the deeds of every person[50] that they are acting blasphemously[51] by setting up His associates? Tell them: 'Name those associates (if Allah Himself has made them His associates)! Or do you inform Allah of something the existence of which He does not even know? Or do people arbitrarily utter empty words?[52] Indeed, their foul contriving[53] has been made to seem fair to the unbelievers and they have been barred from finding the right way.[54] Whomsoever Allah lets go astray will have none to guide him.▶

أَفَمَنْ هُوَ قَآئِمٌ عَلَىٰ كُلِّ نَفْسٍ بِمَا كَسَبَتْ
وَجَعَلُوا لِلَّهِ شُرَكَآءَ قُلْ سَمُّوهُمْ أَمْ
تُنَبِّئُونَهُ بِمَا لَا يَعْلَمُ فِي الْأَرْضِ أَم
بِظَاهِرٍ مِّنَ الْقَوْلِ بَلْ زُيِّنَ لِلَّذِينَ
كَفَرُوا مَكْرُهُمْ وَصُدُّوا عَنِ
السَّبِيلِ وَمَن يُضْلِلِ اللَّهُ فَمَا لَهُ مِنْ
هَادٍ ٣٣

great transformation brought about in the lives of the Companions by the teachings of Islam. How can it be conceived that those who remained unmoved by all the great signs of the truth mentioned above would be stirred by merely observing, let us say, that a mountain had moved, or that the earth was rent asunder, or that dead bodies had risen from their graves?

48. The true reason for not showing miraculous signs was not that God had no power to show such signs, but rather because such a method was inconsistent with God's scheme of things. For the true purpose of that scheme was not so much to drive some people into affirming the prophethood of some Prophet, but to help them attain true guidance. Such a purpose can only be achieved by reforming people's outlook and re-orienting their thinking pattern.

(34) They shall suffer chastisement in the life of the world, and surely the chastisement of the Hereafter is even more grievous. None has the power to shield them from (the chastisement of) Allah. (35) And such will be the Paradise promised to the God-fearing: rivers will flow beneath it, its fruits will be eternal, and so will be its blissful shade. That is the ultimate destiny of the God-fearing while Fire is the destiny of the unbelievers.'

لَّهُمْ عَذَابٌ فِي الْحَيَوٰةِ الدُّنْيَا وَلَعَذَابُ
الْآخِرَةِ أَشَقُّ وَمَا لَهُم مِّنَ اللَّهِ مِن
وَاقٍ ﴿٣٤﴾ مَّثَلُ الْجَنَّةِ الَّتِي
وُعِدَ الْمُتَّقُونَ تَجْرِي مِن تَحْتِهَا الْأَنْهَارُ
أُكُلُهَا دَائِمٌ وَظِلُّهَا تِلْكَ عُقْبَى
الَّذِينَ اتَّقَوا وَّعُقْبَى الْكَافِرِينَ
النَّارُ ﴿٣٥﴾

---

49. Had the purpose merely been that people should believe without understanding and without being rationally convinced then perhaps God did not have to show miraculous signs. That purpose could have been achieved by simply creating all human beings as born believers.

50. God knows the deeds of each and every individual. Nothing escapes His sight – be they good or evil deeds.

51. The unbelievers have the audacity to set up equals with God, to associate the beings created by God Himself with His essence, attributes and rights. People do all this brazenly even though they live within the confines of the universe which has been created by God. They seem to have no fear that they will be called to account by anyone.

52. The unbelievers had associated others with God. In that regard, they could choose, to demonstrate their correctness, any one of the following alternatives:

(1) That they had some definite information that God had invested some persons with a share in His attributes, powers or rights. If that were the case, then it should be made clear as to who these persons were, and how such information was obtained.

(2) That some persons might have become God's associates even without God becoming aware of that, and that those very persons subsequently

provided the information about being God's associates. If that were the case, then that has to be stated in clear terms. In such an eventuality, it has to be seen if there are any people who are foolish enough to accept such a preposterous claim.

(3) If both the above propositions are untrue, then the only option which we are left with is that the unbelievers arbitrarily declare regarding whomsoever they wish to that he is either God's relative, or Lord of providence, or one who answers the prayers of people, or the overlord appointed by God over a particular region, or that he is such a saintly person that God disposes several matters in accordance with his wishes.

53. The association of others with God in His divinity by the unbelievers has been branded as a 'foul contriving'. For the celestial bodies or angels or spirits or saints which are said to be God's associates in His attributes, powers and rights have never made any such claims. They do not ask the unbelievers to worship or bow down before them. It is merely a contriving of some unscrupulous human beings who, in order to establish their own control over ordinary people and usurp their earnings, have invented false gods and have misled people into becoming the devotees of those same false gods. This enabled them to exploit people under the claim that they were the authorized representatives of the gods.

Another reason for branding polytheism as a 'foul contriving' is that it is an act of self-deception. For it provides one with an opportunity to fully engross oneself in worldliness and in evading moral scruples. It also provides a rationale for total permissiveness and licentiousness.

Still another reason for labelling polytheists guilty of 'foul contriving' is explained below. (See n. 54 below – Ed.)

54. Such is human nature that when a person prefers a certain course of action, he comes forward with arguments in support of it. He does so in order to satisfy his own conscience as well as to justify his choice to others. He has recourse to a variety of contrived arguments and specious rhetoric with a view to malign and degrade the course he has rejected. It is for this reason that it was pointed out that when the unbelievers made up their minds to deny the truth, in consonance with the law of nature their 'foul contriving' was made attractive to them. It is in this sense that they were barred from finding the right way.

(36) Those upon whom We bestowed the Scriptures earlier rejoice at the Book revealed to you, while there are also some among different groups that reject part of it. Tell them: 'I have only been commanded to serve Allah and not to associate anyone with Him. To Him do I call, and to Him is my return.'[55] (37) And it is with the same directive that We revealed to you this Arabic Writ. And were you indeed to follow the vain desires of people after the true knowledge had come to you, none will be your supporter against Allah, and none will have the power to shield you from His punishment.

(38) We indeed sent many Messengers before you and We gave them wives and children;[56] and no Messenger had the power to produce a miraculous sign except by the command of Allah.[57] Every age has its own (revealed) Book.▶

وَالَّذِينَ ءَاتَيْنَٰهُمُ الْكِتَٰبَ يَفْرَحُونَ
بِمَآ أُنزِلَ إِلَيْكَ وَمِنَ الْأَحْزَابِ مَن يُنكِرُ
بَعْضَهُۥ قُلْ إِنَّمَآ أُمِرْتُ أَنْ أَعْبُدَ اللَّهَ وَلَآ
أُشْرِكَ بِهِۦٓ إِلَيْهِ أَدْعُوا۟ وَإِلَيْهِ مَـَٔابِ
٣٦ وَكَذَٰلِكَ أَنزَلْنَٰهُ حُكْمًا عَرَبِيًّا
وَلَئِنِ اتَّبَعْتَ أَهْوَآءَهُم بَعْدَ مَا جَآءَكَ
مِنَ الْعِلْمِ مَا لَكَ مِنَ اللَّهِ مِن وَلِىٍّ وَلَا
وَاقٍ ٣٧ وَلَقَدْ أَرْسَلْنَا رُسُلًا مِّن
قَبْلِكَ وَجَعَلْنَا لَهُمْ أَزْوَٰجًا وَذُرِّيَّةً
وَمَا كَانَ لِرَسُولٍ أَن يَأْتِىَ بِـَٔايَةٍ إِلَّا
بِإِذْنِ اللَّهِ لِكُلِّ أَجَلٍ كِتَابٌ ٣٨

55. This is in response to an objection which was expressed at that time by the enemies of Islam. They used to contend that if Prophet Muḥammad (peace be on him) had brought the same message which had been brought by the earlier Prophets, why is it that the Jews and Christians the followers of earlier Prophets do not warmly welcome that message and embrace it? In response, the Qur'ān states that, in the first place, not all Jews and Christians rejected the Prophet's message. While it is true that some were not very happy with the Prophet's message, others had greeted it with great joy. However, the Prophet

(39) Allah effaces whatever He wills and retains whatever He wills. With Him is the Mother of the Book.[58]

(40) (O Prophet!) Whether We make you see a part of the punishment that We have threatened them with come to pass during your life-time, or We take you away before that happens, your duty is no more than to convey the Message, and it is for Us to make a reckoning.[59] ▶

يَمْحُوا اللَّهُ مَا يَشَآءُ وَيُثْبِتُ وَعِندَهُۥٓ
أُمُّ الْكِتَٰبِ ﴿٣٩﴾ وَإِن مَّا نُرِيَنَّكَ
بَعْضَ الَّذِى نَعِدُهُمْ أَوْ نَتَوَفَّيَنَّكَ فَإِنَّمَا
عَلَيْكَ الْبَلَٰغُ وَعَلَيْنَا الْحِسَابُ ﴿٤٠﴾

(peace be on him) is required to disregard the reactions of people to the teaching he had received from God. His task, in any case, is to proclaim that message and to make it clear to all that in all circumstances he will follow it.

56. This is the answer to another objection hurled at the Prophet (peace be on him). The unbelievers decried him for being one like ordinary mortals insofar as his life was also encumbered with such worldly concerns as those relating to spouse and children. They were at a loss to appreciate how someone who was God's Messenger could also have sexual urges which would prompt him to marry.

57. This is the answer to another objection. The opponents contended that Prophet Moses (peace be on him) was supported by the miracles of a white, shining hand, and the miraculous rod. Likewise, Jesus was also supported by miracles. He was granted the power to restore sight to the blind, and to cure the leper. In the same manner, Prophet Ṣāliḥ (peace be on him) was supported by another supernatural token – that of a she-camel. The unbelievers would recount all that and then ask: 'Which miraculous sign can Prophet Muḥammad (peace be on him) produce to support his claim to be a Prophet?'

In response, the unbelievers are informed that the miraculous sign which a Prophet shows does not represent his own innate power. The decision as to when a miraculous sign is shown, and through whom, rests entirely with God. Were God to decide so, He would show some miraculous signs through Prophet Muḥammad (peace be on him) as well. But since the Prophet (peace be

(41) Do they not see that We are advancing in the land, diminishing it by its borders on all sides?[60] Allah judges, and no one has the power to reverse His judgement. He is swift in reckoning. (42) Those who lived before them also devised many a plot,[61] but the master plot rests with Allah. He knows what everyone does. The deniers of the truth will soon come to know whose end is good.

أَوَلَمْ يَرَوْا أَنَّا نَأْتِي ٱلْأَرْضَ نَنقُصُهَا مِنْ
أَطْرَافِهَا ۚ وَٱللَّهُ يَحْكُمُ لَا مُعَقِّبَ
لِحُكْمِهِۦ ۚ وَهُوَ سَرِيعُ ٱلْحِسَابِ
﴿٤١﴾ وَقَدْ مَكَرَ ٱلَّذِينَ مِن قَبْلِهِمْ فَلِلَّهِ
ٱلْمَكْرُ جَمِيعًا ۖ يَعْلَمُ مَا تَكْسِبُ كُلُّ
نَفْسٍ ۗ وَسَيَعْلَمُ ٱلْكُفَّٰرُ لِمَنْ عُقْبَى
ٱلدَّارِ ﴿٤٢﴾

on him) lays no claim to the powers of God, it is not fair to ask him to come forth with miraculous signs.

58. This, again, is in answer to an objection raised by the unbelievers. They had asked why a new Book should have been revealed even though the earlier scriptures were extant. They took note of the Prophet's claim that the earlier scriptures had been distorted, and that with the revelation of the Qur'ān – which replaced them – the earlier scriptures stood abrogated. To this the unbelievers responded: 'How can a book revealed by God be tampered with? Why did God not protect it from such tamperings?' They also expressed their scepticism about the Prophet's claim that the Qur'ān was the Word of the same God Who had earlier revealed the Torah and the Gospels. They contended that they were not convinced with that claim since several injunctions of the Qur'ān were opposed to the injunctions embodied in the earlier scriptures. In this connection, they pointed out that many a thing which had been made unlawful in the Torah was subsequently made lawful in the Qur'ān.

More detailed answers to these questions have been provided in the *sūrahs* which were revealed later. Here the answer consists merely of a succinct explication of the matter.

The expression *Umm al-Kitāb* ('Mother of the Book') which occurs in the verse refers to that 'Original Book' which is the source of all heavenly scriptures.

(43) The unbelievers claim that you have not been sent by Allah. Tell them: 'Allah is sufficient as a witness between me and you; and those too who know the Scriptures.'[62]

وَيَقُولُ ٱلَّذِينَ كَفَرُوا۟ لَسْتَ
مُرْسَلًا قُلْ كَفَىٰ بِٱللَّهِ
شَهِيدًۢا بَيْنِى وَبَيْنَكُمْ
وَمَنْ عِندَهُۥ عِلْمُ ٱلْكِتَـٰبِ ﴿٤٣﴾

---

59. The Prophet (peace be on him) is asked not to fret about those who rejected his message. He should not feel distressed about their fate, nor overly concerned as to when they would be subjected to God's chastisement. Disregarding all that, and leaving the ultimate judgement to God, the Prophet (peace be on him) should steadily proceed with the task entrusted to him.

It should be noted that while the present statement is apparently addressed to the Prophet (peace be on him), it is in fact meant for his enemies. The latter had often challenged the Prophet (peace be on him) and had asked him to bring upon them God's scourge – of which he had warned them – then and there.

60. The opponents are reminded that Islam's influence was spreading to every nook and cranny of Arabia. This naturally meant the shrinking of the unbelievers' influence and growing pressure upon them. Did these not indicate that they were heading towards their doom? What God says here, viz. 'We are advancing in land', is a very subtle and refined way of indicating the direction of the change which was then taking place. Since Islam is from God, Who supports the propounders of that message, the spread of Islam has been characterized as the advance of God Himself.

61. There is nothing new in the fact that the unbelievers had resorted to lies, deception and repressive measures to thwart the voice of truth. In the past, people who wanted to achieve that purpose had resorted to more or less the same measures.

62. Everyone who has any knowledge of the scriptures will testify to the fact that the teaching of the Prophet (peace be on him) is exactly the same as that of the earlier Prophets.

Sūrah 14

Ibrāhīm

(Abraham)

(Makkan Period)

Title

The title of this *sūrah* is derived from its reference to Abraham: 'And call to mind when Abraham prayed: "My Lord! Make this city secure" ' (see verse 35). The choice of Abraham as the title does not mean that this *sūrah* presents a biographical account of Abraham (peace be on him). As in other *sūrahs*, the title simply serves the purpose of marking it out from other *sūrahs*. It is a *sūrah* in which Abraham has been mentioned.

Period of Revelation

The general tenor of the *sūrah* is in line with those revealed in the last phase of the Makkan period of the Prophet's life. It appears to have been revealed around the same time as *al-Ra'd*. It is significant that in this *sūrah* we come across the statement: 'Then the unbelievers told their Messengers: "You will have to return to the fold of our faith or else we shall banish you from our land" ' (verse 13). This clearly indicates that the *sūrah* was revealed at a time when the persecution of Muslims in Makka had reached its apex. In the manner of the earlier unbelievers, the Makkans were bent on banishing the believers from their land. As a consequence, the unbelievers are served with the same warning by God which was given to the unbelievers of the past: 'We will most certainly destroy these wrongdoers' (verse 13). Likewise, the believers are comforted in the same manner as believers before them: 'We will cause you to settle in the land as their successors' (verse 14). The tone of the concluding verses (see verse 42 ff.) also suggests that the *sūrah* was revealed in the last phase of the Makkan period.

Central Theme

The *sūrah* consists of an admonition and a warning addressed to those who rejected the Prophet's message and resorted to a wide variety of vile means to defeat his mission. The note of warning in the *sūrah* is more dominant than in the other *sūrahs* revealed around the same period. This is because the earlier *sūrahs* were devoted to admonition. However, admonition proved to be of no avail; in fact, admonition merely increased their obduracy, hostility, rebellion, and mischief and their propensity to perpetrate oppression and cruelty.

In the name of Allah, the Merciful, the Compassionate.

(1) *Alif. Lām. Rā*. This is a Book which We have revealed to you that you may bring forth mankind from every kind of darkness into the light, and direct them, with the leave of their Lord, to the way[1] of the Mighty, the Innately Praiseworthy[2] (2) Allah to Whom belongs all that is in the heavens and all that is in the earth.

الٓرۚ كِتَٰبٌ أَنزَلۡنَٰهُ إِلَيۡكَ لِتُخۡرِجَ
ٱلنَّاسَ مِنَ ٱلظُّلُمَٰتِ إِلَى ٱلنُّورِ بِإِذۡنِ
رَبِّهِمۡ إِلَىٰ صِرَٰطِ ٱلۡعَزِيزِ ٱلۡحَمِيدِ
﴿١﴾ ٱللَّهِ ٱلَّذِي لَهُۥ مَا فِي ٱلسَّمَٰوَٰتِ
وَمَا فِي ٱلۡأَرۡضِۗ

1. The statement says that the Qur'ān brings forth mankind from every kind of darkness into light and directs them to the way of God. This implies that all those who are not on the way of God are in fact stumbling in the darkness of ignorance. Such persons are indeed ignorant notwithstanding their pompous claims to the contrary. Even those illiterate villagers who find the way of God will be credited with the light of knowledge.

The Qur'ān states that the Prophet (peace be on him) had been granted a Book which 'may direct mankind, with the leave of their Lord, to the way of the Mighty, the Innately Praiseworthy'. This statement lays down, on the one hand, a task to which the Prophet (peace be on him) is required to address his efforts. On the other hand, it also mentions the limits within which this task can be performed, by any human being, including a Prophet, who seeks to direct people to the way of the Lord. All that anyone can do is to explain to people what that way is. No one has the power conclusively to put others on the way of God. For that depends on God's help and leave. It is only by God's help that anyone can attain guidance. No one else can enable him to do so. (See *al-Baqarah* 2: 272; *al-Qaṣaṣ* 28: 56; *al-Zumar* 39: 23; and often in the Qur'ān – Ed.)

The Qur'ān has explained at several places the law by which this favour of God is bestowed upon people. Thanks to that, we know that guidance is granted only to those who earnestly seek it, who are free from blind prejudice and obduracy, who are not the slaves of their carnal desires, who keep their eyes and ears open, who think with an unprejudiced mind and have no mental block against accepting whatever is sound and reasonable.

Woe be to those who reject the truth for a severe chastisement; (3) to those who have chosen the life of the world in preference to the Hereafter,[3] who hinder people from the way of Allah, and seek to make it crooked.[4] They have gone far astray.

وَوَيۡلٞ لِّلۡكَٰفِرِينَ مِنۡ عَذَابٖ
شَدِيدٍ ۝٢ ٱلَّذِينَ يَسۡتَحِبُّونَ
ٱلۡحَيَوٰةَ ٱلدُّنۡيَا عَلَى ٱلۡأٓخِرَةِ
وَيَصُدُّونَ عَن سَبِيلِ ٱللَّهِ
وَيَبۡغُونَهَا عِوَجًاۚ أُوْلَٰٓئِكَ فِي
ضَلَٰلِۭ بَعِيدٖ ۝٣

---

2. The word used here is *ḥamīd* which is synonymous with *maḥmūd* (the praised one). There is, however, a subtle difference in their meaning. The word *maḥmūd* is used for anyone who is praised. The word *ḥamīd* – which has been used here – signifies one who innately deserves praise regardless of whether anyone actually praises him or not. The word is too rich in meaning to be expressed merely by the word 'praiseworthy'. Hence, we have rendered it as 'innately praiseworthy'.

3. The unbelievers are concerned only with this world. They simply do not care for the Hereafter. They are so enamoured of the pleasures and comforts of this world that they are willing to risk their success in the Hereafter for the sake of worldly success. Since they do not care about the Hereafter, they are not prepared to risk even the slightest loss, or expose themselves to the least danger or suffering, or deny themselves any pleasure for the sake of success and well-being in the Next Life. The fact is that the unbelievers have carefully considered both the present world and the Next, and after careful reflection have decided to follow the course of the former rather than the latter. Hence, wherever their worldly interests come into conflict with the interests of the Next Life, they invariably accord preference to worldly interests.

4. The unbelievers are not ready to live in subordination to God's will. Instead, they would like God's religion to be subordinated to their desires and interests. They would like God's Message to accommodate all the ideas, fancies, superstitions and conjectures which attract them, and to purge itself of every doctrine which their puny minds are unable to grasp. They would also like religion to sanction all their customs, usages and habits, and to refrain from asking them to follow anything that they are not particularly fond of. In short, they expect their religion to behave like a bonded slave. If they move under the influence of their lusts and desires in one direction, so should it. They are prepared to heed God's command only if He asks them to adhere to an abject religion of the kind described above.

(4) Never have We sent a Messenger but he has addressed his people in their language that he may fully expound his Message to them.[5] [And after the message is given], Allah lets go astray whomsoever He wills, and guides to the right way whomsoever He wills.[6] He is the Mighty, the Wise.[7]

وَمَآ أَرۡسَلۡنَا مِن رَّسُولٍ إِلَّا بِلِسَانِ قَوۡمِهِۦ لِيُبَيِّنَ لَهُمۡۖ فَيُضِلُّ ٱللَّهُ مَن يَشَآءُ وَيَهۡدِي مَن يَشَآءُۚ وَهُوَ ٱلۡعَزِيزُ ٱلۡحَكِيمُ ٤

5. This verse may be interpreted in two ways. First, it may be interpreted to mean that whenever God sends a Messenger to a nation, He also reveals His Message in the language of that nation. The purpose of so doing is that the people concerned should be able to fully grasp the Message. For if the Message is available to a people in their own language, they are left with no excuse to plead that they failed to believe because the teaching presented to them was incomprehensible.

There is, however, also a second possible meaning of the verse. Suppose God were to send His scripture say to an Arabic-speaking Messenger, in an altogether alien language, say in Chinese or Japanese. Surely this would cause people to wonder and would make the scripture appear miraculous to them. However, in God's scheme of things, the concern to enable people to fully understand the content of His Message has an overriding priority. It is much more important that the people among whom a Prophet has been raised should understand his teaching than have them wonder-struck by a miraculous feat. Hence, it was necessary that God's Message should be conveyed in the language of the people to whom it was addressed.

6. Every Messenger presents, as mentioned earlier (see n. 5 above – Ed.) his teaching in the language which his people fully understand. Nevertheless, not all the addressees of the Message are in fact able to embrace the truth. The reason is quite simple. To have faith in something is quite different from just understanding it. In any case, whether man is able to find the right way or keeps wandering in error is something which, in the ultimate, is in God's Hand. Hence, it is quite apt to say that God guides, through His Word, all whom He pleases, to the right way. For others, His Word becomes a means of their falling into error. (See also n. 1 above and n. 7 below – Ed.)

(5) We indeed sent Moses with Our signs, saying: 'Lead your people out of darkness into the light, and admonish them by narrating to them anecdotes from the annals of Allah.[8] Verily in it there are great signs[9] for everyone who is patient and gives thanks (to Allah).'[10]

وَلَقَدْ أَرْسَلْنَا مُوسَىٰ بِآيَاتِنَا أَنْ أَخْرِجْ قَوْمَكَ مِنَ الظُّلُمَاتِ إِلَى النُّورِ وَذَكِّرْهُمْ بِأَيَّامِ اللَّهِ ۚ إِنَّ فِي ذَٰلِكَ لَآيَاتٍ لِكُلِّ صَبَّارٍ شَكُورٍ ﴿٥﴾

7. It should be clearly borne in mind that human beings are not absolutely free. Their ability to find the right way or to lose it simply of their own accord is, therefore, inconceivable. For, after all, man's life is circumscribed by God's overarching will. On the other hand, God does not use His power to direct people to the right way or let them go astray in an arbitrary manner. For He is not just 'Mighty', He is also 'Wise'. And since He is Wise, He decides to direct or not to direct someone to the right way on reasonable grounds. He who found the way was directed to it since he deserved to find it. Likewise, he who was left to stumble in error deserved to do so.

8. The word *ayyām*, as a technical term, signifies events of great historical significance. The expression *'Ayyām Allāh'* (literally, 'the Days of Allah') refers to those major events in human history which show that God treated the nations and major personalities of the past according to their deeds, punishing or rewarding them on that account.

9. Historical events contain many signs which are of great significance. Through these signs a person can find convincing evidence of God's unity. Through them he can also find overwhelming evidence of the fact that the law of retribution is a universal law, based on a sharp distinction – at both the intellectual and moral levels – between truth and falsehood. However, in order that the law of retribution comes into full play, it is absolutely necessary that there should be another life after the present one. Furthermore, the major events of history also provide ample signs with the help of which man can know the evil results of following false doctrines, and, thus, learn an instructive lesson from the past.

10. These signs are found everywhere. However, not everyone can derive the right conclusions from them. It is only people who possess certain qualities

(6) And call to mind when Moses said to his people: 'Remember Allah's favour upon you when He delivered you from Pharaoh's people who afflicted you with a grievous chastisement, slaughtering your sons, while letting your women live. In it there was a terrible trial from your Lord.' (7) Also call to mind when your Lord proclaimed: 'If you give thanks,[11] I will certainly grant you more; but if you are ungrateful for My favours, My chastisement is terrible.'[12] ▶

وَإِذْ قَالَ مُوسَىٰ لِقَوْمِهِ ٱذْكُرُوا۟
نِعْمَةَ ٱللَّهِ عَلَيْكُمْ إِذْ أَنجَىٰكُم
مِّنْ ءَالِ فِرْعَوْنَ يَسُومُونَكُمْ سُوٓءَ
ٱلْعَذَابِ وَيُذَبِّحُونَ أَبْنَآءَكُمْ
وَيَسْتَحْيُونَ نِسَآءَكُمْ ۚ وَفِى
ذَٰلِكُم بَلَآءٌ مِّن رَّبِّكُمْ
عَظِيمٌ ﴿٦﴾ وَإِذْ تَأَذَّنَ رَبُّكُمْ لَئِن
شَكَرْتُمْ لَأَزِيدَنَّكُمْ ۖ وَلَئِن
كَفَرْتُمْ إِنَّ عَذَابِى لَشَدِيدٌ ﴿٧﴾

who can fully appreciate those signs and, thus, benefit from them. Such people are those who, when they are put to any test by God, observe patience and fortitude. When they are blessed with God's favours, they are fully appreciative of them and are inclined to give thanks to God. People who are frivolous and ungrateful can never derive full benefit from those signs even if they are able to perceive them.

11. Here a promise is being made by God to grant favours even more amply. This is meant for those who appreciate God's bounteous favours and make right use of them, who refrain from defiance of God's commands, and who, with a sense of gratitude to God, obey Him.

12. The terrible chastisement mentioned in the verse has been explained at some length in *Deuteronomy*. Before his death Prophet Moses (peace be on him) reminds the Israelites of all the important events of their history. He recounts to them the commandments of the Torah which God had communicated to the Israelites through him. This is followed by a lengthy discourse detailing how handsomely they would be rewarded if they obeyed their Lord. Conversely, if they disobeyed Him, how terrible is the chastisement which awaits them. (For this discourse see *Deuteronomy* 4, 6, 8, 10, 11 and

28–30.) Some of the passages are very moving. A few extracts from this discourse are reproduced here to illustrate its content.

> Hear, O Israel: the Lord our God is one Lord; and you shall love the Lord your God with all your heart, and with all your soul, and with all your might. And these words which I command you this day shall be upon your heart; and you shall teach them diligently to your children, and shall talk of them when you sit in your house, and when you walk by the way, and when you lie down, and when you rise (*Deuteronomy* 6: 4–7).

> And now, Israel, what does the Lord your God require of you, but to fear the Lord your God, to walk in all his ways, to love him, to serve the Lord your God with all your heart and with all your soul, and to keep the commandments and statutes of the Lord, which I commanded you this day for your good? Behold, to the Lord your God belong heaven and the heaven of heavens, the earth with all that is in it; (*Deuteronomy* 10: 12–14).

> And if you obey the voice of the Lord your God, being careful to do all his commandments which I command you this day, the Lord your God will set you high above all the nations of the earth. And all these blessings shall come upon you and overtake you, if you obey the voice of the Lord your God. Blessed shall you be in the city, and blessed shall you be in the field . . . The Lord will cause your enemies who rise against you to be defeated before you; . . . The Lord will command the blessing upon you in your barns, and in all that you undertake; and he will bless you in the land which the Lord your God gives you. The Lord will establish you as a people holy to himself, as he has sworn to you, if you keep the commandments of the Lord your God, and walk in his ways. And all the peoples of the earth shall see that you are called by the name of the Lord; and they shall be afraid of you. And the Lord will make you abound in prosperity, in the fruit of your body, and in the fruit of your cattle, . . . The Lord will open to you his good treasury the heavens, . . . and to bless all the work of your hands; and you shall lend to many nations but you shall not borrow. And the Lord will make you the head, and not the tail; and you shall tend upward only, and not downward; if you obey the commandments of the Lord your God, . . . (*Deuteronomy* 28: 1–13).

> But if you will not obey the voice of the Lord your God or be careful to do all his commandments and his statutes which I command you this day, then all these curses shall come upon you and overtake you. Cursed shall you be in the city, and cursed shall you be in the field. . . . The Lord will send upon you curses, confusion, and frustration, in all that you undertake to do, until you are destroyed and perish quickly, on account of the evil of your doings, because you have forsaken me. The Lord will make the pestilence cleave to you until he has consumed you off the land which you are entering to take possession of it. . . The Lord will cause you to be defeated before your enemies; you shall go out one way against them and

(8) Moses said: 'Were you to disbelieve – you and all those who live on the earth – Allah is still Self-Sufficient, Innately Praiseworthy.'[13]

(9) Have not the accounts of your predecessors reached you:[14] the people of Noah, the 'Ād, the Thamūd, and those who came after them – they whose number is not known to any except Allah? Their Messengers came to them with clear signs, but they thrust their hands in their mouths,[15] and said: 'We do surely reject the message you have brought, and we are in disquieting doubt about what you are calling us to?'[16] ▶

وَقَالَ مُوسَىٰٓ إِن تَكۡفُرُوٓاْ أَنتُمۡ وَمَن فِي ٱلۡأَرۡضِ
جَمِيعٗا فَإِنَّ ٱللَّهَ لَغَنِيٌّ حَمِيدٌ ﴿٨﴾ أَلَمۡ
يَأۡتِكُمۡ نَبَؤُاْ ٱلَّذِينَ مِن قَبۡلِكُمۡ
قَوۡمِ نُوحٖ وَعَادٖ وَثَمُودَ وَٱلَّذِينَ
مِنۢ بَعۡدِهِمۡ لَا يَعۡلَمُهُمۡ إِلَّا ٱللَّهُۚ
جَآءَتۡهُمۡ رُسُلُهُم بِٱلۡبَيِّنَٰتِ فَرَدُّوٓاْ
أَيۡدِيَهُمۡ فِيٓ أَفۡوَٰهِهِمۡ وَقَالُوٓاْ إِنَّا كَفَرۡنَا
بِمَآ أُرۡسِلۡتُم بِهِۦ وَإِنَّا لَفِي شَكّٖ مِّمَّا
تَدۡعُونَنَآ إِلَيۡهِ مُرِيبٖ ﴿٩﴾

flee seven ways before them; . . . You shall betroth a wife, and another man shall lie with her; you shall build a house, and you shall not dwell in it; you shall plant a vineyard, and you shall not use the fruit of it. Your ox shall be slain before your eyes, . . . you shall serve your enemies whom the Lord will send against you, in hunger and thirst, in nakedness, and in want of all things; and he will put a yoke of iron upon your neck . . . And the Lord will scatter you among all peoples, from one end of the earth to the other . . . (*Deuteronomy* 28: 15–64).

13. This is an allusion to the events relating to the Prophet Moses and his people and is meant to convey the following important message to the unbelievers of Makka. If a nation greets God's favours with ingratitude and transgression, it is struck by a terrible punishment. A good example in this connection is provided by the history of the Israelites, which was well known to the people of Makka. It was, therefore, for the Makkans themselves to decide whether or not they wished to court the same punishment by returning God's favours with ingratitude.

It is also pertinent to point out that reference is made here to one great favour

(10) Their Messengers said: 'Can there be any doubt about Allah, the Creator of the heavens and the earth?[17] He invites you that He may forgive you your sins and grant you respite till an appointed term.'[18] They replied: 'You are only human beings like ourselves.[19] You seek to prevent us from serving those whom our forefathers have been serving all along. If that is so, produce a clear authority for it.'[20] ▶

۞ قَالَتْ رُسُلُهُمْ أَفِي ٱللَّهِ شَكٌّ
فَاطِرِ ٱلسَّمَٰوَٰتِ وَٱلْأَرْضِ يَدْعُوكُمْ
لِيَغْفِرَ لَكُم مِّن ذُنُوبِكُمْ
وَيُؤَخِّرَكُمْ إِلَىٰٓ أَجَلٍ
مُّسَمًّى قَالُوٓا۟ إِنْ أَنتُمْ إِلَّا بَشَرٌ
مِّثْلُنَا تُرِيدُونَ أَن تَصُدُّونَا عَمَّا
كَانَ يَعْبُدُ ءَابَآؤُنَا فَأْتُونَا
بِسُلْطَٰنٍ مُّبِينٍ ﴿١٠﴾

in particular. This was the favour of raising Prophet Muḥammad (peace be on him) among them and revealing a great teaching to him for their guidance. The people of Makka are being asked to fully appreciate God's favour and to give thanks to Him for it. The Prophet (peace be on him) sometimes used to tell his people that if they could simply give him a word (indicating their commitment to his teaching) all men – Arab and non-Arab – would follow them. (See al-Tirmidhī, *Abwāb al-Tafsīr: 'Sūrah Qāf'* – Ed.)

14. This marks the conclusion of the Prophet Moses' speech. Hereafter, the discourse turns directly to the unbelievers of Makka.

15. The Qur'ānic expression 'they thrust their hands in their mouths' has been variously interpreted by the commentators on the Qur'ān. In our view, the expression has been used to signify both a flat rejection of the Prophet's message and even a sense of astonishment at being asked to believe in it. The words that follow express both these notions. Additionally, they express a feeling of anger.

16. When the unbelievers of Makka became aware of the Prophet's teaching they fell victims of doubt putting an end to their mental peace. In fact, whenever the message of Islam is proclaimed, it inevitably creates a stir and commotion. As a result, even those who strongly reject it, do so with a feeling of uneasiness. For even the staunchest enemies of Islam cannot ignore the positive aspects of its message. The truth of the message and the weighty arguments that are marshalled in support of it are bound to have an impact on

all. Again, the exponent of the Message – a Prophet – has an almost irresistible appeal which can hardly be ignored. His forthrightness, his captivating style, and his unblemished character and conduct are bound to make a strong impact. In addition, the beneficial effects of his message are also evident from the healthy transformation that takes place in the lives of those who embrace it. For it is quite visible that no sooner does someone sincerely embrace Islam than the process of the purification of his life starts. All these factors are bound to create an agitating disquiet in the hearts of those who reject the message.

17. The Messengers posed that question precisely because the polytheists of all ages acknowledged that God exists and that He alone created the heavens and the earth. It is for this reason that the Messengers inquired of their detractors as to what it was that they were in doubt about. What they were in fact being asked was to affirm that God, the creator of the heavens and the earth, alone should be the sole object of their worship and service. The whole thing is so self-evident that there is no reasonable basis for anyone to have any doubts about it.

18. The expression 'appointed term' used in the verse could either signify the time appointed for each man's death, or the time appointed for the Day of Resurrection.

Moreover, in the same way as there is an appointed term for individuals, so it is for nations. Depending on how a nation acts, God decides the period during which it will see its rise, and when it will encounter its decline and fall. If in the course of time a good nation becomes enmeshed in corruption, its term is reduced and it is destroyed. Conversely, if an evil nation mends its attitude and replaces its evil ways by good ones, its term is extended. In fact, it is quite possible that the term of a nation might be extended till the Day of Judgement. This seems to be alluded to in the following verse: 'Verily Allah does not change a people's condition unless they change their inner selves' (*al-Ra'd* 13: 11).

19. What astonished the unbelievers of Makka was that even though Prophet Muḥammad (peace be on him) was a human being, he spoke to them with authority, telling them what they should do and what they should not. The compatriots of the Prophet (peace be on him) considered him to be simply like them for he also ate, drank and slept. Like them he also had wives and children. Like them he was also susceptible to hunger and sickness. Like them he also felt the rigours of the climate. The Prophet felt things in the same way as other human beings did and similarly he also faced the same limitations which characterize other human beings. The unbelievers saw in him nothing that was extraordinary enough to convince them that God directly communicated with him or that His angels came to him.

20. The 'clear authority' they asked for was a tangible one – something they could perceive with their own eyes and touch with their own hands. They

(11) Their Messengers told them: 'Indeed we are only human beings like yourselves, but Allah bestows His favour on those of His servants whom He wills.[21] It does not lie in our power to produce any authority except by the leave of Allah. It is in Allah that the believers should place their trust. (12) And why should we not place our trust in Allah when it is indeed He Who has guided us to the ways of our life? We shall surely continue to remain steadfast in face of your persecution. All those who have to place trust, should place their trust only in Allah.'

(13) Then the unbelievers told their Messengers: 'You will have to return to the fold of our faith[22] or else we shall banish you from our land.'

قَالَتْ لَهُمْ رُسُلُهُمْ إِن نَّحْنُ إِلَّا بَشَرٌ
مِّثْلُكُمْ وَلَٰكِنَّ اللَّهَ يَمُنُّ عَلَىٰ مَن
يَشَاءُ مِنْ عِبَادِهِۦ وَمَا كَانَ لَنَا أَن
نَّأْتِيَكُم بِسُلْطَٰنٍ إِلَّا بِإِذْنِ اللَّهِ
وَعَلَى اللَّهِ فَلْيَتَوَكَّلِ الْمُؤْمِنُونَ
(١١) وَمَا لَنَا أَلَّا نَتَوَكَّلَ عَلَى اللَّهِ
وَقَدْ هَدَىٰنَا سُبُلَنَا وَلَنَصْبِرَنَّ
عَلَىٰ مَا ءَاذَيْتُمُونَا وَعَلَى اللَّهِ فَلْيَتَوَكَّلِ
الْمُتَوَكِّلُونَ (١٢) وَقَالَ الَّذِينَ كَفَرُوا
لِرُسُلِهِمْ لَنُخْرِجَنَّكُم مِّنْ
أَرْضِنَا أَوْ لَتَعُودُنَّ فِي مِلَّتِنَا

---

thought that it is only when something is so 'clear' in that sense that they would be ready to believe in the Prophet's teaching.

21. The point that is being made here is the following. The Prophets, without doubt, are merely human beings like any others. However, there is a difference. God chooses Prophets in order that He might grant them full knowledge of the truth and a perfect vision and insight. The Prophets themselves have no say in deciding who should be entrusted with prophethood. Such a decision rests entirely with God. The Prophets can neither appoint themselves to that office, nor does it lie in their power to transfer the prophethood conferred upon them to anyone else.

22. The unbelievers urged the Messengers to recant and rejoin the faith of their people or else the latter would banish them. The expression 'return to the

Thereupon their Lord revealed
to them: 'We will most certainly destroy these wrong-
doers, (14) and will then
cause you to settle in the land
as their successors.[23] That is
the reward for him who fears
to stand for reckoning and
holds My threat in awe.'
(15) They sought Our
judgement. And (thanks to the
judgement) every obstinate
tyrant opposed to the truth was
brought to naught.[24] ▶

فَأَوْحَىٰٓ إِلَيْهِمْ رَبُّهُمْ لَنُهْلِكَنَّ
ٱلظَّٰلِمِينَ ﴿١٣﴾ وَلَنُسْكِنَنَّكُمُ
ٱلْأَرْضَ مِنۢ بَعْدِهِمْ ذَٰلِكَ لِمَنْ خَافَ
مَقَامِى وَخَافَ وَعِيدِ ﴿١٤﴾ وَٱسْتَفْتَحُوا۟
وَخَابَ كُلُّ جَبَّارٍ عَنِيدٍ ﴿١٥﴾

fold of our faith' does not imply that before being designated to the office of prophethood, the Prophets belonged to the fold of unbelievers. In fact, the verse can be fully appreciated if we bear in mind that before designation to their office, Prophets live a relatively quiet life. For prior to that designation, they preach no specific religious doctrines. Nor do they engage in refuting the religious doctrines that are generally accepted by their people. As a result, people are commonly inclined to think that they too are an integral part of their religious fold. Hence, when Prophets embark on teaching true religious doctrines, they are charged by their people with renouncing their ancestral faith. The fact, however, is that they were never a part of the fold of those unbelievers.

23. This is a word of comfort and assurance to the Messengers from God. The unbelievers had threatened the Messengers with banishment. God assures them that their enemies were in no position to harm them for God had decided to uproot the unbelievers from their land and to place it under the control of the believers.

24. It is worth noting that this historical narrative constitutes a rejoinder to the objections raised by the unbelievers against Prophet Muhammad (peace be on him). Although the story concerns the Messengers and the nations of the past, it is clearly applicable to the conditions obtaining at the time of the revelation of this *sūrah*. The unbelievers of Makka, in fact all the polytheists of Arabia, are being warned that their future was solely dependent on one thing – their attitude to the message of Prophet Muhammad (peace be on him). They will be able to live in Arabia only if they accept that message. If they reject the

(16) Hell is before him and he shall be made to drink of the oozing pus, (17) which he will gulp but will scarcely swallow, and death will come upon him from every quarter, and yet he will not be able to die. A terrible chastisement lies ahead in pursuit of him.

(18) This is the example of those who disbelieve in their Lord: their works are like ashes upon which the wind blows fiercely on a tempestuous day. They shall find no reward for their deeds.[25] That indeed is the farthest point in straying. (19) Do you not see that Allah created the heavens and the earth in truth?[26] Were He to will, He could take you away and bring a new creation. (20) That is not at all difficult for Allah.[27]

مِن وَرَآئِهِۦ جَهَنَّمُ وَيُسْقَىٰ مِن مَّآءٍ
صَدِيدٍ ﴿١٦﴾ يَتَجَرَّعُهُۥ
وَلَا يَكَادُ يُسِيغُهُۥ وَيَأْتِيهِ
ٱلْمَوْتُ مِن كُلِّ مَكَانٍ وَمَا هُوَ
بِمَيِّتٍ وَمِن وَرَآئِهِۦ عَذَابٌ
غَلِيظٌ ﴿١٧﴾ مَّثَلُ ٱلَّذِينَ كَفَرُوا۟
بِرَبِّهِمْ أَعْمَٰلُهُمْ كَرَمَادٍ ٱشْتَدَّتْ
بِهِ ٱلرِّيحُ فِى يَوْمٍ عَاصِفٍ لَّا يَقْدِرُونَ
مِمَّا كَسَبُوا۟ عَلَىٰ شَىْءٍ ذَٰلِكَ
هُوَ ٱلضَّلَٰلُ ٱلْبَعِيدُ ﴿١٨﴾ أَلَمْ تَرَ أَنَّ
ٱللَّهَ خَلَقَ ٱلسَّمَٰوَٰتِ وَٱلْأَرْضَ
بِٱلْحَقِّ إِن يَشَأْ يُذْهِبْكُمْ وَيَأْتِ
بِخَلْقٍ جَدِيدٍ ﴿١٩﴾ وَمَا ذَٰلِكَ عَلَى
ٱللَّهِ بِعَزِيزٍ ﴿٢٠﴾

---

message, they will be altogether removed from the scene. Subsequent events, as we know, fully vindicated this. Barely fifteen years after this prophecy, there was no polytheist in Arabia.

25. This refers to those who are ungrateful, unfaithful, and rebellious to their Lord. Defying God, they refuse to follow the way to which the Messengers invite them. They are warned that the deeds of such people will be reduced to naught. Their deeds will be as useless and devoid of meaning as a heap of ashes which in the course of time grows into a hillock which is then blown away by a storm into thin air. A time will come when their seemingly splendid civilization and culture, their gigantic industries, their vast and powerful empires, their imposing universities, their astonishing arts

and sciences, their impressive literary heritage, even their religious ritual and outward acts of virtue, their charitable and philanthropic institutions, in short, all that they are proud of will prove to be no more than a heap of ashes which will be swept away by the storm that will arise on the Day of Judgement. On that Day they will be left with absolutely nothing that will have even an atom's weight of worth in the sight of God.

26. This statement has been put forward as evidence in support of the statement made above, viz. that they shall find no reward for their deeds which will turn out to be no more than a heap of ashes blown away by the wind. In fact, the unbelievers are being told not to be surprised that their works should end in naught. For anyone can see that the magnificent system of the heavens and the earth is based on truth rather than falsehood. Hence, anything that does not conform to the truth and is founded on false conjectures and unfounded fancies cannot endure. Anyone who builds castles in the sand or images on water cannot expect those castles to endure or those images to last. For water is not so constituted that any image might be made on it. Nor is sand so constituted as to provide a dependable foundation for stable structures. Hence, whoever bases his actions on vain expectations in disregard of truth and reality is bound to meet with failure.

Anyone who is convinced of this should not be surprised that the deeds of those whose lives are not based on obedience to God, or whose lives are based on recognition of the godhead of anyone other than God – a premise contrary to reality – should go to waste. Since man is born a creature of God, it is altogether false to regard him as independent of Him, or as one who should serve anyone other than God. Anyone who bases his life and thought on such false assumptions is no different from the stupid man who seeks to draw an image on water or build a castle in the sand. The end such a person is bound to meet is the same as that of the person who draws images on water or who builds castles in the sand.

27. This has been said by way of admonition. Moreover, it removes a misunderstanding which might arise in someone's mind after the statement made above. One may well ask: 'If the truth is what has been stated in the above verses, why is it that the devotees of falsehood and all those steeped in iniquity do not perish instantly?' Now, obviously it is not at all difficult for God to annihilate such persons. Nor does there exist any kinship between God and any group of men in consideration of which He might have granted them a reprieve. Every iniquitous nation is exposed to the danger of being removed from the scene and being replaced by another nation. This, however, takes time. The delay in the infliction of punishment by God alone does not at all mean that the nation which is immersed in evil will be destroyed. This delay should not create any illusion about the fact that a nation which deserves to be destroyed will certainly be destroyed. People should shed all illusions and make the best possible use of every single moment at their disposal. They should also realize the brittle foundations of all systems of life and thought which rest on

(21) Then all of them will appear exposed before Allah,[28] and the weak ones will say to the haughty ones: 'We merely followed you. Will you, then, protect us from Allah's chastisement?' They will say: 'Had Allah shown us the way to our salvation, we would surely have also guided you. Now it is all the same whether we cry or suffer patiently, we have no escape.'[29]

وَبَرَزُوا لِلَّهِ جَمِيعًا فَقَالَ الضُّعَفَٰٓؤُا
لِلَّذِينَ اسْتَكْبَرُوٓا إِنَّا كُنَّا لَكُمْ
تَبَعًا فَهَلْ أَنتُم مُّغْنُونَ عَنَّا مِنْ
عَذَابِ اللَّهِ مِن شَيْءٍ ۚ قَالُوا لَوْ هَدَىٰنَا
اللَّهُ لَهَدَيْنَٰكُمْ ۖ سَوَآءٌ عَلَيْنَآ
أَجَزِعْنَآ أَمْ صَبَرْنَا مَا لَنَا مِن
مَّحِيصٍ ﴿٢١﴾

---

falsehood. They should take steps now to base their lives on the solid foundations of truth.

28. The word *burūz* used here does not simply signify that those people will come forth and appear before God; it also has the nuance of standing exposed. Hence we have rendered the verb as meaning: 'Then all of them will appear exposed before Allah.' It is true that every human being always stands exposed before his Lord. However, on the Last Day when all human beings will appear before Him, they will know well that they stand totally exposed before the Best of all judges, the Lord of the Day of Judgement. It will be quite clear to them that nothing is hidden from God, not even the ideas in their minds and the unexpressed intentions that lie concealed in the deep recesses of their hearts.

29. This is a warning to all those who blindly follow others under the pretext that they have to submit to oppressors who are overwhelmingly powerful. They are told that their leaders and rulers in the present world will be utterly unable to protect them from God's chastisement. Hence, they ought to think clearly about whom they follow and whose command they carry out, whither the latter were heading and the lurch in which they would be left as a result of their misguidance.

(22) After the matter has been finally decided Satan will say: 'Surely whatever Allah promised you was true; as for me, I went back on the promise I made to you.[30] I had no power over you except that I called you to my way and you responded to me.[31] So, do not blame me but blame yourselves. Here, neither I can come to your rescue, nor can you come to mine. I disavow your former act of associating me in the past with Allah.[32] A grievous chastisement inevitably lies ahead for such wrong-doers.'

وقال الشيطن لما قضي الأمر إن
الله وعدكم وعد الحق ووعدتكم
فأخلفتكم وما كان لي عليكم من
سلطن إلا أن دعوتكم فاستجبتم لي
فلا تلوموني ولوموا أنفسكم
ما أنا بمصرخكم وما أنتم
بمصرخي إني كفرت بما
أشركتمون من قبل إن
الظلمين لهم عذاب
أليم ﴿٢٢﴾

---

30. On the Day of Judgement Satan will plainly tell them that God's promise was true whereas his own promises were false. He will not dare deny it. For it will be possible for everyone to observe on that Day that all God's promises of reward and all His warnings of punishment were absolutely true. Satan, himself, will confess that he had lied and deceived them. He will confess that he sought to lure them with promises, with temptations of material advantage. He will confess that he tried to persuade them into believing that the Next Life was simply a hoax; and even if there would be any, they would be able to get out of it scot-free with the help of one holy person or another provided the latter were duly ingratiated by their offerings. Satan will also confess that he deluded people into believing that – thanks to these holy men – their salvation was assured so they might go about acting as they wished. Satan will own up to all that and confess that all such statements through which he misled people – either directly or through his agents – were altogether false.

31. Even while confessing all that has been mentioned above, Satan will tell the unbelievers that they had no evidence to support the claim that they wanted to follow the right way but that it was he – Satan – who forced them into following the wrong one. Satan will challenge them to produce any evidence to that effect. He will also point out that all that he did was present a false doctrine

in opposition to the true one, and invite them to falsehood instead of truth and to evil instead of good. They always had the option to heed his call or to disregard it.

Satan will also emphasize that he had no power to compel people into choosing the way to which he had invited them. Satan was doubtlessly guilty of calling people to evil ways and he will be punished for it. Satan's responsibility and punishment will, however, be confined to that act alone – the act of calling people to evil ways. His guilt, however, will not exonerate those who made the wrong choice, and thus misused the opportunity to choose between right and wrong which God bestowed upon them. They will certainly be held responsible for their actions.

32. This verse provides another instance of polytheism at the level of human actions as distinct from polytheism at the level of doctrine and belief. For, obviously no one professes, at the doctrinal level, that Satan is a partner of God in His divinity. Nor does anyone worship Satan. In fact, so far as verbal expressions go, people generally curse Satan. Ironically, the same people who curse him, also follow his ways, at times consciously, and at other times unconsciously. It is precisely this which has been termed as associating Satan with God in His divinity.

The above statement might be considered by some to be merely one made by Satan which has simply been mentioned by God, and, hence, it need not be true in an objective sense. However, it is quite evident that had the statement been a false one, God would have instantly refuted it. Moreover, in addition to the present verse, at several places elsewhere in the Qur'ān certain types of action have been dubbed as tantamount to associating others with God. Some of these instances are given below:

> They take their rabbis and their monks for their lords beside Allah (*al-Tawbah* 9: 31).
>
> And, likewise, the beings supposed to have a share in Allah's divinity have made the slaying of their offspring seem lawful to many of those who associate others with Allah in His divinity (*al-An'ām* 6: 137). (This relates to those who innovated religious customs without any basis for them in Divine guidance.)
>
> Do you see one who takes for his God his own passion? (*al- Furqān* 25: 43).
>
> Did I not enjoin on you, O children of Adam, that you should not worship Satan? (*Yā Sīn* 36: 60).
>
> What! Do they have associates in godhead who established for them some religion without the permission of Allah? (*al-Shūrá* 42: 21).

All these examples illustrate that polytheism does not merely assume one form, viz. associating others with God in matters of belief. There is also

(23) As for those who had
believed and did good in the
world, they shall be admitted
to the Gardens beneath which
rivers flow. There, with the
leave of Allah, they shall
abide forever, and will be
greeted with: 'Peace'.[33] (24)
Do you not see how Allah has
given the example of a good
word?[34] It is like a good tree,
whose root is firmly fixed, and
whose branches reach the
sky,[35] (25) ever yielding its
fruit in every season with the
leave of its Lord.[36] Allah gives
examples for mankind that
they may take heed.▶

وَأُدْخِلَ ٱلَّذِينَ ءَامَنُوا۟ وَعَمِلُوا۟
ٱلصَّٰلِحَٰتِ جَنَّٰتٍ تَجْرِى مِن تَحْتِهَا
ٱلْأَنْهَٰرُ خَٰلِدِينَ فِيهَا بِإِذْنِ رَبِّهِمْ
تَحِيَّتُهُمْ فِيهَا سَلَٰمٌ ﴿٢٣﴾ أَلَمْ تَرَ كَيْفَ
ضَرَبَ ٱللَّهُ مَثَلًا كَلِمَةً طَيِّبَةً
كَشَجَرَةٍ طَيِّبَةٍ أَصْلُهَا ثَابِتٌ
وَفَرْعُهَا فِى ٱلسَّمَآءِ ﴿٢٤﴾ تُؤْتِىٓ
أُكُلَهَا كُلَّ حِينٍۭ بِإِذْنِ رَبِّهَا
وَيَضْرِبُ ٱللَّهُ ٱلْأَمْثَالَ لِلنَّاسِ
لَعَلَّهُمْ يَتَذَكَّرُونَ ﴿٢٥﴾

another form which consists of exalting someone to a position where it becomes imperative to follow him without any sanction for it from God, or even in opposition to God's command. Such an act, according to the Qur'ān, is tantamount to setting up a partner to God in His godhead. A person who follows someone in this unreserved fashion is guilty of setting up a partner to God even if he keeps on abusing and cursing him. Even if such a person is not treated on a par with those who commit polytheism at the doctrinal level, nevertheless his act will be considered highly reprehensible. (For further details see *Towards Understanding the Qur'ān*, vol. II, *al-An'ām* 6, nn. 87 and 107, pp. 270 and 278–9 and *al-Kahf* 18, n. 50.)

33. The word *taḥīyah* literally means wishing someone to have a long life. In actual practice, however, this is an expression of greeting or welcome which is uttered when a person meets another. Hence, we have considered it as the equivalent of 'greeting someone with peace'.

34. Literally, the expression *'kalimah ṭayyibah'* means 'a good word'. However, it also stands for the statement about truth and sound belief which fully conforms to truth and reality. Such a statement, according to the Qur'ān, could only be one that consists of affirming the doctrines of the unity of God,

(26) And the example of an evil word[37] is that of an evil tree, uprooted from the surface of the earth, wholly unable to endure.[38] (27) Thus, through a firm word, Allah grants firmness to the believers both in this world and in the Hereafter.[39] And the wrong-doers, Allah lets them go astray.[40] Allah does whatever He wills.

وَمَثَلُ كَلِمَةٍ خَبِيثَةٍ كَشَجَرَةٍ خَبِيثَةٍ
ٱجْتُثَّتْ مِن فَوْقِ ٱلْأَرْضِ مَا لَهَا مِن قَرَارٍ
﴿٢٦﴾ يُثَبِّتُ ٱللَّهُ ٱلَّذِينَ ءَامَنُوا۟ بِٱلْقَوْلِ
ٱلثَّابِتِ فِى ٱلْحَيَوٰةِ ٱلدُّنْيَا وَفِى
ٱلْـَٔاخِرَةِ ۖ وَيُضِلُّ ٱللَّهُ ٱلظَّـٰلِمِينَ ۚ
وَيَفْعَلُ ٱللَّهُ مَا يَشَآءُ ﴿٢٧﴾

---

prophethood, heavenly scriptures, and the Hereafter since these are the fundamental truths as expounded by the Qur'ān.

35. In other words, since the entire system which encompasses the heavens and the earth is based on the truth expressed in the basic doctrinal statement of the believer 'there is no god other than Allah', it never comes into conflict with the law of nature. Nor does human nature feel any aversion to the truth which it expresses, nor with any other fact of the universe. Hence, the earth with its entire system extends its co-operation to him and the heaven with its entire system welcomes him.

36. The good word is so highly fruitful and productive that were individuals or groups of people to base their lives on it, they will continually benefit from the good results ensuing from it. For it brings about clarity in thought, stability in attitude, moderation in temperament, firmness in character, purity in morals, truthfulness in speech, strength in commitment, honesty in dealings with others, refinement in social relationships, elegance and finesse in culture, balance and equilibrium in collective life, justice and compassion in economy, honesty in politics, magnanimity in war, sincerity in peace, and faithfulness in covenant. Like Midas, everything that it touches turns into gold.

37. The 'evil word' is obviously just the opposite of the 'good word'. It embraces every variety of falsehood. In the above verse, however, it refers to all false doctrines – atheism, deism, polytheism, idolatry – in short, every world-view other than the one taught by the Prophets.

38. In other words, the Qur'ān says that since every false doctrine is opposed to reality, it is totally out of tune with the law of nature. Every particle

of the universe rejects and refutes it. One might say, if its seeds are sown, the earth will be ever inclined to cast it away. And if these seeds grow into a tree, the heavens will press upon its branches so as to dwarf it. Had man not been granted freedom of choice and respite to show his performance, the evil word would not have been allowed to grow at all. However, since God has allowed man to do what he wants to, when some foolish people expend their energies to make this evil tree grow, it grows a little but only after a considerable struggle against nature. However, as long as the tree remains, it produces poisonous and bitter fruit. Whenever the circumstances change, just one blow of vicissitude suffices to root it out.

Anyone who is acquainted with the religious, moral, intellectual and cultural history of mankind, will appreciate the difference between the 'good word' and the 'evil word'. It is clear that from the very outset, the 'good word', has been one and the same. As for 'evil words', they have simply been innumerable. Despite all efforts to the contrary, it has never been possible to extirpate the 'good word', but history is replete with the carcasses of thousands of 'evil words'. Many of them have totally disappeared. If they exist anywhere, it is in the annals of the past. Many evil doctrines which were once fashionable have been relegated to such obscurity that people today are scarcely even aware of them; and if they do come into contact with them, they simply wonder at the rank follies that had once been cherished by others like them.

In sharp contrast is the 'good word'. Whenever a person or a nation embraces it sincerely, like perfume it radiates its fragrance all around. Its blessings enrich those who embrace it, as well as those around. Whenever the 'evil word' has struck its roots, it has proved a curse for the entire area around it. It is a tree which produces thorns from the prick of which barely anyone escapes. Its foul smell vitiates the entire surroundings.

For a better understanding of this parable, reference may be made to a preceding verse of this *sūrah* which embodies the same idea: 'The example of those who disbelieve in their Lord: their words are like ashes upon which the wind blows fiercely on a tempestuous day' (verse 18). The same point has been driven home (see *al-Ra'd* 13: 17) through the parables of swelling scum caused by torrential rains and the scum from smelting metals.

39. The 'good word' provides believers with a firm intellectual frame of reference, a stable perspective, and an all-embracing world-view. Thanks to all that, they come to possess the master key which helps them solve all the complicated problems of life. Through the 'good word' the conduct and morals of people acquire firmness and are scarcely affected by the violent vicissitudes of time. Through it the believers are able to grasp a set of solid principles which provides them with mental peace on the one hand, and prevents them from stumbling into confusion on the other.

These blessings of the 'good word' are not confined to this life. In the Hereafter, too, the 'good word' will save them from falling prey to any unusual fear and anxiety. For everything will happen as they had already been told. They will step into the Next World and will feel as if they are on familiar

(28) Did you not see those who have exchanged Allah's favour with ingratitude to Him, causing their people to be cast in the abode of utter perdition (29) Hell, wherein they shall roast? How wretched a place to settle in! (30) They have set up rivals to Allah that they may lead men astray from His way. Tell them: 'Enjoy for a while. You are doomed to end up in the Fire!'

(31) (O Prophet!) Tell those of My servants who believe that they should establish Prayer and spend out of what We have provided them with, both secretly and openly,[41] before there arrives the Day when there will be no bargaining, nor any mutual befriending.[42]

۞ أَلَمْ تَرَ إِلَى ٱلَّذِينَ بَدَّلُوا۟ نِعْمَتَ ٱللَّهِ
كُفْرًا وَأَحَلُّوا۟ قَوْمَهُمْ دَارَ ٱلْبَوَارِ ٢٨
جَهَنَّمَ يَصْلَوْنَهَا ۖ وَبِئْسَ ٱلْقَرَارُ
٢٩ وَجَعَلُوا۟ لِلَّهِ أَندَادًا لِّيُضِلُّوا۟ عَن
سَبِيلِهِۦ ۗ قُلْ تَمَتَّعُوا۟ فَإِنَّ مَصِيرَكُمْ
إِلَى ٱلنَّارِ ٣٠ قُل لِّعِبَادِىَ ٱلَّذِينَ
ءَامَنُوا۟ يُقِيمُوا۟ ٱلصَّلَوٰةَ وَيُنفِقُوا۟ مِمَّا
رَزَقْنَٰهُمْ سِرًّا وَعَلَانِيَةً مِّن قَبْلِ أَن يَأْتِىَ
يَوْمٌ لَّا بَيْعٌ فِيهِ وَلَا خِلَٰلٌ ٣١

---

territory. Nothing will come to pass there about which they had not been foretold, and for which they were mentally unprepared. As a result, they will pass through every stage of the Next Life with steady steps. Their experience of the Hereafter will, therefore, be altogether different from that of the unbelievers. The latter will find everything in the Hereafter quite contrary to their expectation.

40. As to those who follow the evil rather than the 'good word', God lets them fall prey to mental confusion and causes their efforts to go to waste. Such people are unable to find the right way. In sum, their efforts prove to be of no avail.

41. The thrust of the statement is that the believers' attitude should be quite different from that of the unbelievers. In sharp contrast to the unbelievers who

(32) It is Allah[43] Who created the heavens and the earth, Who sent down water from the heaven and thereby brought forth a variety of fruits as your sustenance; Who subjected for you the ships that they may sail in the sea by His command; Who subjected for you the rivers; (33) Who subjected for you the sun and the moon and both of them are constant on their courses; Who subjected for you the night and the day;[44] (34) and Who gave you all that you asked Him for.[45] Were you to count the favours of Allah you shall never be able to encompass them. Verily, man is highly unjust, exceedingly ungrateful.

ٱللَّهُ ٱلَّذِى خَلَقَ ٱلسَّمَٰوَٰتِ وَٱلْأَرْضَ
وَأَنزَلَ مِنَ ٱلسَّمَآءِ مَآءً فَأَخْرَجَ
بِهِۦ مِنَ ٱلثَّمَرَٰتِ رِزْقًا لَّكُمْ وَسَخَّرَ
لَكُمُ ٱلْفُلْكَ لِتَجْرِىَ فِى ٱلْبَحْرِ
بِأَمْرِهِۦ وَسَخَّرَ لَكُمُ ٱلْأَنْهَٰرَ ﴿٣٢﴾
وَسَخَّرَ لَكُمُ ٱلشَّمْسَ وَٱلْقَمَرَ
دَآئِبَيْنِ وَسَخَّرَ لَكُمُ ٱلَّيْلَ وَٱلنَّهَارَ
﴿٣٣﴾ وَءَاتَىٰكُم مِّن كُلِّ
مَا سَأَلْتُمُوهُ وَإِن تَعُدُّوا۟ نِعْمَتَ ٱللَّهِ
لَا تُحْصُوهَآ إِنَّ ٱلْإِنسَٰنَ لَظَلُومٌ
كَفَّارٌ ﴿٣٤﴾

are a thankless lot, the believers should give thanks to God. What this implies, in practice, is that they should establish Prayer and spend in the way of God.

42. Man is unable to escape God's judgement. Neither will riches nor the influence of his friends be of any avail.

43. It is God to Whom the unbelievers do not give thanks, Whom they are disinclined to obey and worship, and in Whose divinity they associate others. It must be recalled that the same God has lavished innumerable bounties on them.

44. The Qur'ānic statement وَسَخَّرَ لَكُمُ اللَّيْلَ وَالنَّهَارَ meaning that 'God has subjected for you the night and the day' is often misunderstood. Some think that it means that the forces of nature have been placed under the control of man. Such an assumption leads people to develop a variety of odd ideas. Some

(35) And call to mind when Abraham prayed:[46] 'My Lord! Make this city[47] secure, and keep me and my sons away from worshipping the idols. (36) My Lord! They have caused many people to go astray.[48] Now, if anyone follows me, he belongs to mine; but he who turns against me, surely You are Ever Forgiving, Most Merciful.[49]

وَإِذْ قَالَ إِبْرَٰهِيمُ رَبِّ ٱجْعَلْ هَٰذَا ٱلْبَلَدَ ءَامِنًا وَٱجْنُبْنِى وَبَنِىَّ أَن نَّعْبُدَ ٱلْأَصْنَامَ ﴿٣٥﴾ رَبِّ إِنَّهُنَّ أَضْلَلْنَ كَثِيرًا مِّنَ ٱلنَّاسِ ۖ فَمَن تَبِعَنِى فَإِنَّهُۥ مِنِّى ۖ وَمَنْ عَصَانِى فَإِنَّكَ غَفُورٌ رَّحِيمٌ ﴿٣٦﴾

even go so far as to say that to achieve mastery over the heavens and the earth is the true end of man's existence. However, what the Qur'ānic statement means by the subjection of the natural phenomena is simply that God has bound them to laws which are beneficial for mankind. Had sailing in the sea not been subject to any law, it would not have been possible for man to undertake sea voyages. Had the rivers not been subject to any laws, man could not have used them for irrigation. Likewise, had the sun, the moon, the day and the night not been regulated, there could have been no life on earth, let alone any flourishing human civilization.

45. That is, God provided man with everything that his nature called for. He also provided all that was needed for man's sustenance, and made available, in plenty, the resources that would ensure his survival and growth.

46. After mentioning God's favours to all mankind, reference is made here to the favours which were specially bestowed on the Quraysh. The Quraysh are told that when their ancestor, Abraham (peace be on him), settled in Makka with the robust hope that his descendants would live in obedience to their Lord, God lavished a great variety of favours upon them in response to Abraham's prayer. But in return for all those favours, the Quraysh acted in brazen disregard of Abraham's expectations of them, embraced erroneous doctrines, and engaged in every kind of misdeed.

47. Here reference is made to Makka.

48. These idols turned many people away from worshipping God and enticed them to worship idols. The statement, of course, is figurative. Since

(37) Our Lord! I have made some of my offspring settle in a barren valley near Your Inviolable House! Our Lord! I did so that they may establish Prayer. So make the hearts of people affectionately inclined to them, and provide them with fruits for their sustenance[50] that they may give thanks.▶

رَّبَّنَآ إِنِّيٓ أَسۡكَنتُ مِن ذُرِّيَّتِي بِوَادٍ غَيۡرِ ذِي زَرۡعٍ عِندَ بَيۡتِكَ ٱلۡمُحَرَّمِ رَبَّنَا لِيُقِيمُواْ ٱلصَّلَوٰةَ فَٱجۡعَلۡ أَفۡـِٔدَةٗ مِّنَ ٱلنَّاسِ تَهۡوِيٓ إِلَيۡهِمۡ وَٱرۡزُقۡهُم مِّنَ ٱلثَّمَرَٰتِ لَعَلَّهُمۡ يَشۡكُرُونَ ٣٧

many people became victims of idolatry, the act of misleading people to it has been ascribed to the idols.

49. This reflects the height of Abraham's tenderness, his great compassion for mankind. Abraham was not prepared to see any person seized by God's chastisement. Hence he prayed till the very last that God may forgive and be merciful to all. It was also because of his compassion that Abraham prayed that God may provide sustenance: 'My Lord! Make this a place of security and provide such of its people who believe in Allah and the Last Day with fruits for sustenance' (*al-Baqarah* 2: 126).

As to punishment in the Hereafter, Abraham's compassion prompted him to refrain from asking God to punish those who follow ways opposed to his own. Regarding them, he merely said: 'You are Ever Forgiving, Most Merciful' (verse 36). Abraham was full of compassion not only for his own children, but also for others. When the angels were on their way to obliterate the evil-doing people of Lot, Abraham is mentioned as engaging in a 'dispute' with God for the sake of that people (*Hūd* 11: 74–5). The same compassion and mercy also characterized another Prophet, Jesus (peace be on him). The Qur'ān says that when in the Hereafter God will mention to Jesus the erroneous beliefs of Christians, he will submit: 'If You chastise them, they are Your servants; and if You forgive them, You are the All-Mighty, the All-Wise' (*al-Mā'idah* 5: 118).

50. In the past people from all over Arabia gravitated towards Makka for *ḥajj* and *'umrah*. After the acceptance of Abraham's prayer, armies of people from every nook and cranny of the world were attracted to Makka. Also, thanks to Abraham's prayer, every variety of sustenance – fruits, grains, etc. – reached that city. This was despite the fact that the land in and around Makka was too barren even to grow fodder for cattle.

(38) Our Lord! Surely You know all that we conceal and all that we reveal'[51] – and nothing in the earth or in the heaven[52] is hidden from Allah – (39) 'All praise be to Allah Who, despite my old age, has given me Ishmael and Isaac. Surely my Lord hears all prayers. (40) My Lord! Enable me and my offspring to establish Prayer, and do accept, our Lord, this prayer of mine. (41) Our Lord! Forgive me and my parents and the believers on the Day when the reckoning will take place.'[53]

(42) Do not think Allah is heedless of the evil deeds in which the evil-doers are engaged. He is merely granting them respite until a Day when their eyes shall continue to stare in horror, (43) when they shall keep pressing ahead in haste, their heads lifted up, their gaze directed forward, unable to look away from what they behold,[54] their hearts utterly void.▶

رَبَّنَآ إِنَّكَ تَعۡلَمُ مَا نُخۡفِي وَمَا نُعۡلِنُۗ
وَمَا يَخۡفَىٰ عَلَى ٱللَّهِ مِن شَيۡءٖ فِي ٱلۡأَرۡضِ
وَلَا فِي ٱلسَّمَآءِ ﴿٣٨﴾ ٱلۡحَمۡدُ لِلَّهِ ٱلَّذِي
وَهَبَ لِي عَلَى ٱلۡكِبَرِ إِسۡمَٰعِيلَ
وَإِسۡحَٰقَۚ إِنَّ رَبِّي لَسَمِيعُ ٱلدُّعَآءِ ﴿٣٩﴾
رَبِّ ٱجۡعَلۡنِي مُقِيمَ ٱلصَّلَوٰةِ وَمِن
ذُرِّيَّتِيۚ رَبَّنَا وَتَقَبَّلۡ دُعَآءِ ﴿٤٠﴾
رَبَّنَا ٱغۡفِرۡ لِي وَلِوَٰلِدَيَّ وَلِلۡمُؤۡمِنِينَ
يَوۡمَ يَقُومُ ٱلۡحِسَابُ ﴿٤١﴾ وَلَا
تَحۡسَبَنَّ ٱللَّهَ غَٰفِلًا عَمَّا يَعۡمَلُ
ٱلظَّٰلِمُونَۚ إِنَّمَا يُؤَخِّرُهُمۡ لِيَوۡمٖ
تَشۡخَصُ فِيهِ ٱلۡأَبۡصَٰرُ ﴿٤٢﴾ مُهۡطِعِينَ
مُقۡنِعِي رُءُوسِهِمۡ لَا يَرۡتَدُّ إِلَيۡهِمۡ طَرۡفُهُمۡۖ
وَأَفۡـِٔدَتُهُمۡ هَوَآءٞ ﴿٤٣﴾

51. The statement that God knows 'all that we conceal and all that we reveal' means that God heard all that Abraham was praying for. Moreover, God was also well aware of the feelings and emotions which were hidden in his heart which were not expressed verbally.

52. This parenthetical statement corroborates what Abraham had said, viz. that nothing is hidden from God.

(44) (O Muḥammad!) Warn mankind of the Day when a severe chastisement shall overtake them, and the wrong-doers will say: 'Our Lord, grant us respite for a short while; we shall respond to Your call and will follow Your Messengers.' (But they will be clearly told): 'Are you not the same who swore earlier that they shall never suffer decline?' (45) You said so even though you had lived in the dwellings of those who had wronged themselves (by sinning), and you were aware how We dealt with them, and We had even explained to you all this by giving examples. (46) Indeed the unbelievers contrived their plan, but it is Allah's power to nullify their plan, even though their plans were such that would move even mountains.[55]

وَأَنذِرِ ٱلنَّاسَ يَوْمَ يَأْتِيهِمُ ٱلْعَذَابُ
فَيَقُولُ ٱلَّذِينَ ظَلَمُوا رَبَّنَآ أَخِّرْنَآ إِلَىٰٓ
أَجَلٍ قَرِيبٍ نُّجِبْ دَعْوَتَكَ وَنَتَّبِعِ
ٱلرُّسُلَ أَوَلَمْ تَكُونُوٓا أَقْسَمْتُم
مِّن قَبْلُ مَا لَكُم مِّن زَوَالٍ ﴿٤٤﴾
وَسَكَنتُمْ فِى مَسَٰكِنِ ٱلَّذِينَ
ظَلَمُوٓا أَنفُسَهُمْ وَتَبَيَّنَ لَكُمْ
كَيْفَ فَعَلْنَا بِهِمْ وَضَرَبْنَا لَكُمُ
ٱلْأَمْثَالَ ﴿٤٥﴾ وَقَدْ مَكَرُوا
مَكْرَهُمْ وَعِندَ ٱللَّهِ مَكْرُهُمْ
وَإِن كَانَ مَكْرُهُمْ لِتَزُولَ
مِنْهُ ٱلْجِبَالُ ﴿٤٦﴾

---

53. Abraham included his father in this prayer for forgiveness on account of the promise the latter had made at the time of leaving his homeland: 'I will pray to my Lord for your forgiveness' (*Maryam* 19: 47). However, when he later realized that his father was God's enemy, he recanted. (See *al-Tawbah* 9: 114.)

54. The harrowing spectacle of the Day of Judgement will cast a spell on the unbelievers. They will continuously gaze, unable to blink or turn their eyes away from the terrible scene. It will seem as though their eyes have been petrified.

(47) So, do not think (O Prophet!) that Allah will go back upon His promise to His Messengers.[56] Surely Allah is Mighty, Lord of retribution. (48) (Do warn them of the) Day when the heavens and the earth shall be altogether changed;[57] when all will appear fully exposed before Allah, the One, the Irresistible! (49) On that Day you shall see the guilty ones secured in chains; (50) their garments shall be black as if made out of pitch,[58] and the flames of the Fire shall cover their faces (51) so that Allah may requite each person for his deeds. Allah is swift in reckoning.

فَلَا تَحْسَبَنَّ ٱللَّهَ مُخْلِفَ وَعْدِهِۦ رُسُلَهُۥٓ
إِنَّ ٱللَّهَ عَزِيزٌ ذُو ٱنتِقَامٍ ﴿٤٧﴾ يَوْمَ
تُبَدَّلُ ٱلْأَرْضُ غَيْرَ ٱلْأَرْضِ وَٱلسَّمَٰوَٰتُ
وَبَرَزُوا۟ لِلَّهِ ٱلْوَٰحِدِ ٱلْقَهَّارِ ﴿٤٨﴾ وَتَرَى
ٱلْمُجْرِمِينَ يَوْمَئِذٍ مُّقَرَّنِينَ فِى
ٱلْأَصْفَادِ ﴿٤٩﴾ سَرَابِيلُهُم مِّن
قَطِرَانٍ وَتَغْشَىٰ وُجُوهَهُمُ ٱلنَّارُ
﴿٥٠﴾ لِيَجْزِىَ ٱللَّهُ كُلَّ نَفْسٍ مَّا كَسَبَتْ
إِنَّ ٱللَّهَ سَرِيعُ ٱلْحِسَابِ ﴿٥١﴾

---

55. The nations of the past resorted to all sorts of contriving to evade the consequences of having denied God's laws and to defeating the mission of God's Messengers. But it is well known that just one move from God checkmated them. Despite this, the unbelievers have not ceased their contriving, fancying that their efforts will ultimately meet with success.

56. Though this statement is apparently addressed to Prophet Muḥammad (peace be on him), it is in fact meant for his enemies. They are being told that all the promises which God had made to His earlier Messengers were fulfilled and caused their enemies to be vanquished. In view of this, it is quite evident that the promise that God made to Muḥammad (peace be on him) will also come true, and all those who oppose him will be totally destroyed.

57. The present verse as well as several allusions to the subject at different places in the Qur'ān indicate that the present heavens and earth will not be totally destroyed. It seems that it is only the present physical order of things that will be disrupted. Between the first and the second blowing of the Trumpet there will be a time gap the duration of which is known only to God. During this intervening period the present form of the heavens and the earth will be

(52) This is a proclamation for all mankind that they may be warned by it, and that they may know that their god is none but the One True God, and that men of understanding may take heed.

هَٰذَا بَلَٰغٌ لِّلنَّاسِ وَلِيُنذَرُوا بِهِۦ وَلِيَعْلَمُوٓا أَنَّمَا هُوَ إِلَٰهٌ وَٰحِدٌ وَلِيَذَّكَّرَ أُو۟لُوا۟ ٱلْأَلْبَٰبِ ﴿٥٢﴾

---

transformed. A new physical order will be created along with a different set of natural laws. This will mark the advent of the Hereafter. Also, with the second blowing of the Trumpet, all human beings created since Adam till the Day of Judgement will be resurrected and will be made to stand before God. This is what the Qur'ān calls *ḥashr* ('the gathering').

It becomes evident from the allusions in the Qur'ān and explicit statements in the *Ḥadīth* that people will be gathered together on this very earth and will stand before God's judgement. It is on the earth that God will take stock of people's deeds. It is also on the earth that God's scale will be fixed to weigh men's actions. It is also on the earth that God's judgement will be made.

The teachings of the Qur'ān and the *Ḥadīth* also make it clear that the Next Life will not be merely one of a spiritual nature. Men will be resurrected both physically and spiritually, exactly as they are today. Everyone will assume the same personality which he held in the present world.

58. Some translators and commentators of the Qur'ān have interpreted *qaṭirān* as arsenic and others in the sense of molten brass. However, in Arabic usage it refers to pitch or coal-tar.

Sūrah 15

Al-Ḥijr

(The Rock)

(Makkan Period)

Title

The title of this *sūrah* is derived from verse 80: 'Surely the people of *al-Ḥijr* (the Rock) rejected the Messengers, calling them liars.'

Period of Revelation

The contents and style of this *sūrah* indicate that it was revealed in almost the same period as *Sūrah Ibrāhīm*. Two factors predominate the background. First, the Prophet (peace be on him) had spent quite a long time calling people to embrace Islam. In response to the call, the Makkans continually demonstrated an adamant defiance. They ridiculed the Prophet (peace be on him) and his teaching, relentlessly opposed him, and left no stone unturned to persecute the Muslims. The hostility of the unbelievers had reached a stage where there seemed little point in continuing to exhort them. The situation rather seemed to call for a severe warning, for holding out the threat of chastisement. Second, the Prophet (peace be on him) had been engaged in his struggle for a long time. He had struggled to break down the mountains of defiance and hostility which had stood in his way. The long struggle had begun to have its effect and there were indications of weariness and exhaustion. Occasionally, the Prophet (peace be on him) appeared to be heart-broken. This explains the several verses through which God comforted and consoled the Prophet (peace be on him) and raised his morale.

Central Theme and Subject

The central theme of the *sūrah* comprises two subjects: (i) to warn those who had rejected the Prophet's message, ridiculed him, and tried to suppress his movement in a variety of ways; (ii) to comfort and encourage the Prophet (peace be on him).

This, however, does not mean that the *sūrah* is devoid of the exposition and explicitation of the basic teachings of Islam, nor is it devoid of admonition. Nowhere in the Qur'ān, do we find that God resorted merely to warning and reproach. Exhortation and admonition go hand in hand with dire threats and trenchant rebukes to those who are opposed to the truth. No wonder, the present *sūrah* also has succinct statements embodying arguments in support of such basic doctrines as God's unity. Moreover, the story of Adam and Satan is also narrated for didactic purposes.

In the name of Allah, the Merciful, the Compassionate.

(1) *Alif. Lām Rā*. These are the verses of the Book, and a clear Qur'ān.[1]

(2) Soon will the time come when the unbelievers will wish they were Muslims. (3) Leave them to eat and enjoy life and let false hopes amuse them. They will soon come to know. (4) Whenever We destroyed a town, a definite term had previously been decreed for it.[2] (5) No people can anticipate the term for its destruction nor can it delay it.

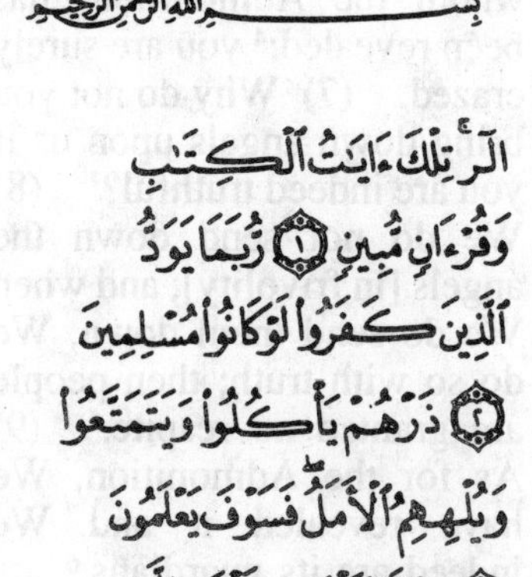

1. This is a brief introductory statement about the *sūrah* which is immediately followed by the main discourse.

The Qur'ān is characterized by its clarity. The purpose of this characterization is to emphasize that the Qur'ān has set out its teachings in lucid terms, rendering them understandable.

2. God never punished a people immediately in the wake of their rejecting the message of a Prophet. They should, however, entertain no misgiving on that account. There is no justification for people to believe that, merely because they had so far remained unpunished for rejecting the Prophet (peace be on him), insulting him, and publicly insisting that he was not a genuine Messenger of God. They should bear in mind that it is God's law to earmark a definite period of time for a people so that they may heed the call of the Messenger, to carefully consider it, and to mend their attitude. During this period that nation is allowed to act as it wishes, and God magnanimously tolerates its behaviour despite full knowledge of its wickedness. Throughout the appointed term of respite, the nation is not punished. (For further elaboration of this idea see *Ibrāhīm* 14, n. 18.)

(6) They say: 'O you to
whom the Admonition[3] has
been revealed:[4] you are surely
crazed. (7) Why do not you
bring down angels upon us if
you are indeed truthful?' (8)
We do not send down the
angels [in frivolity]; and when
We do send them down, We
do so with truth; then people
are granted no respite.[5] (9)
As for the Admonition, We
have revealed it and We
indeed are its guardians.[6]

وَقَالُوا يَٰٓأَيُّهَا ٱلَّذِى نُزِّلَ عَلَيْهِ ٱلذِّكْرُ
إِنَّكَ لَمَجْنُونٌ ﴿٦﴾ لَّوْ مَا تَأْتِينَا
بِٱلْمَلَٰٓئِكَةِ إِن كُنتَ مِنَ ٱلصَّٰدِقِينَ
﴿٧﴾ مَا نُنَزِّلُ ٱلْمَلَٰٓئِكَةَ إِلَّا بِٱلْحَقِّ
وَمَا كَانُوٓا۟ إِذًا مُّنظَرِينَ ﴿٨﴾ إِنَّا نَحْنُ
نَزَّلْنَا ٱلذِّكْرَ وَإِنَّا لَهُۥ لَحَٰفِظُونَ ﴿٩﴾

3. The term 'Admonition' has been used to signify the Book of God. This characterization is quite apt since the whole of the Qur'ān consists of admonition and good counsel. All the earlier scriptures were based on admonition, and so is the Qur'ān. (Literally, *dhikr* means to remind, to caution, to tender good advice.)

4. The unbelievers referred to the Qur'ān as 'admonition' by way of sarcasm. They did not believe that it was a revelation from God to Prophet Muḥammad (peace be on him). Had they so believed, they would not have called him 'crazed'. If this element of sarcasm is borne in mind, it is easy to appreciate what was meant by saying: 'O you to whom the Admonition has been revealed!' What this statement really meant was: 'O you who claim that the Admonition was revealed to him!' Such a statement closely resembles the sarcastic remark that Pharaoh made to his courtiers with regard to Moses (peace be on him): 'Your Messenger – one sent for you – is indeed crazed' (*al-Shu'arā'* 26: 27).

5. Angels are not despatched to a people merely to entertain them. Hence, it makes no sense that whenever a people ask God to send angels down to earth, God accepts it forthwith. Nor are angels sent down in order to disclose the realities which are beyond man's sense-perception and in which men are required to believe. Instead, angels are sent down to a people after a definitive decision has been made by God to destroy them. When that moment comes, the angels do not go to that people with the message: 'Believe, and you will be spared God's punishment!' The respite granted to the unbelievers to accept the

(10) (O Muḥammad!) Certainly We did send Messengers before you among the nations which have gone by. (11) And whenever a Messenger came to them, they never failed to mock at him. (12) Even so We make a way for it [the Admonition] in the hearts of the culprits (like a rod); (13) they do not believe in it.[7] This has been the wont of people of this kind from ancient times.

وَلَقَدْ أَرْسَلْنَا مِن قَبْلِكَ فِي شِيَعِ الْأَوَّلِينَ ﴿١٠﴾ وَمَا يَأْتِيهِم مِّن رَّسُولٍ إِلَّا كَانُوا بِهِ يَسْتَهْزِءُونَ ﴿١١﴾ كَذَٰلِكَ نَسْلُكُهُ فِي قُلُوبِ الْمُجْرِمِينَ ﴿١٢﴾ لَا يُؤْمِنُونَ بِهِ وَقَدْ خَلَتْ سُنَّةُ الْأَوَّلِينَ ﴿١٣﴾

teaching of tne Prophet lasts only as long as the reality remains concealed from their sense-perception. Once that reality stands fully disclosed, the time for believing is over.

The statement that 'angels are sent down in truth' implies that they descend in order to wipe out falsehood and replace it with the truth. In other words, they are sent down with God's decree to destroy a people and make sure that the decree is fully enforced.

6. The unbelievers dubbed the Prophet (peace be on him) – the bearer of the 'Admonition' – as crazed. It is emphasized here that the 'Admonition' was not something which the Prophet (peace be on him) made up; instead it was revealed to him by God. Hence, the taunts and abuse hurled at the Prophet (peace be on him) is in fact aimed at God.

The unbelievers are also asked to disabuse their minds of the idea that they would be able to cause any hurt to the Book of God. For God stands guard over it. No one can, therefore, destroy the Book, nor suppress its message. The taunts and attacks that the unbelievers throw at the Qur'ān will not detract from its value. Nor will their opposition to it impede the spread of its message. Nor will God allow anyone to distort or alter it.

7. To whom does the pronoun (third person, singular) in the expressions نَسْلُكُهُ and لَا يُؤْمِنُونَ بِهِ refer. In the former instance, translators and commentators on the Qur'ān consider the pronoun هُ to refer to the act of mocking (see verse 11 above) and in the latter to refer to 'the Admonition' (see verse 9). On the basis of that assumption, the verse means that God causes

(14) If We were even to open for them a way to the heaven, and they could continually climb up to it in broad daylight; (15) they would still have said: 'Surely our eyes have been dazzled; rather, we have been enchanted.'

(16) Indeed We have set constellations in the heaven[8] and have beautified them for the beholders,[9] (17) and have protected them against every accursed satan[10] (18) save him who may eavesdrop,[11] and then a bright flame pursues him.[12]

وَلَوْ فَتَحْنَا عَلَيْهِم بَابًا مِّنَ ٱلسَّمَآءِ
فَظَلُّوا۟ فِيهِ يَعْرُجُونَ ﴿١٤﴾ لَقَالُوٓا۟ إِنَّمَا
سُكِّرَتْ أَبْصَٰرُنَا بَلْ نَحْنُ قَوْمٌ مَّسْحُورُونَ
﴿١٥﴾ وَلَقَدْ جَعَلْنَا فِى ٱلسَّمَآءِ بُرُوجًا
وَزَيَّنَّٰهَا لِلنَّٰظِرِينَ ﴿١٦﴾
وَحَفِظْنَٰهَا مِن كُلِّ شَيْطَٰنٍ رَّجِيمٍ
﴿١٧﴾ إِلَّا مَنِ ٱسْتَرَقَ ٱلسَّمْعَ فَأَتْبَعَهُۥ
شِهَابٌ مُّبِينٌ ﴿١٨﴾

mocking to enter into the hearts of culprits. As a result, they do not believe in 'Admonition'. From a purely grammatical standpoint, this explanation cannot be faulted. However, both from a grammatical viewpoint as well as otherwise, we are of the view that in both cases the pronoun should preferably be deemed to refer to 'the Admonition'.

The Arabic word *salaka* literally means to penetrate, to put something into another as thread is put into a needle. What the verse, therefore, means is that so far as the believers are concerned, when 'the Admonition' penetrates their hearts, it provides them with peace of mind and spiritual nourishment. On the contrary, when it penetrates the hearts of the unbelievers, they feel as if it was a hot, burning rod.

8. In Arabic the word *burūj* is used to denote a fort or palace, or a strong, fortified building. In ancient astronomy, it was used as a term to indicate the twelve constellations which stood for the twelve spheres of the zodiac. In view of the above, some commentators on the Qur'ān believe that the word *burūj* refers here to the spheres of the zodiac. Other commentators have interpreted the word as denoting the planets. Reflection over the content of the present verse and the verse which immediately follows leads me to think that perhaps the reference here is to the heavenly spheres, which have been separated from each other by means of fortified boundaries. Although the frontiers in the

atmosphere are imperceptible, it is impossible for anything from one sphere to penetrate into that of another. In this sense, we are inclined to consider *burūj* as signifying 'fortified heavenly sphe[illegible]s'.

9. A shining planet or star was placed in every sphere with the result that the entire universe became illuminated. In other words, rather than create a vast, dismal and chaotic wilderness, God created a universe of dazzling beauty. The universe not only bespeaks of the skilled workmanship and infinite wisdom of the Creator, it also reflects the superb aesthetics of the Great Artist. The same idea has been beautifully expressed in the Qur'ān in the following words: 'He Who created in perfect beauty everything that He created' (*al-Sajdah* 32: 7).

10. Like other terrestrial creatures, the satans belonging to the *jinn* species are also confined to the sphere of the earth. They have no access to the heavens. This has been stated in order to rectify the popular misunderstanding, a misunderstanding held both in the past and even today, that Satan and his descendants are free to strut about in the whole universe. Refuting this, the Qur'ān states that satans cannot proceed beyond a certain limit. Their power to soar above is not unlimited.

11. Here reference is made to those satans who try to obtain information regarding matters belonging to the realm beyond the ken of sense-perception, and convey it to others. With the help of this information, many soothsayers, hermits and fake saints try to dupe people by claiming to know much more than they actually do. Those satans try to obtain information by eaves-dropping. They are able to do so because their constitution is closer to angels than to human beings. But in actual fact they are able to lay their hands on nothing.

12. The Qur'ānic expression *shihāb mubīn* means 'bright flame'. (Elsewhere the Qur'ān uses the expression *shihāb thāqib* – literally, 'the flame that penetrates the darkness'.) What the Qur'ān means by this expression is not necessarily that it is a meteor. It might in fact be referring to some cosmic rays, or possibly to some other kind of rays not yet known to us. At the same time, it is also possible that the expression might indeed refer to the meteors which we occasionally observe shooting across the sky and then falling to earth.

According to recent astronomical observations, the number of meteors which rush towards the earth from outer space is one trillion a day. Of these about 20 million reach the upper atmosphere of the earth. Out of these barely one meteor reaches the earth. The speed of these meteors in outer space is around 26 miles per second, sometimes reaching 50 miles per second. Sometimes almost a rainfall of meteors has been witnessed even by the naked eye. It is on record that on 12 November 1833, in the eastern part of North America, 200,000 meteors were seen falling to earth from midnight till morning in just one location. (See *Encyclopaedia Britannica*, XIVth edition,

(19) And the earth – We have stretched it out and have cast on it firm mountains, and have caused to grow in it everything well-measured.[13] (20) And We have provided sustenance for you on it and also for those of whom you are not the providers.

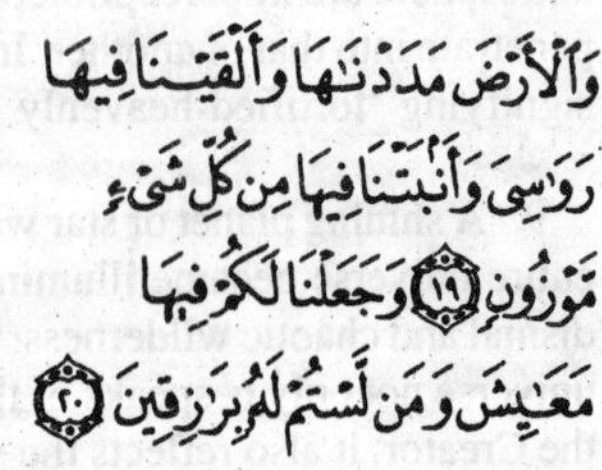

vol. XV, pp. 337–9.) Possibly this mass rain of meteors might be the impediment which prevents the free movement of satans in outer space. For it is quite understandable that the rain of a trillion meteors would have made the outer atmosphere impassable for them.

This throws some light on the nature of the 'fortified spheres' referred to earlier. (See verse 16 and n. 8 above – Ed.) Apparently, the atmosphere is transparently clear, without any visible walls or ceilings. However, God has surrounded it by a number of imperceptible protective walls which safeguard one sphere from the onslaught of another. As a result of these protective walls, out of a trillion meteors which come shooting towards the earth only one manages to reach its surface.

Of the meteorites preserved in museums all over the world, the largest one weighs 645 pounds. This penetrated 11 feet into the ground when it crashed to earth. Moreover, there is also a huge piece of iron weighing 36.5 tonnes. The only plausible explanation that scientists have been able to offer for its presence is that it is also perhaps a meteorite. One may, thus, visualize that but for the safeguard provided by the protective spheres the rain of shooting stars would have wreaked havoc on the earth. These fortified spheres are called *burūj* in the Qur'ān.

13. Here attention is drawn to another significant sign of God's absolute power and wisdom. Plants have such a capacity for growth and multiplication that if one plant were to flourish unchecked, it would leave no room for any other plant to grow. However, since the universe represents a well-thought-out design of the All-Wise and All-Powerful Creator, we witness that the growth of each plant variety stops at a certain point. Another manifestation of the same phenomenon is that plants of every volume, diameter, height and growth potential have a certain limit which they may not exceed. It is quite evident that someone has fixed the shape, size, foliage and output of each and every tree, plant and vine. It is also evident that all this was done with perfect precision.

(21) There is nothing
except that its treasures are
with Us and We do not send it
down except in a known
measure.[14]

(22) We send fertilizing
winds, and then cause rain to
descend from heaven, providing you abundant water to
drink even though you could
not have stored it up for
yourselves.

(23) It is indeed We Who
grant life and cause death and
it is We who shall be the sole
Inheritors of all.[15] (24)
Surely We know those of you
who have passed before and
those who will come later.
(25) Indeed your Lord will
gather them all together. Surely He is All-Wise, All-
Knowing.[16]

وَإِن مِّن شَيْءٍ إِلَّا عِندَنَا خَزَآئِنُهُۥ
وَمَا نُنَزِّلُهُۥٓ إِلَّا بِقَدَرٍ مَّعْلُومٍ ﴿٢١﴾
وَأَرْسَلْنَا ٱلرِّيَٰحَ لَوَٰقِحَ فَأَنزَلْنَا مِنَ
ٱلسَّمَآءِ مَآءً فَأَسْقَيْنَٰكُمُوهُ وَمَآ
أَنتُمْ لَهُۥ بِخَٰزِنِينَ ﴿٢٢﴾ وَإِنَّا لَنَحْنُ
نُحْيِۦ وَنُمِيتُ وَنَحْنُ ٱلْوَٰرِثُونَ ﴿٢٣﴾
وَلَقَدْ عَلِمْنَا ٱلْمُسْتَقْدِمِينَ مِنكُمْ
وَلَقَدْ عَلِمْنَا ٱلْمُسْتَـْٔخِرِينَ ﴿٢٤﴾ وَإِنَّ
رَبَّكَ هُوَ يَحْشُرُهُمْ إِنَّهُۥ حَكِيمٌ عَلِيمٌ ﴿٢٥﴾

14. That God creates everything with perfect precision and in a well-measured manner is not confined to plants. It rather applies to all creatures on the earth. A definite measure and limit has been determined for whatever exists, whether it is air, water, light, heat or cold; and whether they are minerals, plants or animals. In short, it has been determined from on high that every object, every species in existence and every form of energy found in the universe should exist strictly according to the measure and within the limits determined by God.

It is certainly owing to God's wise and superb determination of everything that has produced the balance and proportion which we find in the entire universe. Had the universe been the mere product of an accident, or had it been created by a number of gods, there would never have been the perfect balance and superb proportion that we find between the objects and forces of the universe, let alone that the balance and proportion would have endured in the manner it has.

(26) And indeed We brought man into being out of dry ringing clay which was wrought from black mud,[17] (27) while We had brought the jinn into being before out of the blazing fire.[18] (28) Recall when your Lord said to the angels: 'I will indeed bring into being a human being out of dry ringing clay wrought from black mud. (29) When I have completed shaping him and have breathed into him of My Spirit,[19] then fall you down before him in prostration.'

وَلَقَدْ خَلَقْنَا ٱلْإِنسَٰنَ مِن صَلْصَٰلٍ مِّنْ حَمَإٍ
مَّسْنُونٍ ﴿٢٦﴾ وَٱلْجَآنَّ خَلَقْنَٰهُ مِن قَبْلُ مِن نَّارِ
ٱلسَّمُومِ ﴿٢٧﴾ وَإِذْ قَالَ رَبُّكَ لِلْمَلَٰٓئِكَةِ إِنِّى
خَٰلِقٌۢ بَشَرًا مِّن صَلْصَٰلٍ مِّنْ حَمَإٍ
مَّسْنُونٍ ﴿٢٨﴾ فَإِذَا سَوَّيْتُهُۥ وَنَفَخْتُ فِيهِ
مِن رُّوحِى فَقَعُوا۟ لَهُۥ سَٰجِدِينَ ﴿٢٩﴾

15. God alone will ultimately inherit all since all beings except God Himself are destined to pass away. Men have been granted the opportunity to make use of their possessions only temporarily. A day will come when they will leave everything behind in the world. Then ultimately everything will revert to God's treasury.

16. God's wisdom requires that He should muster together all human beings. His knowledge is so vast and encompassing that no living being can escape his grasp. In fact, such is God that He will not allow to be lost even an atom of the dust of which man was constituted. Hence, whoever doubts the possibility of the Hereafter has no idea of God's wisdom. Likewise, whoever pleads that it is simply impossible to resurrect human beings since their bodies will totally disintegrate after death is also absolutely ignorant of the extent of God's power and knowledge.

17. The Qur'ān here clearly refutes the doctrine that it was after a process of evolution in the course of which man passed through genetic adaptations involving many stages of animal existence that he entered the stage of humanity. This Qur'ānic statement is, therefore, in direct conflict with the opinions that are currently being expressed by some commentators on the Qur'ān who, under the influence of the Darwinian theory of evolution, are striving to lend support to that theory with arguments drawn from the Qur'ān.

(30) So, the angels – all of them – fell down in prostration, (31) except Iblīs; he refused to join those who prostrated.[20] (32) The Lord inquired: 'Iblīs! What is the matter with you that you did not join those who prostrated?' (33) He said: 'It does not behove of me to prostrate myself before a human being whom you have created out of dry ringing clay wrought from black mud.'

فَسَجَدَ ٱلْمَلَٰٓئِكَةُ كُلُّهُمْ أَجْمَعُونَ
﴿٣٠﴾ إِلَّآ إِبْلِيسَ أَبَىٰٓ أَن يَكُونَ مَعَ
ٱلسَّٰجِدِينَ ﴿٣١﴾ قَالَ يَٰٓإِبْلِيسُ
مَا لَكَ أَلَّا تَكُونَ مَعَ ٱلسَّٰجِدِينَ ﴿٣٢﴾
قَالَ لَمْ أَكُن لِّأَسْجُدَ لِبَشَرٍ خَلَقْتَهُۥ
مِن صَلْصَٰلٍ مِّنْ حَمَإٍ مَّسْنُونٍ ﴿٣٣﴾

They do so in spite of the fact that the Qur'ān envisages that man was directly created out of elements derived from the earth.

The material mentioned has been described as صلصال من حمإ مسنون . The word *ḥama'* in Arabic is used for black mud which has a bad odour owing to its rottenness or as a result of fermentation. As for the word *masnūn,* it has two meanings. First, it denotes something smooth and slippery because of its rottenness. Second, the word signifies something that has been fashioned into a particular shape. The word *ṣalṣāl* is used for clay which, once dried, has a ringing sound.

These words are clearly indicative of the fact that the skeleton of a species was fashioned out of rotting clay; once it dried up it was infused with a soul.

18. *'Samūm'* denotes blazing wind. Used in conjunction with *nār,* the word suggests intense heat. This explains the Qur'ānic statements which mention the *jinn* to have been brought into being out of fire. (For details see *al-Raḥmān* 55, nn. 14–16.)

19. From this we learn that the soul infused into man is a reflection of God's attributes. We see that man has been invested with life, knowledge, power, will, volition and other similar attributes. Taken together, these stand for his soul or spirit. It is a mild reflection of the Divine attributes bestowed on man who was created out of clay. By dint of the reflection of Divine attributes, man became God's vicegerent on earth. By virtue of the same, everything on the earth, including angels, were made to prostrate before man.

(34) The Lord said: 'Then get out of here; you are rejected, (35) and there shall be a curse upon you till the Day of Recompense.'[21] (36) Iblīs said: 'My Lord! Grant me respite till the Day when they will be resurrected.' ▶

قَالَ فَٱخۡرُجۡ مِنۡهَا فَإِنَّكَ رَجِيمٞ ﴿٣٤﴾ وَإِنَّ عَلَيۡكَ ٱللَّعۡنَةَ إِلَىٰ يَوۡمِ ٱلدِّينِ ﴿٣٥﴾ قَالَ رَبِّ فَأَنظِرۡنِيٓ إِلَىٰ يَوۡمِ يُبۡعَثُونَ ﴿٣٦﴾

Every attribute found in human beings owes its origin either to one attribute of God or another. This is evident from the tradition which states:

جعل الله الرحمة مائة جزء فأمسك عنده تسعة وتسعين وأنزل في الأرض جزءا واحدا فمن ذلك الجزء يتراحم الخلائق حتى ترفع الدابة حافرها عن ولدها خشية أن تصيبه

'God divided mercy into a hundred parts. Of this He retained ninety-nine parts and sent down to earth just one part. It is because of this that creatures are kind to one another. So much so that an animal raises its hoof away from the body of its young one lest it might hurt it' (al-Bukhārī, *Kitāb al-Adab, 'Bāb Ja'al Allāh al-Rahmah Mi' at juz'* '; Muslim, *Kitāb al-Tawbah, 'Bāb fī Sa'at Rahmat Allāh Ta'āla'* '. (The word الدابة used in the tradition above occurs in Muslim whereas the word 'horse' occurs in al-Bukhārī – Ed.)

What, however, distinguishes man from other creatures and makes him superior to them is the comprehensiveness of God's attributes as reflected in man.

This idea, however, is quite subtle and any misunderstanding in grasping it might result in creating the illusory belief that the reflection of a Divine attribute amounts to acquiring a part of divinity. That is, of course, altogether out of the question since divinity is totally beyond the reach of all creatures.

20. Cf. *al-Baqarah* 2: 30 ff.; *al-Nisā'* 4: 116 ff.; *al-A'rāf* 7: 11 ff., and the relevant notes therein.

21. This means that Satan will remain cursed till the Day of Judgement, and that he will be punished subsequently for his disobedience in the Afterlife.

(37) Allah said: 'For sure you are granted respite (38) until the day of a known time.' (39) Iblīs said: 'My Lord! In the manner you led me to error, I will make things on earth seem attractive to them [mankind] and lead all of them to error,[22] (40) except those of Your servants whom You have singled out for Yourself.' (41) Allah said: 'Here is the path that leads straight to Me.[23] (42) Over My true servants you will be able to exercise no power, your power will be confined to the erring ones, ones who choose to follow you.[24] (43) Surely Hell is the promised place for all of them.'[25]

قَالَ فَإِنَّكَ مِنَ ٱلْمُنظَرِينَ ﴿٣٧﴾ إِلَىٰ
يَوْمِ ٱلْوَقْتِ ٱلْمَعْلُومِ ﴿٣٨﴾ قَالَ رَبِّ
بِمَآ أَغْوَيْتَنِي لَأُزَيِّنَنَّ لَهُمْ فِي
ٱلْأَرْضِ وَلَأُغْوِيَنَّهُمْ أَجْمَعِينَ ﴿٣٩﴾
إِلَّا عِبَادَكَ مِنْهُمُ ٱلْمُخْلَصِينَ
﴿٤٠﴾ قَالَ هَٰذَا صِرَٰطٌ عَلَيَّ
مُسْتَقِيمٌ ﴿٤١﴾ إِنَّ عِبَادِي
لَيْسَ لَكَ عَلَيْهِمْ سُلْطَٰنٌ إِلَّا مَنِ
ٱتَّبَعَكَ مِنَ ٱلْغَاوِينَ ﴿٤٢﴾ وَإِنَّ
جَهَنَّمَ لَمَوْعِدُهُمْ أَجْمَعِينَ ﴿٤٣﴾

---

22. Satan responded by saying that since he was asked to prostrate before an inferior creature, he was virtually compelled to disobey God. He would, therefore, make the worldly life attractive to mankind so that they are tempted by it and disobey God. In other words, Satan said that he would make the ephemeral benefits and advantages of worldly life so attractive to man that he would forget all about his vicegerency of God and his accountability to Him in the Hereafter. Men will thus either altogether forget God or if they do remember Him, they will violate His commands.

23. The Qur'ānic expression may be translated in two ways. One possible meaning is: 'Here is the path that leads straight to Me.' We have understood the verse to mean so and this is reflected in our translation. Another meaning could be: 'This is the right way which I have taken upon Myself to keep under My protection.'

24. This Qur'ānic statement may also be interpreted in two ways. One is that which is reflected in our translation. The other meaning could be: 'You

will have no power over My servants (i.e. mankind) to force them to disobedience. However, those who have fallen into error and have decided to follow you out of their own volition, they will be allowed to do so. We will not forcefully prevent them from proceeding in that direction.'

According to the first interpretation, the basic idea that the verse conveys is that worshipping God constitutes the true way that leads man to God. Satan is unable to exercise any dominating influence over the people who choose to follow this way. God will single out such people exclusively for Himself. Satan also acknowledges that he is unable to lead such people astray.

However, those who disobey God will lose the road to their felicity and success. They will fall prey to Satan, will follow him blindly and will be vulnerable to all his contrivings.

Were one to accept the second interpretation, the verse purports to mention Satan's future plan. He would do everything possible to make the worldly life attractive to human beings. He would do so in order to make people heedless of God and turn them away from obeying Him. God verifies this, pointing out that Satan was being granted a fixed period of time during which he had the opportunity to attempt to mislead human beings. It was clear, however, that God had not granted him the power to force people to err.

It is also evident from the above verse that Satan accepted the fact that he would be unable to mislead those whom God singled out for Himself. This might lead to a misconception that God would arbitrarily choose some people, to the exclusion of others, and make them immune to Satan's contriving. However, there is no basis for this misunderstanding since God makes it unequivocally clear that only those given to error will follow Satan. In other words, those who are on the right path will not fall prey to Satan. These are the ones whom God will single out for Himself.

25. In order to fully appreciate the purpose of this story it is important to bear in mind its context. Looking at the themes set out in verses 1 ff. and 18 ff., it becomes clear that the story of Adam and Satan has been recounted so as to warn the unbelievers that they had been misled by their eternal enemy, Satan, and that they were following his ways. As a result, they were sliding into those depths of error and degradation which, out of his jealousy, Satan had always wanted to push all mankind into. On the contrary, the Prophet (peace be on him) has a compassionate concern for all mankind and seeks to liberate them. He also wishes to lead them to the heights of success and honour to which they were entitled by virtue of the position accorded to them under God's scheme of things. In view of the above, it seems astonishing that people are often inclined to look upon their enemies as friends, and their friends as enemies.

It is also emphasized that there is just one way which can ensure man's salvation and felicity. That way consists of sincerely worshipping and serving God. All other ways are Satan's, and each of them will directly lead to Hell.

Another truth that is brought home through this story is that the unbelievers themselves are to blame for their error. Satan can at best try to delude people by

(44) There are seven gates in it, and to each gate a portion of them has been allotted.[26] (45) As for the God-fearing,[27] they shall be amid gardens and springs. (46) They will be told: 'Enter it in peace and security.' (47) And We shall purge their breasts of all traces of rancour;[28] and they shall be seated on couches facing one another as brothers. (48) They shall face no fatigue in it, nor shall they ever be driven out of it.[29]

(49) (O Prophet!) Declare to My servants that I am indeed Ever Forgiving, Most Merciful. (50) At the same time, My chastisement is highly painful.

لَهَا سَبْعَةُ أَبْوَٰبٍ لِّكُلِّ بَابٍ مِّنْهُمْ جُزْءٌ
مَّقْسُومٌ ﴿٤٤﴾ إِنَّ ٱلْمُتَّقِينَ فِى جَنَّٰتٍ
وَعُيُونٍ ﴿٤٥﴾ ٱدْخُلُوهَا بِسَلَٰمٍ ءَامِنِينَ ﴿٤٦﴾
وَنَزَعْنَا مَا فِى صُدُورِهِم مِّنْ غِلٍّ إِخْوَٰنًا
عَلَىٰ سُرُرٍ مُّتَقَٰبِلِينَ ﴿٤٧﴾ لَا يَمَسُّهُمْ
فِيهَا نَصَبٌ وَمَا هُم مِّنْهَا بِمُخْرَجِينَ
﴿٤٨﴾ ۞ نَبِّئْ عِبَادِىٓ أَنِّىٓ أَنَا ٱلْغَفُورُ
ٱلرَّحِيمُ ﴿٤٩﴾ وَأَنَّ عَذَابِى هُوَ
ٱلْعَذَابُ ٱلْأَلِيمُ ﴿٥٠﴾

---

making the worldly life seem overly attractive to them. However, if people fall into any error, that is entirely their own act, and for all such acts they alone will bear all responsibility. (For further details see *Ibrāhīm* 14: 22 ff. and n. 31.)

26. The gates of Hell will correspond to the kind of error and sin which a person commits, making him deserving of being cast into Hell. Some people deserve being cast into Hell because of polytheism; some because of hypocrisy; some because of excessive self-indulgence; some because of their injustice and oppression and the harm they have done to other human beings. There are still others who deserve to be cast into Hell on the basis that they propagated some outrageously misleading doctrines, or had made unbelief prevail, or had worked to spread corruption and shameful immorality.

27. This refers to those who did not follow Satan; who, out of their God-fearingness, lived as God's faithful servants.

(51) And tell them about Abraham's guests.[30] (52) When they came to Abraham they said: 'Peace be upon you!' He replied: 'Indeed we feel afraid of you.'[31] (53) They said: 'Do not feel afraid, for we give you the good news of a clever boy.'[32] (54) Abraham said: 'What! Do you give me this tiding though old age has smitten me? Just consider what tiding do you give me!' ▶

وَنَبِّئْهُمْ عَن ضَيْفِ إِبْرَٰهِيمَ ﴿٥١﴾ إِذْ دَخَلُوا۟ عَلَيْهِ فَقَالُوا۟ سَلَـٰمًا قَالَ إِنَّا مِنكُمْ وَجِلُونَ ﴿٥٢﴾ قَالُوا۟ لَا تَوْجَلْ إِنَّا نُبَشِّرُكَ بِغُلَـٰمٍ عَلِيمٍ ﴿٥٣﴾ قَالَ أَبَشَّرْتُمُونِى عَلَىٰٓ أَن مَّسَّنِىَ ٱلْكِبَرُ فَبِمَ تُبَشِّرُونَ ﴿٥٤﴾

28. The hearts of the righteous will be purged of any feeling of bitterness and rancour – if they ever had any such feelings – before entering Paradise. (For details see *Towards Understanding the Qur'ān*, vol. III, *al-A'rāf* 7, n. 32, p. 28.)

29. This Qur'ānic statement has been elaborated in the following tradition. The Prophet (peace be on him) said:

يقال لأهل الجنة إن لكم أن تصحوا ولا تمرضوا أبدا، وإن لكم أن تعيشوا فلا تموتوا أبدا، وإن لكم أن تشبوا ولاتهرموا أبدا، وإن لكم أن تقيموا فلا تضعنوا أبدا

'It will be said to the people of Paradise: ''You will now remain healthy for ever and will never fall sick. You will live for ever and never die. You will always remain young and never grow old. You will always remain settled, and will never require to undertake [the strain of] any journey''.' (For the contents of this tradition see Muslim, *Kitāb al-Jannah wa Ṣifat Na'ī mihā wa Ahlihā, 'Bab fī Dawām Na'īm Ahl al-Jannah'*, and al-Tirmidhī, *Abwāb al-Tafsīr, 'Tafsīr Sūrah al-Zumar'*.)(We have been unable, however, to trace the last sentence quoted here, viz.

وإن لكم أن تقيموا فلا تضعنوا أبدا – Ed.)

This is further explained by the Qur'ān and several traditions from the Prophet (peace be on him) which state that the inmate of Paradise will have no need to toil for his bread. Man will receive all that he wishes for without having to toil for it.

(55) They said: 'The good tiding we give you is of truth. Do, not, therefore, be of those who despair.' (56) Abraham said: 'Who despairs of the mercy of his Lord except the misguided?' (57) He added: 'What is your errand O sent ones?'[33] ▶

قَالُوا۟ بَشَّرْنَٰكَ بِٱلْحَقِّ فَلَا تَكُن مِّنَ ٱلْقَٰنِطِينَ ﴿٥٥﴾ قَالَ وَمَن يَقْنَطُ مِن رَّحْمَةِ رَبِّهِۦٓ إِلَّا ٱلضَّآلُّونَ ﴿٥٦﴾ قَالَ فَمَا خَطْبُكُمْ أَيُّهَا ٱلْمُرْسَلُونَ ﴿٥٧﴾

30. This marks the commencement of the story of Abraham (peace be on him). This is immediately followed by the story of the people of Lot (peace be on him).

In order to fully understand the underlying purpose of this narration, it is necessary to bear in mind some of the verses in the earlier part of the present *sūrah*. First of all we encounter the statement of the Makkan unbelievers: 'Why do you not bring down angels upon us if you are indeed truthful?' (verse 7). At that point a brief rejoinder has been made: 'We do not send down angels [in frivolity] and when We do send them down, We do so with truth, and then people are granted no respite' (verse 8). An elaboration of the same point is made here with reference to these two stories. The unbelievers are told that the angels had brought one kind of 'truth' to Prophet Abraham (peace be on him) (verses 52–6), but brought 'truth' of quite another kind to the people of Lot (peace be on him). Now it was for the unbelievers themselves to decide which 'truth' should be communicated to them. It was quite obvious that they had not brought along the kind of truth which was sent to Abraham (peace be on him) through the angels. Were they, then, desirous that the kind of truth which was brought to the people of Lot (peace be on him) by the angels – one that spelled mass destruction – should also be sent to them?

31. Cf. *Hūd* 11: 69 ff. and the relevant notes there.

32. This alludes to the prophecy about the birth of Isaac (peace be on him), which has been clearly stated in *Hūd*. (See verse 71 – Ed.)

33. It is evident from Prophet Abraham's question that angels appear in human form only in extraordinary circumstances. Whenever they come in that form, it is to carry out some extraordinary mission.

(58) They said: 'Verily we have been sent to a guilty people[34] (59) excepting the household of Lot. We shall deliver all of them, (60) except his wife (about whom Allah says that) We have decreed. She shall be among those who stay behind.'

(61) So when the envoys came to the household of Lot,[35] (62) he said: 'Surely you are an unknown folk.'[36] (63) They said: 'Nay, we have brought to you that concerning which they have been in doubt. (64) We truly tell you that we have brought to you the truth. ▶

قَالُوٓا إِنَّآ أُرْسِلْنَآ إِلَىٰ قَوْمٍ مُّجْرِمِينَ ﴿٥٨﴾
إِلَّآ ءَالَ لُوطٍ إِنَّا لَمُنَجُّوهُمْ أَجْمَعِينَ
﴿٥٩﴾ إِلَّا ٱمْرَأَتَهُۥ قَدَّرْنَآ إِنَّهَا لَمِنَ
ٱلْغَٰبِرِينَ ﴿٦٠﴾ فَلَمَّا جَآءَ ءَالَ لُوطٍ
ٱلْمُرْسَلُونَ ﴿٦١﴾ قَالَ إِنَّكُمْ قَوْمٌ
مُّنكَرُونَ ﴿٦٢﴾ قَالُوا بَلْ جِئْنَٰكَ
بِمَا كَانُوا فِيهِ يَمْتَرُونَ ﴿٦٣﴾ وَأَتَيْنَٰكَ
بِٱلْحَقِّ وَإِنَّا لَصَٰدِقُونَ ﴿٦٤﴾

---

34. The brevity of the reference indicates that the guilt of the people of Lot had exceeded all limits, and that they had become quite notorious for it. As a result, it was sufficient to mention them as a 'guilty people' without specifically naming them.

35. Cf. *al-A'rāf* 7: 73 ff. and *Hūd* 11: 69 ff.

36. The narration of the incident here is very brief. Its details are to be found in *Hūd* (see verse 77 ff.) where it has been mentioned that Prophet Lot (peace be on him) felt much consternation at the visit of the angels. As soon as he saw them, he felt convinced that something grave lay in store. The reason for Lot's consternation has been alluded to in the Qur'ān, but mentioned in clearer terms in the traditions. The angels had come down to the people of Lot in the form of handsome youths. Lot was fully aware of the perversity and wickedness of his people which made him feel very bad. Lot was also worried at his helplessness for he was neither in a position to send his guests back nor to keep them away from the reach of his wicked people. (See *Hūd* 11: 77 ff. – Ed.)

(65) So set out with your family in a watch of the night, and keep yourself behind them,[37] and no one of you may turn round,[38] and keep going ahead of you as you have been commanded.' (66) And We communicated to him the decree that by the morning those people will be totally destroyed.

(67) In the meantime the people of the city came rejoicing to Lot.[39] (68) He said: 'These are my guests, so do not disgrace me. (69) Have fear of Allah, and do not humiliate me.' (70) They replied: 'Did we not forbid you again and again to extend hospitality to all and sundry?'

فَأَسْرِ بِأَهْلِكَ بِقِطْعٍ مِّنَ ٱلَّيْلِ وَٱتَّبِعْ
أَدْبَٰرَهُمْ وَلَا يَلْتَفِتْ مِنكُمْ أَحَدٌ
وَٱمْضُوا۟ حَيْثُ تُؤْمَرُونَ ﴿٦٥﴾ وَقَضَيْنَآ
إِلَيْهِ ذَٰلِكَ ٱلْأَمْرَ أَنَّ دَابِرَ هَٰٓؤُلَآءِ
مَقْطُوعٌ مُّصْبِحِينَ ﴿٦٦﴾ وَجَآءَ أَهْلُ
ٱلْمَدِينَةِ يَسْتَبْشِرُونَ ﴿٦٧﴾ قَالَ إِنَّ
هَٰٓؤُلَآءِ ضَيْفِى فَلَا تَفْضَحُونِ ﴿٦٨﴾ وَٱتَّقُوا۟
ٱللَّهَ وَلَا تُخْزُونِ ﴿٦٩﴾ قَالُوٓا۟ أَوَلَمْ
نَنْهَكَ عَنِ ٱلْعَٰلَمِينَ ﴿٧٠﴾

---

37. Lot (peace be on him) was asked to follow the members of his family, ensuring thereby that none of them remained behind.

38. This does not mean that as soon as they looked behind, they would be turned into pillars of salt, as the Bible says (*Genesis* 19: 26). What was being asked was simply that they should not be prompted by the noise behind them to pause and see what was going on. There was no time to lose, no time to feel sorrow at the tragic end which was about to befall that wicked nation. For if they lost any time, they might also be seized by the calamitous punishment aimed at the people of Lot.

39. This gives some idea of the moral degeneration of Lot's people. The mere fact that some good-looking guests had come to someone in the neighbourhood was enough to prompt a mob of people to converge on his house. Not only that, they also publicly demanded that the youths be handed over to them so that they may gratify their sensual desires. Immorality had become so rampant that no section of the population felt the need to protect

(71) Lot exclaimed in exasperation: 'If you are bent on doing something, then here are my daughters.'[40]

(72) By your life (O Prophet!), they went about blindly stumbling in their intoxication. (73) Then the mighty Blast caught them at sunrise, (74) and turned the land upside down, and rained down stones of baked clay.[41]

قَالَ هَٰٓؤُلَآءِ بَنَاتِيٓ إِن كُنتُمۡ فَٰعِلِينَ ٧١
لَعَمۡرُكَ إِنَّهُمۡ لَفِي سَكۡرَتِهِمۡ يَعۡمَهُونَ ٧٢
فَأَخَذَتۡهُمُ ٱلصَّيۡحَةُ مُشۡرِقِينَ ٧٣
فَجَعَلۡنَا عَٰلِيَهَا سَافِلَهَا وَأَمۡطَرۡنَا
عَلَيۡهِمۡ حِجَارَةٗ مِّن سِجِّيلٍ ٧٤

themselves against it. Nor did the people have the moral sensitivity that would prompt them to refrain from publicly indulging in such shameless vices.

Now, if these people had the audacity to storm the house of someone as well-known for his piety and righteousness as Lot (peace be on him), it is easy to imagine the extent of the moral corruption that was rampant in that land.

The Talmud provides an account of the people which clearly mirrors the depth of their moral depravity. It mentions that once a stranger was passing through their town. As night was falling, he had to stay in Sodom. He had his own provisions so that he did not need anyone to host him. He lay under a tree, when a Sodomite persuaded him to accompany him to his house. During the night the Sodomite stole his ass and its reins, and all his guest's merchandise. Nobody paid any attention to the stranger's protests. Instead, the other inhabitants of the town looted whatever belongings were left with him and turned him out of the town.

Once Sarah sent one of her slaves to Sodom to inquire about the welfare of Lot's family. When the slave entered the town he found a Sodomite beating a stranger. When he interfered, asking the Sodomite not to be so unkind to a helpless traveller, he was also subjected to a beating and sustained head injuries.

On another occasion, a poor man came to Sodom. No one gave him anything to eat. Worn out by starvation, he collapsed. The daughter of Lot (peace be on him) spotted him and provided him with food. However, the inhabitants reproached Prophet Lot (peace be on him) and his daughter for their act of kindness. They also threatened that if they did the same again, they would forfeit the right to live among them.

After recounting several such episodes, the author of the Talmud remarks that Lot's people in their day-to-day lives were extremely oppressive, habitually resorted to deception, and did not keep their word. If a poor man passed through their town, none would give him any food. They even stripped the dead of their shrouds, leaving them stark naked. If any merchant came to them from another town, they robbed him of his merchandise and his protests went unheeded. They even built a spacious garden in their valley which spread over many miles. In that garden they publicly committed every possible act of indecency. There was not a single soul among them except Lot (peace be on him), who tried to dissuade them from indulging in such wickedness. The Qur'ān has succinctly portrayed their evil ways: 'Before this they were wont to commit evil deeds' (*Hūd* 11: 78). 'Do you approach men [to gratify your sexual desire] and 'cut off the highway, and commit wickedness even in your councils?' (*al-'Ankabūt* 29: 29).

40. This point has been elaborated in *Hūd,* n. 87 above. It must be remembered that Lot (peace be on him) made these remarks in a state of total desperation, when a mob of people, fully bent upon corruption, was pouncing upon his guests in total disregard of all his pleas and protestations.

It is pertinent to clarify one thing at this point. The sequence of events mentioned in *Sūrah Hūd* (see verse 77 ff.) indicates that at the time when those people attempted an assault on his guests, Lot was quite unaware that they were angels. He was under the impression that the youths were strangers who, in the course of their travelling, had accidentally come to his house. Hence when a gang of wicked fellows carried out an assault on them, Lot exclaimed: 'Would that I had the strength to set you straight or could seek refuge in some powerful support' (*Hūd* 11: 80). It is at this point that the angels disclosed their identity. Then they directed Lot (peace be on him) to get away from the place along with his family so that they might adequately carry out the mission to inflict a severe chastisement on his people.

If we remember the true sequence of events as mentioned in *Sūrah Hūd* (see verse 77 ff.), it is easy to appreciate how desperate Lot (peace be on him) must have been when he uttered the words mentioned above. But in the present *sūrah* the events have not been referred to in their earlier sequence. This presumably is because the purpose of the narrative here is to emphasize the point for which the story has been narrated. (This purpose is to underscore that God's chastisement inevitably seizes a people who go too far in their iniquity – Ed.) However, the sequence in which the events have been mentioned here might lead a common reader to the mistaken view that the angels had already revealed their identity to Lot (peace be on him). This might even lead some to wonder about the plea made by Lot in order to prevent his people from laying their hands on his guests. They might even be led to consider Lot's statement to be no more than an act that he had put on.

41. The 'stones of baked clay' might have been meteorites. Or else volcanic eruptions may have taken place, throwing up some material that subsequently might have fallen on Lot's people like a rain of stones. Alternatively, a fierce storm may have been the instrument for this extraordinary rain of stones.

(75) There are great signs in this incident for men of intelligence. (76) The place (where this occurred) lies along a known route.[42] (77) Verily there is a sign in this for the believers.

(78) And the people of Aykah[43] were also wrong-doers. (79) So We chastised them. The desolate locations of both communities lie on a well-known highway.[44]

(80) Surely the people of al-Hijr[45] also rejected the Messengers, calling them liars. (81) We also gave them Our signs, yet they turned away from them.

إِنَّ فِي ذَٰلِكَ لَآيَٰتٍ لِّلْمُتَوَسِّمِينَ ﴿٧٥﴾
وَإِنَّهَا لَبِسَبِيلٍ مُّقِيمٍ ﴿٧٦﴾ إِنَّ فِي ذَٰلِكَ
لَآيَةً لِّلْمُؤْمِنِينَ ﴿٧٧﴾ وَإِن كَانَ أَصْحَٰبُ
ٱلْأَيْكَةِ لَظَٰلِمِينَ ﴿٧٨﴾ فَٱنتَقَمْنَا مِنْهُمْ
وَإِنَّهُمَا لَبِإِمَامٍ مُّبِينٍ ﴿٧٩﴾ وَلَقَدْ كَذَّبَ
أَصْحَٰبُ ٱلْحِجْرِ ٱلْمُرْسَلِينَ ﴿٨٠﴾
وَءَاتَيْنَٰهُمْ ءَايَٰتِنَا فَكَانُوا۟ عَنْهَا
مُعْرِضِينَ ﴿٨١﴾

---

42. This devastated piece of land lies on the route from the Hijaz to Syria and Iraq to Egypt. The caravans that pass by this region witness traces of the devastation. In fact, some of these traces can still be observed even today. The area referred to is situated to the east and south of the Dead Sea. As to its southern part, geographers are of the view that it is characterized by a desolation for which there is no parallel on earth.

43. The people of Aykah were the people of Prophet Shu'ayb (peace be on him). They were known as the Midianites after the name of their capital, Midian. As to the word 'Aykah', it was the former name of the city called Tabūk. Lexically, the word denotes 'dense forest'.

44. The territory of the Midianites also lies on the route from the Hijaz to Palestine and Syria.

45. Al-Ḥijr was the capital city of the people of Thamūd. Its ruins are found to the north-west of Madina, a few miles from the present town of al-'Ulā'. The town lies *en route* from Madina to Tabūk through which caravans still pass. However, in accordance with the directive of Prophet Muḥammad (peace

(82) They used to hew out houses from the mountains and lived in security. (83) Then the Blast caught them in the morning, (84) whatever they had been earning proved of no avail.[46]

(85) We have not created the heavens and the earth and all that is in between them except with truth.[47] Surely the Hour will come. So (O Muḥammad!) do graciously overlook them (despite their lowly behaviour). ▶

وَكَانُوا۟ يَنْحِتُونَ مِنَ ٱلْجِبَالِ بُيُوتًا ءَامِنِينَ
﴿٨٢﴾ فَأَخَذَتْهُمُ ٱلصَّيْحَةُ مُصْبِحِينَ ﴿٨٣﴾
فَمَآ أَغْنَىٰ عَنْهُم مَّا كَانُوا۟ يَكْسِبُونَ ﴿٨٤﴾
وَمَا خَلَقْنَا ٱلسَّمَٰوَٰتِ وَٱلْأَرْضَ وَمَا
بَيْنَهُمَآ إِلَّا بِٱلْحَقِّ ۗ وَإِنَّ ٱلسَّاعَةَ
لَءَاتِيَةٌ ۖ فَٱصْفَحِ ٱلصَّفْحَ ٱلْجَمِيلَ ﴿٨٥﴾

---

be on him), travellers do not halt there. In the eighth century *Hijrah,* Ibn Baṭṭūṭah visited the place on his way to Makka. He says: 'I have seen the buildings of Thamūd hewed in red mountains; the paintings look so bright as if they have been put on only recently . . . and rotten bones of human beings are found in them even today'. Ibn Baṭṭūṭah, *Muhadhdhab Riḥlat Ibn Baṭṭūṭah,* ed. Aḥmad al-'Awāmir and Muḥammad Jād al-Mawlá' (Cairo, al-Amiriyah, 1934), vol. 1, p. 89. (For further details see *Towards Understanding the Qur'ān,* vol. III, *al-A'rāf* 7, n. 57, p. 45 ff.)

46. That is, their sturdy, rock-hewn houses totally failed to protect them from God's chastisement.

47. This is stated so as to comfort Prophet Muḥammad (peace be on him). He is told that even though falsehood apparently seemed to dominate and that there lay many obstacles and difficulties in the path of truth, one should not be daunted by them. For this state is purely transient and cannot endure. This is because the heavens and the earth have been created with truth. In fact, the whole universe is in consonance with the truth and discordant with falsehood. It is the truth rather than falsehood which endures. (For further details see *Ibrāhīm* 14, nn. 25–6 and 35–9 above.)

(86) Your Lord is indeed the Creator of all, the All-Knowing.[48] (87) We have indeed bestowed on you the seven oft-repeated verses[49] and the Great Qur'ān.[50] ▶

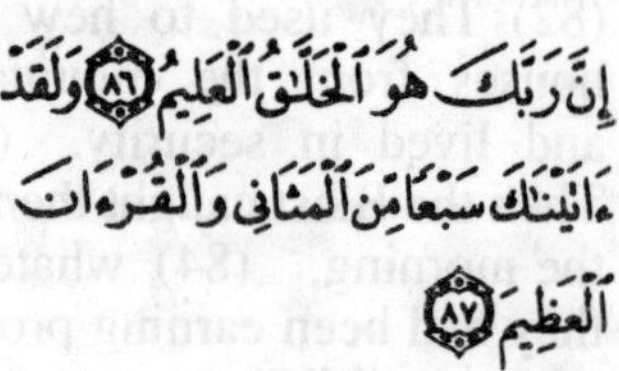

48. Being the Creator, God holds total sway over all His creatures. None can elude His grip. Moreover, being the Creator, God is All-Knowing. He is fully aware of all the efforts made by Prophet Muḥammad (peace be on him) to reform his people. He is also fully cognizant of the stratagems of the Prophet's enemies designed specifically to frustrate his efforts. Hence, there is no reason for the Prophet (peace be on him) to lose his patience. For in the course of time full justice will be done.

49. The expression 'seven oft-repeated verses' stands for the seven verses of the opening *sūrah* of the Qur'ān, *al-Fātiḥah*. Some scholars, however, consider the expression to refer to the seven long *sūrahs* each of which has more than two hundred verses. These *sūrahs* are *al-Baqarah, Āl 'Imrān, al-Nisā' al-Mā'idah, al-An'ām, al-A'rāf* and *Yūnus* or *al-Anfāl* or *al-Tawbah*. All the above-mentioned *sūrahs* are among the longer *sūrahs* of the Qur'ān.*

The vast majority of Muslim scholars, however, are agreed that the expression refers to *al-Fātiḥah*. Al-Bukhārī mentions two traditions which show that the Prophet (peace be on him) himself clarified that the 'seven repeated verses' signified *al-Fātiḥah*. (See al-Bukhārī, *Kitab al-Tafsīr, 'Bāb Mā Jā' fī Fātiḥat al-Kitāb'*, *Tafsīr Sūrat al-Ḥijr*, and *'Bāb Qawluh Wa la qad Ātaynāk Sab'an min al-Mathānī wa al-Qur'ān al-'Aẓīm* – Ed.)

50. This was also said with a view to comforting and consoling the Prophet (peace be on him) and his Companions. At that time they were in a state of miserable suffering. Some time after the assumption of his onerous responsibilities, the Prophet's trade activities virtually came to a halt. The savings of his wife Khadījah were also exhausted during the course of about ten years. This much should suffice to explain the financial predicament of the Prophet (peace be on him).

*It is not accurate to say that each of these *sūrahs* has two hundred or more verses. For the number of verses in *al-Nisā'* is 176; in *al-Mā'idah*, 120; in *al-An'ām*, 165; in *al-Tawbah*, 129 and in *Yūnus*, 109 – Ed.

(88) Do not even cast your eyes towards the worldly goods We have granted to different kinds of people, nor grieve over the state they are in,[51] and turn your loving attention to the believers instead, (89) and clearly tell the unbelievers: 'I am most certainly a plain warner,' ▶

لَا تَمُدَّنَّ عَيْنَيْكَ إِلَىٰ مَا مَتَّعْنَا بِهِۦٓ
أَزْوَٰجًا مِّنْهُمْ وَلَا تَحْزَنْ عَلَيْهِمْ
وَٱخْفِضْ جَنَاحَكَ لِلْمُؤْمِنِينَ ﴿٨٨﴾
وَقُلْ إِنِّىٓ أَنَا ٱلنَّذِيرُ
ٱلْمُبِينُ ﴿٨٩﴾

So far as the rest of the Muslims are concerned, some young men were expelled from their homes. Those who were engaged in trade, or had some vocation, were financially crippled as a result of the economic boycott. In addition to these, many Muslims lacked any financial *locus standi* since their social status was that of slaves or clients (*mawālī*). Thus, the Prophet (peace be on him) and his Companions had quite a miserable existence in Makka and the areas around it owing to the severe persecution to which they were subjected. Everywhere they were ridiculed, insulted, and vilified. As if mental torture was not enough, they were also subjected to cruel physical chastisements. In sharp contrast to the lot of the Muslims, was the situation of the unbelievers of the Quraysh. Their chiefs were conspicuously prosperous. All kinds of worldly enjoyments were plentifully available to them.

It is in the context of these circumstances that the believers are being asked not to lose heart. For, God has blessed them with something which is far more valuable than all worldly riches. The moral and intellectual wealth granted to the Muslims is incomparably superior to the unlawfully earned material wealth in possession of the unbelievers. The latter kind of wealth will be of no avail to them for they will be utterly bankrupt when they appear before their Lord on the Day of Judgement.

51. The Prophet (peace be on him) is being asked not to grieve over the lot of the unbelievers. They mistook their sincere well-wisher for an enemy. They considered doctrinal errors and moral corruption as matters one ought to be proud of. They were well advanced on a path that would inevitably lead them to a disastrous end. Above all, they had spared no efforts to frustrate the teachings of the Prophet (peace be on him) who was engaged in striving to direct them to the way which would lead to their salvation.

(90) even as We had sent warning on those who had divided their religion into fragments; (91) those who had split up their scripture [Qur'ān] into pieces.[52] (92) By your Lord, We will question them all (93) concerning what they have been doing.

(94) (O Prophet!) Proclaim what you are commanded, and pay no heed to those who associate others with Allah in His divinity. (95) Surely We suffice to deal with those who scoff at you; (96) those who set up another deity alongside Allah. They shall soon come to know.

كَمَآ أَنزَلْنَا عَلَى ٱلْمُقْتَسِمِينَ ﴿٩٠﴾
ٱلَّذِينَ جَعَلُوا۟ ٱلْقُرْءَانَ عِضِينَ ﴿٩١﴾
فَوَرَبِّكَ لَنَسْـَٔلَنَّهُمْ أَجْمَعِينَ ﴿٩٢﴾
عَمَّا كَانُوا۟ يَعْمَلُونَ ﴿٩٣﴾ فَٱصْدَعْ بِمَا
تُؤْمَرُ وَأَعْرِضْ عَنِ ٱلْمُشْرِكِينَ ﴿٩٤﴾
إِنَّا كَفَيْنَٰكَ ٱلْمُسْتَهْزِءِينَ ﴿٩٥﴾
ٱلَّذِينَ يَجْعَلُونَ مَعَ ٱللَّهِ إِلَٰهًا
ءَاخَرَ فَسَوْفَ يَعْلَمُونَ ﴿٩٦﴾

52. The reference here is to the Jews. They have been branded as '*muqtasimūn*' since they had torn their religion into shreds by believing in certain parts of it and not in others. They had also added a great deal to their original religion and divested it of many of its original features, which gave rise to the scores of sects in their midst. They had also split their scripture, which for them was like the Qur'ān is to Muslims, into fragments. The act mentioned here is in fact no other than what has been mentioned elsewhere in the Qur'ān in the following words: 'Do you believe in a part of the Scripture and reject the rest?' (*al-Baqarah* 2: 85).

The purpose of the above statement is to warn the Muslims regarding matters for which the Jews had been warned earlier. The record of the Jews was highlighted in order that the Muslims might learn a lesson. The Jews had failed to heed warnings from God. This led to disastrous consequences. That this contained a lesson for the Muslims was quite evident. To fail to take heed of it amounted to choosing an end as tragic as that of the Jews.

(97) We certainly know that their statements sorely grieve you. (98) When (you feel so) glorify your Lord, with His praise, and prostrate yourself before Him, (99) and worship your Lord until the last moment (of your life) that will most certainly come.[53]

وَلَقَدْ نَعْلَمُ أَنَّكَ يَضِيقُ صَدْرُكَ بِمَا
يَقُولُونَ ﴿٩٧﴾ فَسَبِّحْ بِحَمْدِ رَبِّكَ وَكُن
مِّنَ السَّاجِدِينَ ﴿٩٨﴾ وَاعْبُدْ رَبَّكَ
حَتَّىٰ يَأْتِيَكَ الْيَقِينُ ﴿٩٩﴾

53. Believers are bound to encounter hardships in the course of their efforts to propagate Islam and bring about reform in the lives of people. They can face the hardships and sufferings which come their way only with the help of Prayer and perseverance in the service of God. These will infuse them with patience, will raise their morale and also develop in them the steadfastness needed to carry out the mission that will please God, even in the face of opposition, condemnation and vilification.

Sūrah 16

al-Naḥl

(The Bee)

(Makkan Period)

Title

The title of this *sūrah* is derived from the word 'bee' which occurs in verse 68: 'Your Lord inspired the bee . . .' Like other *sūrahs*, the title merely distinguishes one *sūrah* from another. It bears no reference to its contents.

Period of Revelation

There are several pieces of internal evidence which suggest the period of the *sūrah*'s revelation. For instance, verse 41 reads: 'Those who have forsaken their homes for the sake of Allah after enduring persecution . . .' This verse clearly indicates that the *sūrah* was revealed after the migration to Abyssinia.

Likewise, verse 106 makes a reference to 'anyone who disbelieves in Allah after having had faith . . .' This is also significant as it indicates that the believers have been under a state of persecution for a long time. As a result, the following question arose among their ranks: 'How should one judge those who were coerced, under the pressure of unendurable persecution, into disbelieving?'

Verses 112–14 of the *sūrah* read: 'Allah sets forth the parable of [the people of] a town who were secure and content and whose sustenance came in abundance from every quarter. But then the people of the town showed ingratitude towards Allah for His bounties, so Allah afflicted them with hunger and fear in punishment for their evil deeds. Most certainly a Messenger came to them from among them; but they rejected him, calling him a liar. Therefore, chastisement seized them while they engaged in wrongdoing. So eat out of the lawful and good sustenance that Allah has bestowed upon you, and thank Allah for His bounty, if it is Him that you serve.' These verses indicate that the great famine of Makka which began after the designation of Muḥammad (peace be on him) as the Messenger of God had ended before the *sūrah* was revealed.

There is also an allusion to verse 115 of this *sūrah* in verse 119 of *al-An'ām*. Similarly, there is allusion to verse 118 of this *sūrah* in verse 146 of *al-An'ām*. Thus it appears that both *sūrahs* – *al-Naḥl* and *al-An'ām* – were revealed around the same time.

In light of the above pieces of internal evidence it may be deduced that this *sūrah* was revealed in the last phase of the period of the Prophet's life in Makka. The *sūrah*'s contents also corroborate this point.

Major Themes

The *sūrah* is mainly concerned with the following purposes: to refute polytheism, to affirm God's unity, to warn people of the dire consequences of rejecting the call of the Prophets, and to reproach those who seek to oppose the truth.

Subject-Matter

The *sūrah* opens, without any preliminary remarks, and instead with a severe warning. The Makkan unbelievers asked the Prophet (peace be on him) why they had not been seized by God's scourge of which they had been warned earlier. They expressed curiosity as to why no scourge had struck them even though they had rejected the Prophet (peace be on him), had called him a liar, and were openly opposed to him. They made this statement thinking that it was a persuasive proof of the falsity of Muḥammad's claim to be a Prophet. In response, the unbelievers were told that God's scourge was about to be let loose upon them. It was, therefore, foolish of them to constantly clamour for God's scourge to seize them. They should rather make good use of the time they still had to grasp the message and mend their ways accordingly.

This warning is followed by a discourse aimed at driving home to people the basic message of Islam. The following subjects are discussed one after the other:

1. The truth of monotheism and the falsity of polytheism are driven home to people with the help of persuasive arguments and by

drawing attention to a myriad of signs in the universe as well as in man's own being.

2. The objections, doubts, pseudo-arguments and pretexts of the unbelievers are taken up, one by one, and repudiated.

3. The unbelievers are warned of the dreadful consequences of their persistence in falsehood and their arrogant rejection of the truth.

4. A blueprint of the reform that the Prophet's message seeks to bring about in human life – at both a moral and practical level – is outlined in succinct and convincing terms. The polytheists, who claim to believe in God, are informed of the requisites of such a belief. Belief in God does not consist merely of verbally assenting to a set of metaphysical propositions; rather, it makes a number of demands which should be evident from a man's beliefs, his morals, and his practical life.

5. The Prophet (peace be on him) and his Companions are being consoled and encouraged. They are also being told how they should face the campaign of opposition and persecution launched by the unbelievers.

In the name of Allah, the Merciful, the Compassionate.

(1) Allah's judgement has (all but) come;[1] do not, then, call for its speedy advent. Holy is He, and far above their associating others with Him in His Divinity.[2] ▶

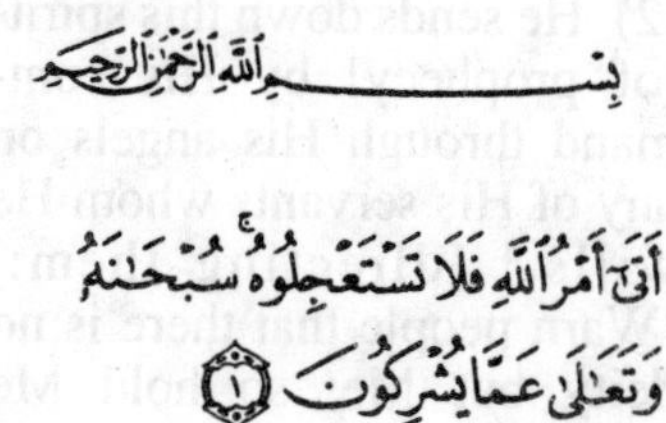

1. This is an emphatic way of saying that God's judgement will become known very soon. The past tense employed for conveying this idea underscores that God's judgement is both imminent and near. Another possible reason for using the past tense may be that the rebelliousness and iniquity of the unbelieving Quraysh had reached its apex and, hence, it was necessary for God to take decisive and final action against them.

This naturally raises the question as to what this 'judgement' was, and what form it took. In our opinion, the 'judgement' refers to Prophet Muḥammad's migration from Makka. This seems to be evident from the fact that soon after the revelation of this *sūrah* he was directed to migrate to Madina.

On studying the Qur'ān, it would appear that a Prophet is asked, as a last resort, to migrate when all his efforts to reform his people have failed, and his people persist in rejection and unbelief. Hence, when a Prophet is to migrate, the fate of his people is sealed. Therefore, either God's scourge smites them, or they are destroyed at the hands of that Prophet and his followers. This is borne out by history. When Prophet Muḥammad (peace be on him) migrated to Madina, the unbelievers assumed that they had won the day. However, within eight to ten years of the Prophet's migration, polytheism and every form of unbelief were wiped out not only from Makka, but also from the whole of the Arabian peninsula.

2. In order to fully understand the link between the two parts of this verse it is necessary to bear in mind its background. The unbelievers often challenged the Prophet (peace be on him) to bring about God's scourge upon them. Implicit in such a statement was the conviction that their religion was the right one, and the religion which Muḥammad (peace be on him) propagated was false and devoid of God's sanction. The pith of their argument was as follows: 'Muhammad (peace be on him) claims that we have deviated from the truth. He also claims to be a Prophet designated by God. If both these statements are true, we should by now have been seized by God's scourge.'

Hence, the proclamation of God's judgement was immediately followed by

(2) He sends down this spirit[3] [of prophecy] by His command through His angels on any of His servants whom He wills,[4] [directing them:] 'Warn people that there is no deity but Me; so hold Me alone in fear.'[5] (3) He created the heavens and the earth with truth. Exalted is He above whatever they associate with Allah in His Divinity.[6]

(4) He created man out of a mere drop of fluid, and lo! he turned into an open wrangler.[7] (5) He created the cattle. They are a source of clothing and food and also a variety of other benefits for you.

يُنَزِّلُ الْمَلَٰٓئِكَةَ بِالرُّوحِ مِنْ أَمْرِهِۦ عَلَىٰ
مَن يَشَآءُ مِنْ عِبَادِهِۦٓ أَنْ أَنذِرُوٓا۟ أَنَّهُۥ
لَآ إِلَٰهَ إِلَّآ أَنَا۠ فَاتَّقُونِ ﴿٢﴾ خَلَقَ
السَّمَٰوَٰتِ وَالْأَرْضَ بِالْحَقِّ
تَعَٰلَىٰ عَمَّا يُشْرِكُونَ ﴿٣﴾
خَلَقَ الْإِنسَٰنَ مِن نُّطْفَةٍ فَإِذَا
هُوَ خَصِيمٌ مُّبِينٌ ﴿٤﴾ وَالْأَنْعَٰمَ
خَلَقَهَا لَكُمْ فِيهَا دِفْءٌ
وَمَنَٰفِعُ وَمِنْهَا تَأْكُلُونَ ﴿٥﴾

clarification that the unbelievers were altogether mistaken about the reason for the delay in the enforcement of that judgement. The delay in punishment did not warrant belief in polytheism. God is holier and far above being One with Whose divinity anyone could be associated.

3. The 'spirit' mentioned here is the spirit of prophecy. The Messenger is infused with it, and it animates all that he says or does. Revelation and the spirit of prophecy have the same significance in man's moral life as does the 'soul' in his physical life. Hence, the Qur'ān has used the term 'spirit' for it. Since the Christians were unable to grasp this, they were led to believe in the Holy Ghost and to make him one of three persons constituting a Trinity.

4. The unbelievers in effect demanded: 'Bring down God's punishment upon us here and now if you can.' This demand was based on their belief that the Prophet's claim to have been designated by God was false. Hence it was not deemed sufficient to refute polytheism. It was also considered necessary to affirm Muḥammad's prophethood. God responded to their statement by saying that it was after being infused with God's spirit that the Prophet (peace be on him) embarked upon his mission.

As to the Qur'ānic statement that 'He sends down this spirit [of prophecy] on any of His servants whom He wills' is a rejoinder to the unbelievers' charge that the Prophet (peace be on him) was false in claiming that he was a Messenger. The unbelievers took strong exception to the choice of Muḥammad (peace be on him), the son of 'Abd Allāh for this divine assignment. How could he be so appointed when there were outstanding scions in the leading families of Makka and Tā'if who, in their view, were much better suited for such a position. This frivolous statement is dismissed at several points in the Qur'ān by asserting that God knows best what He ought to do. He does not stand in need of anyone's advice in deciding whom to entrust with prophethood.

5. This amounts to saying that the message of all those who were granted the spirit of prophecy was one and the same – that only One Being is invested with godhead and He alone deserves to be held in awe. The anchor of man's morality, and the focal point of man's thoughts and actions should be fear of God's displeasure and punishment, and fear of the dire consequences which follow disobedience of Him.

6. This amounts to saying that the rejection of polytheism and the affirmation of monotheism which form the core of all the Prophets' message is attested to by virtually everything that is in the heavens and the earth. For the universe is not a chaotic figment of someone's imagination. It rather represents an ordered existence founded on truth. The universe, therefore, provides no support of polytheism. On the contrary, one can see that there is only One True God at work everywhere. Nothing in the universe points to anyone other than God as its creator. Since the entire system, which is based on an incontrovertible truth, has been working on the principle that God is One, no room is left for associating others with God. Polytheism is nothing more than a conglomeration of fancies and conjectures and is totally devoid of any basis in fact. There are numerous signs in both the physical world and man's own being which provide incontestable testimony in support of God's unity on the one hand, and of the doctrine of prophethood on the other.

7. The Qur'ānic statement affords two possible interpretations. It seems that both are at once correct. The verse states that although God created man from a mere drop of semen, he is quite argumentative and is prone to marshal proofs in support of his view. Another meaning is that although man was created by God from a mere drop of semen, he became so arrogant that he wrangles even with God.

Taken in the first sense, the verse is part of the argument elaborated in the several verses which follow. (We shall turn to their explanation at the end of the present discourse.) In the latter sense, the verse asks man to reflect over his humble origins before wrangling with God and behaving arrogantly. He should call to mind the form in which he was born; the place where he was originally nurtured; the passage through which he made his way to the earth. He should also consider the stages through which he passed before reaching the age of his youth. Does it behove anyone with such origins to be impertinent to God?

(6) And you find beauty in them as you drive them to pasture in the morning and as you drive them back home in the evening; (7) and they carry your loads to many a place which you would be unable to reach without much hardship. Surely your Lord is Much-Loving, Most-Merciful. (8) And He created horses and mules and asses for you to ride, and also for your adornment. And He creates many things (for you) that you do not even know about.[8] (9) It rests with Allah alone to show you the right way, even when there are many crooked ways.[9] Had He so willed, He would have [perforce] guided you all aright.[10]

وَلَكُمْ فِيهَا جَمَالٌ حِينَ تُرِيحُونَ
وَحِينَ تَسْرَحُونَ ﴿٦﴾ وَتَحْمِلُ
أَثْقَالَكُمْ إِلَىٰ بَلَدٍ لَّمْ تَكُونُوا
بَالِغِيهِ إِلَّا بِشِقِّ الْأَنفُسِ ۚ إِنَّ
رَبَّكُمْ لَرَءُوفٌ رَّحِيمٌ ﴿٧﴾ وَالْخَيْلَ
وَالْبِغَالَ وَالْحَمِيرَ لِتَرْكَبُوهَا
وَزِينَةً ۚ وَيَخْلُقُ مَا لَا تَعْلَمُونَ ﴿٨﴾
وَعَلَى اللَّهِ قَصْدُ السَّبِيلِ وَمِنْهَا
جَائِرٌ ۚ وَلَوْ شَاءَ لَهَدَاكُمْ
أَجْمَعِينَ ﴿٩﴾

8. God has yoked many a thing to man's service, making it beneficial to him. Man, however, is not even aware of all these things and the services which they render him.

9. While adducing arguments to establish that God is one, that He is merciful, and that He alone nurtures all, an argument is also subtly adduced in support of the doctrine of prophethood. The argument that has been summarily hinted at is as follows: Logically, there are many ways and man chooses one or the other of them. Obviously, all of these cannot be right. Only one of them can be so, and this will be the one which is consonant with the truth. Likewise, one can choose the course of one's action out of the myriad of paths that have been charted. Now, the only right path of action is the one rooted in the right world-view.

To know the right way that would ensure both sound intellectual orientation and right behaviour is man's greatest need. Obviously man also has other needs, arising out of his animality, even if that animality might be of a higher

(10) He it is Who sends down water for you from the sky out of which you drink and out of which grow the plants on which you pasture your cattle, (11) and by virtue of which He causes crops and olives and date-palms and grapes and all kinds of fruit to grow for you. Surely in this there is a great sign for those who reflect.

هُوَ ٱلَّذِىٓ أَنزَلَ مِنَ ٱلسَّمَآءِ مَآءً
لَّكُم مِّنْهُ شَرَابٌ وَمِنْهُ شَجَرٌ فِيهِ
تُسِيمُونَ ﴿١٠﴾ يُنۢبِتُ لَكُم بِهِ
ٱلزَّرْعَ وَٱلزَّيْتُونَ وَٱلنَّخِيلَ
وَٱلْأَعْنَٰبَ وَمِن كُلِّ ٱلثَّمَرَٰتِ
إِنَّ فِى ذَٰلِكَ لَءَايَةً لِّقَوْمٍ
يَتَفَكَّرُونَ ﴿١١﴾

order than other species. But knowledge of the right way as mentioned above is necessary if man is to fulfil his need *qua* man. If this need remains unfulfilled, it means that man's whole life has been wasted. Now, God's providence is well worth reflecting upon. For, as we know well, God keeps many a provision in readiness for man even before he is born. As for the arrangements that God makes to cater to the requirements of the animal aspects of man's nature, they are both extensive and highly elaborate. Can it even be imagined that a God who cares for man's material needs would have made no arrangements to fulfil the greatest and most fundamental needs of man's humanity?

It is precisely such an arrangement which was made by means of the institution of prophethood. In fact, those who do not believe in prophethood should be able to identify what arrangement was made by God for man's guidance other than prophethood. It is not appropriate for anyone to say, in response to this query, that God has invested man with reason in order that he might find the right way. For, as we know, human reason has discovered several ways. This fact is patent proof of the inadequacy of human reason.

Nor would it be justifiable to say that God has made no arrangements for man's guidance. Such a statement would be an outrageous thing to say about God. For, as we have pointed out earlier, the arrangements made to provide for man's sustenance and growth as an animal are both perfect and elaborate. How can it be conceived, then, that God would take no interest in man's distinctly human requirements and leave him to wander and stumble in darkness? (For further elaboration of this point see *Tafhīm al-Qur'ān, al-Raḥmān* 55, nn. 2–3.)

10. One possible way for God to guide man to the right way was to make him inherently rightly-directed, that is the manner of beings that are devoid of

(12) He has subjected for you the night and the day and the sun and the moon for you, and the stars have also been made subservient by His command. Surely there are signs in this for those who use their reason. (13) And there are also signs for those who take heed in the numerous things of various colours that He has created for you on earth.

(14) And He it is Who has subjected the sea that you may eat fresh fish from it and bring forth ornaments from it that you can wear. And you see ships ploughing their course through it so that you may go forth seeking His bounty[11] and be grateful to Him.

وَسَخَّرَ لَكُمُ ٱلَّيْلَ وَٱلنَّهَارَ
وَٱلشَّمْسَ وَٱلْقَمَرَ وَٱلنُّجُومُ
مُسَخَّرَٰتٌۢ بِأَمْرِهِۦٓ إِنَّ فِى ذَٰلِكَ
لَءَايَٰتٍ لِّقَوْمٍ يَعْقِلُونَ ﴿١٢﴾ وَمَا
ذَرَأَ لَكُمْ فِى ٱلْأَرْضِ مُخْتَلِفًا
أَلْوَٰنُهُۥٓ إِنَّ فِى ذَٰلِكَ لَءَايَةً
لِّقَوْمٍ يَذَّكَّرُونَ ﴿١٣﴾ وَهُوَ
ٱلَّذِى سَخَّرَ ٱلْبَحْرَ لِتَأْكُلُوا۟
مِنْهُ لَحْمًا طَرِيًّا وَتَسْتَخْرِجُوا۟ مِنْهُ
حِلْيَةً تَلْبَسُونَهَا وَتَرَى ٱلْفُلْكَ
مَوَاخِرَ فِيهِ وَلِتَبْتَغُوا۟ مِن
فَضْلِهِۦ وَلَعَلَّكُمْ
تَشْكُرُونَ ﴿١٤﴾

---

all free-will. This, however, was not God's will. He willed that there should come into being a species possessed of free-will and volition, one capable of making its own choice – even the wrong choice.

In order that man might make use of this freedom, he was endowed with the means of acquiring knowledge, with the faculties of reason and thinking, with the potential for will and desire, with the power to use a large number of things both within and outside him. God also created in man's nature and in the world around a number of things which could lead man either to true guidance or to error. All this would have been meaningless had it been decided that man, in terms of his nature, could only follow the true guidance, and that no other option was available to him. Nor would it have been possible for man to reach those heights of spiritual growth which can be reached only by the exercise of free-will.

God, therefore, did not will that men should be compelled to follow only the right way. Instead, God decided to establish the institution of prophethood. It

(15) And He has placed firm mountains[12] on the earth lest it should move away from you, and has made rivers and tracks[13] that you may find your way, (16) and He has set other landmarks[14] in the earth. And by the stars too do people find their way.[15]

وَأَلْقَىٰ فِي ٱلْأَرْضِ رَوَٰسِيَ أَن تَمِيدَ
بِكُمْ وَأَنْهَٰرًا وَسُبُلًا لَّعَلَّكُمْ
تَهْتَدُونَ ﴿١٥﴾ وَعَلَٰمَٰتٍ وَبِٱلنَّجْمِ
هُمْ يَهْتَدُونَ ﴿١٦﴾

was, thus, ensured that man would retain his freedom. At the same time, it was also ensured that the purpose of putting man to the test should also be realized. All this was done side by side with making adequate arrangements for the availability of true guidance to mankind.

11. The expression 'seeking the bounty of your Lord' means earning a living by lawful means.

12. We learn by this that the main advantage of the mountains is to regulate the earth's rotation and the speed of that rotation. That the main function of the mountains is to keep the earth in a stable position has also been emphasized at other points in the Qur'ān. All other advantages are incidental and peripheral. (See Zaghloul R. El-Naggar, *The Geological Concept of Mountains in the Holy Qur'ān* (Herndon, Virginia, 1991) – Ed.)

13. This refers to the natural tracks besides rivers, streams and ravines. These natural tracks are especially useful in mountainous regions, though this does not detract from their importance in the plains.

14. All parts of the earth have not been created alike. Instead, each region has been distinguished by unique landmarks. Of the numerous benefits of these landmarks, the most important is that they help man to identify his path and destination. Man recognizes the true importance of these landmarks especially in desert regions which are largely devoid of them. As a result, he is always in fear of losing his way. More importantly, man also realizes their significance on sea-bound voyages for landmarks are also not evident here and man is always aware that he can stray. Nonetheless, God has arranged for man's guidance even in the desert and on the sea. Since time immemorial man has found his way with the help of the stars.

Here also subtle evidence in support of prophethood is put forward, and in the midst of a discourse focused on reinforcing God's unity and His merciful providence. Reading this verse, one readily realizes that God Who has so meticulously arranged for man's material needs could not have disregarded man's moral needs by failing to provide for his guidance. Obviously, the perils and harm involved in losing one's way in a literal and physical sense bear no connection to losing one's way morally. And yet we know that God, out of His compassion, is so concerned with man's material well-being that He has made a variety of arrangements to prevent him from losing his way. He has made tracks into the mountains. He has created landmarks on the plains. He has provided luminous stars in the sky to enable man to know his direction in both deserts and seas. How can we even conceive that a God Who is so compassionate, so deeply concerned with man's well-being, would have devised no path that would lead man to his salvation? How can we imagine that God would have placed no landmarks to mark out the way leading to man's success? How can we think that He would have provided for no 'illuminating lamp' *(sirāj munīr)* to keep that way always illuminated?

15. Numerous signs in both the universe and man's own being are mentioned in order to drive home the fact that no matter which direction man might look, he will find everything in the universe corroborating the teaching of the Prophet (peace be on him) that God is one and unique and that He alone ought to be served. There is nothing in the universe which lends support to notions of polytheism or atheism.

In this context reference is made to man's own creation. One wonders how a drop of fluid was transformed into a moving, talkative and even wrangling being called man. How a variety of animals were created with their hair, skin, blood, milk, flesh and backs – all in accordance with man's multifarious requirements, including his aesthetic taste. We also see rainfall coming down from the sky. We see how the earth is able to produce every kind of fruit and grain as well as plants that produce fodder. We also notice how the natural phenomena are interrelated, and at the same time, correspond to man's need.

The constant alternation of day and night, the regulated movements of the moon, the sun, and the stars are all closely linked with the production of food and are conducive to man's other interests. Likewise, we observe the seas which provide a great deal that satisfies man's physical and aesthetic requirements. We also find how the vast masses of water have been subjected to a set of laws. Thanks to all this, man is able to boldly steer his way across them from one land to another, voyaging and trading. We also see mountains securely anchored in the earth, raising their heads skyward and realize how immensely useful they are to mankind. Our attention is also drawn to the numerous signs and landmarks all over the universe right from the structure of the earth's surface to the great heights of the heavens and the usefulness of all this for man.

All these provide incontrovertible evidence of the fact that the entire scheme has been planned by One and the same Being. It is He Who has designed

(17) Is then the One Who creates like the one who does not create?[16] Will you not, then, take heed? (18) For, were you to compute the favours of Allah, you will not be able to compute them. Surely Allah is Ever-Forgiving, Most-Merciful.[17] (19) Allah knows all that you conceal and all that you disclose.[18]

أَفَمَن يَخْلُقُ كَمَن لَّا يَخْلُقُ أَفَلَا
تَذَكَّرُونَ ﴿١٧﴾ وَإِن تَعُدُّوا
نِعْمَةَ اللَّهِ لَا تُحْصُوهَا إِنَّ اللَّهَ
لَغَفُورٌ رَّحِيمٌ ﴿١٨﴾ وَاللَّهُ يَعْلَمُ
مَا تُسِرُّونَ وَمَا تُعْلِنُونَ ﴿١٩﴾

---

everything in accordance with His grand scheme, and it is He Who has created them according to that design. It is He Who constantly brings new things into being in such a manner that they are not at all discordant with the total scheme of creation. Again, it is He Who operates and regulates this gigantic system.

One indeed has to be utterly stupid or stubborn to believe that all this is the outcome of a mere accident; or to fancy that the different parts and functions of such a well-ordered universe were created by, or are under the control of a variety of gods.

16. This argument is addressed to polytheists. The polytheists believe – as did the polytheists of Makka and elsewhere – that God alone is the creator of the universe. They also acknowledge that the deities whom they associate with God have created nothing. This being so, how can those who have no share in creation have the same authority as God in the realm of His own creation? How can those who have not created have the same rights as God against His creatures? How can one be led to believe that the power of Him Who creates is the same as the power of those who have not created? Or that the Creator and the created belong to the same species so much so that the relationship between Creator and created might be that of parent and offspring.

17. Much has been left unsaid with regard to the two statements in the above verse. For the message is too obvious to require any further elaboration. It is enough to point out after enumerating the many bounties of God, that He is Ever-Forgiving and Most-Merciful. This statement underscores the fact that man owes God a profound debt of gratitude in view of all His favours. And yet man is prone to be ungrateful, treacherous, faithless, and rebellious towards his Benefactor. But God is forbearing and compassionate in the extreme. Despite

(20) Those whom they call upon beside Allah have created nothing; rather, they themselves were created; (21) they are dead, not living. They do not even know when they will be resurrected.[19]

وَالَّذِينَ يَدْعُونَ مِن دُونِ اللَّهِ لَا يَخْلُقُونَ شَيْئًا وَهُمْ يُخْلَقُونَ ﴿٢٠﴾ أَمْوَاتٌ غَيْرُ أَحْيَاءٍ وَمَا يَشْعُرُونَ أَيَّانَ يُبْعَثُونَ ﴿٢١﴾

---

man's ingratitude God continues to lavish His favours, year after year, on ungrateful individuals, and century after century on nations that are rebellious against Him. There are many who, even though they deny the existence of God, continue to receive God's favours. There are also those who associate others with the Creator in His attributes, authority and rights. They also thank others than the One True God for the benevolence that He alone shows them. All this notwithstanding, they do not cease to receive God's favours. There are also those who verbally recognize God to be the Creator and the Benefactor, and yet remain rebellious and disobedient to Him. Despite this, they continue to enjoy God's bounties and favours in full measure.

18. No one should be so stupid as to believe that if such people continue to receive favours despite their denial of God, despite their polytheistic beliefs and practice, or their disobedience of Him, that this is because God is not aware of man's blasphemous attitude. Nor does this indicate a chaotic state of affairs in God's realm. God's bestowal of bounties on all represents God's forbearance and forgiveness despite the fact that He has full knowledge of not only people's apparent misdeeds, but also of their hidden misdeeds. In fact, God even knows the intentions which lie hidden in men's hearts. This is the kind of generosity and magnanimity which befits only the Lord of the universe.

19. The words of this verse make it quite plain that the false gods whose godhead is being denied and refuted here are not angels or *jinn* or Satan or idols made of wood and stone. Instead, they are human beings who at some stage in the past were consigned to graves. This is so because both angels and devils are alive. Hence the Qur'ānic description of them as those 'who are dead, not living' does not apply to them. Likewise, the statement that 'they do not even know when they will be resurrected' also excludes the images made of wood and stone as objects of worship. Hence, the expression 'those whom they call upon besides Allah' inevitably refers to the people of the past – to Prophets, saints, martyrs, righteous men, and all human beings of extraordinary stature whom their devotees call upon for the fulfilment of their needs. It might be

(22) Your God is the One God. But the hearts of those who do not believe in the Hereafter are steeped in rejection of the truth; and they are given to arrogance.[20] (23) Surely Allah knows all that they conceal and all that they disclose. He certainly does not love those who are steeped in arrogance.

إِلَٰهُكُمْ إِلَٰهٌ وَٰحِدٌ ۚ فَٱلَّذِينَ لَا يُؤْمِنُونَ
بِٱلْءَاخِرَةِ قُلُوبُهُم مُّنكِرَةٌ وَهُم
مُّسْتَكْبِرُونَ ﴿٢٢﴾ لَا جَرَمَ أَنَّ ٱللَّهَ
يَعْلَمُ مَا يُسِرُّونَ وَمَا يُعْلِنُونَ ۚ
إِنَّهُۥ لَا يُحِبُّ ٱلْمُسْتَكْبِرِينَ ﴿٢٣﴾

claimed by some that gods of this genre were not found in pre-Islamic Arabia. Such a statement, in our opinion, only betrays unfamiliarity with the Arabia of that time. It is well known that there were Christians and Jews in Arabia who belonged to the tribes of Rabī'ah, Kalb, Taghlib, Quḍā'ah, Kinānah, Ḥarth, Ka'b and Kindah. It is also well known that they were engrossed in the worship of Prophets, saints and martyrs. Likewise, many of the deities worshipped by the pagan Arabs were in fact human beings who were initially venerated for their goodness. Subsequently, they were turned into deities. There is a report in Bukhārī on the authority of Ibn 'Abbās that Wadd, Suwā', Yaghūth, Ya'ūq and Nasr were all names of virtuous people who were later verified. (See al-Bukhārī, *K. al-Tafsīr, 'Tafsīr sūrah Nūḥ, Bāb . . . Lā Wadd wa lā Suwā' wa lā Yaghūth . . .'* – Ed.) Likewise, there is a tradition from 'Ā'ishah that both Isāf and Nā'ilah were human beings. (Ibn Hishām, *al-Sīrah,* vol. I, p. 82 ff. – Ed.) Similar reports are also found about al-Lāt and al-'Uzzá. It has even been reported that all these were so dear to God that He spent winter with al-Lāt and summer with al-'Uzzá. (This tradition is mentioned in the notes of Ibn Hishām, *Sīrah,* vol. I, p. 226 – Ed.)

20. The denial of the Hereafter has made unbelievers so irresponsible, indifferent and so exceedingly enamoured of this world that they feel no qualms in denying any truth whatsoever. All truths have ceased to have any worth in their eyes. Nor are they willing to put up with any kind of discipline. Moreover, they are not the least interested in finding out whether the way they were following is true or not.

(24) When[21] they are asked: 'What is it that your Lord has revealed?' They answer: 'They are merely tales of olden times!'[22] (25) [They say so] that they may bear the full weight of their burdens on the Day of Resurrection and also of the burdens of those whom they misled on account of their ignorance. What a heavy burden do they bear! (26) Surely many people before them had plotted in a similar manner to [vanquish the truth], but Allah uprooted the whole structure of their plot from its foundations so that the roof fell in upon them, and the chastisement [of Allah] visited them from unknown directions.

وَإِذَا قِيلَ لَهُم مَّاذَآ أَنزَلَ رَبُّكُمْ قَالُوٓا۟
أَسَٰطِيرُ ٱلْأَوَّلِينَ ﴿٢٤﴾ لِيَحْمِلُوٓا۟
أَوْزَارَهُمْ كَامِلَةً يَوْمَ ٱلْقِيَٰمَةِ وَمِنْ
أَوْزَارِ ٱلَّذِينَ يُضِلُّونَهُم بِغَيْرِ عِلْمٍ
أَلَا سَآءَ مَا يَزِرُونَ ﴿٢٥﴾ قَدْ
مَكَرَ ٱلَّذِينَ مِن قَبْلِهِمْ فَأَتَى
ٱللَّهُ بُنْيَٰنَهُم مِّنَ ٱلْقَوَاعِدِ فَخَرَّ
عَلَيْهِمُ ٱلسَّقْفُ مِن فَوْقِهِمْ
وَأَتَىٰهُمُ ٱلْعَذَابُ مِنْ حَيْثُ
لَا يَشْعُرُونَ ﴿٢٦﴾

21. At this point the discourse turns to another theme. The Qur'ān enumerates, one after the other, every single mischief enacted against the Prophet (peace be on him) by the Makkan unbelievers, all the arguments and pleas to which they resorted in the course of their opposition to him, all the pretexts to which they had recourse so as to evade believing in him, and all the objections which they raised against him. After mentioning all this the unbelievers are then admonished, censured and counselled.

22. As the news about the Prophet's call spread all around, people asked the Makkans wherever they went about the Qur'ān and its contents. To this the Makkan unbelievers were wont to reply in a manner that would repel others from the Prophet (peace be on him) and the Qur'ān. They tried to sow the seeds of doubt in people's hearts about the Qur'ān, or at least to develop in them an attitude of aversion towards the Prophet (peace be on him).

(27) And again, on the Day of Resurrection, He will bring them to disgrace, and say: 'Tell Me, now, where are those to whom you ascribed a share in My Divinity, and for whose sake you disputed [with the upholders of the truth]?' Those who were endowed with knowledge[23] [in the world] will say: 'Surely today humiliation and misery shall be the lot of the unbelievers'; (28) The same believers[24] who, when the angels seize them[25] and cause them to die while they are engaged in wronging, they will proffer their submission saying: 'We were engaged in no evil.' [The angels answer them:] 'Surely Allah knows well all that you did. (29) Go now, and enter the gate of Hell, and abide in it for ever.'[26] Evil indeed is the abode of the arrogant.

ثُمَّ يَوْمَ الْقِيَامَةِ يُخْزِيهِمْ وَيَقُولُ أَيْنَ
شُرَكَائِيَ الَّذِينَ كُنتُمْ
تُشَاقُّونَ فِيهِمْ قَالَ الَّذِينَ أُوتُوا
الْعِلْمَ إِنَّ الْخِزْيَ الْيَوْمَ وَالسُّوءَ عَلَى
الْكَافِرِينَ ﴿٢٧﴾ الَّذِينَ تَتَوَفَّاهُمُ
الْمَلَائِكَةُ ظَالِمِي أَنفُسِهِمْ فَأَلْقَوُا
السَّلَمَ مَا كُنَّا نَعْمَلُ مِن سُوءٍ بَلَىٰ
إِنَّ اللَّهَ عَلِيمٌ بِمَا كُنتُمْ تَعْمَلُونَ ﴿٢٨﴾
فَادْخُلُوا أَبْوَابَ جَهَنَّمَ خَالِدِينَ
فِيهَا فَلَبِئْسَ مَثْوَى الْمُتَكَبِّرِينَ ﴿٢٩﴾

---

23. There is a subtle gap between the answer and the preceding question. The reader is left to fill this gap with a little reflection. God will ask: 'Tell Me, now where are those of whom you ascribe a share in My divinity and for whose sake you disputed [with the upholders of the truth]?' This will leave all unbelievers and polytheists dumbfounded. Then a conversation will take place among those endowed with knowledge. That conversation is alluded to here.

24. This is what God, Himself, will say in addition to what was said by 'people endowed with knowledge'. What God says is by way of further explanation. Some commentators of the Qur'ān consider this to be a part of the statement by 'people endowed with knowledge'. Scholars who took this view,

however, had to resort to far-fetched explanations, and despite all their efforts, their statements remain unpersuasive.

25. That is, when angels seize their souls at the time of death.

26. This and the following verse which mention the conversation between the righteous and the angels after the latter have seized the souls, are among several verses in the Qur'ān which prove beyond doubt that people will be both rewarded and punished in the grave.

In the *Ḥadīth* the expression *qabr* is used metaphorically for *barzakh*, for the state in which men's souls will remain starting from the last moment of earthly life until their resurrection in the Hereafter. Those who reject the *Ḥadīth* consider it to be a period of non-existence, a period when men will be devoid of any feeling or perception, and during which men will receive neither reward nor punishment. However, in light of the above verse, it is clear that when the souls of the unbelievers are seized, they find the new world beyond the present one totally at odds with their expectations. Hence, they try to deceive the angels and plead their innocence. In response, however, the angels rebuke them and tell them that they are destined for Hell. When the souls of the righteous are seized, however, the angels welcome them and felicitate them in advance for their being destined for Paradise. Is it necessary, then, to look for any further evidence to prove that people will have life, feeling, consciousness, reward and punishment in the state known as *barzakh*?

A statement similar to the one made here occurs in *al-Nisā'* (4: 97) which recounts the conversation between the angels and those Muslims who had failed to migrate in the cause of God. The most unambiguous statement of punishment is made in *al-Mu'min* (40: 45–6). Regarding Pharaoh and his people, God says: '. . . but the brunt of the punishment encompassed the people of Pharaoh on all sides. They are exposed to the Fire, morning and evening, and when the Day of Judgement will arrive, the sentence will be issued: ''Cast the people of Pharaoh into the severest punishment''.'

The portrayal of the intervening period between man's death and the Day of Resurrection in the Qur'ān and the *Ḥadīth* is identical. Death is merely separation of the soul from the body. It does not signify the annihilation of the soul. Also, after separation from the body, and unlike it, the soul does not suffer decomposition. It rather exists along with the personality shaped by its experience during earthly life and by its mental and moral attainments. Consciousness, feeling, observation and experience of the soul in this state resembles that of a dream. The interrogation of a convict's soul, its experience of punishment and torture, and its exposure to Hell are similar to the nightmare which a murderer experiences before his execution. Likewise, the reception accorded to the soul of a righteous person, the glad tidings about its entry into Paradise, and its experience of the breeze and fragrance of Paradise are similar to the sweet dreams of the official who sees in them that he has been summoned to receive a great award in recognition of his excellent performance.

All dreams come to an end with the blowing of the Trumpet for the

(30) And when the God-fearing are asked: 'What has your Lord revealed?' – they answer: 'Something excellent!'[27] Thus good fortune in this world awaits those who do good; and certainly the abode of the Hereafter is even better for them. How excellent is the abode of the God-fearing: (31) everlasting gardens that they shall enter; the gardens beneath which rivers shall flow, and where everything shall be as they desire.[28] Thus does Allah reward the God-fearing; (32) those whose souls the angels seize while they are in a state of purity, saying: 'Peace be upon you. Enter Paradise as a reward for your deeds.'

۞ وَقِيلَ لِلَّذِينَ ٱتَّقَوْا۟ مَاذَآ أَنزَلَ
رَبُّكُمْ ۚ قَالُوا۟ خَيْرًا ۗ لِّلَّذِينَ أَحْسَنُوا۟ فِى
هَـٰذِهِ ٱلدُّنْيَا حَسَنَةٌ ۚ وَلَدَارُ ٱلْـَٔاخِرَةِ
خَيْرٌ ۚ وَلَنِعْمَ دَارُ ٱلْمُتَّقِينَ ﴿٣٠﴾ جَنَّـٰتُ
عَدْنٍ يَدْخُلُونَهَا تَجْرِى مِن تَحْتِهَا
ٱلْأَنْهَـٰرُ ۖ لَهُمْ فِيهَا مَا يَشَآءُونَ ۚ
كَذَٰلِكَ يَجْزِى ٱللَّهُ ٱلْمُتَّقِينَ ﴿٣١﴾
ٱلَّذِينَ تَتَوَفَّىٰهُمُ ٱلْمَلَـٰٓئِكَةُ طَيِّبِينَ ۙ
يَقُولُونَ سَلَـٰمٌ عَلَيْكُمُ ٱدْخُلُوا۟
ٱلْجَنَّةَ بِمَا كُنتُمْ تَعْمَلُونَ ﴿٣٢﴾

Resurrection and the evil-doers will suddenly find themselves alive both in body and soul. In utter surprise they will exclaim: 'Ah! Woe unto us! (*Yā Sīn* 36: 52). The righteous, however, will say with full conviction: 'This is what Allah, Most Gracious, had promised; and true was the word of the Messengers' (*Yā Sīn* 36: 52). The immediate reaction of the evil-doers will be as if they had been asleep in their beds for an hour or so. They will find themselves awakened and will run for their lives. However, the believers' reaction will be marked by firm conviction. They will say: 'Indeed you did tarry, within Allah's decree, to the Day of Resurrection, and this is the Day of Resurrection; but you were not aware!' (*al-Rūm* 30: 56).

27. The reply of the God-fearing and the righteous to the queries of people outside Makka concerning the Prophet (peace be on him) and his teachings is radically different from that of the unbelievers who lied. What distinguishes the former is that they do not engage in false propaganda. Nor do they try to deceive or confuse people. They simply express their appreciation of the

(33) (O Muḥammad!) Are they waiting for anything else than that the angels should appear before them, or that your Lord's judgement should come.[29] Many before them acted with similar temerity. And then what happened with them was not Allah's wrong-doing; they rather wronged themselves. (34) The evil consequences of their misdeeds overtook them and what they mocked at overwhelmed them.

هَلْ يَنظُرُونَ إِلَّآ أَن تَأْتِيَهُمُ ٱلْمَلَٰٓئِكَةُ
أَوْ يَأْتِىَ أَمْرُ رَبِّكَ ۚ كَذَٰلِكَ فَعَلَ ٱلَّذِينَ مِن
قَبْلِهِمْ ۚ وَمَا ظَلَمَهُمُ ٱللَّهُ وَلَٰكِن
كَانُوٓا۟ أَنفُسَهُمْ يَظْلِمُونَ ﴿٣٣﴾
فَأَصَابَهُمْ سَيِّـَٔاتُ مَا عَمِلُوا۟ وَحَاقَ
بِهِم مَّا كَانُوا۟ بِهِۦ يَسْتَهْزِءُونَ ﴿٣٤﴾

Prophet (peace be on him) and his message, and apprise people of the facts as they are.

28. This succinctly expresses what Paradise will be like. Its basic characteristic is that man will be able to have what he wishes. Nothing will happen in it which is opposed to his desire and liking. It is obvious that no matter how resourceful any person may be in this world, he can never enjoy a similar privilege. Hence, every inmate of Paradise will attain the zenith of joy and satisfaction insofar as everything will happen as he desires. All his yearnings will be satisfied. All his dreams will come true.

29. This is said by way of advice as well as warning. For as far as explaining truths is concerned, the Prophet (peace be on him) carried out that task quite adequately. He did not fail to reinforce his discourse with persuasive arguments. He also adduced every possible evidence drawn from the phenomena of the universe in support of his message. In short, he left no room for any reasonable person to persist in polytheism. What is it, then, that prevents the unbelievers from accepting an obvious truth? Are they waiting for the angel of death to approach them such that they embrace the true faith with their last breath? Will they see reason only after they have experienced the first blow of God's punishment?

(35) Those who associate others with Allah in His divinity say: 'Were Allah to will so, neither we nor our forefathers would have worshipped any other than Him, nor would we have prohibited anything without His command.'[30] Their predecessors proffered similar excuses.[31] Do the Messengers have any other duty but to plainly convey the Message? (36) We raised a Messenger in every community (to tell them): 'Serve Allah and shun the Evil One.'[32]

وَقَالَ ٱلَّذِينَ أَشۡرَكُواْ لَوۡ شَآءَ ٱللَّهُ
مَا عَبَدۡنَا مِن دُونِهِۦ مِن شَيۡءٖ
نَّحۡنُ وَلَآ ءَابَآؤُنَا وَلَا حَرَّمۡنَا مِن
دُونِهِۦ مِن شَيۡءٖۚ كَذَٰلِكَ فَعَلَ ٱلَّذِينَ
مِن قَبۡلِهِمۡۚ فَهَلۡ عَلَى ٱلرُّسُلِ إِلَّا ٱلۡبَلَٰغُ
ٱلۡمُبِينُ ٣٥ وَلَقَدۡ بَعَثۡنَا فِي
كُلِّ أُمَّةٖ رَّسُولًا أَنِ ٱعۡبُدُواْ
ٱللَّهَ وَٱجۡتَنِبُواْ ٱلطَّٰغُوتَۖ

---

30. The whole argument of the polytheists was mentioned in *al-An'ām* 6: 148–9, and then it was refuted. (For an appreciation of the matter see *Towards Understanding the Qur'ān,* vol. II, *al-An'ām* 6: 148–9, and nn. 124–6, pp. 287–9.)

31. There is nothing new in the argument that if anyone falls into error or evil it was because of God's will. This pretext has always been made use of by evil-doers in order to deceive their conscience and silence the well-wishers who admonish them.

What is being said here is the first rejoinder to the point made by the polytheists. In order to have a deeper understanding of this, it is worth recalling that in the preceding verses the polytheists dismissed the Qur'ān as 'merely the tale of olden times'. In other words, they argued that the Prophet (peace be on him) was merely relating what had already been said thousands of times since olden days. Here these detractors are being told that they themselves have come up with nothing new. Their present plea is itself a repetition of what people had been saying over and over again since ancient times.

32. It is not apt for polytheists to hold God's will to be responsible for their evil deeds, and for not honouring God's directives in respect of what is lawful and what is unlawful. Their plea is unjustified as God has raised His Messengers in every community. Each of these Messengers informed his people that they should serve only the One True God; that they had not been created to serve *Ṭāghūt*. Thus, human beings had already been adequately

Thereafter Allah guided some of them while others were overtaken by error.[33] Go about the earth, then, and observe what was the end of those who rejected the Messengers, calling them liars.[34] (37) (O Muḥammad!) Howsoever eager you may be to show them the right way, Allah does not bestow His guidance on those whom He lets go astray; and in fact none will be able to help them.

فَمِنْهُم مَّنْ هَدَى ٱللَّهُ وَمِنْهُم مَّنْ
حَقَّتْ عَلَيْهِ ٱلضَّلَٰلَةُ فَسِيرُوا۟ فِى
ٱلْأَرْضِ فَٱنظُرُوا۟ كَيْفَ كَانَ
عَٰقِبَةُ ٱلْمُكَذِّبِينَ ﴿٣٦﴾ إِن
تَحْرِصْ عَلَىٰ هُدَىٰهُمْ فَإِنَّ ٱللَّهَ
لَا يَهْدِى مَن يُضِلُّ وَمَا لَهُم
مِّن نَّٰصِرِينَ ﴿٣٧﴾

informed that God does not approve their falling into doctrinal error or committing evil deeds. The plea that if God had willed it so, they would not have fallen into error, does not, therefore, hold water. What it amounts to is that they wanted God not to send Messengers who would teach and explain but rather send those who would forcefully put them off the wrong way and compel them to follow the right way. (In order to appreciate the distinction between God's will and God's good pleasure see *Towards Understanding the Qur'ān,* vol. II, *al-An'ām* 6, n. 80, pp. 266–7 and *Tafhīm al-Qur'ān, al-Zumar* 39, n. 20.)

33. Whenever a Messenger came, his people were split into two groups. One group consisted of those who accepted his teachings (and this was possible only because of God's succour). The other group was made up of those who clung to their inherited error. (For further elaboration see *Towards Understanding the Qur'ān,* vol. II, *al-An'ām* 6, n. 28, p. 231.)

34. Experience is the best criterion for knowing what is true. If this view is correct, then it is easy for man to realize what is proved by the cumulative record of man's past. Who was the victim of God's wrath: Pharaoh and his people or Moses and the Israelites? Did God's punishment strike Ṣāliḥ and his followers or those who rejected him, calling him a liar? Did it befall Hūd, Noah and other Messengers and their followers or those who rejected their call? Do the events of the past justify the conclusion that those persons who, thanks to God's will, commit polytheism and develop the criterion to distinguish between lawful and unlawful independent of God's guidance, enjoy God's

(38) They swear most solemnly in the name of Allah and say: 'Allah shall not raise to life any who dies.' [He will certainly raise men to life for] that is a promise by which He is bound, even though most men do not know that. (39) [That is bound to happen in order that] He may make clear to them the reality regarding the matters on which they differ and that the unbelievers may realize that they were liars.[35] (40) [As for the possibility of resurrection bear in mind that] whenever We do will something, We have to do no more than say: 'Be', and it is.[36]

وَأَقْسَمُوا بِاللَّهِ جَهْدَ أَيْمَانِهِمْ
لَا يَبْعَثُ اللَّهُ مَنْ يَمُوتُ بَلَىٰ وَعْدًا
عَلَيْهِ حَقًّا وَلَٰكِنَّ أَكْثَرَ النَّاسِ
لَا يَعْلَمُونَ ﴿٣٨﴾ لِيُبَيِّنَ لَهُمُ الَّذِي
يَخْتَلِفُونَ فِيهِ وَلِيَعْلَمَ الَّذِينَ كَفَرُوا
أَنَّهُمْ كَانُوا كَاذِبِينَ ﴿٣٩﴾ إِنَّمَا
قَوْلُنَا لِشَيْءٍ إِذَا أَرَدْنَاهُ أَنْ نَقُولَ
لَهُ كُنْ فَيَكُونُ ﴿٤٠﴾

---

approval and good pleasure? On the contrary, facts clearly prove that those who cling to error despite counsel and admonition, are allowed to commit guilt to a point, but when they go too far in their defiance, they are altogether destroyed by God.

35. This shows that both rational and moral considerations require that Resurrection and Final Judgement ought to take place. This is necessary because from the outset of man's existence, there have been countless differences among human beings about what constitutes the truth. These differences have led to division within races, nations and families. They have also given rise to different creeds, cultures and societies based on a diversity of views. Millions of people have had such strong feelings about their religious doctrines that they have staked their lives, wealth, honour and everything else that they value so as to defend and promote them. On numerous occasions, fierce conflicts have broken out between the adherents of different religious views, each religious group doing its best to destroy the others completely. Yet those who were vanquished or obliterated, refused to give up their religious positions. Reason demands that, at least at some point, man should be in a position to know for sure the extent to which each of the doctrines was true or

(41) As for those who have forsaken their homes for the sake of Allah after enduring persecution, We shall certainly grant them a good abode in this world; and surely the reward of the Hereafter is much greater.[37] If they could but know [what an excellent end awaits] (42) those who remain steadfast and put their trust in their Lord.

وَالَّذِينَ هَاجَرُوا فِي اللَّهِ مِنْ بَعْدِ مَا
ظُلِمُوا لَنُبَوِّئَنَّهُمْ فِي الدُّنْيَا حَسَنَةً
وَلَأَجْرُ الْآخِرَةِ أَكْبَرُ لَوْ كَانُوا
يَعْلَمُونَ ﴿٤١﴾ الَّذِينَ صَبَرُوا وَعَلَىٰ
رَبِّهِمْ يَتَوَكَّلُونَ ﴿٤٢﴾

---

false; to know who are the people who followed the right way and who deviated from it. It seems impossible that the truth will ever become indisputably clear to all in the present world. Hence, there has to be another life to fulfil this human requirement.

Life-after-Death, however, is not only a requirement of reason. It is also a moral requirement. A great many people have been party to the differences mentioned earlier. Some of them were oppressors and wrong-doers while others were victims of oppression and wrong-doing. Some people made sacrifices while others subjected them to these sacrifices. In addition, everyone adopted according to his lights, a moral philosophy and attitude which affects – for good or bad – the lives of billions, even trillions of other human beings. Now, a time must come when the moral consequences of these attitudes should be visible in the form of reward or punishment. If the present world is not so constituted that the true and full moral consequences of man's actions can become apparent, then there must be another world to ensure that this is so.

36. The unbelievers assume that the resurrection all at one time of all human beings who ever lived in the world will be exceedingly difficult. They obviously do not bear in mind the extent of God's power. For God does not require, in order to carry out whatever He wills, any of the resources that are ordinarily needed. All that the implementation of any act requires is His command. If He commands, all the resources are instantly provided and the conditions for the implementation of God's intended act are created forthwith. It ought to be remembered that the present world also came to be merely because God so willed. And were He to so will, another world can instantly come into existence merely by virtue of His command.

(43) (O Muḥammad!) Whenever We raised any Messengers before you, they were no more than human beings; [except that] to them We sent revelation.[38] So ask those who possess knowledge if you do not know.[39] (44) We raised earlier Messengers with clear signs and Divine Books, and We have now sent down this Reminder upon you that you may elucidate to people the teaching that has been sent down for them,[40] and that the people may themselves reflect.

وَمَآ أَرْسَلْنَا مِن قَبْلِكَ إِلَّا رِجَالًا
نُّوحِىٓ إِلَيْهِمْ فَسْـَٔلُوٓا أَهْلَ ٱلذِّكْرِ
إِن كُنتُمْ لَا تَعْلَمُونَ ﴿٤٣﴾ بِٱلْبَيِّنَٰتِ
وَٱلزُّبُرِ وَأَنزَلْنَآ إِلَيْكَ ٱلذِّكْرَ
لِتُبَيِّنَ لِلنَّاسِ مَا نُزِّلَ إِلَيْهِمْ وَلَعَلَّهُمْ
يَتَفَكَّرُونَ ﴿٤٤﴾

37. This is an allusion to those who migrated to Abyssinia under the pressure of persecution from the Makkan unbelievers; this persecution had assumed unbearable proportions. The mention of the *Muhājirūn* following the rejoinder to those who denied the Hereafter is done with a special purpose. It is to warn the Makkan unbelievers that after having perpetrated all kinds of cruelties, there is no reason for them to entertain the illusion that they would go unpunished, and that the grievances of the oppressed would never be redressed.

38. Here an objection of the unbelievers is refuted without making explicit mention of it. The same objection had been made in the past against other Prophets, and the contemporaries of the Prophet (peace be on him) also often gave vent to it. The objection consisted of pleading that a Prophet is no more than any other human being. How could they, then, accept him to be God's Messenger?

(45) Do those who have been devising evil plans [against the mission of the Messenger] feel secure that Allah will not cause the earth to swallow them up or that chastisement will not come upon them from a direction that they will not even be able to imagine; (46) or that He will not suddenly seize them while they are going about to and fro and they will be unable to frustrate His design, (47) or that He will not seize them when they are apprehensive of the impending calamity? Surely your Lord is Most-Compassionate, Most-Merciful.

أَفَأَمِنَ ٱلَّذِينَ مَكَرُواْ ٱلسَّيِّـَٔاتِ أَن
يَخْسِفَ ٱللَّهُ بِهِمُ ٱلْأَرْضَ أَوْ يَأْتِيَهُمُ
ٱلْعَذَابُ مِنْ حَيْثُ لَا يَشْعُرُونَ
﴿٤٥﴾ أَوْ يَأْخُذَهُمْ فِى تَقَلُّبِهِمْ فَمَا
هُم بِمُعْجِزِينَ ﴿٤٦﴾ أَوْ يَأْخُذَهُمْ عَلَىٰ
تَخَوُّفٍ فَإِنَّ رَبَّكُمْ لَرَءُوفٌ
رَّحِيمٌ ﴿٤٧﴾

39. They are directed to ask the religious scholars of the People of the Book, and all those knowledgeable persons acquainted with the teachings of the scriptures and the history of previous Prophets.

40. The Prophet (peace be on him) is instructed to elucidate the teachings embodied in the Qur'ān – the 'Admonition'. He is required to elucidate those teachings not merely by word of mouth. He is also required to do so by his conduct, by establishing a full-fledged Islamic society under his supervision, and by establishing and operating a whole order of human life in consonance with that 'Admonition'.

Thus, God explains the wisdom underlying the choice of human beings to serve as God's Messengers. As for 'Admonition' *(al-dhikr)*, it could have been sent through angels. It could also have been distributed on a mass scale among human beings in the form of a printed work. This would not, however, have fulfilled God's purpose, Who, in His wisdom and compassion, willed that the Qur'ān be revealed for man's guidance. That purpose could be best realized by having it communicated to mankind through someone who would be the best specimen of humanity. The Book of God was revealed to the Prophet (peace be on him) in fragments so that he might communicate it to the people gradually. While so doing he should explain any aspect of the Book to people which might be incomprehensible to them. He should also remove the doubts of those who had any, disabuse their minds of misconceptions, and answer the objections of those who might have misgivings or objections.

It was also quite obvious that many would not believe in the Book of God, and that they would always oppose and resist it. The Messenger (peace be on him) was required to deal with such people in a manner that befits the bearers of such an exalted Book. As for those who decide to believe in it, it was required by the Prophet (peace be on him) to provide them with directives relating to every aspect of their lives, and to present before them a shining embodiment of these directives through his own life. He is also required to train his followers – both on an individual and a collective level – in order that an ideal human society comes into being; the kind of society which translates into practice the ideals of social order in consonance with the purposes which the Qur'ān seeks to achieve.

This verse furnishes a weighty argument against those who do not believe that human beings can serve as God's message-bearers. Likewise, it refutes the standpoint of those who reject the *Ḥadīth* and seek to derive guidance from the Book of God alone without considering it necessary to be guided by the elucidation and elaboration of the Book by the Prophet (peace be on him). Such people take a variety of positions. One of these is that the Prophet (peace be on him) did not elucidate the Book. His task was simply confined to delivering it to people. Some of them take the position that what people are bound by is the Book of God, but not its elucidation by the Prophet (peace be on him). Others are of the view that the Book is sufficient to guide people and its elucidation was, therefore, unnecessary. They also argue that only the Qur'ān is proved to be extant in an authentic form, and that the Prophet's true elucidation of it is either no longer extant or at least is not found in any trustworthy form. Regardless of which of these positions they may take, each one of them comes into sharp conflict with the verse in question.

Let us take the first position, viz. that the Prophet (peace be on him) did not elucidate the Qur'ān and confined his efforts merely to presenting the text of the Book. This view destroys the very purpose of revealing the Book to the Prophet instead of having it sent to people either directly or via angels.

Let us now consider the second option: that men should obtain guidance only from the Book of God but not from the Prophet's elucidation of it. This reflects poorly on the institution of Messengers established by God. For if this supposition was sound, the Book might as well have been sent directly to human beings without the intermediation of His Messengers.

As for those who regard the Prophet's elucidation as untrustworthy, this amounts to an annulment of the Qur'ān as well as of the prophethood of Muḥammad (peace be on him). In fact, were we to follow this assumption, it would require acceptance of a new Prophet and a new revelation. For in this verse, God describes the Prophet (peace be on him) as indispensable for

(48) Do the people not see how the objects Allah has created cast their shadows right and left prostrating themselves in utter submission to Allah?[41] (49) All living creatures and all angels in the heavens and on the earth are in prostration before Allah;[42] and never do they behave in arrogant defiance. (50) They hold their Lord, Who is above them, in fear, and do as they are bidden.

أَوَلَمْ يَرَوْا إِلَىٰ مَا خَلَقَ ٱللَّهُ مِن شَيْءٍ
يَتَفَيَّؤُا ظِلَٰلُهُۥ عَنِ ٱلْيَمِينِ
وَٱلشَّمَآئِلِ سُجَّدًا لِّلَّهِ وَهُمْ دَٰخِرُونَ ﴿٤٨﴾
وَلِلَّهِ يَسْجُدُ مَا فِي ٱلسَّمَٰوَٰتِ
وَمَا فِي ٱلْأَرْضِ مِن دَآبَّةٍ
وَٱلْمَلَٰٓئِكَةُ وَهُمْ لَا يَسْتَكْبِرُونَ ﴿٤٩﴾
يَخَافُونَ رَبَّهُم مِّن فَوْقِهِمْ
وَيَفْعَلُونَ مَا يُؤْمَرُونَ ﴿٥٠﴾

elucidating the Book, emphasizing that a Messenger is necessary to explain the intent of the Qur'ān.

Now, we come to those who reject the *Ḥadīth* on the grounds that the Prophet's explanation and elucidation can no longer be found in the world. This inevitably leads to two conclusions. First, that the ideal character of the Prophet (peace be on him) is no longer available to mankind for emulation. Thus, for all practical purposes, our relationship with Muḥammad (peace be on him) is similar to that with the Prophets of the past such as Hūd, Ṣāliḥ, and Shu'ayb (peace be on them). For we believe in them but do not consider them models to be emulated in our own lives for the simple and obvious reason that we lack reliable information about them. If we were to hold the same view about the Prophet (peace be on him), this necessarily calls for the advent of a new Messenger. For if that is the case, only a fool would still insist that Muḥammad (peace be on him) is the final Messenger. The second conclusion to which this line of thinking leads is that the Qur'ān has become incapable of guiding mankind. This is so because the Qur'ān itself declares that without the elucidation of its teachings by the Prophet (peace be on him), it, in itself, does not suffice for man's guidance. Hence, once it is accepted that the elucidation of the Qur'ān does not exist in a trustworthy form, the need for a new revelation and the advent of a new Messenger is automatically established. Those who deny the *Hadīth* are, therefore, undermining the very foundations of Islam.

41. The shadow of every physical object, be it a mountain or tree or animal or human being, testifies to the fact that everything is subject to a universal law.

(51) Allah has commanded: 'Do not take two gods;[43] for He is but One God. So fear Me alone.' (52) His is whatever is in the heavens and on the earth, and obedience to Him inevitably pervades the whole universe.[44] Will you, then, hold in awe any other than Allah?[45]

(53) Every bounty that you enjoy is from Allah; and whenever any misfortune strikes you, it is to Him that you cry for the removal of your distress.[46] (54) But as soon as He removes the distress from you, some of you associate others with their Lord in giving thanks,[47] (55) that they may show ingratitude for the bounties We bestowed upon them. So enjoy yourselves for a while, soon you will come to know (the truth).

۞ وَقَالَ اللَّهُ لَا تَتَّخِذُوا إِلَٰهَيْنِ اثْنَيْنِ
إِنَّمَا هُوَ إِلَٰهٌ وَاحِدٌ فَإِيَّايَ فَارْهَبُونِ ﴿٥١﴾
وَلَهُ مَا فِي السَّمَاوَاتِ وَالْأَرْضِ وَلَهُ الدِّينُ
وَاصِبًا أَفَغَيْرَ اللَّهِ تَتَّقُونَ ﴿٥٢﴾ وَمَا بِكُم
مِّن نِّعْمَةٍ فَمِنَ اللَّهِ ثُمَّ إِذَا مَسَّكُمُ
الضُّرُّ فَإِلَيْهِ تَجْأَرُونَ ﴿٥٣﴾ ثُمَّ إِذَا
كَشَفَ الضُّرَّ عَنكُمْ إِذَا فَرِيقٌ مِّنكُم
بِرَبِّهِمْ يُشْرِكُونَ ﴿٥٤﴾ لِيَكْفُرُوا بِمَا
آتَيْنَاهُمْ فَتَمَتَّعُوا فَسَوْفَ تَعْلَمُونَ ﴿٥٥﴾

All are characterized by subservience to the Lord of the universe and none has any share of His divinity. That something casts a shadow indicates its materiality. And materiality, in turn, is a proof of its being a creature bound in servitude to God.

42. Apart from terrestrial beings, even heavenly beings which have been mistakenly conceived since time immemorial for gods, goddesses and kith and kin of God, are in fact beings in bondage to God. None has any share of His divinity at all.

Incidentally, the above verse also alludes to the fact that living beings are not special to the earth, but are also found on other planets. The same point has been made in *al-Shūrá* (42: 29).

(56) They set apart for those, whose reality they do not even know,[48] a portion of the sustenance We have provided them.[49] By Allah, you will surely be called to account for the lies that you have invented!

(57) They assign daughters to Allah[50] – glory to Him – whereas they assign to themselves what they truly desire![51] (58) When any of them is told about the birth of a female his face turns dark, and he is filled with suppressed anger, (59) and he hides himself from people because of the bad news, thinking: should he keep the child despite disgrace, or should he bury it in dust? How evil is their estimate of Allah.[52] (60) Those who do not believe in the Hereafter deserve to be characterized with evil attributes whereas Allah's are the most excellent attributes. He is the Most-Mighty, the Most-Wise.

وَيَجْعَلُونَ لِمَا لَا يَعْلَمُونَ نَصِيبًا مِّمَّا
رَزَقْنَٰهُمْ تَٱللَّهِ لَتُسْـَٔلُنَّ عَمَّا كُنتُمْ
تَفْتَرُونَ ﴿٥٦﴾ وَيَجْعَلُونَ لِلَّهِ ٱلْبَنَٰتِ
سُبْحَٰنَهُۥ وَلَهُم مَّا يَشْتَهُونَ ﴿٥٧﴾
وَإِذَا بُشِّرَ أَحَدُهُم بِٱلْأُنثَىٰ ظَلَّ
وَجْهُهُۥ مُسْوَدًّا وَهُوَ كَظِيمٌ ﴿٥٨﴾
يَتَوَٰرَىٰ مِنَ ٱلْقَوْمِ مِن سُوٓءِ مَا بُشِّرَ بِهِۦٓ
أَيُمْسِكُهُۥ عَلَىٰ هُونٍ أَمْ يَدُسُّهُۥ فِى
ٱلتُّرَابِ أَلَا سَآءَ مَا يَحْكُمُونَ ﴿٥٩﴾
لِلَّذِينَ لَا يُؤْمِنُونَ بِٱلْءَاخِرَةِ مَثَلُ
ٱلسَّوْءِ وَلِلَّهِ ٱلْمَثَلُ ٱلْأَعْلَىٰ وَهُوَ
ٱلْعَزِيزُ ٱلْحَكِيمُ ﴿٦٠﴾

43. The negation of two gods naturally includes the negation of more than two gods.

44. In other words, obedience to God is the axis around which the whole system of the universe revolves.

45. People are asked whether fear of any being other than the One True God, and desire to escape His wrath constitute an appropriate basis for man's life?

(61) Were Allah to take people to task for their wrong-doing, He would not have spared even a single living creature on the face of the earth. But He grants them respite until an appointed term. And when that term arrives, they have no power to delay it by a single moment, nor to hasten it. (62) They assign to Allah what they dislike for themselves and their tongues utter a sheer lie in stating that a happy state awaits them. Without doubt the Fire awaits them and it is to it that they shall be hastened.

وَلَوْ يُؤَاخِذُ ٱللَّهُ ٱلنَّاسَ بِظُلْمِهِم
مَّا تَرَكَ عَلَيْهَا مِن دَآبَّةٍ وَلَٰكِن
يُؤَخِّرُهُمْ إِلَىٰٓ أَجَلٍ مُّسَمًّى فَإِذَا
جَآءَ أَجَلُهُمْ لَا يَسْتَـْٔخِرُونَ
سَاعَةً وَلَا يَسْتَقْدِمُونَ ﴿٦١﴾
وَيَجْعَلُونَ لِلَّهِ مَا يَكْرَهُونَ
وَتَصِفُ أَلْسِنَتُهُمُ ٱلْكَذِبَ
أَنَّ لَهُمُ ٱلْحُسْنَىٰ لَا جَرَمَ أَنَّ
لَهُمُ ٱلنَّارَ وَأَنَّهُم مُّفْرَطُونَ ﴿٦٢﴾

---

46. The fact that man instantly turns to God alone in moments of distress is a clear testimony embedded in man's own being. When faced with a serious crisis, all false notions woven by human fancies are shattered, and the true nature of man comes forward. This is the nature which knows none other than the One True God to be the true deity, the lord, the all-powerful master! (For further explanation see *Towards Understanding the Qur'ān,* vol. II, *al-An'ām* 6, nn. 29 and 41, pp. 231–3 and 239–40, and *Yūnus* 10, n. 31 above.)

47. Once the crisis is over, men are wont to join others – saints, gods and goddesses – with God in giving thanks and making offerings and sacrifices. By so doing, they are saying that in addition to God there are also others who had a hand in the kindness shown by God. The fact is that they believe that had these beings not been kind to them and had they not urged God to kindness, He would not have shown them any kindness.

(63) By Allah (O Muhammad!) We sent Messengers to other communities before you but Satan made their evil deeds attractive to them [so they paid no heed to the call of the Messengers]. The same Satan is their patron to-day and they are heading towards a painful chastisement. ▶

تَاللَّهِ لَقَدْ أَرْسَلْنَا إِلَىٰ أُمَمٍ مِّن قَبْلِكَ فَزَيَّنَ لَهُمُ الشَّيْطَانُ أَعْمَالَهُمْ فَهُوَ وَلِيُّهُمُ الْيَوْمَ وَلَهُمْ عَذَابٌ أَلِيمٌ ﴿٦٣﴾

48. The unbelievers have no reliable means of knowing whether God has associated anyone in His divinity and whether He has delegated any of His tasks to others; or whether or not He has placed any part of His realm into the care of others.

49. This refers to the sacrifices and offerings which people make to deities out of their earnings, and to the portion of their agricultural produce which they exclusively allocate for their gods and goddesses.

50. In the pantheon of Arabia, goddesses outnumbered gods. These goddesses were conceived to be the daughters of God. Likewise, angels were also considered to be God's daughters.

51. That is, sons.

52. The attitude of the unbelievers was tantalizingly self-contradictory. On the one hand, they considered it a matter of shame to have daughters, and on the other, they had no compunction in saying that God had daughters. Notwithstanding the gross ignorance and blasphemy in the claim that God had children, the unbelievers are specially reproached for cherishing a concept of God which, in terms of their own conception, showed God in an unfavourable light. Polytheistic beliefs had made them so blasphemous, insolent, and insensitive to God's majesty that they had no hesitation in saying whatever they wished about God.

(64) We have sent down the Book that you may explain to them the truth concerning what they are disputing and that the Book may serve as a guidance and mercy for those who believe in it.[53]

(65) Allah sends down water from the heaven, and thereby He instantly revives the earth after it lay dead. Verily in it there is a sign for those who have ears.[53a]

وَمَآ أَنزَلْنَا عَلَيْكَ ٱلْكِتَٰبَ إِلَّا لِتُبَيِّنَ
لَهُمُ ٱلَّذِى ٱخْتَلَفُوا۟ فِيهِ ۙ وَهُدًى
وَرَحْمَةً لِّقَوْمٍ يُؤْمِنُونَ ﴿٦٤﴾
وَٱللَّهُ أَنزَلَ مِنَ ٱلسَّمَآءِ مَآءً فَأَحْيَا بِهِ
ٱلْأَرْضَ بَعْدَ مَوْتِهَآ ۚ إِنَّ فِى ذَٰلِكَ لَءَايَةً
لِّقَوْمٍ يَسْمَعُونَ ﴿٦٥﴾

53. In the absence of revelation, men are liable, under the influence of personal fancies or inherited beliefs, to divide themselves into a myriad of religious groups. However, revelation of the Qur'ān has provided a solid basis of truth which can prove a rallying-point for all human beings. It is unfortunate that despite this favour granted by God, some people prefer to cling to their former state. It is obvious that such an attitude is bound to bring destruction and disgrace upon them. Only those who decide to accept and be guided by this Book will be directed to the right way and receive the blessings and bounties of the Qur'ān.

53(a). Man witnesses an instructive spectacle every year. He observes that during the course of each year a time comes when the earth turns altogether barren, becoming bereft of every sign of life and fertility. One does not even see a blade of grass, nor plants or leaves, nor vines or flowers, nor even insects. Then suddenly the rainy season sets in. The very first shower causes life to well up from the depths of the earth. Innumerable roots that lay crushed under layer upon layer of earth are suddenly revived, causing the plants which had appeared on the surface a year ago and had then withered away, to make their appearance once again. Likewise, innumerable insects, every trace of which had been destroyed by the heat of summer, make their reappearance. Men observe this spectacle year after year – that life is followed by death and death by life.

Despite all this, when the Prophet (peace be on him) tells men that God will restore people to life after death, they are struck with surprise. This reaction clearly indicates that their observation of the phenomenon of life following

(66) Surely there is a lesson for you in the cattle: We provide you to drink out of that which is in their bellies between the faeces and the blood – pure milk[54] – which is a palatable drink for those who take it. (67) And out of the fruits of date-palms and grapes you derive intoxicants as well as wholesome sustenance.[55] Surely there is a sign for those who use reason.

وَإِنَّ لَكُمْ فِي ٱلْأَنْعَٰمِ لَعِبْرَةً نُّسْقِيكُم مِّمَّا فِي بُطُونِهِۦ مِنۢ بَيْنِ فَرْثٍ وَدَمٍ لَّبَنًا خَالِصًا سَآئِغًا لِّلشَّٰرِبِينَ ﴿٦٦﴾ وَمِن ثَمَرَٰتِ ٱلنَّخِيلِ وَٱلْأَعْنَٰبِ تَتَّخِذُونَ مِنْهُ سَكَرًا وَرِزْقًا حَسَنًا إِنَّ فِي ذَٰلِكَ لَءَايَةً لِّقَوْمٍ يَعْقِلُونَ ﴿٦٧﴾

death is one akin to the observation of irrational brutes who can hardly make any intelligent sense of what they see. For even if they note the phenomena of nature which makes them wonder, they are still unable to perceive the signs of the power and wisdom of God behind them. Had it not been so, their reaction to the Prophet's statement regarding the Next Life should have been different. They should have cried out that the innumerable signs which they themselves observed testified to it.

54. By mentioning what is in the cattle's bellies between the filth and the blood, the Qur'ān emphasizes the point that what animals eat is transformed, on the one hand, into blood, and on the other, into faeces. At the same time, she-cattle produce milk which differs from both in its properties, colour, smell as well as in its uses and purpose. They produce milk in such large quantities that it not only suffices the nutritional needs of their young ones, but also provides a palatable nutrition for human beings.

55. Implicit in the above verse is the fact that the juice provided by date-palms and grapes serves as wholesome sustenance. Additionally, however, the same juice can be fermented so as to produce alcohol. Now it depends on man whether he prefers to derive a nutritional drink from these fruits, or whether he prefers to make wine out of them which then makes him lose his senses. It should also be noted that the verse quite subtly suggests that wine does not constitute 'wholesome sustenance'. This is a hint of its unlawfulness.

(68) Your Lord inspired[56] the bee saying: 'Set up hives in the mountains and in the trees and in the trellises that people put up; (69) then suck the juice of every kind of fruit and keep treading the ways of your Lord which have been made easy.[57] There comes forth from their bellies a drink varied in colours, wherein there is healing for men.[58] Verily there is a sign in this for those who reflect.[59]

وَأَوْحَىٰ رَبُّكَ إِلَى ٱلنَّحْلِ أَنِ ٱتَّخِذِى مِنَ
ٱلْجِبَالِ بُيُوتًا وَمِنَ ٱلشَّجَرِ وَمِمَّا يَعْرِشُونَ
﴿٦٨﴾ ثُمَّ كُلِى مِن كُلِّ ٱلثَّمَرَٰتِ فَٱسْلُكِى
سُبُلَ رَبِّكِ ذُلُلًا ۚ يَخْرُجُ مِنۢ بُطُونِهَا
شَرَابٌ مُّخْتَلِفٌ أَلْوَٰنُهُۥ فِيهِ شِفَآءٌ
لِّلنَّاسِ ۗ إِنَّ فِى ذَٰلِكَ لَءَايَةً لِّقَوْمٍ
يَتَفَكَّرُونَ ﴿٦٩﴾

---

56. The Qur'ānic term *waḥy* literally means making a veiled or subtle suggestion which is comprehended only by the concerned party. It is for this reason that the term was also used to convey the concepts of *ilqā'*, 'putting something in someone's heart', and *ilhām* or inspiration (i.e. teaching something under the veil of secrecy). Now God does not impart His message to His creatures in tangible forms. The message is conveyed, instead, in subtle modes so that the actual transmission of the message eludes people's observation. Hence the process of the revelation of the Qur'ān has been variously expressed by terms such as *ilqā'*, *ilhām* and *waḥy*. These terms, however, subsequently developed technical connotations. As a result, the term *waḥy* began to be used to denote the message communicated to Prophets and *ilhām* to denote the inspiration made to saints and other spiritually exalted beings. As for *ilqā'*, it has come to denote the ideas and feelings which God puts into the hearts and minds of ordinary people.

The Qur'ān, however, does not make any such distinction. Hence, it mentions the *waḥy* made to the heavens according to which the heavens are administered. 'To teach heaven He made *waḥy* of its duty' (*Ḥā Mīm* 41: 12). Likewise, the earth also receives the revelation *(waḥy)* which makes it narrate its record: 'On that Day will it declare its tidings: for your Lord will have made the *waḥy*' (*al-Zalzalah* 99: 4–5). Angels are also bestowed with *waḥy* and they function accordingly. 'And recall when your Lord made *waḥy* to the angels: "I am with you!" ' (*al-Anfāl* 8: 12).

Significantly, *waḥy* is also made to the bee to set up hives in the mountains and in the trees and in the trellises that people put up. However, this kind of inspiration *(waḥy)* is not confined to the bee alone. Such divine inspiration teaches fish to swim, birds to fly, and new-born to suckle. Also, whenever man hits upon sound opinion or the right way to help him out of a situation without resort to the normal processes of reflection and investigation, this also constitutes a form of *waḥy*. It is in this sense that the mother of Moses received *waḥy*: 'So We sent *waḥy* to the mother of Moses to suckle him' (*al-Qaṣaṣ* 28: 7).

In this sense no one is deprived of *waḥy*. All major achievements of rulers and statesmen and all significant discoveries and inventions reflect this kind of *waḥy*. Many ordinary human beings also encounter experiences which show that they received direct guidance from on high. Sometimes a person suddenly finds that some idea has made an inroad into his heart, or he intuitively feels inclined to take a certain step, or receives a suggestion in his dream and subsequently discovers that all that was instrumental in providing him with right guidance come to him from an unidentifiable source.

Of the many forms of *waḥy*, one special form is the revelation which is specifically communicated to Prophets. This form of *waḥy* radically differs from other forms. In this kind of *waḥy*, one to whom it is communicated is fully cognizant of the fact that guidance is from God. The recipient is fully convinced that it is from God. This kind of *waḥy* consists of guidance embodying beliefs, injunctions and directives with the help of which Prophets are able to guide mankind.

57. 'To keep treading the ways of the Lord which have been made easy' refers to the entire system and procedure followed by a group of bees. The design of their hives, the organization of their groups, the astonishing division of labour among them, their constant and well-regulated movements to produce, carry and store honey represent the ways which have been made easy for them by God. They have been so well prepared to undertake this task that they do not even have to reflect for a moment about the acts in which they engage. There is a well-known, thoroughly regulated procedure which they have been following down the ages to keep these innumerable small honey-making factories in operation so as to produce a sweet source of sustenance.

58. Honey is too useful and tasty an item of food to need any explicit mention. However, the healing properties of honey are relatively less known. This aspect, therefore, was brought to light. Honey is inherently useful in the treatment of certain diseases for it preserves the juice and glucose of flowers and fruits in its best form for a long time.

Additionally, honey has certain properties which prevent it from rotting. It also serves as a preservative and keeps other things fresh for a long time. It is for this reason that it has been used for centuries in the pharmaceutical industry in place of alcohol. If bees have their hives at a place where there is an abundance of a particular herb, honey will contain the essence of that herb. The

(70) Allah has created you, and then He causes you to die.[60] Some of you have your lives prolonged to an abject old age, when one loses all knowledge after having acquired it.[61] Allah is All-Knowing, All-Powerful.

وَاللَّهُ خَلَقَكُمْ ثُمَّ يَتَوَفَّاكُمْ وَمِنكُم مَّن
يُرَدُّ إِلَىٰ أَرْذَلِ الْعُمُرِ لِكَيْ لَا يَعْلَمَ بَعْدَ عِلْمٍ
شَيْئًا إِنَّ اللَّهَ عَلِيمٌ قَدِيرٌ ٧٠

---

honey so produced will therefore be useful for the treatment of those ailments for which that herb is used. If bees are systematically employed for pharmaceutical purposes and the honey containing the essence of different herbs is preserved, it will possibly be much more useful than the medicines produced in laboratories.

59. The present discourse aims at corroborating the second part of the Prophet's call. The unbelievers and polytheists opposed the Prophet (peace be on him) on two grounds. First, he preached the doctrine of Life-after-Death which calls for moral transformation. Second, he emphasized that God alone is worthy of worship and obedience, that He alone has the power to remove their distress and heed their complaints. This strikes at the very roots of the way of life founded on polytheism and atheism.

Attention is drawn here to the natural phenomena which bear testimony to the truth behind both aspects of the Prophet's teachings. The above discourse invites man to reflect over the signs around him. People should seriously think whether they lend support to the truth of the Prophet's statement regarding God's unity and After-life or whether they lend support to the superstitions and fancies of the polytheists. The Prophet (peace be on him) vociferously states that after his death man will be resurrected. The unbelievers contemptuously dismiss this as utterly impossible. However, as soon as the first drops of rain fall on the earth, it is fully established that resurrection is not only logically possible, but is also a recurrent phenomenon. The Prophet (peace be on him) also forcefully states that the universe has a God Who created it and holds sway over it. This is denied by atheists as a claim unsupported by any evidence.

One has only to consider the design and function of cattle, of dates and grapes, and bees and it would be quite evident that all has been created by the All-Wise and All-Merciful Lord. Had it not been so, how would it have been possible for the cattle, the trees and the bees to join hands in producing such a fine, delicious and nutritious thing for man with such unfailing regularity?

The Prophet (peace be on him) also emphatically states that it is God Whom

(71) Allah has favoured some of you with more worldly provisions than others. Then those who are more favoured do not give away their provisions to their slave so that they become equal sharers in it. Do they, then, deny the favour of Allah?[62]

وَٱللَّهُ فَضَّلَ بَعْضَكُمْ عَلَىٰ بَعْضٍ فِي ٱلرِّزْقِ ۚ فَمَا ٱلَّذِينَ فُضِّلُوا۟ بِرَآدِّى رِزْقِهِمْ عَلَىٰ مَا مَلَكَتْ أَيْمَٰنُهُمْ فَهُمْ فِيهِ سَوَآءٌ ۚ أَفَبِنِعْمَةِ ٱللَّهِ يَجْحَدُونَ ﴿٧١﴾

---

they should worship, upon Whom they should lavish all praise, and Whom they should always thank. This is resented by the polytheists who insist on making offerings to their numerous deities. However, can one truly say that anyone other than God provided them with milk, dates, grapes and honey, which furnish them with the best kind of nourishment? Is it true that it is not the One True God but rather gods, goddesses and saints who made the elaborate arrangements for man's subsistence that we observe?

60. Not only are the arrangements for man's sustenance and growth entirely in God's Hand, but God alone also has total control over man's life and death. No one else has the power to grant life, nor to cause death.

61. Man is proud of his knowledge, and his knowledge indeed distinguishes him from other creatures. It must be remembered that even knowledge is bestowed upon man by none other than God. It is a common sight – and yet highly instructive – that in old age even the wisest person who, in his younger days imparted wisdom to others, is reduced to a mere lump of flesh. Gone is all his sharpness. His senses become dull, rendering him incapable of even looking after his ordinary affairs.

62. This verse has been grossly misinterpreted in recent times. The interpretation to which the verse has been subjected clearly indicates the danger inherent in considering every single verse of the Qur'ān separately and attempting to understand it in isolation from its context. This is bound to open the flood-gates of irresponsible and fanciful interpretation.

The present verse has been considered by some people to represent the foundation of the Islamic economic philosophy, and as an important provision of the Islamic economic system. According to such people, the true purpose of the verse is to tell those who have been granted ample worldly provisions to return them to their servants and slaves so as to make them equal sharers of those provisions. It is contended that if they fail to do so, they will be guilty of denying God's favour.

The fact of the matter is that the context in which this verse occurs renders any discussion of economic questions quite out of place. The discourse is in fact devoted to emphasizing God's unity and refuting polytheism. The preceding verses are directed to the above subjects, and the same discussion continues. It would be quite odd if an economic principle were suddenly enunciated at this point in the midst of a discussion devoted to quite another subject matter.

If one bears in mind the correct context of the verse it can be easily appreciated that what is being said here is something quite different. Here, people are first reminded of an actual fact of life. They are told that they do not share their wealth – even though it has been bestowed upon them by God – with their slaves and servants. In view of this, how can they justify that they should associate God's helpless servants with Him in giving thanks for the favour conferred upon them by God alone? How can they consider these creatures of God equal to Him in respect of both rights and authority?

Exactly the same point is made asking the same question elsewhere in the Qur'ān: 'He does propound to you a similitude from your own experience. Do you have partners from among those whom your right hands possess so that they would share the wealth We have bestowed on you till they become equals? Do you fear them as you fear your peers? Thus do We explain the signs in detail to a people that understand' (*al-Rūm* 30: 28).

A comparison of the present verse with the verse just quoted (viz. *al-Rūm* 30: 28), makes it clear that both the verses are geared to the same purpose. The example and the argument which have been marshalled are also identical. In fact the two verses are complementary, each assisting in the understanding of the other.

Perhaps the misinterpretation which arises has been caused by the Qur'ānic statement: 'Do they, then, deny the favour of Allah?' (verse 71). Since this statement soon follows the citing of an example, it has led some people to the mistaken view that the failure to hand over one's possessions to one's slaves and servants amounts to denying God's favours. However, anyone well versed in the Qur'ān knows well that to thank someone other than God for a favour bestowed by God is tantamount, according to the Qur'ān, to denying God's favours. This point has been repeated so often in the Qur'ān that anyone who is familiar with it can never fall prey to any such misconception. Only those who are not well acquainted with the Qur'ān and who, therefore, have to have recourse to studying it with the help of indices and concordances will be unaware of the true Qur'ānic teaching on the matter.

Once a person rightly grasps what is meant by 'denying God's favours' the verse becomes quite intelligible. The point that is being emphasized here is that people know the basic difference between master and slave. They also maintain such a distinction between the two in their practical lives, and make an effort to keep the two apart. However, they seem to brush all this aside in God's case. Instead, they insist on associating His creatures – those who are

(72) And Allah has given you spouses from your kind, and has granted you through your spouses, sons and grandsons, and has provided you wholesome things as sustenance. [After knowing all this] do they still believe in falsehood[63] and deny Allah's bounty.[64] (73) And instead of Allah, worship those helpless beings who have no control over providing them any sustenance from the heavens and the earth; do you worship those who have no power to do anything of this sort? (74) So do not strike any similitudes to Allah,[65] Allah knows whereas you do not know.

وَٱللَّهُ جَعَلَ لَكُم مِّنْ أَنفُسِكُمْ أَزْوَٰجًا
وَجَعَلَ لَكُم مِّنْ أَزْوَٰجِكُم بَنِينَ
وَحَفَدَةً وَرَزَقَكُم مِّنَ ٱلطَّيِّبَٰتِ
أَفَبِٱلْبَٰطِلِ يُؤْمِنُونَ وَبِنِعْمَتِ ٱللَّهِ هُمْ
يَكْفُرُونَ ﴿٧٢﴾ وَيَعْبُدُونَ مِن دُونِ
ٱللَّهِ مَا لَا يَمْلِكُ لَهُمْ رِزْقًا مِّنَ
ٱلسَّمَٰوَٰتِ وَٱلْأَرْضِ شَيْـًٔا وَلَا
يَسْتَطِيعُونَ ﴿٧٣﴾ فَلَا تَضْرِبُوا۟ لِلَّهِ
ٱلْأَمْثَالَ إِنَّ ٱللَّهَ يَعْلَمُ وَأَنتُمْ لَا
تَعْلَمُونَ ﴿٧٤﴾

His born servants – with Him. They also insist on giving thanks to God's creatures for the favours that He alone has bestowed upon them.

63. To charge the unbelievers that they 'believe in falsehood' means that they subscribe to beliefs which are totally baseless and devoid of all truth. They subscribe, for instance, to the belief that it is gods, goddesses, *jinn* and saints of the past who have full powers to make or mar people's destiny, to respond to their invocations, to bless them with offspring and the means for their livelihood, to effectively help them in any litigation and in preventing them falling prey to disease.

64. The Makkan polytheists did not deny that they owe to God all the bounties which they had received. They also had no hesitation in gratefully acknowledging God's favours. However, their mistake lay in the fact that, in addition to giving thanks to God for those favours, they also gave thanks to others whom they considered to be His partners. The Qur'ān considers this to be tantamount to denying God's favour.

(75) Allah sets forth a parable:[66] There is one who is a slave and is owned by another, and has no power over anything; and there is one whom We have granted good provision Ourselves, of which he spends both secretly and openly. Can they be equal? All praise be to Allah.[67] But most of them do not even know (this simple fact).[68]

۞ ضَرَبَ اللَّهُ مَثَلًا عَبْدًا مَّمْلُوكًا لَّا يَقْدِرُ عَلَىٰ شَيْءٍ وَمَن رَّزَقْنَاهُ مِنَّا رِزْقًا حَسَنًا فَهُوَ يُنفِقُ مِنْهُ سِرًّا وَجَهْرًا هَلْ يَسْتَوُونَ الْحَمْدُ لِلَّهِ بَلْ أَكْثَرُهُمْ لَا يَعْلَمُونَ ﴿٧٥﴾

The Qur'ān enunciates the principle that to give thanks to someone other than to whom it is due is identical to denying the favour of the true benefactor. Likewise, the Qur'ān enunciates another principle. It declares that any gratuitous assumption that the benefactor did not bestow favour out of his benevolence, but did so at the behest or intervention of someone else, also amounts to denying the favour of the true benefactor.

It will be seen that both principles enunciated by the Qur'ān are consonant with the dictates of justice and common sense. Everyone is capable of appreciating their reasonableness. Suppose someone helps a needy person out of compassion and then the person so helped stands up and gives thanks to someone who had nothing to do with the favour granted him. Someone might disregard this outrageous behaviour out of magnanimity. He might even be so forbearing as to continue to help him. Nevertheless, he is bound to feel in his heart of hearts that the person whom he had helped was utterly thankless. Moreover, if a benefactor comes to know that the needy person thanks others rather than himself in the belief that the latter had acted under the influence of someone else rather than out of genuine compassion and generosity, he is bound to feel insulted if such was not the case. Such a foolish explanation on the part of that person will only mean that he had an overly low opinion of his benefactor. It is indicative of the fact that he considers his benefactor to be bereft of compassion and mercy; that he looks upon him as one given to nepotism, as one who does not care for human beings and their sufferings. All he cares for is a group of persons whom he wishes to gratify in and out of season.

65. The command 'not to strike any similitudes to Allah' amounts to warning people not to conceive of Him in the image of worldly sovereigns. For

many people do indeed develop faulty notions about God owing to the basically false image that they entertain about Him. They tend to conceive in Him the image of a worldly ruler who is surrounded in his palace by courtiers, officers and servants. Using this as their analogy, they think that God is also helplessly surrounded by angels, saints and other chosen ones. In the same way as a worldly sovereign cannot be approached directly without having to go through intermediaries, so it is in the case of God.

66. God explains the truth by means of sound parables for the benefit of those who are inclined to understand things through parables. The unbelievers had arrived at wrong conclusions precisely because they had attempted to grasp things with the help of wrong parables.

67. There is a gap between the question which has been posed here and the statement that follows: 'All praise be to Allah.' In itself this expression contains a good hint as to how the gap can be filled.

Obviously, it was in no way possible for the polytheists to say, in response to the Prophet's questions, that the two are equal. The only sensible answer to the question – even that given by many unbelievers – must have been an acknowledgement of the fact that the two are certainly not equal. There would, however, have been others who would have preferred to remain silent. They would have chosen to do so because the logical corollary to such an acknowledgement was that their polytheistic doctrines were false. On hearing both these kinds of responses the Prophet (peace be on him) says: 'All praise be to Allah.' With regard to the first response, he thanks God for the fact that even a polytheist was able to grasp at least that point. With regard to the second response, he thanks God that despite his obduracy the polytheist was unable to say that the two were equal, and thus failed to find any fault with the basic premise of monotheism.

68. The unbelievers are fully aware of the difference between the powerful and the powerless among their fellow human beings. Nor do they fail to distinguish between these two categories of people in their practical lives. So it is astonishing that when it comes to applying this reasonable distinction to Creator and created, they show utter foolishness and stupidity insofar as they fail to recognize the essential difference between the two. As a result, they tend to conceive created beings as partners with God in His essence and attributes, in His power and rights. They also adopt towards created beings a stance which ought to be adopted only towards the Creator.

Astonishingly enough, when it comes to worldly life, the unbelievers are quite clever. When they need something they know that they should ask the master of the house for it rather than his servant. However, when it comes to asking for bounties which lie beyond the range of normal causation, rather than seek them from the Lord of the universe, they turn to His servants.

(76) Allah sets forth another parable: There are two men, one of whom is dumb and has no power over anything; he is a burden to his master, and wheresoever his master directs him, he fails to bring forth any good. Can such a person be the equal[69] of one who enjoins justice and himself follows the right way?

(77) Allah has full knowledge of the truths beyond the reach of human perception both in the heavens and the earth;[70] and the coming of the Hour will take no more than the twinkling of an eye; it may take even less.[71] Indeed Allah has power over everything.

وَضَرَبَ ٱللَّهُ مَثَلًا رَّجُلَيْنِ أَحَدُهُمَآ
أَبْكَمُ لَا يَقْدِرُ عَلَىٰ شَىْءٍ وَهُوَ
كَلٌّ عَلَىٰ مَوْلَىٰهُ أَيْنَمَا يُوَجِّههُّ لَا
يَأْتِ بِخَيْرٍ هَلْ يَسْتَوِى هُوَ وَمَن
يَأْمُرُ بِٱلْعَدْلِ وَهُوَ عَلَىٰ صِرَٰطٍ
مُّسْتَقِيمٍ ﴿٧٦﴾ وَلِلَّهِ غَيْبُ ٱلسَّمَٰوَٰتِ
وَٱلْأَرْضِ ۚ وَمَآ أَمْرُ ٱلسَّاعَةِ إِلَّا كَلَمْحِ
ٱلْبَصَرِ أَوْ هُوَ أَقْرَبُ ۚ إِنَّ ٱللَّهَ عَلَىٰ
كُلِّ شَىْءٍ قَدِيرٌ ﴿٧٧﴾

---

69. In the former parable the difference between God and the false deities is brought out with reference to the all-powerfulness of the One and the powerlessness of the other. In the second parable, the same difference is explained even more emphatically. However, this is done with reference to attributes. The point that emerges, therefore, is not merely that God is the Master Who is possessed of power, while the false deities are powerless servants but in addition there is a further difference between them. Being powerless servants the false deities cannot hear their prayers, nor answer them, nor do they have the power to do anything out of their own power. In fact they owe even their existence to their Lord. Were the Master to assign them any task, they have no power – unless God confers it upon them – to accomplish that task. In sharp contrast to that, the Master is all-powerful and all-wise. He enjoins all to practice justice. He not only has the power to act as He chooses, but He also acts in accordance with truth and rectitude. Thus, the difference between God and the false deities is quite glaring. How can it be wise, then, for anyone to hold the Lord and His servants as equal?

(78) Allah has brought you forth from your mothers' wombs when you knew nothing, and then gave you hearing, and sight and thinking hearts[72] so that you may give thanks.[73]

(79) Have they never noticed the birds how they are held under control in the middle of the sky, where none holds them [from falling] except Allah? Surely there are signs in this for those who believe.

وَاللَّهُ أَخْرَجَكُم مِّنۢ بُطُونِ أُمَّهَٰتِكُمْ
لَا تَعْلَمُونَ شَيْـًٔا وَجَعَلَ لَكُمُ
السَّمْعَ وَالْأَبْصَٰرَ وَالْأَفْـِٔدَةَ ۙ
لَعَلَّكُمْ تَشْكُرُونَ ﴿٧٨﴾ أَلَمْ يَرَوْا۟
إِلَى الطَّيْرِ مُسَخَّرَٰتٍ فِى جَوِّ
السَّمَآءِ مَا يُمْسِكُهُنَّ إِلَّا اللَّهُ ۗ إِنَّ فِى
ذَٰلِكَ لَءَايَٰتٍ لِّقَوْمٍ يُؤْمِنُونَ ﴿٧٩﴾

70. Taken together with the following verse this verse constitutes a rejoinder to the oft-repeated question of the Makkan unbelievers as to when Resurrection would take place. The question is answered here without explicitly mentioning it.

71. Resurrection would not come about gradually. Men will not be able to observe it approaching. It will rather overtake them suddenly and no one will have the time to make amends. Hence it is imperative that people give serious thought to the matter and make up their minds as to what they ought to do. No one should relax under the illusion that the Day of Judgement is far off. For when it is evident that the Day of Judgement is close at hand, no one will be able to make amends.

The question of the After-life has been introduced with seeming abruptness in this discussion for good reason. The purpose is to drive home to people that the choice between monotheism and polytheism is not just a theoretical issue. They should rather be conscious, quite conscious, that the Day of Judgement will suddenly overtake them and decide man's success or failure in the Next Life. With this note of warning, the discourse on God's unity is resumed.

72. This refers to the resources which enable man to obtain knowledge and to administer the affairs of the world. At the time of his birth a human child is much more helpless and ignorant than the new-born of any animal. However, it is by dint of the means of obtaining knowledge bestowed upon him by God –

(80) Allah has made your houses a repose, and has provided you with the skins of the cattle for your habitation[74] which are light to handle both when you travel and when you camp;[75] and out of their wool, and their fur and their hair He has given you furnishings and goods for use over a period of time. (81) And Allah has provided shade for you out of some of the things He has created; and has provided you with shelters in the mountains, and has given you coats that protect you from heat[76] as well as coats that protect you in battle.[77] Thus does He complete His favour upon you that you may submit to Him.[78]

وَٱللَّهُ جَعَلَ لَكُم مِّنۢ بُيُوتِكُمْ سَكَنًا
وَجَعَلَ لَكُم مِّن جُلُودِ ٱلْأَنْعَـٰمِ بُيُوتًا
تَسْتَخِفُّونَهَا يَوْمَ ظَعْنِكُمْ وَيَوْمَ
إِقَامَتِكُمْ ۙ وَمِنْ أَصْوَافِهَا وَأَوْبَارِهَا
وَأَشْعَارِهَآ أَثَـٰثًا وَمَتَـٰعًا إِلَىٰ حِينٍ ٨٠
وَٱللَّهُ جَعَلَ لَكُم مِّمَّا خَلَقَ ظِلَـٰلًا
وَجَعَلَ لَكُم مِّنَ ٱلْجِبَالِ
أَكْنَـٰنًا وَجَعَلَ لَكُمْ سَرَٰبِيلَ
تَقِيكُمُ ٱلْحَرَّ وَسَرَٰبِيلَ تَقِيكُم
بَأْسَكُمْ ۚ كَذَٰلِكَ يُتِمُّ نِعْمَتَهُۥ
عَلَيْكُمْ لَعَلَّكُمْ تُسْلِمُونَ ٨١

---

hearing, sight, reason – that he gains mastery over all other earthly creatures.

73. Man is asked to give thanks to God Who has bestowed on him such invaluable bounties. It is the height of ingratitude that man should use his faculty of hearing and listening to everything except God's message: that he should use the faculty of sight to observe everything except God's signs; that he should use his intellect to reflect about every possible thing except the question as to who it is who has lavished all possible bounties on him.

74. This refers to a tent of skin which is quite a common feature in Arabia.

75. When they embark on a journey, they easily fold the tent and carry it, and when they decide to stay somewhere they easily unfold and pitch the tent they were carrying.

(82) But if they turn away, your only duty is to clearly deliver the message of the truth. (83) They are aware of the favours of Allah, and yet refuse to acknowledge them.[79] Most of them are determined not to accept the truth.

فَإِن تَوَلَّوْا فَإِنَّمَا عَلَيْكَ ٱلْبَلَٰغُ ٱلْمُبِينُ ﴿٨٢﴾ يَعْرِفُونَ نِعْمَتَ ٱللَّهِ ثُمَّ يُنكِرُونَهَا وَأَكْثَرُهُمُ ٱلْكَٰفِرُونَ ﴿٨٣﴾

76. Here no reference is made to winter clothing. One possible reason could be that summer clothing represents the height of human civilization. Having mentioned that, there is, therefore, no need to refer to something which represents a lower stage of civilization. Another possible reason could be that lands such as Arabia are subject to the ravaging simoom, the blazing wind of the hot, scorching desert. Given this, summer clothing is of much greater importance than winter clothing. If one does not cover one's head, neck, ears – in fact the whole of one's body – one may be scorched to death by the simoom.

77. That is, coat of mail.

78. The completion of God's favour upon man means that God takes note of all man's needs in life and provides him with them all. An instance in point is the protection of the human body against the inclemencies of the weather. In this regard, God has made such elaborate arrangements in response to such a wide variety of needs that were one to write about them in some detail, it would run into a voluminous book. In fact, a whole volume is needed simply in connection with clothing and shelter. However, man also needs food. In this regard we know that God has provided an abundance of resources to feed human beings on such a wide scale and with such a baffling variety that no requirement of man for food remains unfulfilled. Were one to enumerate the different varieties and forms of food, this would also run into a huge book. This would be the completion of God's favour concerning food. In like manner, if we were to scan man's needs in all his different spheres of life, it is quite evident that God has lavished His bounties on all.

79. Here 'refusal to acknowledge' God's favours signifies not so much the refusal to acknowledge it in words as in practice. The Makkan unbelievers did not verbally deny that God had done them a great variety of favours. Yet they

(84) (They are heedless of) the Day when We shall raise a witness[80] from each community and then the unbelievers will neither be allowed to plead[81] nor will they be asked to repent and seek pardon.[82]

وَيَوْمَ نَبْعَثُ مِن كُلِّ أُمَّةٍ شَهِيدًا ثُمَّ لَا يُؤْذَنُ لِلَّذِينَ كَفَرُوا وَلَا هُمْ يُسْتَعْتَبُونَ ﴿٨٤﴾

believed that God's favours upon them were due to the intercession of their saints and deities. Hence, they thanked the beings which, in their view, interceded on their behalf more amply than they thanked God. It is precisely this which God regards as denial of His favour and downright ingratitude to Him.

80. The word 'witness' in the verse stands for the Prophet of a people, or anyone else who after his passing away, asks them to eschew polytheistic superstitions and rituals, invites them to exclusively worship the One True God, and warns them of accountability on the Day of Judgement. Such a person will bear testimony on the Day of Judgement that he did indeed convey the truth to his people. Whatever they did thereafter was, therefore, not out of ignorance. It was rather done despite full knowledge, and so deliberately.

81. This does not mean that people will not be allowed to explain their conduct. What the verse means is that the wrong-doing of the unbelievers will be established by incontrovertible and undeniable evidence. It will leave them no room to explain away or defend their conduct.

82. At this stage they will not be asked to repent and seek pardon from their Lord. For this will be the Hour of Judgement. Both the Qur'ān and the *Hadīth* make it clear that one may repent and seek pardon during the present life. It is not possible to do so in the Hereafter. Even in this life, the opportunity for repenting and seeking pardon is available as long as one is not in the throes of death. When a man becomes certain that he is on the verge of breathing his last, his repentance is of no avail. For as soon as a person reaches the frontiers of death, the term for doing good comes to an end. Only one thing follows that event – God's reward or punishment.

(85) And once the wrong-doers have beheld the chastisement, neither will it be lightened for them nor will they be granted any respite. (86) And when those who associated others with Allah in His Divinity will see those to whom they ascribed this share, they will say: 'Our Lord! These are the beings to whom we ascribed a share in Your divinity and whom we called upon instead of You', whereupon those beings will fling at them the words: 'You are liars.'[83] (87) As for that Day they will offer their submission and all that they had fabricated will have vanished.[84] ▶

وَإِذَا رَءَا ٱلَّذِينَ ظَلَمُوا۟ ٱلْعَذَابَ
فَلَا يُخَفَّفُ عَنْهُمْ وَلَا هُمْ يُنظَرُونَ
﴿٨٥﴾ وَإِذَا رَءَا ٱلَّذِينَ أَشْرَكُوا۟
شُرَكَآءَهُمْ قَالُوا۟ رَبَّنَا
هَٰٓؤُلَآءِ شُرَكَآؤُنَا ٱلَّذِينَ
كُنَّا نَدْعُوا۟ مِن دُونِكَ ۖ فَأَلْقَوْا۟
إِلَيْهِمُ ٱلْقَوْلَ إِنَّكُمْ
لَكَٰذِبُونَ ﴿٨٦﴾ وَأَلْقَوْا۟
إِلَى ٱللَّهِ يَوْمَئِذٍ ٱلسَّلَمَ ۖ وَضَلَّ
عَنْهُم مَّا كَانُوا۟ يَفْتَرُونَ ﴿٨٧﴾

83. This does not mean that the false deities will deny that the unbelievers called upon them to help them and rescue them from distress. What they will deny is that they neither knew nor expressed their consent, nor did they ask them to call upon them rather than upon God. Hence, they were in no way responsible for whatever the polytheists might have done. If people believed that they had the power to hear and answer prayers, or to remove distress or effectively assist them, all this was a lie which people had themselves invented. Hence, they alone should be responsible for that and bear its consequences.

84. All the fabrications of the unbelievers will vanish on the Day of Judgement. Those in whom the unbelievers and polytheists had placed their trust will be gone. They will be unable to find anyone even to heed their complaints and lamentations. None will be there to solve their difficulties. No holy men or saints will step forward to intercede on their behalf. No one will dare to plead with God that no harm should come to them for they were sincerely devoted to Him.

(88) As for those who disbelieved and barred others from the way of Allah, We shall add chastisement[85] to their chastisement for all the mischief they did.

(89) (O Muḥammad!) Warn them of the coming of a Day when We shall bring forth a witness against them from each community and We shall bring you forth as a witness against them all; (and it is for that purpose that) We sent down the Book to you which makes everything clear;[86] and serves as a guidance and mercy and glad tidings to those who have submitted to Allah.[87]

الَّذِينَ كَفَرُوا وَصَدُّوا عَن سَبِيلِ
اللَّهِ زِدْنَاهُمْ عَذَابًا فَوْقَ الْعَذَابِ بِمَا
كَانُوا يُفْسِدُونَ ﴿٨٨﴾ وَيَوْمَ
نَبْعَثُ فِي كُلِّ أُمَّةٍ شَهِيدًا عَلَيْهِم
مِّنْ أَنفُسِهِمْ ۖ وَجِئْنَا بِكَ شَهِيدًا
عَلَىٰ هَٰؤُلَاءِ ۚ وَنَزَّلْنَا عَلَيْكَ الْكِتَابَ
تِبْيَانًا لِّكُلِّ شَيْءٍ وَهُدًى وَرَحْمَةً
وَبُشْرَىٰ لِلْمُسْلِمِينَ ﴿٨٩﴾

---

85. The punishment inflicted on such unbelievers will be two-fold. Apart from being punished for unbelief, they will also be punished for barring others from the way of God.

86. The Qur'ān clearly explains what the basic factors are which cause man to find or lose the right way, to attain success or end up in failure. It also clearly illuminates all that a man needs to know in order to be rightly-directed and to be able to distinguish truth from falsehood. However, some people tend to make an altogether erroneous interpretation of تِبْيَانًا لِّكُلِّ شَيْءٍ ('which makes everything clear') and similar statements in other verses of the Qur'ān. They take the statement in a purely literal sense to mean that every single thing has been laid down and explained in the Qur'ān. Proceeding on this assumption, they try to call out from the Qur'ān all sorts of strange facts – scientific and otherwise – in order to vindicate their assumption.

87. The Qur'ān will provide sound guidance to those who accept the Qur'ān and adopt the stance of obedience in all spheres of life. Adherence to Qur'ānic

(90) Surely Allah enjoins justice, kindness and the doing of good, to kith and kin,[88] and forbids all that is shameful, evil and oppressive.[89] He exhorts you so that you may be mindful. (91) And fulfil the covenant which you have made with Allah and do not break your oaths after having firmly made them, and after having made Allah your witness. Surely Allah knows all that you do. ▶

۞ إِنَّ ٱللَّهَ يَأْمُرُ بِٱلْعَدْلِ وَٱلْإِحْسَـٰنِ
وَإِيتَآئِ ذِى ٱلْقُرْبَىٰ وَيَنْهَىٰ عَنِ
ٱلْفَحْشَآءِ وَٱلْمُنكَرِ وَٱلْبَغْىِ ۚ
يَعِظُكُمْ لَعَلَّكُمْ تَذَكَّرُونَ ﴿٩٠﴾
وَأَوْفُوا۟ بِعَهْدِ ٱللَّهِ إِذَا عَـٰهَدتُّمْ
وَلَا تَنقُضُوا۟ ٱلْأَيْمَـٰنَ بَعْدَ تَوْكِيدِهَا
وَقَدْ جَعَلْتُمُ ٱللَّهَ عَلَيْكُمْ كَفِيلًا ۚ إِنَّ
ٱللَّهَ يَعْلَمُ مَا تَفْعَلُونَ ﴿٩١﴾

guidance will bring upon them God's mercy. Moreover, the Book of God will announce to them the glad tidings of their success on the Day of Judgement. Those who reject the Qur'ān, however, will be deprived of God's guidance and mercy. Not only that but on the Day of Judgement when God's Messenger will bear witness against them, this Book will serve as an overpowering evidence against them. For the Messenger will conclusively establish that he had conveyed to them the Book which clearly explains the distinction between truth and falsehood.

88. This directive which has been so succinctly expressed enjoins on people three principles which provide the basis for the sound ordering of human society. The first and foremost principle is 'justice' which comprises two independent truths. One, that there be balance and right proportion among human beings in respect of their rights. Two, that every person be granted his rights without any distinction. The word used in Urdu as an equivalent of *'adl* (justice) is *inṣāf*. This word creates some confusion. It somehow leads people to believe that in the distribution of rights between two or more persons, the basis should be *nisf* and *nisf* ('half and half').

It is presumably for this reason that justice has come to signify equal distribution of rights. This is, however, quite contrary to nature. What justice really demands is balance and right proportion rather than absolute equality. True, in certain respects, equality among members of society, such as in respect of the rights of citizenship, is a requirement of justice. However, equality in certain other matters is diametrically opposed to the requirements of justice. For instance, it would be sheer injustice if we were to grant children equal rights with their parents, or to equally compensate those who work hard and well and those who do not. Hence, what God has commanded is not equality in rights. He has rather commanded balance and right proportion. This requires that the moral, social, economic, legal, political and cultural rights to which a person is entitled should be granted to him with sincerity.

The second principle is benevolence (to be literal, 'doing good') which broadly embraces all such good acts as politeness, generosity, sympathy, tolerance, courtesy, forbearance, mutual accommodation, mutual consideration, giving to others more than what is their due, and being content for oneself with a little less than what one is entitled to. This principle goes a step further than justice and is hence, in some respects, even more important for man's social life than justice. If justice is the foundation on which the structure of a society should rest, then benevolence represents the beauty and perfection of that structure. Justice wards off the bitterness of discord and disharmony from human life. Benevolence adds to it the elements of pleasance and sweetness. No society can be sustained merely on the principle that every member of it should be jealously watchful of, and insistent upon, receiving every bit of his right and be willing to grant others exactly what is their due, but absolutely no more. Perhaps such a cold and stark society might – thanks to the application of justice as conceived above – be able to avoid internal conflicts. However, such a society will be utterly devoid of such life-giving and life-sustaining values as love and compassion, gratitude and magnanimity, and sacrifice and goodwill for others.

The third principle enunciated in this verse is liberality to kith and kin. This is a corollary of the former principle – 'benevolence' – when it is applied to one's relatives. This consists not only of sharing one's joys and sorrows with one's kin, and in helping and supporting the fulfilment of their legitimate desires within permissible limits. But also that one should recognize that one's wealth ought not to be spent exclusively on oneself and one's immediate family. Other members of the family also have a share in it. God's law requires rich persons to take care of the needs of their relatives and not to leave them to go about without proper food and clothing. According to the Qur'ānic standard of judgement a society in which some people are immersed in luxury whereas other members of their family remain unprovided for even with the basic necessities of life is an unhealthy society.

The needy members of a family have a prior claim to receive assistance from their relatives, and it is only after this that they have a claim to assistance from others. To put it conversely, the prosperous members of a family are required to assist their own relatives in need before assisting any others.

This principle has been explicitly enunciated by the Prophet (peace be on him) in a number of his statements. It has been stated in several traditions that a person's parents, his wife, his children and his brothers and sisters have the first and foremost right against him. These are followed by those who are next to them in kinship, the principle being the closer the relationship, the more is the claim; and *vice versa*. Guided by this principle 'Umar made it incumbent on the cousin of an orphan to undertake the latter's maintenance. Likewise, he

(92) And do not become like the woman who, after having painstakingly spun her yarn, caused it to disintegrate into pieces.[90] You resort to oaths as instruments of mutual deceit so that one people might take greater advantage than another although Allah puts you to the test through this.[91] Surely on the Day of Resurrection He will make clear the truth concerning the matters over which you differed.[92] ▶

وَلَا تَكُونُوا كَالَّتِي نَقَضَتْ غَزْلَهَا
مِنۢ بَعْدِ قُوَّةٍ أَنكَٰثًا تَتَّخِذُونَ
أَيْمَٰنَكُمْ دَخَلًۢا بَيْنَكُمْ أَن تَكُونَ
أُمَّةٌ هِيَ أَرْبَىٰ مِنْ أُمَّةٍ ۚ إِنَّمَا يَبْلُوكُمُ
ٱللَّهُ بِهِۦ ۚ وَلَيُبَيِّنَنَّ لَكُمْ يَوْمَ ٱلْقِيَٰمَةِ مَا
كُنتُمْ فِيهِ تَخْتَلِفُونَ ﴿٩٢﴾

---

stated that if that orphan had no close relative but only a distant one, the latter would be responsible for the orphan's maintenance. If each family looks after its members, it can be well imagined how widely spread would economic prosperity be in that society; how harmonious and pleasant would the interrelationship of its members be, and how sublime and lofty would the moral standards operating in it be.

89. In contrast to the three moral principles mentioned above, God forbids three vices which corrupt both individuals and society at large.

The first and foremost of these vices is *fahshā'* which embraces the whole range of evil and shameful deeds. Every vice which is intrinsically of a highly reprehensible character falls into this category whether it be miserliness, fornication, nudity, homosexuality, marrying those with whom marriage is forbidden, stealing, drinking, begging, or hurling abuses and outrageously rude words at others. Likewise, it also covers those evil acts which are committed publicly or which lead to the propagation of corruption such as slander, calumny, publicizing the hidden sins of others, inciting people to moral corruption be it by so-called *belles-lettres,* plays or films, nude pictures, appearance of women in public with alluring make-up, promiscuous mixing between men and women, appearance of women on the stage to dance and twist their bodies, and the display of other forms of female coquetry.

The next category of vice referred to is evil which is universally acknowledged as bad and immoral. Included in it are all evils which have been unanimously condemned by the human conscience and which have been forbidden by the Divine Law in all ages.

The third category of vice which is forbidden is transgression. This stands for the exceeding on anyone's part one's proper limits and usurping the rights of others – whether those rights be those of God or of fellow human beings.

90. This verse explains three kinds of covenants and exhorts the believers to fulfil their obligations to each of them. These covenants are described in a descending order of importance. The covenant of highest importance is the one made by man with God. The second in importance is the covenant that has been reinforced by invoking God's name. The last category consists of agreements made with others without invoking the name of God. This is less important than the other two. However, it is imperative that the obligations incurred by all of these covenants be fulfilled. For it is not permitted to breach any of the above categories of covenant.

91. Here the worst kind of breach of covenant is specifically mentioned and denounced. The reason for its denunciation is that this kind of breach causes the greatest corruption and mischief.

Strangely, this kind of breach is committed by people of stature who do so considering it an act of virtue and who win acclaim from their people for doing so.

In the course of the political, economic and religious conflicts between groups and nations it often happens that the leader of one group or nation enters into an agreement with another. Subsequently, the leader of that group or nation brazenly violates that agreement or acquires some illegitimate advantages by violating it, and does so under the plea of promoting the interests of his group or nation. Even those who are righteous in their personal lives feel no qualms in committing such a breach of agreement. Their own community does not censure them. It does not charge them for having committed an evil act. On the contrary, they are patted on the back, and their petty cunning is acclaimed as the height of diplomatic astuteness.

God warns against such an attitude. Every agreement puts the morality and integrity of the person and the group who are a party to it to the test. Those who fail the test will not escape being brought to account for it in the majestic court of God.

92. It is only on the Day of Judgement that one will know which among the conflicting views prevalent in the world was right. However, even those who are altogether right in their views have recourse to breach of commitment, or to lie and slander and are deceitful against their opponents even if their world-view is totally erroneous and false. Such an attitude is altogether faulty. For devotion to truth requires not only that one's world-view and purpose be based on truth, but that the means used to promote it should also be fair and honest. Such a warning is especially needed with regard to religious groups which are often under the illusion that God is permanently on their side and that

(93) Had Allah so willed, He would have made you all one single community.[93] However, He lets go astray whomsoever He wills and shows the right way to whomsoever He wills.[94] Surely you shall be called to account regarding what you did.

وَلَوْ شَآءَ ٱللَّهُ لَجَعَلَكُمْ أُمَّةً
وَٰحِدَةً وَلَٰكِن يُضِلُّ مَن يَشَآءُ
وَيَهْدِى مَن يَشَآءُ ۚ وَلَتُسْـَٔلُنَّ عَمَّا
كُنتُمْ تَعْمَلُونَ ﴿٩٣﴾

---

their opponents are God's rebels. The former, therefore, have a right to hurt the latter by all possible means. They consider themselves free of all restraint in dealing with those whom they consider to be God's enemies. Against such people, they need not be bound by the dictates of truthfulness, trustworthiness and faithfulness to commitment. That is exactly what the Jews of Arabia used to say: 'We will not be taken to task for whatever we may do to the non-Jews *(ummīs)*' (*Āl 'Imrān* 3: 75). In other words, they considered themselves free to deal with Gentiles as they pleased. They considered themselves free to commit breach of faith, and to resort to any other means – fair or foul – which would serve the interests of those who were dear to God (i.e. Jews) and hurtful to their opponents (i.e. Gentiles). They were sure they would not be taken to task by God regardless of what they did.

93. This further explains the contents of the preceding note. If someone considers himself to belong to God's party and strives to promote His religion and to wipe out all other religions, resorting in that connection to foul means, he is guilty of going against God's will. For had God wanted that all religious differences among human beings be totally wiped out, leaving no choice in matters of religion and forcing all men willy-nilly to embrace one single religion, He could have done so without the help of those who claim to be of God's own party. God was well able to achieve that purpose by the use of His power. He could have created all men to be born believing in and submitting to God's imperatives and so deprived them of the capacity to disbelieve and disobedience. Had God so willed, who could have deviated in the least from faith and obedience?

94. The opportunity that man enjoys to make a choice between alternative ways out of his own free-will has been granted to him by none other than God Himself. Hence, the ways that men will choose are bound to be diverse. For anyone who seeks to end up in error, God makes it possible to choose error.

(94) Do not make your oaths a means of deceiving one another or else your foot may slip after having been firm,[95] and you may suffer evil consequences because of hindering people from the way of Allah. A mighty chastisement awaits you. (95) Do not barter away the covenant of Allah[96] for a paltry gain.[97] Verily that which is with Allah is far better for you, if you only knew. (96) Whatever you have is bound to pass away and whatever is with Allah will last. And We shall surely grant those who have been patient[98] their reward according to the best of what they did. ▶

وَلَا تَتَّخِذُوٓا أَيْمَٰنَكُمْ دَخَلًا بَيْنَكُمْ
فَتَزِلَّ قَدَمٌ بَعْدَ ثُبُوتِهَا وَتَذُوقُوا ٱلسُّوٓءَ
بِمَا صَدَدتُّمْ عَن سَبِيلِ ٱللَّهِ وَلَكُمْ
عَذَابٌ عَظِيمٌ ﴿٩٤﴾ وَلَا تَشْتَرُوا بِعَهْدِ
ٱللَّهِ ثَمَنًا قَلِيلًا إِنَّمَا عِندَ ٱللَّهِ هُوَ خَيْرٌ
لَّكُمْ إِن كُنتُمْ تَعْلَمُونَ ﴿٩٥﴾
مَا عِندَكُمْ يَنفَدُ وَمَا عِندَ ٱللَّهِ بَاقٍ
وَلَنَجْزِيَنَّ ٱلَّذِينَ صَبَرُوٓا أَجْرَهُم
بِأَحْسَنِ مَا كَانُوا يَعْمَلُونَ ﴿٩٦﴾

But, whoever seeks to be directed to the straight path, God also makes it possible.

95. This verse emphatically admonishes the believers to adhere to righteous conduct. At times, those who are otherwise intellectually convinced that Islam is sound, may observe the misbehaviour and corruption of Muslims and this may deter them from joining the fold of Islam. The reason being that they did not find the Muslims with whom they came into contact any better in their moral conduct than the unbelievers.

96. Reference is made here to the commitment made by the Muslims in the name of God, or as representatives of the religion enjoined by God.

97. To urge people not to barter away the covenant of God for a paltry gain does not mean that one may do so for a substantial gain. The purpose of this directive is to emphasize that worldly gains, howsoever big they may be, are paltry in comparison with God's covenant. Thus, bartering away God's

(97) Whosoever acts righteously – whether a man or a woman and embraces belief, We will surely grant him a good life;[99] and will surely grant such persons their reward according to the best of their deeds.[100]

مَنْ عَمِلَ صَٰلِحًا مِّن ذَكَرٍ أَوْ أُنثَىٰ وَهُوَ مُؤْمِنٌ فَلَنُحْيِيَنَّهُۥ حَيَوٰةً طَيِّبَةً وَلَنَجْزِيَنَّهُمْ أَجْرَهُم بِأَحْسَنِ مَا كَانُوا۟ يَعْمَلُونَ ﴿٩٧﴾

covenant will always lead man to suffer loss no matter what he receives in return for it.

98. 'Those who have been patient' are those who adhere to truth and honesty in utter disregard of all temptations, desires, and lusts. They are the ones who endure all losses which accrue to them as a result of strictly confining themselves to fair and honest means and spurning all advantages which ensue from adopting unfair methods. Such persons are prepared to wait till the very end of their worldly life after which they will be able to observe the good consequences of their deeds.

99. This verse aims at removing the misunderstanding that might be entertained by believers and unbelievers alike. This misunderstanding consists of the belief that one who follows the path of truth, honesty and righteousness, is bound to ruin his worldly life. At best such a person may be able to achieve success in the Next Life, but as far as this world is concerned, no good results can be expected.

In response, it is pointed out that such a supposition is altogether erroneous. Anyone who adopts the right attitude will not only be able to enjoy success in the Next Life, but will also achieve success in the present life. Those who are righteous, straightforward in their dealings, and virtuous in their conduct are perceptibly better even in their worldly life than those who are devoid of faith and good morals. For it is they alone who enjoy the confidence and genuine respect of people because of their unblemished character. The kind of success which they enjoy, therefore, cannot fall to the share of those who pursue success by all possible means, including those that are outrageously foul. The righteous, even when their material conditions are unenviable, enjoy an inner peace and tranquillity which is beyond the reach of evil-doers even when they live in ostentatious luxury.

100. In the Next Life the righteous will achieve a status consonant with their best deeds. In other words, a person who does good deeds in this present world

(98) Whenever you read the Qur'ān seek refuge with Allah from Satan, the accursed.[101] (99) Surely he has no power over those who have faith and who place their trust in their Lord. (100) He has power only over those who take him as their patron and who, under his influence, associate others with Allah in His Divinity.

فَإِذَا قَرَأْتَ ٱلْقُرْءَانَ فَٱسْتَعِذْ بِٱللَّهِ مِنَ
ٱلشَّيْطَٰنِ ٱلرَّجِيمِ ﴿٩٨﴾ إِنَّهُۥ لَيْسَ لَهُۥ
سُلْطَٰنٌ عَلَى ٱلَّذِينَ ءَامَنُوا۟ وَعَلَىٰ
رَبِّهِمْ يَتَوَكَّلُونَ ﴿٩٩﴾ إِنَّمَا
سُلْطَٰنُهُۥ عَلَى ٱلَّذِينَ يَتَوَلَّوْنَهُۥ
وَٱلَّذِينَ هُم بِهِۦ مُشْرِكُونَ ﴿١٠٠﴾

– be they of major or minor significance – will be generously rewarded. Even for minor acts of goodness such a person will receive the reward which people merit for good deeds of major significance.

101. This does not simply mean that before starting to recite the Qur'ān one should simply utter the words: 'I seek refuge with Allah from Satan, the accursed.' Seeking refuge with God against Satan should not merely involve a man's tongue, but also his heart. In addition, the desire to free oneself from Satan's evil prompting should be backed up by practical efforts to keep oneself secure against uncalled-for doubts and suspicions. Such a person should make a serious effort to view the Qur'ān in its right perspective, allowing the Qur'ān to leave the imprint of its true teachings on his mind. He should take every precautionary measure to avoid distorting the Qur'ān. One should beware of this, since many people are wont to interpret the Qur'ān in the light of their own ideas, fancies or inclinations derived from extraneous sources. The result is that they understand the Qur'ān in disregard of, or even as contrary to the intent which God embodies in it.

One should also never forget that Satan's greatest wish is that man should always remain deprived of obtaining guidance from the Qur'ān. Hence, whenever a person turns to the Qur'ān, Satan leaves no stone unturned to prevent him from deriving guidance from it and to directing his thoughts instead along erroneous paths. One should, therefore, be highly vigilant while studying the Qur'ān and should constantly invoke God's help lest one fail to be directed to the guidance it embodies owing to Satan's machinations. If someone fails to obtain guidance from the Qur'ān he will obtain guidance from nowhere. And if someone is so unfortunate that he derives false and erroneous doctrines from the Qur'ān, nothing in the world will be able to rescue him from misguidance and doctrinal error.

(101) Whenever We replace one verse by another verse – and Allah knows what He should reveal – they are wont to say: 'You are nothing but a fabricator [who has invented the Qur'ān].' The fact is that most of them are ignorant of the truth.[102]

وَإِذَا بَدَّلْنَآ ءَايَةً مَّكَانَ ءَايَةٍ وَٱللَّهُ أَعْلَمُ بِمَا يُنَزِّلُ قَالُوٓا۟ إِنَّمَآ أَنتَ مُفْتَرٍۭ ۚ بَلْ أَكْثَرُهُمْ لَا يَعْلَمُونَ ﴿١٠١﴾

The present verse forms part of a discourse which is geared to refuting certain objections of the polytheists which were directed against the Qur'ān. It states in a preparatory manner that only he who is alert to Satan's machinations and seeks God's refuge from him will be able to perceive the true light of the Qur'ān. For those who are complacent about Satan are led off the right track to such a degree that it becomes simply impossible for them to appreciate the message of the Qur'ān.

102. The replacement of one verse by another might possibly signify replacing one command by another. For the commands embodied in the Qur'ān were revealed gradually. Sometimes it also happened that on one particular issue, two or three commandments were revealed one after the other in the course of a few years. The instances which immediately come to mind are those regarding drinking and unlawful sexual indulgence.

We feel disinclined, however, to accept this interpretation. The simple reason is that the verse in question was revealed during the Makkan period. As far as we know, no instances of gradual revelation of commands are on record for this period.

We, therefore, tend to believe that what is meant by replacing one verse by another is that a certain idea was explained in the Qur'ān at different places with the help of different parables. The same story is conveyed with one set of expressions and then later with another. At times a particular aspect of an issue is highlighted and at other times some other aspect of it is emphasized. To prove a point, sometimes recourse is made to one argument and sometimes to another. The same idea is presented briefly at one place and in greater detail at another.

This led the Makkan unbelievers to charge the Prophet (peace be on him) with being the author of the Qur'ān. For them if the Qur'ān had been derived from a divine source of knowledge, it would have set forth every question in such a manner that it would be absolutely clear and there would be no need for

(102) Tell them: 'It is the spirit of holiness that ha brought it down, by stages, from your Lord,[103] that it might bring firmness to those who believe,[104] and guidance to the right way,[105] and give glad tidings of felicity and success to those who submit to Allah.'[106]

قُلْ نَزَّلَهُۥ رُوحُ ٱلْقُدُسِ مِن
رَّبِّكَ بِٱلْحَقِّ لِيُثَبِّتَ
ٱلَّذِينَ ءَامَنُوا۟ وَهُدًى
وَبُشْرَىٰ لِلْمُسْلِمِينَ ﴿١٠٢﴾

taking it up again. They considered it unworthy of God to reveal His messages piecemeal; to send His guidance gradually; and to resort to a variety of revelations. They contended that piecemeal and gradual revelation did not behove God. The unbelievers thought such an attitude weak and imperfect which in turn reflected the efforts of human beings to express their imperfect knowledge.

103. The Qur'ānic expression *'Rūḥ al-Qudus'* literally means 'holy spirit' or the 'spirit of holiness'. This appellation is exclusively used for the angel Gabriel. By preferring to use this appellation rather than his proper name, the Qur'ān emphasizes that the message of the Qur'ān has been conveyed through the spirit which is free from all human weaknesses and imperfections. The Qur'ān was communicated to the Prophet (peace be on him) by one who is fully trustworthy so that there is no danger of his tampering with God's message. The Qur'ān was not communicated through anyone who is prone to lying and fabrications so that he would make up some messages and then falsely ascribe them to God. Nor was it communicated through someone who would resort to deception and fraud under the influence of selfish motives. Instead, the Qur'ān was communicated by a holy and purified spirit which always conveys the Word of God with utmost trustworthiness.

104. That the Qur'ān was revealed gradually rather than in one piece does not prove any deficiency in God's knowledge or wisdom – a view erroneously held by the unbelievers. It is rather man's power of comprehension and assimilation which is deficient. Hence, if the Qur'ān had been revealed in one piece, it would have been difficult for people to assimilate its whole message in a short span of time. Nor would it have been easy to fully digest even a single aspect of that message in a limited period of time. Thus God, in His wisdom, entrusted Gabriel to communicate the Qur'ān to the Prophet (peace be on him)

(103) Surely We know well that they say about you: 'It is only a human being who teaches him,'[107] [notwithstanding] that he whom they maliciously hint at is of foreign tongue, while this [Qur'ān] is plain Arabic speech.▶

وَلَقَدْ نَعْلَمُ أَنَّهُمْ يَقُولُونَ إِنَّمَا يُعَلِّمُهُۥ بَشَرٌ لِّسَانُ ٱلَّذِى يُلْحِدُونَ إِلَيْهِ أَعْجَمِىٌّ وَهَٰذَا لِسَانٌ عَرَبِىٌّ مُّبِينٌ ﴿١٠٣﴾

in pieces. At times, the Qur'ānic messages were set out succinctly and at other times in some detail The literary style employed to explain the messages also varied. One and the same point is driven home by variously employing different methods. All this is done so that all those who seek the truth might be able to obtain it despite their varying intellectual endowments, and subsequently grow mature in their knowledge, conviction and understanding.

105. This constitutes another reason underlying the gradual revelation of the Qur'ān. The believers who attempt to follow the way of God encounter many problems in the course of their calling to Islam as well as in connection with the practical problems of life. The Qur'ān provides them with adequate and timely guidance in this regard. It is quite obvious that it would have been altogether unwise to reveal directives in connection with all the different problems and stages of life before people even encountered them. Nor would it have been useful to reveal all the directives together in a short span of time.

106. This constitutes still another reason for the gradual revelation of the Qur'ān. The Muslims encountered different kinds of resistance and opposition, and they were also subjected to persecution in a myriad of forms. Formidable obstacles were placed by their opponents to prevent the propagation of Islam. These daunting circumstances required that the Muslims should constantly receive good tidings from God to keep their morale high. It was also necessary that the believers should be assured of their ultimate victory in order to prevent them falling prey to pessimism and despair.

107. These are reports which mention different names. These were the Makkan unbelievers who were suspected of being the true source of the teachings of the Prophet (peace be on him). In one of the reports, the name of

(104) Surely Allah will not enable those who do not believe in the signs of Allah to be directed to the right way, and a painful chastisement awaits them. (105) [It is not the Prophet who invents lies], it is rather those who do not believe in the signs of Allah[108] who invent lies. They are liars.

إِنَّ ٱلَّذِينَ لَا يُؤْمِنُونَ بِـَٔايَٰتِ ٱللَّهِ
لَا يَهْدِيهِمُ ٱللَّهُ وَلَهُمْ عَذَابٌ أَلِيمٌ
١٠٤ إِنَّمَا يَفْتَرِى ٱلْكَذِبَ ٱلَّذِينَ
لَا يُؤْمِنُونَ بِـَٔايَٰتِ ٱللَّهِ وَأُوْلَٰٓئِكَ
هُمُ ٱلْكَٰذِبُونَ ١٠٥

the person mentioned is Jabr who was a Roman slave of 'Āmir ibn al-Ḥaḍramī. In another report, the name mentioned is 'Ā'ish or Ya'īsh, a slave of Ḥuwayṭib ibn 'Abd al-'Uzzá. Another report mentions Yasār, a Jew, whose agnomen *(kunyah)* – was Abū Fukayhah, and who was the slave of a Makkan woman. Still another report mentions someone by the name of Bal'ān or Bal'ām, a Roman slave.

Be that as it may, the unbelievers of Makka formed their judgement on the basis of one simple thing. They tried to find out who, among the acquaintances of the Prophet (peace be on him) knew about the Torah and the Gospels. They needed to know nothing else about the person to be able to declare that he was the real author of the Qur'ān, a Book which the Prophet (peace be on him) ascribed to God. (See Ibn Hishām, *Sīrah,* vol. 1, p. 393 and al-Qurṭubī's comments on verse 103 of the present *sūrah* – Ed.)

This shows how grossly mistaken people are in forming opinions about the true worth of their contemporaries. The Makkans had the unique privilege of being directly acquainted with a man like whom none had lived on earth before, nor would ever live after. Disregarding the sterling qualities of such a person, they saw greater merit in some foreign slaves of Makka who had some small knowledge of the scriptures. Strangely enough, they were inclined to consider them to be the source of knowledge and wisdom embodied in the Qur'ān.

108. Alternatively, this verse may be translated as follows: 'It is only those who do not believe in the signs of Allah who invent lies.'

(106) Anyone who disbelieves in Allah after having had faith – except he who does so under duress while his heart remains content with faith – and as for one who opens his heart to disbelief – they shall incur Allah's wrath. A mighty chastisement awaits them.[109] (107) That is because they love the life of this world more than the Hereafter; and Allah does not guide those who are ungrateful to Allah for His favours. (108) They are the ones upon whose hearts and hearing and eyes Allah has set a seal. They are utterly steeped in heedlessness. ▶

مَن كَفَرَ بِٱللَّهِ مِنۢ بَعْدِ إِيمَٰنِهِۦٓ
إِلَّا مَنْ أُكْرِهَ وَقَلْبُهُۥ مُطْمَئِنٌّۢ
بِٱلْإِيمَٰنِ وَلَٰكِن مَّن شَرَحَ بِٱلْكُفْرِ
صَدْرًا فَعَلَيْهِمْ غَضَبٌ مِّنَ ٱللَّهِ
وَلَهُمْ عَذَابٌ عَظِيمٌ ﴿١٠٦﴾ ذَٰلِكَ
بِأَنَّهُمُ ٱسْتَحَبُّوا۟ ٱلْحَيَوٰةَ ٱلدُّنْيَا
عَلَى ٱلْءَاخِرَةِ وَأَنَّ ٱللَّهَ لَا يَهْدِى
ٱلْقَوْمَ ٱلْكَٰفِرِينَ ﴿١٠٧﴾ أُو۟لَٰٓئِكَ
ٱلَّذِينَ طَبَعَ ٱللَّهُ عَلَىٰ قُلُوبِهِمْ
وَسَمْعِهِمْ وَأَبْصَٰرِهِمْ ۖ وَأُو۟لَٰٓئِكَ
هُمُ ٱلْغَٰفِلُونَ ﴿١٠٨﴾

109. This verse deals with those Muslims who, at that time, were being severely persecuted; were being forced under torture to revert to unbelief. Such believers are being assured that if under such unendurable pressure, and out of the desire to save their lives, they are sometimes inclined to indicate that they no longer believe in Islam, they will be pardoned by God provided their hearts remain secure from all false doctrines. However, if they not only declare their verbal dissociation from Islam, but even in their hearts become convinced that it was some other religious doctrine rather than Islam which was true, they will not be able to escape God's punishment.

It is not the purpose of the verse to urge people to declare their dissociation from Islam in order to save their lives. All the verse says is that a person would not be punished for so doing provided that in his heart he retains his faith. However, if someone wants to follow a more praiseworthy cause and prefers to live on a higher level of faith, he ought to adhere to his position even if he is most brutally tortured to death.

If we were to carefully study the time of the Prophet (peace be on him), we would find examples of men like Khabbāb ibn Aratt who was made to lie on a red-hot fire until the fire was extinguished by the molten fat of his body. Despite such torture, Khabbāb valiantly clung to his faith. Likewise, Bilāl was made to put on his armour and then stand in the scorching sun. He was then

(109) No doubt they shall be losers in the Hereafter.[110] (110) And surely your Lord will be Ever-Forgiving and Most-Merciful towards those who left their homes after they were persecuted, and who thereafter struggled hard and remained constant.[111] (111) [Allah's judgement will come about them all] on the Day when every one shall come pleading in his defence, and every one shall be fully requited for his deeds and none shall be wronged in the least.

لَاجَرَمَ أَنَّهُمْ فِي ٱلْآخِرَةِ هُمُ
ٱلْخَٰسِرُونَ ﴿١٠٩﴾ ثُمَّ إِنَّ
رَبَّكَ لِلَّذِينَ هَاجَرُوا۟ مِنۢ
بَعْدِ مَا فُتِنُوا۟ ثُمَّ جَٰهَدُوا۟
وَصَبَرُوٓا۟ إِنَّ رَبَّكَ مِنۢ بَعْدِهَا
لَغَفُورٌ رَّحِيمٌ ﴿١١٠﴾ ۞ يَوْمَ تَأْتِي
كُلُّ نَفْسٍ تُجَٰدِلُ عَن نَّفْسِهَا
وَتُوَفَّىٰ كُلُّ نَفْسٍ مَّا عَمِلَتْ
وَهُمْ لَا يُظْلَمُونَ ﴿١١١﴾

made to lie down on hot sand and dragged around. In spite of all this, Bilāl continued his declaration of God's unity. In like manner we come across Ḥabīb ibn Zayd ibn 'Āṣim. Under orders from Musaylimah, the false pretender to prophethood, one limb after another was severed from this man's body so as to force him to affirm that Musaylimah was a Prophet designated by God. Ḥabīb continued to resist such demands, bearing this unspeakable torture until he died.

On the other side of the scale, we see 'Ammār ibn Yāsir, who had seen how both his father and mother were cruelly tortured to death. Thereafter, he himself was subjected to torture. The torture was simply too severe for 'Ammār to bear; under those unbearable circumstances he uttered all that the unbelievers had wanted him to say. Then he burst into tears and appeared before the Prophet (peace be on him): 'O Messenger of God, I was not spared until I reviled you and praised their gods.' The Prophet (peace be on him) asked him: 'What do you feel is the state of your heart?' He replied: 'Satisfied with what I believe in.' The Prophet (peace be on him) said: 'If the unbelievers repeat their persecution, do again what you did.' (Ibn Sa'd, vol. 3, p. 249 – Ed.)

(112) Allah sets forth the parable of [the people of] a town who were secure and content and whose sustenance came in abundance from every quarter. But then the people of the town showed ingratitude towards Allah for His bounties, so Allah afflicted them with hunger and fear in punishment for their evil deeds. (113) Most certainly a Messenger came to them from among them; but they rejected him, calling him a liar. Therefore chastisement seized them while they engaged in wrongdoing.[112]

(114) So eat out of the lawful and good sustenance that Allah has bestowed upon you, and thank Allah for His bounty,[113] if it is Him that you serve.[114] ▶

وَضَرَبَ ٱللَّهُ مَثَلًا قَرْيَةً كَانَتْ
ءَامِنَةً مُّطْمَئِنَّةً يَأْتِيهَا رِزْقُهَا
رَغَدًا مِّن كُلِّ مَكَانٍ فَكَفَرَتْ
بِأَنْعُمِ ٱللَّهِ فَأَذَٰقَهَا ٱللَّهُ لِبَاسَ
ٱلْجُوعِ وَٱلْخَوْفِ بِمَا كَانُوا۟
يَصْنَعُونَ ﴿١١٢﴾ وَلَقَدْ جَآءَهُمْ
رَسُولٌ مِّنْهُمْ فَكَذَّبُوهُ فَأَخَذَهُمُ
ٱلْعَذَابُ وَهُمْ ظَٰلِمُونَ ﴿١١٣﴾
فَكُلُوا۟ مِمَّا رَزَقَكُمُ ٱللَّهُ حَلَٰلًا
طَيِّبًا وَٱشْكُرُوا۟ نِعْمَتَ ٱللَّهِ
إِن كُنتُمْ إِيَّاهُ تَعْبُدُونَ ﴿١١٤﴾

---

110. These statements were made about those who, finding that the path of faith was difficult, recanted and rejoined the ranks of their people – the unbelievers and the polytheists.

111. Reference is made to those who had migrated to Abyssinia.

112. There are no clear indications that help one identify the 'town' alluded to in the previous verse; even commentators on the Qur'ān have been unable to identify it. It is Ibn 'Abbās' opinion that the town referred to in the parable is Makka itself. (See al-Qurṭubī's comments on verse 113 of the present *sūrah* – Ed.) As for the hunger and fear mentioned in the verse (i.e. verse 113), this possibly refers to the famine that held the Makkans in its grip for quite some time after the advent of the Prophet (peace be on him).

(115) Allah has forbidden you only carrion, and blood, and the flesh of swine; also any animal over which the name of any other than Allah has been invoked. But whoever eats of them under compelling necessity – neither desiring it nor exceeding the limit of absolute necessity – surely for such action Allah is Ever-Forgiving, Most-Merciful.[115] (116) And do not utter falsehoods by letting your tongues declare: 'This is lawful' and 'That is unlawful', thus fabricating lies against Allah.[116] Surely those who fabricate lies against Allah never prosper. (117) Brief is their enjoyment of the world, and thereafter they shall suffer a painful chastisement.

إِنَّمَا حَرَّمَ عَلَيْكُمُ ٱلْمَيْتَةَ وَٱلدَّمَ
وَلَحْمَ ٱلْخِنزِيرِ وَمَآ أُهِلَّ لِغَيْرِ ٱللَّهِ
بِهِۦ فَمَنِ ٱضْطُرَّ غَيْرَ بَاغٍ وَلَا عَادٍ
فَإِنَّ ٱللَّهَ غَفُورٌ رَّحِيمٌ ﴿١١٥﴾ وَلَا
تَقُولُوا۟ لِمَا تَصِفُ أَلْسِنَتُكُمُ
ٱلْكَذِبَ هَٰذَا حَلَٰلٌ وَهَٰذَا حَرَامٌ
لِّتَفْتَرُوا۟ عَلَى ٱللَّهِ ٱلْكَذِبَ إِنَّ ٱلَّذِينَ
يَفْتَرُونَ عَلَى ٱللَّهِ ٱلْكَذِبَ لَا يُفْلِحُونَ
﴿١١٦﴾ مَتَٰعٌ قَلِيلٌ وَلَهُمْ عَذَابٌ أَلِيمٌ ﴿١١٧﴾

---

113. We thus learn that the famine mentioned above had come to an end by the time the present *sūrah* was revealed.

114. The believers are directed to abstain from deciding on their own what is lawful and what is not. They may partake of all that God has declared to be lawful and good, and should give thanks to Him. Conversely, they should abstain from all things unlawful in the Law of God.

115. The same command recurs elsewhere as well. See *al-Baqarah* 2: 173; *al-Mā'idah* 5: 3; and *al-An'ām* 6: 119.

116. The verse lays down categorically that no one other than God has the authority to declare something lawful or otherwise. In other words, God alone is the Law-Maker. If anyone else makes bold to declare on his own certain

وَعَلَى ٱلَّذِينَ هَادُوا۟ حَرَّمْنَا مَا قَصَصْنَا عَلَيْكَ
مِن قَبْلُ ۖ وَمَا ظَلَمْنَـٰهُمْ وَلَـٰكِن كَانُوٓا۟
أَنفُسَهُمْ يَظْلِمُونَ ﴿١١٨﴾ ثُمَّ إِنَّ
رَبَّكَ لِلَّذِينَ عَمِلُوا۟ ٱلسُّوٓءَ
بِجَهَـٰلَةٍ ثُمَّ تَابُوا۟ مِنۢ بَعْدِ ذَٰلِكَ
وَأَصْلَحُوٓا۟ إِنَّ رَبَّكَ مِنۢ بَعْدِهَا
لَغَفُورٌ رَّحِيمٌ ﴿١١٩﴾

(118) We[117] have already recounted to you what We prohibited to the Jews.[118] In so doing We did not wrong them; it is they who wronged themselves. (119) But to those who commit evil out of ignorance and then repent and amend their ways, thereafter your Lord will be Much-Forgiving, Most-Merciful.

---

things to be lawful and others unlawful, he certainly goes beyond his legitimate limits. No such statements may be made unless one can demonstrate that such opinions are based on God's commands. By arrogating the right to declare things lawful or unlawful, one becomes guilty of inventing lies against God. For anyone who declares certain things to be lawful and others unlawful is guilty of any one of the following. He will either claim that his declarations of lawful and unlawful are in accordance with God's own declarations. Alternatively, he will claim that God has withdrawn His own prerogative to give man the Law which he might follow, and has, thereby, now delegated it to man himself. In either case, the statement is false and is tantamount to inventing lies against God.

117. All this is in response to the objections that were being made against the above-mentioned command, viz. to consider God alone to be the Law-Giver. The Makkan unbelievers pointed an accusing finger towards the Muslims, charging that they had made lawful many a thing which was unlawful in the Old Testament. They further agreed that if the Mosaic Law was also from God then the Muslims were themselves guilty of violating God's Law. They also pointed out that if the Law revealed to Moses and the Law revealed to Muḥammad (peace be on him) were both from one and the same source – God – how can one explain the differences between them?

Another major objection they made was that the Prophet (peace be on him) had dispensed with the law of the Sabbath which figures in the Old Testament. The kernel of their objection was that there were now two possibilities of which the Muslims had to choose one. They should either admit that they had changed one of God's laws out of their own volition. Or they should admit that they acknowledge that God gave two contradictory commands in two different versions of His Law.

(120) Indeed Abraham was a whole community by himself,[119] obedient to Allah, exclusively devoted to Him. And he was never one of those who associated others with Allah in His Divinity.

إِنَّ إِبْرَٰهِيمَ كَانَ أُمَّةً قَانِتًا لِّلَّهِ حَنِيفًا وَلَمْ يَكُ مِنَ ٱلْمُشْرِكِينَ ﴿١٢٠﴾

118. This alludes to the following verse in *al-An'ām* (6: 146): 'And to those who had Judaized we have forbidden all beasts with claws.' The verse in fact mentions that it was because of the continual disobedience of the Jews that certain things which were originally lawful, were made unlawful for them as punishment for their misdeeds.

This, however, poses a problem. In the above verse, as we have seen, reference is made to a verse of *al-An'ām*. This would imply that *Sūrah al-An'ām* was revealed prior to the revelation of the present *sūrah*. However, in *al-An'ām* we also come across the following verse: 'And how is it that you do not eat of that over which Allah's name has been pronounced even though He has clearly spelled out to you what He has forbidden you?' (*al-An'ām* 6: 119). This seems to clearly refer to *al-Naḥl*. For, of the Makkan *sūrahs, al-Naḥl* is the only *sūrah,* apart from *al-An'ām,* which enumerates in some detail which things are unlawful.

This raises the question as to which of the two *sūrahs* – *al-Naḥl* or *al-An'ām* – was revealed earlier. In our opinion, *al-Naḥl* was revealed earlier, and it is to this *sūrah* that reference is made in the above-mentioned verse of *al-An'ām*. At a later stage, the Makkan unbelievers levelled objections against verses of *al-Naḥl* which we have referred to. At that time, *al-An'ām* had already been revealed. By way of rejoinder it was pointed out that the matter had been clarified earlier, that is, in *al-An'ām*. That clarification consisted of stating that certain things had been made unlawful especially for the Jews. However, since the objection had been made with regard to some of the contents of *al-Naḥl,* the rejoinder was subsequently included as a parenthetical statement in *al-Naḥl* itself.

119. Abraham was indeed a whole community by himself. For when there was not a single Muslim on earth, all being steeped in unbelief, Abraham stood out as the sole standard-bearer of Islam. He single-handedly performed a task that was stupendous enough to have been performed by a whole community.

(121) He rendered thanks to Allah for His bounties so that Allah chose him [for His favours] and directed him to the right way. (122) We bestowed good upon him in this world, and in the Hereafter he shall certainly be among the righteous. (123) Then We revealed to you: 'Follow the way of Abraham with exclusive devotion to Allah. He was not one of those who associated others with Allah in His Divinity.'[120]

شَاكِرًا لِّأَنْعُمِهِ ٱجْتَبَىٰهُ وَهَدَىٰهُ
إِلَىٰ صِرَٰطٍ مُّسْتَقِيمٍ ﴿١٢١﴾ وَءَاتَيْنَٰهُ فِى
ٱلدُّنْيَا حَسَنَةً وَإِنَّهُۥ فِى ٱلْءَاخِرَةِ لَمِنَ
ٱلصَّٰلِحِينَ ﴿١٢٢﴾ ثُمَّ أَوْحَيْنَآ إِلَيْكَ
أَنِ ٱتَّبِعْ مِلَّةَ إِبْرَٰهِيمَ حَنِيفًا وَمَا كَانَ
مِنَ ٱلْمُشْرِكِينَ ﴿١٢٣﴾

120. This constitutes a full-scale refutation of the unbelievers' objection. The refutation consists of two main points. First, that contrary to their inference on the basis of the apparent difference between some injunctions of the Old Testament and the Qur'ān, there is no contradiction in God's Law. The Jews had been prohibited certain bounties in retribution for their transgression. There was obviously no reason to deprive others of those bounties. The second point brought home in this verse is that Muḥammad (peace be on him) has been commanded to follow the way of Abraham. It is common knowledge that several things which are unlawful in Mosaic Law were not so in Abrahamic Law. To cite a few examples, the Jews are not supposed to eat the flesh of the camel, whereas it was permissible for the Abrahamic community to do so. Likewise, ostrich, duck and rabbit are forbidden in Jewish Law while they were perfectly lawful for the followers of Abraham.

After clarifying this point, the Makkan unbelievers are emphatically told that neither they nor the Jews have any true affinity with Abraham. This is for the simple reason that both are guilty of polytheism. The only true followers of the Abrahamic way are Muḥammad (peace be on him) and his Companions whose beliefs and actions show no trace of polytheism.

(124) As for the Sabbath, it was made incumbent only on those who differed about its laws.[121] Certainly your Lord will judge on the Day of Resurrection between them regarding the matters they disputed.

(125) (O Prophet!) Call men to the way of your Lord with wisdom and goodly exhortation,[122] and reason with them in the best manner possible.[123] Surely your Lord knows best who has strayed away from His path, and He also knows well those who are guided to the right way.

إِنَّمَا جُعِلَ ٱلسَّبْتُ عَلَى ٱلَّذِينَ
ٱخْتَلَفُوا۟ فِيهِ ۚ وَإِنَّ رَبَّكَ لَيَحْكُمُ
بَيْنَهُمْ يَوْمَ ٱلْقِيَـٰمَةِ فِيمَا كَانُوا۟
فِيهِ يَخْتَلِفُونَ ﴿١٢٤﴾ ٱدْعُ إِلَىٰ سَبِيلِ
رَبِّكَ بِٱلْحِكْمَةِ وَٱلْمَوْعِظَةِ ٱلْحَسَنَةِ ۖ
وَجَـٰدِلْهُم بِٱلَّتِى هِىَ أَحْسَنُ ۚ إِنَّ
رَبَّكَ هُوَ أَعْلَمُ بِمَن ضَلَّ عَن
سَبِيلِهِۦ ۖ وَهُوَ أَعْلَمُ بِٱلْمُهْتَدِينَ ﴿١٢٥﴾

121. This is in response to another objection made by the Makkan unbelievers. It was hardly necessary to point out that the law of the Sabbath itself was meant for the Jews alone. The restrictions of the Sabbath were simply unknown to Abraham and his followers. All this was far too well known to the Makkans to be clearly mentioned here. Hence, it was deemed sufficient to implicitly express the idea that the Sabbath did not belong to the early period – the period of Abraham. It was only at a relatively later time that the restrictions of the Sabbath were introduced in view of the known misdeeds of the Jews.

This cursory statement of the Qur'ān can perhaps best be appreciated only after taking note of the passages in the Bible which deal with the Sabbath laws. In order to become acquainted with the laws of the Sabbath see *Exodus* 20: 8–11; 23: 12–13; 31: 12–17; 35: 2–3 and *Numbers* 15: 32–6. These should, however, be read in conjunction with the passages which mention the audacity with which the Jews violated those laws. See, for example, *Jeremiah* 17: 21–7; and *Ezekiel* 20: 12–14.

122. In calling people to the truth one should bear in mind two things – wisdom and good counsel. Wisdom requires that in calling people to the truth, one should be conscious of the predilections and biases as well as the mental

(126) If you take retribution, then do so in proportion to the wrong done to you. But if you can bear such conduct with patience, indeed that is best for the steadfast.▶

وَإِنْ عَاقَبْتُمْ فَعَاقِبُوا۟ بِمِثْلِ مَا عُوقِبْتُم بِهِۦ ۖ وَلَئِن صَبَرْتُمْ لَهُوَ خَيْرٌ لِّلصَّـٰبِرِينَ ﴿١٢٦﴾

capacities and circumstances of the people to whom the message is being addressed. One should also be sensitive to the context in which the message is given to the people. Nor should one fail to note the diversities between different individuals and groups. Instead, when one comes into contact with an individual or a group, one should try to understand the background of that individual or group. This should be followed by a reasoned discourse that penetrates the hearts and minds of the persons concerned.

As for 'good counsel', this denotes two things. First, that one should not be content with merely trying to convince people with the help of rational arguments. Instead, one should also appeal to the nobler emotions of man. For instance, one should not merely muster rational arguments so as to negate and show the falsity of erroneous doctrines or unrighteous behaviour. In addition, one should also evoke the instinctive repugnance to evil which is embodied in human nature and shake people into realizing the horrible consequences of their misdeeds. Likewise, in addition to supporting sound doctrines and righteous behaviour with the help of rational arguments, an attempt should also be made to create a relish for them.

Another meaning of 'good counsel' is counselling people in such a manner that one's deep sympathy, compassion and concern for the people in question does not go unnoticed by them. One should be quite conscious of the fact that 'counselling' people should not be allowed to be misunderstood as an act emanating from the presumption of one's own superior status, or of the inferior status of the audience.

123. This represents an important note of caution. When someone presents a doctrine, that necessarily generates discussion with those who do not agree with that doctrine. Those who seek to promote the cause of God should be exceedingly cautious about allowing this discussion to degenerate into a polemical or intellectual bout. Such discussions should not be marred by obstinate refusal to see the strength of the other party's arguments or by slanderous allegations, or attacks and taunts.

The purpose of the discussion too should not be to render the other party speechless, or to establish one's superior eloquence. On the contrary, one's discourse should be gracious and refined. It should also reflect the person's

(127) (O Muḥammad!) So bear with patience – and your patience is only because of the help of Allah – and do not grieve over them, nor feel distressed by their evil plans. (128) For surely Allah is with those who hold Him in fear and do good.[124]

وَاصْبِرْ وَمَا صَبْرُكَ إِلَّا بِاللَّهِ ۚ
وَلَا تَحْزَنْ عَلَيْهِمْ وَلَا تَكُ فِي
ضَيْقٍ مِّمَّا يَمْكُرُونَ ﴿١٢٧﴾
إِنَّ اللَّهَ مَعَ الَّذِينَ اتَّقَوا وَّالَّذِينَ
هُم مُّحْسِنُونَ ﴿١٢٨﴾

---

higher moral stature and courteous disposition. Moreover, the arguments should appeal to good sense. Likewise, the statements made in the course of the discussion should be so couched as not to arouse obstinacy. In such discussions, one should try to express one's viewpoint in a straightforward and elegant manner, taking good care not to arouse adamance and egotistical feelings in the audience. However, as soon as one realizes that the other party has been so provoked as to cling, out of sheer obstinacy, to his viewpoint, one should put an end to the discussion. For continuing it any further might cause the other person to veer even further away from the truth.

124. They are the ones who, out of their God-fearingness, refrain from evil and adhere to good behaviour. No matter how others treat them, they return even their evil with good.

Glossary of Terms

'Ahd means covenant. The *'ahd* with reference to God (*al-Baqarah* 2: 27) consists of the command issued by God to His servants. This *'ahd* consists of God's eternal command that His creatures are obligated to render their service, obedience and worship to Him alone.

Al-Ākhirah (After-life, Hereafter, Next World). The term embraces the following ideas:

1. that man is answerable to God;
2. that the present order of existence will some day come to an end;
3. that when it happens, God will bring another order into being in which He will resurrect all human beings, gather them together and examine their conduct, and reward them with justice and mercy;
4. that those who are reckoned good will be sent to Paradise whereas the evil-doers will be consigned to Hell; and
5. that the real measure of success or failure of a person is not the extent of his prosperity in the present life, but his success in the Next.

'Arsh literally means throne. It has been generally used in the Qur'ān with reference to the Throne of God. It is obviously difficult to appreciate fully the exact nature of God's Throne. What seems certain is that God's Throne signifies dominion and authority. The Qur'ān also mentions that God 'ascended the Throne', an expression which seems to signify His taking over the reins of the universe after creating it. The main thrust of such a statement is that God is not merely the creator, but also the sovereign and ruler of the universe; that after creating the universe He did not detach Himself from, nor become indifferent to, His creation, but continues to exercise effective control over it.

Burūj (sing. *burj*) literally denote forts, palaces, fortified structures. The word has been used once in the Qur'ān, in this literal meaning (see *al-Nisā'* 4: 78). In ancient astronomy, however, the term *burj* was used to indicate the twelve constellations which stood for the twelve spheres of the zodiac. However, the *burūj* seems to have been used in its other usages in the Qur'ān (i.e. in *al-Ḥijr* 15: 16; *al-Furqān* 25: 61 and *al-Burūj* 85: 1) to signify heavenly spheres which have been separated from each other by means of fortified boundaries. Thus the word *burūj* in these verses signifies 'fortified heavenly spheres'.

Dhikr means remembrance and admonition. In the Islamic context, it is used in the sense of 'remembrance of God'. In *al-Baqarah* 2: 198, *dhikr* refers to remembering God on a specific occasion, namely during the Pilgrimage at Minā. *Dhikr* has also been used to refer to the Qur'ān since it is 'Admonition' *par excellence* (see *al-Ḥijr* 15: 9).

Dīn has the core meaning of obedience. As a Qur'ānic technical term, *dīn* refers to the way of life and the system of conduct based on recognizing God as one's sovereign and committing oneself to obeying Him. According to Islam, true *dīn* consists of living in total submission to God, by recognizing that the guidance communicated through the Prophets was binding on people and ought to be followed.

Faḥshā' (plural *fawāḥish*) applies to all those acts whose abominable character is self-evident. In the Qur'ān all extra-marital sexual relationships, sodomy, nudity, false accusation of unchastity, and taking as one's wife a woman who had been married to one's father are specifically reckoned as shameful deeds. In *Ḥadīth,* theft, taking intoxicating drinks and begging have been characterized as *fawāḥish* as have many other brazenly evil and indecent acts.

Ḥadīth literally means communication or narration. In the Islamic context it has come to denote the record of what the Prophet (peace be on him) said, did, or tacitly approved. According to some scholars, *Ḥadīth* also covers reports about the sayings and deeds, etc. of the Companions of the Prophet in addition to those of the Prophet (peace be on him) himself. The whole body of traditions is termed *Ḥadīth* and its science *'Ilm al-Ḥadīth*.

Ḥajj (Major Pilgrimage) is one of the five pillars of Islam, a duty one must perform during one's life-time if one has the financial resources for it. It resembles *'umrah* (q.v.) in some respects but differs from it insofar as it can only be performed during certain specified dates of Dhū al-Ḥijjah. In addition to *ṭawāf* and *sa'y* (q.v.), which are also required for *'umrah,* there are a few other requirements but especially one's 'standing' (i.e. stay) in 'Arafāt during the day-time on 9th of Dhū al-Ḥijjah. For details of the rules of *Ḥajj,* see the books of *Fiqh*.

Ḥashr (literally 'gathering'), signifies the Islamic doctrine that with the blowing of the second Trumpet all those who were ever created will be resurrected and will be brought forth to the Plain where all will be made to stand before God for His judgement.

Ḥijrah signifies migration from a land where a Muslim is unable to live according to the precepts of his faith to a land where it is possible to do so. The *hijrah par excellence* for Muslims is the *ḥijrah* of the Prophet (peace be on him) and his Companions to Madina. This provided not only refuge from persecution, but also an opportunity to build a society and state according to the ideals of Islam.

'Ibādah is used in three meanings: (1) worship and adoration; (2) obedience and submission; and (3) service and subjection. The fundamental message of Islam is that man, as God's creature, should direct his *'ibādah* to God in all the above-mentioned meanings of the term, and associate none with God in rendering it.

Iblīs literally means 'one thoroughly disappointed; one in utter despair'. In Islamic terminology it denotes the *jinn* (q.v.) who out of vainglory, refused the command of God to prostrate before Adam. He also asked God to allow him a term during which he might mislead and tempt mankind to error. The term was granted to him by God whereafter he became the chief promoter of evil and prompted Adam and Eve to disobey God's order. He is also called *al-Shayṭān* (Satan). He is possessed of a specific personality and is not just an abstract force.

Iḥsān literally denotes doing something in a goodly manner. When used in the Islamic religious context, it signifies excellence of behaviour arising out of a strong love for God and a profound sense of close relationship with Him. According to a tradition, the Prophet (peace be on him) defined *iḥsān* as worshipping God as though one sees Him.

Īlā' denotes a husband's vow to abstain from sexual relations with his wife. The maximum permissible limit for abstaining from such relations under that vow is four months, after which *īlā'* would automatically mean the repudiation of the marriage.

Injīl signifies the inspired orations and utterances of Jesus (peace be on him) which he delivered during the last two or three years of his earthly life in his capacity as a Prophet. The *Injīl* mentioned by the Qur'ān should, however, not be identified by the four Gospels of the New Testament which contain a great deal of material in addition to the inspired utterances of the Prophet Jesus (peace be on him). Presumably the statements explicitly attributed to Jesus (peace be on him) constitute parts of the true, original *Injīl*. It is significant, however, that the statements explicitly attributed to Jesus in the Gospels contain substantively the same teachings as those of the Qur'ān.

Isāf was originally the name of a person of the Jurhum tribe (Isāf ibn Baghy). A woman of the same tribe, was called Nā'ilah bint Dīk. Before Islam, idols bearing both these names were placed near Zamzam and animals were sacrificed to both idols – Nā'ilah and Isāf – by way of offering.

Jinn are an independent species of creation about which little is known except that unlike men, who were created out of earth, the *jinn* were created out of fire. But like men, a Divine Message has also been addressed to the *jinn* and they too have been endowed with the capacity, again like men, to choose between good and evil, and between obedience and disobedience to God.

Kufr literally means 'to conceal'. This word has been variously used in the Qur'ān to denote: (1) state of absolute lack of faith; (2) rejection or denial of any of the essentials of Islam; (3) attitude of ingratitude and thanklessness to God; and (4) non-compliance with certain basic requirements of faith. In the accepted technical sense, *kufr* consists of rejection of the Divine Guidance communicated through the Prophets and Messengers of God. More specifically, ever since the advent of the last of the Prophets and Messengers, Muhammad (peace be on him), the rejection of his teaching constitutes *kufr*.

Al-Lāt was the chief idol of the Thaqīf tribe in Ṭā'if, and one of the most famous idols in pre-Islamic Arabia.

Mut'ah was a form of marriage-contract in pre-Islamic Arabia, signifying a marriage contract according to which the male partner takes a woman in marriage for a fixed period of time and undertakes to pay *mahr*. At the expiry of the stipulated period, the marriage tie is automatically dissolved without specifically requiring its repudiation. Islam, however, prohibits this practice.

Nā'ilah was an idol; (q.v. **Isāf**).

Nasr was an idol of the Ḥimyar (South Arabia).

Qarn usually denotes 'the people of a given age'. However, the word in its several usages in the Qur'ān, connotes a 'nation' which wields in its hey-day, either fully or partially, the reins of world leadership.

Rabb has three meanings: (i) Lord and Master; (ii) Sustainer, Provider, Supporter, Nourisher and Guardian; and (iii) Sovereign and Ruler, He who controls and directs. God is *Rabb* in all three meanings of the term.

The rationale of the basic Qur'ānic message – 'serve none but God' – is that since God is man's *Rabb* – Lord, Sustainer, Provider, Supporter, Nourisher, etc. – He alone should be the object of man's worship and service. See, for example, *al-Baqarah* 2: 21.

Rūḥ al-Qudus literally means 'the spirit of holiness'. This appellation is exclusively used for the angel Gabriel. By using this appellation, the Qur'ān emphasizes that the message of the Qur'ān has been conveyed through the spirit which is free of all human weaknesses and imperfections.

Sabt or **Sabbath** i.e. Saturday. It was laid down that the Israelites should consecrate that day for rest and worship. They were required to altogether abstain on that day from all worldly acts, including fishing (which they might neither do themselves nor have others do for them).

Sa'y is a rite which is part of both *hajj* and *'umrah* and consists of seven laps of brisk walk (literally, 'running') seven times between Ṣafā and Marwah, two hillocks near the Ka'bah. This commemorates Abraham's wife, Hagar's search for water for her baby child.

Shirk consists of associating anyone or anything with the Creator either in His being, or attributes, or in the exclusive rights (such as worship) that He has against His creatures.

Suwā' was an idol of Hudhayl ibn Mudrikah ibn Ilyās ibn Muḍar. It was placed in Yanbu'.

Ṭāghūt literally denotes one who exceeds his legitimate limits. In the Qur'ānic terminology it refers to the creature who exceeds the limits of his creatureliness and arrogates to himself godhead and lordship. In the negative scale of values, the first stage of man's error is *fisq* (i.e. disobeying God without necessarily denying that one should obey Him). The second stage is that of *kufr* (i.e. rejection of the very idea that one ought to obey God). The last stage is that man not only rebels against God but also imposes his rebellious will on others. All those who reach this stage are *ṭāghūt*.

Ṭawāf is a rite which is part of both *ḥajj* and *'umrah* and consists of circumambulating the Ka'bah seven times.

Tawriyah denotes 'covering up' or 'concealing' a fact. One may resort to *tawriyah* in a situation where there remains no other alternative in order to save a victim from his oppressor, or to ward off some serious mischief or harm, than to have recourse to a statement or device which does not accord with facts. In such a situation a pious man, while abstaining from explicitly lying, may resort to an ambiguous statement or device aimed at concealing facts so as to ward off some evil.

Ummah (literally 'collectivity', sharing the same origin or source) has been generally used in the Qur'ān to refer to all those who receive the message of a Messenger of God, or happen to be living in an age when the teachings of that Messenger are extant.

Umm al-Kitāb generally signifies the opening *sūrah* of the Qur'ān – *al-Fātihah*. The expression also signifies the 'Original Book' or the 'Preserved Tablet' (*al-Lawh al-Mahfūz*). The expression has also been used to refer to the verses of the Qur'ān embodying commandments couched in unambiguous phraseology.

'Umrah (Minor Pilgrimage) is an Islamic rite and consists of pilgrimage to the Ka'bah. It consists essentially of *ihrām, ṭawāf* (q.v. circumambulation) around the Ka'bah (seven times), and *sa'y* (q.v. i.e. running) between Ṣafā and Marwah (seven times). It is called minor *Hajj* because it need not be performed at a particular time of the year and its performance requires fewer ceremonies than the *Ḥajj* proper.

Al-'Uzzá has been identified with Venus, but it was given the form of an acacia tree, and worshipped. It was the deity of the Ghaṭfān tribe.

Wadd was an idol of a clan of the Quḍā'ah and was located in Dawmat al-Jandal.

Waḥy signifies the revelation which consists of communicating God's Messages to a Prophet or Messenger of God. The highest form of revelation is the Qur'ān, which, in every sense of the expression, is the 'speech or word' of God.

Yaghūth was an idol of the people of Jurash in Arabia.

Ya'ūq was an idol of a clan of the Hamdān tribe and was located in Yemen.

Biographical Notes

'Abd Allāh Ibn 'Abbās see Biographical Notes vols. I and II.

'Abd Allāh Ibn Mas'ūd see Biographical Notes vols. I and II.

'Abd al-Raḥmān Ibn 'Awf see Biographical Notes vol. III.

Abū Sufyān ibn Ḥarb see Biographical Notes vol. I.

Abū 'Ubaydah ibn al-Jarrāh, d. 18 A.H./639 C.E., was a Companion and one of the most outstanding military commanders of the early Islamic period. He replaced Khālid ibn al-Walīd as the commander of the Muslim forces which were heading towards Syria which was conquered under his command.

'Ā'ishah see Biographical Notes vols. I and III.

'Alī ibn Abī Ṭālib see Biographical Notes vols. I and II.

'Ammār ibn Yāsir see Biographical Notes vol. II.

Bilāl see Biographical Notes vols. I and II.

Ḥabīb ibn Zayd ibn 'Āṣim, was a Companion of the Prophet (peace be on him). He was in 'Umān when he heard of the death of the Prophet (peace be on him). Musaylimah, the false claimant to prophethood, sought from him the affirmation of his claim. When Ḥabīb declined to do so, Musaylimah had him killed, the limbs of his body being amputated one after the other.

Hūd see Biographical Notes vol. III.

Ḥuwayṭib ibn 'Abd al-'Uzzá, d. 54 A.H./674 C.E., was a Companion of the Prophet (peace be on him), who died at a ripe age exceeding a hundred years. For long he was opposed to Islam but ultimately embraced it after the conquest of Makka. He subsequently took part in the battles of Ḥunayn and Ṭā'if on the side of the Muslims.

Ibn Baṭṭūṭah, Muḥammad ibn 'Abd Allāh ibn Muḥammad ibn Ibrāhīm, d. 779 A.H./1377 C.E., was a great traveller of Tangier, Morocco. He undertook voyages which covered North West Africa,

Egypt, Syria, Hijaz, Iraq, Persia, Yemen, Bahrain, Turkistan, Transoxiana, parts of India, China, Java, the land of the Tatars, and Central Africa. He returned to his homeland after a period of thirty-one years and then dictated an elaborate account of his travels which is available both in its original Arabic and in its translated version in several international languages.

Ibn Isḥāq, Muḥammad, d. 151 A.H./768 C.E., was a scholar of Madina, and one of the earliest historians and biographers of the Prophet (peace be on him). His biography of the Prophet (peace be on him) has had a lasting influence on the works of that genre.

Ibn Kathīr see Biographical Notes vols. I and II.

Ibn Taymīyah see Biographical Notes vol. I.

Ja'far al-Ṭayyār, d. 8 A.H./629 C.E., was a Companion and an elder brother of 'Alī, the fourth caliph (q.v.). He was among the early converts to Islam and took part in the second migration to Abyssinia. He is known for his mature understanding of Islam and his contribution to the propagation of his faith, and above all, for his role as a valiant soldier.

Khabbāb ibn al-Aratt, d. 37 A.H./657 C.E., a Companion of the Prophet (peace be on him) and one of the early converts to Islam, was mercilessly persecuted by the opponents of Islam in Makka.

Mujāhid see Biographical Notes vol. II.

Muṣ'ab ibn 'Umayr, d. 3 A.H./625 C.E., was a Companion of the Prophet (peace be on him) and one of the early converts to Islam who migrated first to Abyssinia, then returned to Makka and migrated once again to Madina where he played a major role in the spread of Islam. He was martyred in the battle of Uḥud.

Sa'd ibn Abī Waqqāṣ see Biographical Notes vol. III.

Ṣāliḥ see Biographical Notes vol. III.

Shu'ayb see Biographical Notes vol. III.

Ṣuhayb ibn Sinān see Biographical Notes vol. II.

al-Ṭabarī see Biographical Notes vol. II.

Ṭalḥah see Biographical Notes vol. III.

'Ubaydah ibn al-Ḥārith see Biographical Notes vol. III.

'Umar ibn al-Khaṭṭāb see Biographical Notes vols. I and II.

'Uthmān ibn 'Affān see Biographical Notes vols. I and II.

Al-Zamakhsharī, Maḥmūd ibn Muḥammad ibn Aḥmad, d. 538 A.H./1144 C.E., was an outstanding theologian and a scholar of language and literature. He has a host of works to his credit but is best known for his exegesis of the Qur'ān called *al-Kashshāf*.

Zayd ibn Ḥārithah ibn Sharāḥīl (or Shuraḥbīl) al-Kalbī, was a Companion of the Prophet (peace be on him) and one of the earliest converts to Islam. The Prophet (peace be on him) adopted him as his son and held him in considerable affection. He also appointed him commander of different military expeditions. He was martyred in the battle of Mu'tah in 8 A.H./630 C.E.

Bibliography

Abū Dā'ūd, Sulaymān ibn al-Ash'ath al-Sijistānī, *al-Sunan.*

Al-Bukhārī, Abū 'Abd Allāh Muḥammad ibn Ismā'īl, *al-Jāmi' al-Ṣaḥīḥ.*

Al-Dāraquṭnī, 'Alī ibn 'Umar, *al-Sunan,* 4 vols., Beirut, 'Ālam al-Kutub, n.d.

Al-Dārimī, Abū Muḥammad 'Abd Allāh ibn 'Abd al-Raḥmān, *al-Sunan,* 2 vols., Cairo, Dār al-Fikr, 1978.

Encyclopaedia Britannica, XIVth edition.

Al-Fīrūzābādī, *al-Qāmūs al-Muḥīṭ,* Cairo, al-Ḥalabī, 1952. Second Edition.

Hershon, Paul Isaac, *Talmudic Miscellany,* London, 1880.

The Holy Bible, Revised Standard Edition, New York, 1952.

Ibn al-'Arabī, Abū Bakr, *Aḥkām al-Qur'ān.*

Ibn Baṭṭūṭah, *Muhadhdhab Riḥlat Ibn Baṭṭūṭah,* ed. Aḥmad al-'Awāmir Muḥammad Jād al-Mawlá', Cairo, al-Amiriyah, 1934.

Ibn Hishām, Abū Muḥammad 'Abd al-Malik, *Sīrah,* eds. Muṣṭafá al-Saqqā et al., II edition, Cairo, 1955.

Ibn Isḥāq, *The Life of Muḥammad,* tr. and notes by A. Guillaume, Oxford University Press, 1955.

Ibn Kathīr, *Mukhtaṣar Tafsīr Ibn Kathīr,* ed. Muḥammad 'Alī al-Ṣābūnī, 7th edition, 3 vols., Beirut, 1402–1981.

Ibn Mājah, Abū 'Abd Allāh Muḥammad ibn Yazīd al-Qazwīnī, *al-Sunan.*

Ibn Manẓūr, *Lisān al-'Arab,* Beirut, Dār Ṣādir, n.d.

Ibn Rushd, *Bidāyat al-Mujtahid,* 2 vols., Cairo, n.d.

Ibn Sa'd, Abū 'Abd Allāh Muḥammad, *Al-Ṭabaqāt al-Kubrá,* 8 vols., Beirut, 1957–60.

Ibn Taymīyah, Taqī al-Dīn, *Majmū' al-Fatāwá Ibn Tymīyah,* ed. Muḥammad ibn 'Abd al-Raḥmān ibn Qāsim, 37 vols., Riyadh, 1398.

Al-Jaṣṣāṣ, Abū Bakr, *Aḥkām al-Qur'ān,* 3 vols., Cairo, 1347 A.H.

Al-Jazīrī, 'Abd al-Raḥmān, *al-Fiqh 'alá al-Madhāhib al-Arba'ah,* 5 vols., Beirut, Dār Iḥyā' al-Turāth, 1980.

Mālik ibn Anas, *al-Muwaṭṭa',* ed. Muḥammad Fu'ād 'Abd al-Bāqī, 2 vols., Cairo, 1951.

Muslim, ibn al-Ḥajjāj, *al-Ṣaḥīḥ.*

Al-Nasā'ī, Abū 'Abd al-Raḥmān Aḥmad ibn Shu'ayb, *al-Sunan.*

Al-Nawawī, Yaḥyá ibn Sharaf, *Al-Arba'īn.*

Polano, H., *The Talmudic Selections,* London, Frederick Warne & Co.

Al-Qurṭubī, *al-Jāmi' li Aḥkām al-Qur'ān,* 8 vols., Cairo, Dār al-Sha'b, n.d.

Al-Ṣābūnī, Muḥammad 'Alī, *Ṣafwat al-Tafāsīr,* 3 vols., 4th edition, Beirut, 1402–1981.

Al-Ṣāliḥ, Ṣubḥī, *Mabāḥith fī 'Ulūm al-Qur'ān,* Beirut, 1977.

Al-Ṭabarī, Muḥammad b. Jarīr, *Tafsīr.*

Al-Tirmidhī, Abū 'Īsá Muḥammad ibn 'Īsá, *al-Jāmi' al-Ṣaḥīḥ.*

Al-Wāqidī, Muḥammad ibn 'Umar, *al-Maghāzī,* ed. M. Jones, 3 vols., Cairo, 1966.

Wensinck, A.J., *Concordance et indices de la tradition musulmane,* 7 vols., Leiden, 1939–1969.

Zaghloul, R. El-Naggar, *The Geological Concept of Mountains in the Holy Qur'ān,* Herndon, Virginia, 1991.

Subject Index

General Index